CONTEMPORARY FIELDS OF PSYCHOLOGY AND EXPERIMENTS

About the Author

M. Rajamanickam, is currently the Managing Editor of the *Journal of Community Guidance and Research*. He had founded this Journal in January 1984 and since then he is the Founder-Editor of it. A 1966 Ph.D. of the Annamalai University, he has been teaching Psychology to the Post-Graduate students for more than three decades and also has been guiding research students for M.Phil. and Ph.D. Degrees. He was the Dean of the Faculty of Education of the Annamalai University and was elected to the Syndicate of the University for three terms. He has spent of much of this time in research, specializing in Psychological Measurements as well as designed and developed quite a number of Psychological Test Materials.

He has published number of research papers in National and International Journals, presented papers in Conferences and also took part in Symposiums. He has been associated with many Academic Institutions and Professional Organizations like the Indian Psychological Association, Indian Academy of Applied Psychology and National Vocational and Educational Guidance Association. He is a prolific writer and has published a number of books in Psychology.

CONTEMPORARY FIELDS OF PSYCHOLOGY AND EXPERIMENTS

Dr. M. RAJAMANICKAM, M.A. M.LITT., Ph.D.
Formerly Dean, Faculty of Education and Professor
and
Head of the Department of Psychology,
Annamalai University

CONCEPT PUBLISHING COMPANY, NEW DELHI-110059

ISBN : 81-7022-796-8 (H.B.)
ISBN : 81-7022-797-6 (P.B.)

First Published 1999

Published and Printed by
Ashok Kumar Mittal
Concept Publishing Company
A/15-16, Commercial Block, Mohan Garden
New Delhi-110059 (INDIA)
Phone : 5648039, 5649024
Fax : 091-11-5648053

PREFACE

The beginning of twentieth century was a remarkable period in the history of psychology, since different schools of thought have emerged almost at the same time. Though each one was dealing with human behavioural problems in its own way, all of them have co-existed somehow for a considerable period of time till the end of the second quarter of this century. After 1950s, around the period 1960s the validity of these systems, particularly, the dominant schools, the Psychoanalysis and the Behaviourism were questioned by some critics and revolutionary thinkers in the field of psychology. Evidences were collected against the services and the contributions made by these schools. Strong opinions were expressed for and against the positive services rendered by these systems of psychology for more than fifty years.

At last a third force has emerged both in the mental health field and in the field of experimental psychology. Their main argument was that psychoanalysis studies only mentally abnormal persons, and behaviourism studies animal behaviour and attributes animal characteristics to human beings. They came out with a strong view that psychological studies should mainly deal with mentally healthy persons and the study of human personality should not be molecular or fragmentary, but it should be holistic, the person as a single whole.

These views were gaining more importance in the United States. There were several conferences, seminars, and controversies were going on for some time. Then, a group of psychologists have come out as Humanistic Psychologists under the leadership of Prof. Abraham Maslow and another group came out calling themselves as Community Psychologists. Following these, human behavioural problems were also conceived from other angles like ecological point of view involving the broad spectrum of environment and its influence on humans and the reaction of humans to it. A fourth group of psychologists have paid more attention on the miseries and vices of humans, and humans were losing their happiness of life periodically due to the serious population problems and they found strong evidences in the history of humankind. Thus all these four ways of thinking about human problems resulted in founding different fields of psychology almost at the same period around 1960s.

The fields are Community Psychology, Humanistic Psychology, Environmental Psychology and Population Psychology. New type of researches have been invented to evolve more information and new methods have been formulated to solve human problems. Some of these fields are more interested in theoretical aspects and some put more emphasis on application of the principles. Looking into the objectives of these fields, it is very conspicuous that all these fields are studying only human problems from different perspectives and making contributions to the development of knowledge in the field of psychology.

Of the four fields, except Humanistic Psychology, all other fields are more prone toward application of the methods to solve various types of human problems. Sigmund Freud once told his colleagues that his theory of Psychoanalysis and his findings are not the final, they are the beginnings for further research in this area for the young scientists. Freud was not rigid in his research findings in the field of mental health tradition. He wanted that young scientists should come forward in the field of mental health and make new contributions. This was what happened when Eysenck, the English Psychologist, criticised the therapeutic techniques adapted by the American Psychotherapists in dealing with mental health problems for more than fifty years. Eysenck's criticism became an impetus for starting a new field of thought called Community Psychology in mental health tradition.

The emergence of Environmental Psychology is based upon several factors. The impact of natural and physical, and the man-made and social environmental conditions have been causing enormous amount of human problems. The environmentalists felt that man digs his own grave while he is alive. They were very much worried over the behaviour of modern man, who is destroying the clean, green and fresh airy natural environment and constructing smoke, dust, and toxic and chemical wastage producing industries and polluting the environmental components and causing respiratory ailments and other infectious diseases to humankind. The new type of constructions and the skyscrapers prevent the movement of free air and the natural light and make people to get crowded in large number in small areas, which result in causing conflict, frustration and tension among the people who live there in a limited space.

People who are living in the newly constructed residential buildings are not only subjected to physical ill health, but also lose their psychological well-being. People in these man-made environmental conditions are constantly facing all sorts of pollutions, like air pollution, water pollution and environmental pollution and they are exposed to physical and other respiratory diseases. All these contribute to various types of human problems. Therefore, a group of American Psychologists felt that a separate field of study, the Environmental (or ecological) Psychology alone can deal with such problems and find out remedial measures for them. Guided by these ideas and principles large number of psychologists have put up their efforts in studying the problems caused by the environmental pollutions. As a result of it in a short period, enormous amount research contributions have been brought out in this field.

The American Population Council has started a separate division for studying the population problems from psychological point of view. The human crises, miseries and vices affect the harmonious life of the people very much and people are getting disgusted with the unwholesome human crowds everywhere, which are causing adjustment problems in their interaction with others. Therefore, it has been realized whether these human problems could be brought under the fold of psychological perspective and remedies can be find out. Though these problems involve the services of several other social sciences, effective strategies can be evolved from psychological perspective and the problems may be dealt with. This has awakened many social scientists all over the world and a separate field of study was felt which resulted in the birth of population psychology. Then, these four fields have defined their areas of study and they were started functioning almost at the same time around 1960s. Thus the third quarter of 20th century also may be regarded as the remarkable period in the history of psychology.

In this book, "Contemporary Fields of Psychology and Experiments", I tried to bring out all the salient features of the four fields and also incorporated relevant experiments covering every field, in such a way that they would arouse the curiosity in the minds of the academic people, so that they may identify the problems of the respective field and plan some wider substantial work which may be of some use to the people of the nation, who are facing many real serious problems in their life situations.

People in India are easily and constantly immunized to all sorts of pollutions and unhealthy environmental conditions and they find no means of avoiding them. It is obligatory for the social scientists of India to create a sense of awareness among the people and rescue them from the degeneration of the public and mental health hazards which are the root causes of human miseries and vices that are encompassing the people of the nation. A leading American Psychologist, Prof. Coleman said that the nineteenth century may be called the age of progress and the twentieth century, the age anxieties. But the twentieth century is something more than what Prof. Coleman has stated. We may add a few more epithets to Coleman's statement, that twentieth century is not only the age of anxieties, but also the age of uncertainties, stresses and tensions as people are in the strong grip of these unhealthy and unpleasant psychological forces and these states of affair do not seem to have an ending with 20th century, but it may also continue with more vigour in twenty-first century.

Chennai-600040 M. RAJAMANICKAM

Contents

1

COMMUNITY PSYCHOLOGY

1. INTRODUCTION

The second quarter of twentieth century, particularly the decade 1960, is a very remarkable period in the history of psychology for more than one reason. It is just like the beginning of twentieth century, during which period the time was ripen for the emergence of several schools of psychology, The schools of Associationism, Functionalism and the Behaviourism in the United States, the schools of Structuralism and Gestalt in Germany and psychoanalysis in Austria and the purposivism in England have emerged. Since all these schools of psychology have emerged almost at the same time between 1900 and 1915. Woodworth (1935), first published all the theoretical aspects of these schools under the title of *Contemporary Schools of Psychology.* This shows that within a short period, several schools of thought have come up, each one having its own way of approach to study human behaviour. Around the period of 1960 and 1970 a number of fields of psychology have emerged. They are Humanistic Psychology, Community Psychology, Environmental Psychology, Ecological Psychology and Population Psychology

But all the systems of psychology did not have the same level of importance. Somehow around 1950s the schools that were dominant in the United States were the psychoanalysis and the behaviourism. Freud's psychoanalysis during course of forty years has developed very rapidly as a profession and there were several offshoots from psychoanalysis to deal with the mental health problems. Similarly, Watson's behaviourism began to dominate in the field of experimental psychology and there were also several offshoots from Watson's behaviourism. One was dealing with mental health problems and the other was concentrating in experiments on animals. A group of psychologists in America looked upon both the systems from different angle and expressed their dissatisfaction in various ways. Abraham Maslow (1908-1970) has become the champion of this movement. Along with him a group of psychologists expressed passionately protesting the two dominant schools of psychology, psychoanalysis and behaviourism as having limited images of plan and it resulted in the emergence of *humanistic psychology, a vigorous third force in psychology* in 1962. In 1950s, the British psychologist, Eysenck (1952) has made a scathing comment on psychotherapeutic techniques, questioning the effects of them during the period of fifty years from 1900 to 1950. Eysenck's scathing criticism added fuel to the ventures of humanistic psychologists.

Around 1970, a group of psychologists turned to human engineering and human factors research and keenly observed into the effects of certain environmental conditions such as extreme heat, cold, noise and spatial effects on human performance and work efficiency. Researchers like Proshansky, Ittelson and Revlin (1970), Sommer (1969), Kaplan (1972), Whohlwill (1970) observed the influence of built environment on human behaviour and brought out publications on environmental psychology and at the same time courses in environmental psychology were started in the city University of New York. Bell *et al* (1976) brought out standard textbooks. A field called *Environmental Psychology* was born.

We know that behaviour inevitably influences the environment. Barker (1968) and his colleagues were strongly advocating the social ecological approach to human behaviour. Barker's approach is that behaviour setting is an entity in itself. The ecological psychology views environment-behaviour relationships as two-way passages. Behaviour of human being influences the environment and in return environment influences the behaviour of the people. Barker (1960, 1964, 1973) made many contributions to ecological approach to human behaviour in 1960s and in 1970s. Tornatzky (1976) states that there are also *Ecological Psychology* Training Programmes in progress to experimental field research. Barker and his colleagues are considered to be the founders of *Ecological Psychology* and it was *born around 1968-1970.*

Psychologists are turning their attention to the problems generated by the interpersonal relationships of the individuals in the communities. The interpersonal problems are numerous and complex. But many stand out because of their potential threat to man's wellbeing. A great deal of anxiety is being expressed regarding the population explosion and the possible effects resulting from over-crowding which may have on the individual's health and behaviour. There are many aspects of population crisis that are of great interest to psychologists, as they are interested in behaviour. We hear great deal, world-wide, about population disaster, with predictions of starving of millions, revolutions and wars brought out by population pressures. Overpopulation exists because of a very fundamental form of behaviour—the sexual behaviour. Psychologists and many researchers have studied sexual behaviour directly but nothing related to birth control. Some psychologists like Smith (1972) are interested in areas such as fertility control and abortion and population policies. Bartz (1970) accused the psychologists for taking lightly the population crisis. Buckhout (1972) states that there are more talks on population problems than research action. However at present psychologists are very much interested in population problems. Great deal of research projects are going on. What distinctive contributions that psychology can make to the broader field of population. The over population is the consequences of continued high birth rates and the improved control over death rates. Fawcatt (1970) states that population density results from high fertility and low mortality. Smith (1969) states that the study of fertility is a legitimate domain for psychologists. Within a short period many psychological studies and publications have been brought out by Pohlman (1969) and others. The American Psychological Association put up a task force on psychology and Family Planning, encouraging greater research and service by psychologists in this area of social problem. Thus the field of *Population Psychology* was recognized by the APA and it came into being in 1960s. Therefore it is evident that between 1960 and 1970 four fields of psychology have emerged. Hence these four as fields may be stated as the *contemporary fields of psychology.*

The scathing criticism made by Eysenck served as a double edged sword at this time. One sharp end was used by Humanistic psychologists for their purpose and the other sharp end was used by community psychologists for their purpose. There was a growing dissatisfaction in the United States against Freud's psychoanalysis and the psychotherapeutic techniques with regards to its therapeutic effects as many quack professionals also started practising psychotherapy as a profession. This was the time when Eysenck's (1952) criticism also appeared and this has become an additional source of authentic information for those who were already dissatisfied with psychoanalysis and psychotherapy, Though there was strong protest for Eysenck's criticism from many professionals, Eysenck's statement was well accepted as fact. Those who were already protesting against psychotherapy used Eysenck's comment as an additional weapon to fight for their goal.

Many community mental health centres were already functioning in the United States with the approval of the President's assent. Many psychologists who were already working in community mental health centres met in Boston at a conference in 1965 discussed the educational qualifications of psychologists for the community mental health work. Hersch (1969) states that this meeting of conference acknowledged the *birth date of community psychology as May 1965.* Thus community psychology was born in 1965 as the most revolutionary development in psychology and in mental health field in general. Nicholas Hobbs (1964) calls this as the *Third Mental Health Revolution.* Community psychology was given equal importance in all respects to those of other humanitarian organizations in the United States.

The Boston Conference assigned the area of service for the community mental health workers and for the community psychologists. The Boston conference called for the community psychologists for an active participation in the more general problems areas of the society. The conference report was published in 1966 by Bennett *et al* (1966) in which the community psychologists were called as Social Change Agents, Political Activists, and Participant Conceptualizer. Many community psychologists have associated themselves with the community mental health movement as professionals in accordance with the Boston conference. Community Psychology was given a status in the American Psychological association (APA). The Community Mental Health Journal, the first journal was brought out by Cowen in 1965, in which a chapter on Social and Community Intervention was also introduced. Around 1972, another journal named, American Journal of Community Psychology was edited and published by Charles D. Spielberger. Subsequently many research papers, volumes of books and monographs were brought out to enrich the field.

Thus Community Psychology has emerged as a revolutionary field of psychology and as the third mental health revolution in 1960s when the Humanistic Psychology also has emerged as a 'third force' in psychology to counteract against the two major schools, psychoanalysis and behaviourism. Community Psychology is evolved from the field of Clinical Psychology and the mental health field. Community Psychology has formulated new approach to deal with human problems.

The individual is not its main concern. It is the community that is taken as the subject matter. The community is the social environment which is responsible for the individual's problem. The community has neglected the individual. It has not made equity distribution of the natural and psychological resources to the individuals who are suffering from various types of problems.

Community Psychology emphasises that the role played by the social and physical environments is the cause of all adjustment and mental health problems and therefore by making the social and physical environments to suit to the needs of the individuals their problems can be alleviated. By making the community resources available to every individual and also by making the individuals to avail the opportunities to enjoy the resources of the society without any deprivation the problems of the individual can be solved. Many of the mental health or adjustment problems of the individuals are based upon the economic and social deprivations. Many unemployed are suffering from malnutrition, partial starvation, and physical weakness to carry out their even normal work.

Therefore, Community Psychology considers that the main crisis in the families, the sub-communities, are the emotional and social frustrations, economic deprivation, loss of family members, broken homes, mobility, divorce and social changes — all contribute to psychological problems. Community Psychology aims to work out strategies to study human behaviour problems as it occurs at homes, on the street, in the communities, in the work places and to study the complex relationship between the problem people and their physical and social environments and tries to solve them. First it tries to inform people that there is help for mental health problems and guides them. Secondly, it teaches them how to cope with the problems. We shall see now the historical background of the emergence of the community mental health and community psychology, the themes and the strategies of them.

2. HISTORICAL BACKGROUNDS FOR THE EMERGENCE OF COMMUNITY PSYCHOLOGY

The mental health problem of human beings is as old as man himself. Mental ill-health or behaviour disorder had been viewed by every society in every age with its own ideas, experiences and theories. If we want to have a better idea about the behaviour disorder, an understanding of the history of the problems becomes an essential matter. At various times at various places in history there have been men of experts in handling the mentally ill with their own methods and techniques. They were invariably called as Wizards or magicians, witch doctors, religious leaders, medical practitioners, mental doctors and so on. In the present days they are called psychologists, psychiatrists, psychoanalysts and so on.

The primitive or the prehistoric man lived in a state of peril, attributing all sorts of hazards to evil spirits. He believed that even the natural disasters such as storm, heavy rains, thunder, lightning earthquakes he was facing were all caused by evil spirits. This period was called animism. Animism was the earliest form religion. Men were living in constant fear of the spirits and every hazard they met were due to the revenge of the spirits whom they failed to satisfy by offerings. The primitive man believed that any abnormal behaviour in man was due to some evil spirit which haunted him as he failed to propitiate the spirit. He is called the 'possessed' which means that his body is possessed by the evil spirit. To drive the spirit out of him the help of shamans or Godman was sought. On the name of treatment the person was tortured and sometimes even put to death. Such was the treatment met by the persons who were suffering from mental disorders in the ancient times. The same type of treatment was continued till the medieval period but in different names.

There are also several historical evidences, available regarding the behaviour disorder. Many forms of mental disorders that we speak of today have been also observed and reported in earlier periods. In Greek mythology there were several instances of behavioural disorders exhibited by the heroes. In Homer's work the Greek hero Ajax, the son of Telamom, the hero of the Trojan war killed himself in an extreme mental demarrage state when Achillas' armour was given to Odysseus. In his deranged state he was killing sheep instead of his enemies. Ulysses, one of the heroes of Trojan war lost his battle and gone mad and was yoking a bull and a horse together ploughing and sowing salt rather than seeds.

The ancient Greek period was a remarkable one which was filled with outstanding rational intellectuals of which the well known were the mathematician and philosopher, Pythagoras lived in 6th century B.C., the philosopher Socrates who preached philosophy by dialectical process, lived in 5th century B.C., the philosopher Plato who initiated the Western Philosophy, lived around 427-347 B.C., the philosopher

Aristotle, pupil of Plato and the Tutor of Alexander the Great, also founded the school of Athens, lived around 384-322 B.C. All of them were belonging to the Rationalistic Tradition unlike the other ancient traditions who lived in the world of superstitions. They have also contributed to psychological thought.

The ancient Babylonians believed that there was a specific demon for each mental disease. Idta for them was the demon causing insanity. There are similar examples available from the records of ancient Egyptians, Chinese and Greeks and Romans. In Bible also there are references that the persons who were possessed by evil demons were cured. In Old Testament, there is a reference to Saul, the first King of Israel lived in 17th century B.C. He led Israel and faught successfully against the Phillistines. But he was continuously in conflict with the high Samuel. Then he was affiliated with madness and committed suicide and died. Pythoness, a Greek mythological woman, believed to be possessed by an oracular spirit. Hercules, the Greek mythological hero was also called Alcides noted for his great strength and courage and a man equivalent to twelve men. He suffered from mental disorder of homicidal type. He killed his two sons, his brother's children, his friend and teacher. Whitwell (1936) states that the king of Persia, Cambyses who lived in 6th century B.C. was said to be an alcoholic and mentally deranged. He was also stated as an incestuous and homicious person. He married his own sister and killed his other sister and his friend's son.

Apart from these ancient heroes there were also many historical heroes who exhibited serious behavioural disorders. One of the most notorious historical heroes was Tamerlane, a Mongolian conquerer also called Timur who lived in 14th century wanted to conquer the world and construct pyramids out of human skulls. He was a great homicide gone mad after killing thousands of people and it was estimated, that he had killed forty thousand people. Richard III, the king of England who lived in 15th century was noted for his insane acts. He killed two of his nephews in the Tower of London. Later on he was killed by Henry VII. He ruled England only for two years. Another notorious king who ruled England was Henry the eighth. He ruled England for forty years from 1507-1547. He married first his brother's wife and beheaded her and married seven ladies one by one killing on the ground that they are not beautiful. He went against the church and became the supreme of the church of England. He changed his advisors often. George, the third, was King of Great Britain and Ireland for sixty years from 1760 to 1820. He lost the American colonies during his reign and became insane in 1811 and displayed with all sorts of behavioural disorders. He suffered from severe manic depressive psychosis. Therefore his son George IV acted as his regent for rest of the period and became the king of Great Britain and Ireland and ruled from 1820 to 1830. He had difference of opinion with his father as he was leading a reckless and wasteful life.

The French Philosopher, Rousseau who lived in eighteenth century (1712-1788) believed in the natural goodness of man and he brought out his famous work Social Contact in 1762. His ideas and philosophy strongly influenced the French Revolution. In the later part of his life Rousseau developed severe parania and also had delusions, had severe anxieties and he suspected everybody that they are plotting against him. He was an agnostic, but in the later years turned God as people are untrustworthy and stated that God also was conspiring against him. George Gordon Byron (1781-1824) was Great English Romantic poet. He was noted for his passionate and disastrous love affairs. He lived only for thirty six years. He was suffering from severe emotional disorders and prayed to God to give him peace and happiness. He expressed his mental agony in his important work 'Childe Harold's Pilgrimage' and had very unpleasant death. John Keats (1795-1821), a famous English Romantic poet, well known for his lyric poems, characterized by both lofty feelings and dignified style. He had many mental conflicts and emotional disorders and prayed to God to give him strength to forget his unpleasant memories. He was suffering from sleeplessness and had many outburst of crying hallucinations. He lived only for twenty six years and had very unpleasant death.

Queen Mary, the First (1516-1558) known as Tutor Mary ruled England for five years (1553-1558). She was the daughter of Henry the Eighth born to Catherine of Dragon and she married Phillip II of Spain in 1554. She was staunch follower of Roman Catholic and dead against Protestantism. Queen Tutor Mary I was contemporary to Queen Stuart Mary of Scotland, who was Protestant. Mary Tutor worked to restore Roman Catholicism to England. In her extreme affiliation for catholicism and extreme hatred for Protestantism she burnt alive about 300 protestants as heretics during her ruling period of five years. Because of this she was called Bloody Mary. By this means she exposed her ruthless sadistic attitude towards her rival, Stuart Mary.

William Wordsworth (1770-1850), a celebrated English natural poet who inspired many contemporary poets like Samuel Taylor Coleridge by his dignified style, suffered from many emotional frustrations followed by social frustration and ideological conflicts. He loved a French woman five years senior to him in France but could not go there and marry her as there was a war between England and France at that time. He expressed all his emotional disturbances in his poem 'Lines written about Tintern Abbey'. As a result of his conflict and emotional frustrations and agony he lived a painful celibate life. His sister Dorothy Wordsworth also was writer and a journalist lived a celibate life along with Wordsworth.

These instances of ancient and historical behaviour disorders show that man was not free from mental disorders and abnormal symptoms. These evaluations of the olden days abnormalities are made in the light of the present day abnormal symptoms and behaviour disorders. Many made notable contributions, achievements and valuable services to society, though they at one stage exhibited abnormal symptoms. They might have struggled hard to make adjustment in their societies. Apart from the behaviour disorders that existed among the people who lived in those days they also imagined and thought of abnormal characteristics and remedies for them in their contemporary writings. This has been revealed in many of the poems, plays, novels and paintings.

Many writers of those periods have carefully and keenly observed the abnormal symptoms and behaviours and vividly presented the emotional reactions of the normal and abnormal people. We have stated above that poets Byron and Wordsworth have expressed their personal mental conflicts in their writings. Byron speaks through the character, 'Childe Harold' in his poem 'Childe Harold's Pilgrimage'. But William Shakespeare (1564-1611) has described the abnormal symptoms and behaviour of those people whom he observed in his days and presented them in his plays. For example, in his plays The Tempest, Timon of Athens, Julius Caeser, Macbeth, Othello, Hamlet, A Midsummer Night's Dream, King Lear and in many other plays Shakespeare has presented characters with some kind of mental disorders and abnormal behaviour. Let us quote one or two examples here. In 'The Tempest' he has presented a character called Caliban as a subnormal person in whom many abnormalities were seen.

In the play Macbeth, Shakespeare has presented Lady Macbeth with severe abnormal symptoms of washing her hands several times everyday and also she states at one stage that even the water of seven oceans cannot wash her hands and all the perfumes of Arabia will not change smell of her hand. Shakespeare, thus revealed the strong guilt feelings of Lady Macbeth who had murdered the King Duncan who was their guest that night in their castle, sleeping in a room after the dinner. Lady Macbeth was suffering from severe compulsive neurosis. King Lear was described as suffering from old age disorder, Senile Dementia.

Many English authors have introduced characters with abnormal behaviour patterns of various types in their plays and novels. Some of the characters were introduced by them as caricatures of some living personalities of their times. Thomas Shadwell (1642-92) was a famous seventeenth century English poet laurete, and dramatist. After Shakespeare, Shadwell has written many famous plays and staged them in London theatres. In his plays he has introduced many characters with symptoms of abnormal behaviour. Some of his contemporaries who could not tolerate his fame, severely criticised and satirized him. John Dryden (1631-1700), an English poet, dramatist and critic was his contemporary, noted for his satirical poems. Dryden written several verses satirizing Shadwell and his plays and ridiculed him as insane and all his plays are collections of insanity.

Therefore there is a tradition of presenting characters with symptoms of abnormal behaviour in their writings right from the time of Homer (8th century B.C.) to the present time in the ancient classics, epics, plays, novels and stories. Abnormal behavioural symptoms were also traced in the historical events, in the lives of kings and queens, poets and philosophers. Even now, modern writers introduce abnormality in their dramas and stories to give a turning point to their stories, and when they wanted certain inexplicable events to take place in their stories. In no minute they create abnormalities of some type and also with the same speed they make them to disappear. It is very interesting to know that in the ancient and medieval periods and also till the end of 19th century the writers had very carefully handled the descriptions about abnormality in their writings and they all seem to be in line with the present day concepts of mental disorder. It appears that these masters of plays and fictions have developed many brilliant characteristics of abnormal behaviour by keen observation of human behaviour from various angle and introduced in their writings. It is very astonishing to see that these classical writers of these periods have made their descriptions of human abnormalities with all the infinite sharp delicacies which are beyond the observation of ordinary human beings. The vividness of the emotional shades which were expressed through the Shakespearean characters like Hamlet, Othello, Timon of Athens and many others only indicate how subtly Shakespeare had observed human emotions of both men and women of various personality types, the feelings and emotions, the ambitions and aspirations of various ages, the plans, the strategies and the conspiracies, the valour and the conquest, the defects and destructions, the conflict and frustrations, the emotional and mental disorders, the delusions, and hallucinations that were prevalent during the respective historical periods. It is stated that many of the abnormal behaviour patterns found in the ancient classics and medieval literature are having clinical characteristics of the present times.

From the descriptions of various personalities and the type of life they were living and the physical and mental sickness from which they were suffering, were all quite similar to what the modern science attributes to many of the physical and mental illnesses. What they were mentioning as insanity is quite similar to psychoses to schizophrenia. There were also mentionings of depression, suicide, alcoholism, drug addiction, mental retardation or sub-normal, homicide, sadism, rape, stress, compulsive neurosis delusions, visual hallucinations, phobias, anxieties, delusions of persecution, delusions of sin and guilt. Therefore there were instances of abnormality right from the ancient time onwards and many of them were referred in the contemporary writings of those periods and also in the historical notes on the historical personalities. The biographies of some of the medieval and modern poets and philosophers, the conquerers and the rulers were also victims of the attacks of abnormalities. The causes of the various types of abnormalities in the ancient, medieval and modern times were not vividly found in the sources. The treatments have varied depending upon the development of culture and civilization of the age, some primitive, some animistic, religious, some physical, medicinal and some philosophical.

Assessment and Treatment of Abnormality

Mental abnormality is stated in varied names such as mental illness, mental disorders, mental disease, insanity, maladaptive behaviour, behaviour disorder, abnormal behaviour, madness, mentally deranged and psychopathology. All these refer to the same state of mind. This is generally referred to any one state of maladaptive behaviour. There are specific disorders. The American Psychiatric Association (1968) has classified mental disorders into ten categories. They are (1) mental retardation, (2) organic brain syndromes, (3) psychoses, (4) neuroses,

(5) personality disorders, (6) psychophysiologic disorders, (7) special symptoms, (8) transient situational disturbances, (9) behaviour disorders in childhood and adolescence and (10) conditions without manifest psychiatric disorders and nonspecific conditions. This is not the final classification. The first classification was published in 1952 and 1968. The list was again revised.

Since it was recognized that different disorders are required different treatments it has become more important to improve the diagnostic procedures and to make the classifications more specific. The classification made in the abnormal behaviour during nineteenth century had many inconsistencies. It has caused serious problems. Therefore revisions were made in the list of classification of abnormal behaviour in France and in Great Britain and the American Psychiatric Association has accepted the British classification with some revision in it in 1918. But the revised classification in collaboration with the World Health Organization (WHO), the American Psychiatric Association again revised it in 1952 and published an elaborated list under the heading of Diagnostic and Statistical Manual of Mental Disorders. This was stated as DSM-I, Another version of the classification was made by the American Psychiatric Association in 1968 which was stated as DSM-II. The revised British system was published again in 1968. The WHO has published a new list of classification in 1969. Each of these classifications stated different symptoms. This again caused some problem in diagnostic practices. Therefore the American Psychiatric Association has published another classification list with revised diagnostic manual in 1980, which was stated as DSM-III. On the basis of the 1980 revision another revision called DSM-III-B appeared in 1987 and investigators and diagnosticians therefore were forced to revise their nomenclature time to time and they themselves will have to brush up their knowledge in this field. All those earlier writings using the classification systems prior to 1980 and 1987 revision will have to be rewritten on the basis of the new classification systems.

The latest revision (1987) DSM-III-R of the classification of abnormal behaviour is having several new findings. This is called DSM-III-R multiaxial classification system. According to the multiaxial system of diagnosis, each individual is to be tested on five separate dimensions and each of which has to be employed in categorizing the persons and diagnostic judgments should be made on each of the five axes. By this method the diagnostician has to collect a very wide range of information and consider the patient's disorder and classify it. Every axis has an area of abnormal behaviour patterns. Let us see how far the 1987 classification of mental disorders is a different from the earlier classification and more convenient for diagnosis and treatment.

One of the important disorders found in the earlier system was neuroses. But in the latest classification DSM-III-R neuroses are classified into several new classes under the heading of 'anxiety disorders'. This was a great disappointment to the clinicians who were working on it for many years. On protest it was restored and added as second heading. Similarly psychosis was another concept which was in usage in the everyday discussions and was also prominent in DSM-II. This was transformed into pervasive developmental disorders, Organic mental disorders, schizophrenic and paranoid disorders and mood disorders. On protest an option was given for diagnosing the depressed patient as psychotic, dropping the idea, neurotic depression and was retained in DSM-III-R. The earlier concept 'drug abuse' is now stated as psychoactive substance abuse, the 'drug addiction' is now used as psychoactive substance dependence. In American culture there was controversy with regard to the patterns of emotional behaviour. Till 1973 in the DSM-II list, homosexuality was stated as sexual deviations. The gay men and women of the activist groups recommended to eliminate the concept of homosexuality and substitute it with 'sexual orientation disturbance'.

The 'organic brain syndrome' of the earlier classification has been eliminated in the DSM-III-R and in place of it two new concepts, such as *organic mental disorder* and *organic mental syndrome* are introduced. These are the two new major categories in the DSM-III-R. The organic mental disorders refer to the organic psychological problems that are connected with a specific factor known as somatic cause. The alcohol induced organic mental disorder is a good example for this.

The organic mental syndromes refer to the organic psychological problems that are caused by more than one specific somatic factors. The organic mood syndrome is an example for this. These are few examples of the changes introduced in the 1987 revision of the classification of the mental disorders. Only a few familiar concepts were substituted with new concepts. These changes seem to be more refined and improved models. But it will take some time for the clinicians and the researchers in this field to accommodate themselves with the 1987 revision of the classification.

The 1987 classification DSM-III-R is a very exhaustive classification compared to DSM-II. The axes I and II include all the mental disorders belonging to the real nature. In Axis III included are the physical disorders that seem to have influenced upon the mental disorders. In axis IV the various types of psychosocial stresses experienced by the children, adolescents and adults are included. In axis V psychological, social, occupational, functional mental health and mental illnesses ranging from mild anxiety to severe type so as to cause injury to the self and others are included. But, however, the classification of DSM-III-R is not as clear as the classification of DSM-II.

In the primitive period it was believed that mental illness was caused by evil spirits. Therefore the shamans or the exorcists were appeasing the spirits around them and keeping them away. A person who was possessed by evil spirits, by his behaviour, was a problem to his family and to the whole group of people. Out of ignorance and superstition the only way of dealing with him was to put him to death. By this means the demon was driven away. Thus the extreme deviates were murdered often as early as possible to drive away the demon in the ancient times.

With regard to specific case of mental disorder both the primitive man and the modern man behaved in the same manner. But the type of treatments varied very widely. Recorded evidences are available from fifth century B.C. that mental illness was approached in a rational manner. The Greek Physician Hippocrates (460-357 B.C.) treated mental patients without involving religion, religious shamans and witch doctors. According to Hippocrates mental illness was the result of malfunctioning of the body and he treated mental illness just like physical disease. According to him all mental abnormalities were due to malfunction of the four basic humours of the body such as yellow bile, black bile, blood and phlegm. Madness was caused by the excess of yellow bile. Excess of black bile was the cause of depression. Excess of blood caused too much of optimistic and excess of phlegm caused sluggish tendency. The scientific or rational approach made by Hippocrates did not catch up to establish a tradition. Therefore what was the treatment prevailing in the prehistoric period began to dominate again in this matter.

In the ancient days the emotionally disorganized persons and the mentally ills were dealt with by religious men, shamans, superstitious people, witch doctors and the exorcists. These people were claiming to be the specialists in handling the mentally ill. In almost all the early religions exorcism was the treatment to emotional and mental disorders and the priests were claiming to be the correct persons to deal with this. In many primitive and quasi-civilized religions the exorcists were considered as the specialists in casting out the evil spirits or demons from the possessed person. The priests and the exorcists treating the mentally ill was mostly prevalent in all primitive religions, among the early Hebrews, among the early Chinese, Egyptians, Greeks and among the Indians. In all these cultures and civilizations mental disorders were believed to be caused by the demons, taking possession of the individual. The treatment invariably was afflicting bodily pain to the persons. Rites and chanting of magic words or *mantras*, making noisy prayers and flogging with whips, chaining and making them to starve were the common treatments in almost all cultures. In some cultures the priests added magic and medicine to the prevalent treatments. Only the Greeks, here and there at sometimes were treating the mentally ills humanistically. In Greek, in the temples of Asdepius during the period of Hippocrates and Alexander the Great, the treatments were somewhat different for a limited period.

The middle age did not show any progress or change from the primitive way of treatment to the mentally ills. Since the period of middle age was not denoted clearly with any line of demarcation, it is very difficult to state when or in which century A.D. changes in the treatment of the mentally disturbed took place. The medieval period was roughly estimated between fifth century and fifteenth century (476 A.D.-1450 A.D.) with a range of one thousand years. During this period much recorded information on this issue were not available and therefore these periods are called dark ages. Therefore treatments were varied from place to place in the same culture. In some parts of Europe, during the middle ages the clergymen were treating the mentally disturbed and monasteries were used as places of confinement and the mental patients were treated kindly in the early middle ages. The clergymen used holy water, prayer, the saliva of the patients, touching the sacred materials, visiting holy places and exorcism in their treatments. The clergymen have developed more technique in exorcism in treating the patients.

The clergymen's approach in treating the mental patients was gaining favourable attitude and the people not connected with religion or monasteries began to approve of it. The treatment was becoming more and more harsh and cruel. The belief was that the devil which possessed the person will not leave the man by simple punishments to the body. Therefore it was felt by the priests that more severe and unpleasant methods should be followed. By this means they believed that the demon will not stay any more in an unpleasant body and would run away. Therefore the mentally disturbed was put to more severe bodily afflictions such as flogging, starving, chaining, putting into hot water and similar torturous situations. It appears that this type of treatments for the mentally disturbed were going on till the end of the middle ages and during these times exorcism has become a highly developed art.

At the close of fifteenth century the old beliefs were maintained with regard to the cause of mental disorder and treatment and something new to the demonology was added. All sorts of superstitious beliefs about devil, satan, supernatural powers, evil spirits, demons were in high spirits. Satan was given more importance in the later part of this period. Theologically, it has been accepted that the persons who were possessed by devils were actually in association and agreement with the devils to whom satan, the supreme of the devils gave them certain supernatural powers with which they could cause all sorts of injuries to their enemies, ruining their crops, causing epidemic diseases and causing natural disasters like storms, heavy rains and flood and also they were taking the forms of animals and because of all these they were strongly believed as witches and wizards. This was the belief of even important clergymen and it was also stated that even Martin Luther (1483-1546), the German leader of the Protestant Reformation had the same view. Thus witchery and wizardry have emerged as evil forces. At the same period there was some rational awakening all over Europe. It had its origin in Italy and it was called the period of Renaissance and men began to think of the finer aspects of the ancient Greeks and Romans, their art, culture and learning. A new trend which was aroused, began to question everything. The demonology and Satanic accomplishments seemed to be in an incongruous state with the new trends. There were great concerns over the increase of witches and wizards everywhere, causing disaster consequences. All the Catholic and Protestant countries were collecting information about the witches and wizards and the clergymen have developed intense fervour to eliminate the witches and wizards who were possessed by the devils. A test was conducted to identify the mentally ill and the physically ill by those who believed in demon possession. By shouting a Bible verse into the ear of the person who was supposed to be possessed, and observing his reaction to it, the really possessed was identified by the signs of turning back to reality for a moment. This means the devil has left him for fear of the holy Bible. At the same time the physically ill shown no sign of change. Having this test into confidence the clergymen expedited the vital hunting. Pope Innocent VIII had sanctioned the publication of a handbook on Witches and two German monks written it with a title of *The Witches' Hammer*.

Persons who were found to be suffering from mental illnesses similar to various types of neuroses and psychoses were suspected as Witches and Wizards. On these suspected persons tests were conducted to identify the persons who were really mentally ill and who were witches. If there were great damages to life and property by storms, floods, rains, or any natural disasters, it was believed that they were all caused by the witches and wizards. If there was an increase in death by any epidemic diseases, serious criminal activities, ruining of the crops then it was assumed that more number of witches were roaming about and they were hunted and taken to lunatic asylums. This sort of hunting of the witches was going on for nearly three hundred years, from last quarter of fifteenth century to the end of eighteenth century. The treatment for them ranged from severe whipping to burning to death. According to Bromberg (1937), the statistics were that about seven thousand women were burned alive during these periods. This was carried out by the Roman Catholic and the Protestant churches in France, Germany, England and also in America. According to Strange (1965), the last witch put to death was in the year 1792.

Even during the period of Witchcraft and Wizardly there were instances of humanistic treatment given by physicians and condemned the treatment given by the clergymen. The mental asylums in USA were like concentration camps, the mentally iils were imprisoned and tortured. Russell (1941) and Bennett (1947) have stated that they were chained, plunged into cold water, hours together in spring water, making them bleeding, purging, vomiting, causing blisters and put to similar torturings. Even in early nineteenth century, in 1930s the patients were head shaven, put on low diet to starve, forced with active forgetives, put in dark cells, and solitary confinements and other tortures were common methods of treatments.

The last quarter of eighteenth century and the whole of nineteenth century was characterised as the Age of Reform. During this period every country had its share in expressing its spirit of free-will in some manner. The important events were the French Civil War faught for ten years (1789 to 1799) till Napoleon (1769-1821) came to power in 1799. The American Civil War was fought between the North and the South America from 1861 to 1865, which was sparked off by Abraham Lincoln's (1805-65) election to the Presidentship. There was also war between Great Britain and America, between 1812 and 1814, after the American Independency War, fought between 1777 and 1785. All those civil wars had profound influence in the political and social life of the people in France and all over the Europe and in America.

The period of renaissance was also stated as the age of enlightenment during which there were two forces at work, one was said to be the period in which the demonology, exorcism, witchcraft, identifying witches, witch hunting as stated in *The Witches' Hammer* and treating the mentally disordered by flogging, chaining, hanging and burning and other methods of torturings were widely dominant.

While these were going on one side, on the other side the force was towards awakening of scientific spirit and technological development. This period was marked by contradicting movements. There were several conflicting philosophies like, scepticism, pragmatism, empiricism, materialism and naturalism making man and the human mind as centre of the enquiry. This resulted in raising criticisms from several corners deploring and condemning the belief that mental disorder was caused by the devils and the cruelty in the name of treatment met by the inmates of the asylums.

There were also signs of changes in the mental health field. It was felt very seriously both in Europe and America. Philippe Pinel (1745-1826), a French physician became the chief of the La Bicetra mental hospital in Paris in 1793 and made radical changes in the mental hospital by instituting humanistic treatment. He released the mental patients from the chains and confinements. He advocated that mental patients should be treated kindly like ordinary physical patients. He was against the practice of treating the mental patients like animals and criminals. Selling (1943) states that the change in the nature of the treatment of the mental patients had tremendous effect upon the patients' discipline. Zilborg and Henry (1941) have stated that many wonderful changes have taken place in the behaviour of the mental patients. Strange (1965) states that at one stage Pinel himself was suspected as a mad man. The authorities also were very reluctantly permitting all the changes he made. Later on Pinel was asked to take charge of another mental hospital Salpetriere. Pinel made similar reforms there and thus these two mental hospitals became the modern hospitals in France. Later on Pinel has extended his activities of reformation to all the mental hospitals in France and made France as the fore-runner of humanistic treatment to the mental patients. Therefore the services rendered by Philippe Pinel was called the *First Mental Health Revolution* in the history mental health services.

At the same time in America, Benjamin Rush (1745-1813) a physician and also a psychiatrist wanted to reform the mental hospitals. Lazarus (1976) states that in nineteenth century the mental health movement was first organized by Dorothea Lynde Dix (1802-1882) a retired teacher, strongly protested against the treatment of the mental patients like animals and wanted to reform it. She went from place to place and fought against the cruelty. While her reform crusade was going on the Civil War broke out at America and she joined the civil war to lend her services.

While Pinel was seriously engaged in reforming the mental asylums in France, Anton Mesmer (1734-1815) an Austrian physician who developed the idea of the universal magnetic fluid, which he believed was distributed in the body, was mainly the cause of the ill health and disease. Mesmer attempted to cure all kinds of mental diseases by animal magnetism. In 1778 he went to Paris and continued his treatment. Mesmer, while treating the hysterial and paralytic patients, found that hypnosis was very much useful for him. The Paris physicians started persecuting him that he was a quack doctor, fraudulantly practicing medicines. As result of it he left Paris. At the same time, in France, Liebault (1823-1904) a physician was also using hypnosis in treating the hysterial patients and established the relationship between hypnosis and hysteria. Bernheim (1840-1919) was very much attracted by Liebault's hypnotic approach and both jointly declared the effects of hypnosis on hysteria. Many accepted this view and they were called Nancy School. Bernheim worked hard and developed Liebault's view and also extended it to all neurotic problems. He tried to explain abnormal behaviour from psychological and clinical observations. While Bernheim was progressing well with his Nancy school on hysteria and neurotic problems by the methods of hypnosis and self suggestions, Jean Charcot (1822-1893) who succeeded Pinel and Jean Esquirol (1772-1840) in running the mental hospitals, Bicetre and Salpetriere in Paris had also shown interest in the works of Nancy school. Charcot originally a neurologist, on experimentation with the works of Nancy School did not accept the views of Nancy school on hysteria. Charcot had strong view that mental disorders and hysteria were caused by brain damages and there were no psychological causes. There were great controversies between Nancy school and Charcot on this matter and finally the Nancy school won over the issue and Charcot himself had accepted the psychological bases of mental disorders. Then the nature of Charcot's works on mental disorders were having both psychological and organic bases. He made many contributions to psychology which brought him great reputations. Many students on knowing about Charcot's works and fame went to Paris and worked under him and subsequently there was another rival school in Paris to Nancy School. Pierre Janet (1859-1947) was one of the famous students of Charcot. He continued Charcot's work and also took charge of the work at Salpetriere hospital on Charcot's death. His important contribution was on psychoneuroses and formulated the process called dissociation.

Though towards the end of nineteenth century it was accepted that mental disorders have psychological and organic bases neither the Nancy school under Liebault and Bernheim nor the Paris school under Charcot and Janet did not explain fully the dynamic functions of the mental disorders. At this stage Sigmund Freud (1856-1939) an Austrian neurologist and psychiatrist from Vienna made systematic attempt to explain many things about somotogenic disorders and factors related to hysteria and mental disorders. Freud was treating mainly neurotic and hysterial patients in Vienna. He heard about Charcot's work on hysteria and neuroses and therefore in 1895 he went to Paris to study under Charcot and later on he was also associated with the Nancy school. Freud was very much satisfied by the hypnotic methods used by Liebault and Bernheim on hysterial patients. He was very much convinced that patients in conscious state will not reveal many mental processes because they were strongly concealed.

Freud in using the hypnotic method had associated himself with Joseph Breuer (1842-1925) an older physician who was using hypnosis to treat hysterial patients. Breuer in his practice had developed certain new techniques in hypnotism. He found that in the hypnotic state the patient was able to talk freely and relieve considerable amount of emotions. The patient after this was relieved of certain emotional tensions. Therefore this was called Cathartic method. Freud and Breuer have jointly published about what they observed in the hysterial and neurotic patients in applying the hypnotic technique, under the title of *Studies in Hysteria* in 1895. This was considered to be an important milestone in abnormal psychology.

Soon, Freud was very much dissatisfied with the hypnotic technique in dealing with the hysterial patients as he found no relationship between the patient's problems and hysterial symptoms. What seemed to be progress in this technique was only a momentary reaction in the clinic. Finally Breuer had to dispense with the Cathartic method as most of the neuroses were found to be having connection with sexual conflicts and frustrations. Therefore Freud had given up the hypnotic techniques and followed a new method, by which he allowed and encouraged the patient to talk freely whatever comes to his/her mind without paying any regard to the nature of the talk. Freud found soon that the patient was able to overcome gradually the defences or the inhibitions built up over many years and discussed the patient's neurotic or hysterial problems. Freud called it 'free association method' and it was found to be very much successful.

On close observation on his patients, Freud often saw that the patient himself was not aware of the source of his conflicts and anxieties. He felt that some factors seem to play powerful role and determine the behaviour of the patient and the patient himself was not aware of them and they were incessible. Freud believed that basically most of the important determinants of behaviour, even a small act of slip of the tongue has a specific cause, to be the unconscious. The patient was not aware of the drives and motives which were *unconscious* and they were putting the individual at work constantly. He believed that all the unpleasant desires, wishes, emotions and motives that were not normally accepted and approved were repressed from the conscious level into the unconscious and from there, they motivate the individual which the person himself was not aware of it. Freud also observed the process of function, called *repression.*

In the application of free association method on neurotic and hysterial patients Freud became aware of the unconscious processes and the process of repression in the patients and also observed that the patients often were mentioning of their dreams. Freud made them to narrate all the dreams they had that day and on previous occasions. These dreams of the patients provided Freud with valuable information for the patients' problems. By interpreting the patients' dreams and his own dreams Freud found that behind the dream events, which, he called as the *manifest content* and, the meaning of the actual events were hidden in what he called, as the *latent content.* To know the real life events of the patients from the dream events Freud had to record and analyse innumerable number of dreams, about more than one thousand dreams from the patients and from the normal people. Thus Freud worked on dream analysis and step by step was able to make his method perfect and succeeded in bringing out the repressed material from the unconscious level to the conscious level. With all these accumulated materials in the year 1900 Freud was able to publish his famous book *The Interpretation of Dreams.*

The Interpretation of Dreams was considered to be the masterpiece of Freud's works, because it consisted of many of his valuable new findings. While explaining the dream process Freud also has given an outline of his personality theory and also developed the method of *psychotherapy.* In analysing and interpreting what the patient talked about overcoming the inhibitions in the free association method Freud used several principles to expand his method and theory which was later on called *Psychoanalysis.* Students from many countries on knowing Freud's new method of treatment for mental disorders came to him to learn the new techniques. Among them, the most remarkable scientists were Karl Abraham from Berlin, Carl Jung (1875-1961) from Zurich, Ernest Jones from London, Brill from America, Alfred Adler (1870-1937) from Vienna. In 1909 Freud went to America on an invitation from Stanley Hall to give a series of lectures on psycho-analysis in the Clark University. After few years Jung and Adler had difference of opinion with Freud on many issues and left Freud and started separate schools of their own. Freud was revising his theories in an attempt to improve and refine them.

Freud lived his life only in Vienna. When Hitler's Nazi troops entered Austria during the World War II Freud was taken by his friends to London where he died of Cancer in September 1939. He lived and saw that his psychodynamic approach to the study of personality and psychoanalysis as a therapeutic technique have spread out throughout the world. Freud made magnificent contributions to psychology, psychiatry, art, literature and science. Edwin Boring (1950) in his book *History of Experimental Psychology* wrote about Freud that in Sigmund Freud (1856-1939) we met a man with the attributes of greatness. He was a pioneer in a field of thought, in a new technique for the understanding of human nature. William McDougall (1926) the British psychologist also wrote about Freud, that in his opinion, Freud has, quite unquestionably done more for the advancement of our understanding of human nature than any other man since Aristotle.

Sigmund Freud started his career as a physician, as a neuro-pathologist and gradually became a neuropsychiatrist and developed the therapeutic technique to cure hysteria and then neuroses and psychoneuroses. He lived and died only for curing mental disorders and for inventing new techniques to deal with them. The monumental contributions made by Sigmund Freud in the late nineteenth and early twentieth centuries follow immediately after the humanitarian reforms in mental hospital brought out by Philippe Pinel and his followers in the late eighteenth and first-half of the nineteenth centuries. Freud's followers continued his work and developed his psychoanalysis and therapeutic techniques in various ways and made it as a leading profession in United States. Therefore Freud's Psychoanalysis has emerged as the *Second Mental Health Revolution* in the history of mental health services and also considered to be one of the two major schools of psychology in the United States.

3. EMERGENCE OF THIRD MENTAL HEALTH REVOLUTION

Man's mental health problem is as old as man himself and man has been trying to find out some methods of treatment and also inventing some medicines to solve all his mental health problems. He was successful in his attempts sometimes and sometimes failed deplorably. In the preceding passages we have discussed how the mental health problem right from the ancient time onwards has been threatening man and the society and man with all his ability, intelligence and resources has been fighting it. The primitive man since he could not get rid of his superstitious beliefs and practices he was often succumbed to the traditional convictions. It had taken thousands of years for man to bring changes in his way of life and in his attitude towards the mental health problems. The practice prevailing at present was the result of continued efforts and the relentless struggles made by the men of scientific and rationalistic spirit against the guardians of the traditions for generations. Thus so far two revolutionary developments have taken place in the field of mental health and what is going on now is the third revolutionary development in psychology and mental health field.

Why is this third mental health revolution in psychology and mental health field? Several causes have been attributed to this state of affair. This spirit was developed among a group of psychologists in the United States around 1950s out of the dissatisfaction they have felt about the progresses made in the field of clinical psychology.

Clinical psychology in the second quarter of twentieth century was a rapidly growing applied field of science in psychology. Its important bearing on mental health problems all over the world was greatly increasing and the clinical psychologists were being asked to play a major role in solving the problems in this field. Still psychology itself is a relatively a new science and its areas of application are in rapid transition. As far the information available, the first decade (1900-1910) of twentieth century may be said to be the period from which clinical psychology began to function scientifically. Only during this period men from America and England went to Vienna to study under Freud. Though the treatments to mental patients were going on from the time of Freud, a systematic clinical approach took place only during his period. But there were only few professional men in the field of psychology. Mental patients were mainly treated by medical men.

Julian Rottar (1964) traces the early beginning of clinical psychology to late eighteenth century and the nineteenth centuries. He is referring to the study of abnormal behaviour which included mental retardation and to the works of Francis Galton (1822-1911) who studied the individual differences. According to Rottar, before World War II clinical psychologists were primarily working with children's problems and only during and after World War II important changes were made in the practice of clinical psychologists. In the late 1930s, large number of European psychologists and psychiatrists were migrated to the United States to escape from the Nazi regime. Many of them were trained under Freud and had psychoanalytic interests and practice. Their writings and thinking were initiated by psychoanalytic concepts and personality disorders and the early works of testing intelligence and the deficits were reduced. Therefore it was the World War II that increased the interest in clinical psychology in United States.

Therefore whatever the progress clinical psychology was making in the United States earlier, it was only during and after the World War II that the interest in clinical psychology was increased and psychologists began to apply it on diviants. Psychoanalysis, psychoanalytic psychotherapy began to develop rapidly and there was widespread acceptance in the United States. These Freudian approaches seemed to have better effects on mental patients and effectively alleviating psychopathology. Professionals in the mental health field were eagerly came forward to learn these new techniques and this has become the basic for the mental health workers. The widespread impression has been that psychoanalysis provides the hope that it could deal with psychological problems effectively and therefore most mental health workers have accepted the idea that psychotherapy could solve the mental health problems. Several different techniques have been discovered and formulated in the field of psychoanalysis and psychotherapy.

Around 1950s a sort of dissatisfaction seemed to take place in the United States against psychoanalysis and psychotherapy, Eysenck (1952) reviewed a quite number of cases and studies that were reported as improvement made by the psychotherapeutic techniques. He has collected the results of the studies conducted from 1900 to 1950. His conclusion was that among the patients who were treated by psychotherapeutic techniques two-thirds of them were improved regardless of the treatment. Eysenck states that we can come to any such conclusion only by comparing patients of the recovery rates of the patients who had similar problems and treated by other methods. He compared the results of two studies referring to such patient groups. One group was suffering from severe neurotic problem, was treated in New York State Hospital system between 1917 and 1934. The physicians rated that 72 per cent of the patients as improved and hence discharged. In another study 500 persons who were suffering from severe psychoneuroses and also they were disabled and they were treated by the physicians with drugs. All these patients were not treated by psychotherapy. These patients were watched for 5 years and some for 10 years. It was observed that 45 per cent of the patients after one year and 27 per cent after 2 years were recovered, making the total cases 72 per cent.

Eysenck also compared the results of many studies.of psychotherapy and found that psychotherapeutic treatments did not produce better results than ordinary hospital treatments made by physicians. He also compared the long term treatments of psychoanalysis. He says that none of the treatments had reached the improvement rate of 72 per cent. On these grounds Eysenck concluded that psychotherapeutic techniques are in no way better than the Hospital system. He published his paper on this issue in 1952 in the *Journal of Consulting Psychology*, and questioned the effectiveness of most types of psychotherapy. Many of the professionals in the United States felt that Eysenck's statement was a serious provocation and they questioned the validity of his assertion and a number of scholars like Bergin (1966, 1971) have rebutted Eysenck's criticisms. Some of them stated that it was not correct to equate the outcomes of psychotherapy with that of ordinary hospital cure. Many criticised Eysenck's logical conclusions. There were many scholars who came forward with sufficient evidences to disproof Eysenck's fundamental conclusions.

Eysenck's statements seem to have been accepted as fact by some. Schofield (1964) has expressed that they do not have agreeable facts that psychotherapy has significant reduction rate of neurotic symptoms. Many persons who were working in the mental health field have began to express their views that even if psychotherapy is effective the way in which it is practised is not the answer to solve the large scale problems of the society at present. Many in the mental health fields doubted the overall effects of psychotherapy. Even those who have accepted that psychotherapy is effective, feel with all this that the present approach to the problem will not alleviate the overwhelming mental health needs of the society. Thus the strong faith that psychotherapy and psychoanalysis have built and held till 1950, enjoying a professional status in the United States has become unnerved by an intriguing paper published by Eysenck.

Those professionals who were practicing psychotherapeutic techniques were now calling for a new method of dealing with the widespread mental health problems. Some of those who have doubted the effectiveness of psychotherapy were seeking for large scale community mental health work. There were many who had strong faith in the application of psychotherapy, were seeking more wide sources by employing non-professionals in the programmes. They have also felt that it is not a good decision to give up all the well established psychotherapeutic techniques all of a sudden when there is no well organized and qualified alternative source.

But there were already several therapies in practice in the United States. Since psychotherapy was dominating all the other therapeutic approaches and also was found to be more attractive, other therapies could not emerge so prominently as psychotherapy was. Now, since many began to doubt about the effects of psychotherapy and its other disadvantages, other therapies started gaining importance. The most important of them are 'behaviour therapy' and the one very recently emerged Aaron Beck's (1967, 1985) 'cognitive therapy' which is also stated as the cognitive behaviour therapy. These two therapies started gaining importance after Eysenck's criticisms. Coleman (1976) has stated that it was until the 1960s Watson's behaviour therapy could not come into its own position. He also states that the major reason for this long delay has been the dominant position held by psychoanalysis in the field of clinical psychology and mental health field. After 1960s behaviour therapy techniques have been significantly applied on various types of maladaptive behaviours.

During this time a group of psychologists who were dissatisfied with psychoanalysis and psychotherapeutic techniques and also who were actively engaged in promoting mental health programmes for the society at large met in Boston. The Boston Conference has shown much interest for the establishment of a section of community psychology within the American Psychological Association. It has also created several training programmes in the universities. While discussing the role of community psychologists, the Boston conference also defined community psychology. Hersch (1969) has made a survey of the history of clinical psychology and he fixed *May 1965 as the birth date of community psychology*. There were also many contributions on community psychology prior to the Boston Conference. Community Psychology stresses that psychologists should play important role in the mental health movement. The mental health movement as a social and cultural phenomena should move in the positive direction for the promotion of bringing back the original shape of the community and the creative living. The patients who could not adjust themselves to the clinical or medical cares, should be brought under community mental health movement. Kelly (1966) stressed that psychologists should bring their scientific skills and knowledge to bear them on the problems and to develop training programmes towards mental health.

During the decade of 1960s more and more research papers and books on community psychology have been published and the stresses for starting community mental health centres have been increased. Many community psychologists who have been practicing therapeutic techniques were turning away from psychotherapy. The National Mental Health Act of 1946 in the United States has created the National Institute of Mental Health and also a system for training psychologists. In 1955 the Mental Health Study Act was passed and a Joint Commission on Mental Health and Illness was set up. This Joint commission was an interdisciplinary body and psychologists were the significant members. They published ten monographs and a report under the heading of 'Action for Mental Health' in the year 1961. This report mainly evaluated the current status of mental health services in the United States. The mental health professionals who participated in the commission represented another source of criticism and dissatisfaction with the traditional approach. The statement of the commission report was that when the clients were in need of psychiatric treatment they will have to wait for a long time for a small amount of treatment. The mental health workers usually would be absent there. The public mental health hospitals were overcrowded and there was also shortage of staff. Many felt that this was a highly critical statement against the traditional hospital system. Another criticism was made by Goffman (1961) against the hospital system. According to him many basic hospital practices were made for the conveniences of the staff and not for therapeutic benefits of the patients. There were several conferences held to express the dissatisfaction against the traditional mental health services. The Swampscott conference held in 1965 expressed the growing dissatisfaction felt by many clinical psychologists. Bennett *et al* (1966) stated that the traditional delivery of mental health services was limited and the clinical psychologists are needed for the promotion of human welfare on a large scale. The joint commission after making a survey for six years concluded that the care provided in the mental hospitals was custodial and that the report carried many recommendations directly for providing effective treatment by developing community mental health centres and through which for the development of community psychology.

One of the same kind of dissatisfactions with the traditional mental health practices was going on with bold injustice and conspicuously. This was with reference to the delivery of mental health services. According to some survey the traditional mental health services were distributed in an inequity and unfair manner. Hollingshead and Redlich (1958) have conducted a survey among the mental patients in New Haven, Connecticut. They had to answer ten questions like: is mental illness related to social class? Is the mental patient's position affecting, how he is treated for his illness? They found that there was inverse relationship between social class and the number of patients treated in public agencies with regard to neurotic disorders.

They observed that the lower the social class the more the patients seen in public agencies. It is because the lower class patients could not pay the fees of the private therapists. The nature of treatment also varied on the basis of social class. Individual psychotherapy was mostly prevalent treatment for all classes. But the lower social class patients were receiving more of directive psychotherapy, shock treatment, lobotomy or drug treatment than the higher class patients. The private practitioners were treating the higher class patients with intensive analytical psychotherapy whereas the lower classes were given more directive therapies. In the case of schizophrenic patients the higher social classes received more of psychotherapy whereas the lower classes received custodial cares. They have also observed that mental impairment was highest among the lower classes and lowest among the highest social classes.

While reviewing the functions of mental institutions in America, Grobb (1973) found that inequity was widely prevalent and many psychiatrists supported the idea of differential treatment for paying and non-paying clients. Lorion (1973) had observed in his reviews that the traditional mental health practitioners turn off patients of lower classes or rejected them as unsuitable for psychological treatment. But if the rejected patients were allowed to stay in psychotherapy the result was as good as the cases of higher social classes. Therefore mental health workers should not reject the lower class patients for psychotherapeutic treatment. The mental health workers should develop new therapeutic techniques and tools to suit to the lower class patients.

These brief descriptions are some of the sources of dissatisfaction expressed against the traditional mental health services in the United States. There were also such dissatisfactions expressed in other countries, but not as actively as in the United States. In the year 1963, based upon the recommendations of the joint commission, Community Mental Health Centres Act was passed during the tenure of President Kennedy. This is for providing comprehensive mental health services in the community and for the prevention and treatment of mental illnesses, According to this Act one mental health centre for every one lakh of people. These mental health centres should provide outpatient therapy, short-term patient care, day time hospitalization, emergency service for twenty-four hours, consultation and education to other agencies. The treatment for the patients may take place in a hospital or Community Mental Health Centre or it may be even in a private clinic, but several different professionals are involved. They are mainly a psychiatrist, a clinical psychologist and a psychiatric social worker—all work together on a given care.

Thus the growing dissatisfaction felt by many clinical psychologists towards traditional mental health services and the subsequent conferences and the appointment of a commission to evaluate the existing mental health services and the report of the joint commission and recommendations made by, resulted in organizing community mental health centres with assigned responsibilities. The trend in 1960s was that many community psychologists have unified in their attitudes of disfavour towards traditionalism, clinical and mental health disciplines in general. This revolt against the traditional mental health service has been associated with a number of innovations in assessment and interventions. In addition to service innovations, there have been changes at theoretical level for models more in harmony with the environmentalist, non-medical personnel, taking direct and militant action to achieve the end in activists attitudes, that are signifying the community psychologists model.

Community psychologists work is in the search of customary activity and there is no pretence as some individual or group therapists often behave. Why there is such a radical shift in the treatment of mental illnesses to the community oriented activism? In the preceding passages we have stated the reasons for the emergence of the community psychology. The same reason can be stated as an answer for this question. It was clearly explained what sort of psychotherapeutic and psychiatric services people have been receiving for many years. The services were very expensive, time consuming and prolonged, not in proper order, and rich, young, attractive and intelligent clients were treated with special care while people of lower social class and status were treated with directive method. There was enviable inequity in the treatment provided to the clients of lower social classes. Further the effectiveness of the treatment was in no way better than the regular hospital treatments. These are the main causes for the *emergence of the third force—the community psychology*.

Hilgard *et al* (1975) have stated that there was great improvement in the treatment for mental disorders since the establishment of the neuropsychiatric hospitals by the old and experienced administrators after the World War II. They say that the treatment in those hospitals were much superior to the state hospitals. One reason for the better treatment after the World War II must be the European trained psychiatrists and psychoanalysts who migrated to America to escape the Nazist regime during the Second World War. They might have put into practice their expertise. Many Americans during this time were trained by the European scientists. Since psychoanalysis was very attractive as a profession, quack psychiatrists and psychoanalysts started treating the mental disorders. This has let to several irregularities in the delivery of traditional mental health services. This state of affair also might have contributed to the growing dissatisfaction towards the traditional mental health services.

Another reason for the development of dissatisfaction can be that psychiatry and psychotherapeutic techniques were of European origin. There is a tendency in America to reject anything of foreign in origin. This was what happened when Fetchner carried Wundt's structuralism to America. Eminent psychologists and philosophers like John Dewey and others have severely criticised it and structuralism underwent several changes. This was in the beginning of this century. Now at the middle of this century dissatisfactions were mounted against psychotherapeutic techniques and new mental health movement, called community mental health and community psychology, was organized in 1960s.

The public health medicine in the second-half of the nineteenth century was striving towards a new type of thinking. The public health medicine was mobilizing the community force to fight the scrious epidemic diseases like the plague and cholera which were threatening with consequences of mass killing. This fear of death made people to gather themselves for a concentrated action, even if they did not know the root cause of the diseases, they were ready to fight it. The cholera epidemic that had swept London city in the nineteenth century was an instance that caused great terror. This has become a good example for the mental health movement to fight and prevent the behaviour disorders or mental illnesses in the same manner as the public health medicine did. Therefore, the pressure to prevent the mental illness was growing day by day which also had contributed to the emergence of community psychology.

The mental health movement, initiated by Dorothea Dix made stress toward changing the attitude of the general public towards mental patients. Clifford Beers, as a mental patient had very bad treatment, received in three mental hospitals, on recovery, started propagating among the public the wrong way of treating the mental patients and also published a book *A Mind that Found Itself* in 1908. This campaign had received the support of many public including the American Psychologist, William James and Adolph Meyer, an eminent psychiatrist. Therefore there was a great public force for a change in the mental health services. This was another impetus for the development of community psychology. There is also another movement to combine community psychology and behaviour therapy which are American in origin in place of psychotherapy. However the recent influence of continental European psychology in America cannot be completely ruled out. Riegal (1972) makes a brief comment on this while stating the influence of Social Forces on Basic Psychology. These are the historical backgrounds for the rise of community psychology in the United States.

What is Community Psychology?

Community Psychology is an offshoot of clinical psychology and psychoanalysis born out of the expression of dissatisfaction of the American mental health professionals—the psychologists, the psychiatrists, the clinical psychologists and the psychiatric social workers. Though the birth date of community psychology has set as May 1965 quite number of books and research papers have already been published. Nicholas Hobbs (1964) was the first to express his view point for the community mental health movement and he called the community mental health as the *third mental health revolution.* It was almost at the same time the humanistic psychology also has emerged. Frick (1971) has stated that *Humanistic Psychology*, a 'vigorous third force' in psychology, has emerged as a passionate protest against the limited major schools of psychology, the psychoanalysis and the behaviourism. The organizers of both the community psychology and humanistic psychology expressed their dissatisfaction against the psychoanalysis and psychotherapeutic techniques. Julian Rappaport (1977) states that Ruth Caplan's (1969) thinking stimulated the energies and thinking of many professionals for genuine change. Large number of professionals joined together to support the community mental health ideology. But those who were engaged in community work began to think every one individually and therefore there were diverse views on this and so many different meanings for community mental health. Ruth Caplan in her work stressed the role of environment in the cause of mental illness and she illustrated it with many examples that how the nineteenth century beliefs and the beliefs of the present day mental health movement were similar with regard to mental illness.

Though there were diverse views prevailing among the community psychologists on community mental health one typical trait appeared to have united them was the dissatisfaction toward the mental health disciplines in general. Rappaport states that community psychology has grown out of the diversified views of the community mental health movement.

Hobbs formulated certain guidelines for community psychology. He saw specifically the concept, public health. He stressed mainly not only prevention of disease, but also creation of a health environment. He expects that the mental health professionals should be concerned not just the mental illness, but also generally the human well-being. Hobbs is of the view that mental illness is not the private organic distress of an individual person, but it is a social, ethical and moral problems. The whole community is responsible for this. Therefore community, according to Rappaport, is the child of community mental health.

Since community mental health discipline has redefined its scope involving not only the individual's mental health problem, but also the society as whole the responsibility mainly rests on the community itself. As Caplan has stated it has become a social, ethical and moral problem. The environment is implicated in the cause of mental illness. Therefore, since community psychology is an offshoot of community mental health all those characteristics attributed to community mental health also may be applicable to community psychology. Hence the definition and scope of community psychology may be completely different from those of other fields of psychology. Just like the definition of social psychology involves the behaviour of the individual and also the role of society, community psychology also involves the community and the individual person. But, except that these two fields have the society and the individual as common factors these fields are in no way having any relationship. The subject matter and the functions of the field of community psychology vary very much from social psychology.

One of the important characteristics of community psychology, according to Nietzal *et al.* (1977) is the spirit of nontraditional approach to social problem. They state that it is a non-medical and activist attitude towards the problems. They are behaviourists, and define community psychology from the behaviouristic point of view. Malvin Zax and Gerald A. Specter (1974) state that community psychology is the most recent revolutionary development in psychology and in the mental health field in general. It involves various approaches to deal with individual person's behavioural problems and also social problems. The community is implicated as the cause of all these problems and it also serves as a potential alleviating force. This may serve as a guideline for formulating any definition.

Hence, there may be many definitions, possible, for community psychology. Everyone who worked in the field of community psychology or made some experimental studies may provide a definition of his own. Zax and Specter (1974) state that community psychology is an approach to human behaviour problems which stresses that it is the environmental forces that cause the development of the problems and the same environmental forces as therapeutic forces can alleviate the problems. Zax and Specter have used the concept of environment in a very broad sense. The environmental forces mainly refer to the society or community in which the individual lives, his interaction with others, the surrounding forces which are acting upon him and also the transaction he is having with them. The conceptional foundation of community psychology has explained this with numerous examples and description as to how the environmental forces contribute to the development of human behavioural problems.

The community psychologists have something in common and they believe that it is the transactional process between the individual and the environment that causes and develops the human behaviour. The transaction may result in a happy or unhappy living of the individual or it may result in an unhealthy or healthy well-being of the person. Cowen (1973) states that as a consequential effort to alleviate social problems it is necessary to make suitable modifications both in the environmental events and in the human behavioural system. Bloom (1973) states that there should be person-oriented and system-oriented intervention if the social problems are to be alleviated and towards which the environment should show continued preference for the social change programmes. This is the indication that there is an approval for focussing the intervention to change the individual skills and the environmental social system.

Community Psychology according to Bennett *et al.* (1966) is set apart to the study of the processes of general psychology that connect social systems with the behaviour of the individual in complex interaction. The connections are such that they provide the basis for action programmes guided towards the improvement of the individual person's well-being, the group in which the individual is a member and the social system that is functioning. Smith and Hobbs (1966) state that the front-line action of the community psychology approach to mental health is seeking ways in which the characteristics of social environment of the people are changed towards the improvement of mental health by putting force strongly on the large groups.

In every society there are people in the borderline in every aspect of life. They are also called marginal people. Generally in psychological studies this refers to people who are mentally retarded or mentally ill or deviants. There may be behaviour deviants, social deviants and sexual deviants. Generally the definitions and explanations for deviant or deviance has become relativistic. Therefore the explanations vary from time to time. Rappaport (1977) states that at present difference in the explanation to social deviance is viewed from a person's biological make up, sometimes from the functions of learned beliefs and behaviour and sometimes from current environmental point of view. But community psychology, he says, on one side tries to find out other alternatives in dealing with the deviance from socially accepted norms. According to him, community psychology, when viewed in this way, is an attempt to encourage the right of every individual person to be different and free from having any chance for suffering from material and psychological approvals.

Therefore one of the important aims of community psychology is to safeguard the right and liberty of the individual person, and also to make the individual liberty to be consistent with the larger community. The larger community inspite of maintaining the regard for the individual differences it also provides the facilities of network of the social systems by which all the resources are available to all its members. Since the individual has got the right to be different from others in the society he has also got the right to be the same like other members in the society. By this means he has right to enjoy the resources of the society in which he is a member or lives. Therefore community psychology is interested that all the people who live in a society should have the right to get material, educational, physical and mental health, and psychological resources or wealth. From these points of view it appears that community psychology is an action-oriented community reform movement largely interested in the creation of a healthy society with physically and mentally well-being of individuals.

Since community psychology emerged out of the criticisms against the traditional mental health services, most of the definitions of it recently have been viewed from different angle by putting more emphasis on the social environment, which is conceived as both causative and potentially a therapeutic factor. In addition, several factors are attributed to the cause of the individual's maladaptive behaviour or mental ill health. Rappaport (1977) states that defining community psychology by putting more emphasis on environment is too general and such an emphasis is the distinctive part of modern general psychology. Therefore he wishes to see the subject matter from a new perspective. According to him the new perspective through which he sees the aspects for the definitions of community psychology are cultural relativity, diversity and ecology. In other words it is fitting the persons to the environments. He tries to deal with the subject matter through ecological point of view. Ecology is the science that studies the relationship between living organisms and their environment. When this is applied to human beings it is called human ecology. Therefore human ecology may be defined as the study of the relationships between human individuals or groups and their physical and social environments. This definition of ecology is quite applicable to community psychology. Therefore Rappaport is quite right in applying the ecological meaning of environment to community psychology.

As Kelly (1969) and Murrell (1973) have stated that there are neither inadequate individuals nor inadequate environments. But the problem is fitting the persons to the environments relatively agreeable or disagreeable. This may be also making the individual persons agreeable to the relevant environment or making the environment suitably to the individual persons. Community psychology is interested in the well-being of an individual person, groups and sub-groups, and the larger society. A larger society is made up many sub-groups, and sub-groups may be different from larger society. A larger community which includes many sub-groups and sub-groups with many diverse individuals cannot exist without social conflicts. Each sub-group's demands may vary from the larger group and therefore the conflicts are to be resolved without any coercion or force in such a way that every sub-group with all its members should function in relation to the larger community in sharing the available resources.

Community psychology is also interested in the change of social systems. Community psychologists are actively engaged in promoting certain changes in components of social systems relating to wealth, education and, physical and mental health. The change is strived towards fair distribution of available material as well as psychological resources. The community psychologists should not be satisfied with the changes in the social systems they brought out once. It is a continuous process and will never come to an end as problems may grow from time to time on various issues.

With regard to the Indian society it will not be possible to bring it into this ecological point of view. Because the sub-groups are not based upon only the social class. There are sub-groups based upon various religious affiliations, communities, castes, regions and languages. Within the same religion there are various sects and each sect is a sub-group. For example, the major religion in India is Hinduism. There are several sects and innumerable number of castes and communities. Each sect and each caste is having a separate presiding deity and for each deity there are festivals periodically celebrated. In celebrating the festival for the deity there may be competition and rivalry, one group surpassing another. Similarly in Islam and Christianity there are group conflicts. There are group clashes within the religious sects and also between different religious sects. So also there are conflicts among the bigger sub-community like the forward and backward and scheduled caste communities. Particularly the problem of reservation of seats to Government jobs and admission to colleges and universities has turned into a very big political issue. The Government which sought to implement its policy of providing chances or opportunity for the socially, economically and educationally deprived communities was thrown out by the politically dominant affluent communities. A large section of the people of the society was having the grievances for a long time that the nation's resources were available only to those who hold power in the Government for generations and those who were deprived of it were denied of the chances of accessibility to the resources by all means. Though some means and methods seem to have taken to alleviate the grievances of those who were deprived of the chances, a change towards an equitable distribution of material and psychological resources has not taken place.

The conflict with regard to the issues remain unresolved and the dissatisfaction in the section of the society is taking different dimensions. Therefore the process is open-ended because the goal of the section of the social groups cannot be fully resolved and social change is needed always. What may be resolved today may become a problem tomorrow or some other new problem may emerge with more severe consequences. Therefore community psychologists in addition to ecological point of view as suggested by Rappaport will have to discover some new strategies and new paradigms—a new way of understanding the problem and a new way of executing it. So long as power and wealth are lopsidedly concentrated, change of any type in the Indian sub-communities can never be imagined. No body wants to part with the power and wealth.

In the case of the issue stated above community psychology is concerned with the application of social sciences to both sub-communities and to the social and political environments. Community psychology is also concerned with the development of human resources. There are certain human service fields which are related to community psychology. They are particularly medicine, psychiatry, community mental health, psychology, community social work, education, public health, juvenile justice system or criminal justice system. These are basic to community psychology for the development of human resources. In this context it is important that political involvement is a major component in this type of social change.

Further, community psychology is not having any faith in the traditional methods of dealing with human mental health problems. Instead of the clients going in search of clinics and hospitals and waiting for hours and getting an expensive treatment, which also is not effective, community psychology wanted to carry out the services directly to the community where the clients are. Community psychology goes to the place where the individual persons who are in need of services and also it does the work of preventing the chances which are supposed to cause problems in the society. It also tries to make certain immediate changes in the existing social systems of the community by which a greater disaster that is likely to take place can be averted. For example, in places where public health services are rare and if there is any fear of some epidemic diseases like cholera, plague, which can affect many persons simultaneously in a community, precautious measures can be taken at once and the spread of disease can be controlled, This type of action involves the action of human resources and also political activity. There may be also instances to which community psychologists could synthesize the services of sociology and economics.

Community psychologists declare that people in certain major sub-communities are unhappy because of the lopsided distribution of wealth and power. Therefore professionals must take efforts with the view of directing political parties, the courts and the legislatures and other humanitarian organizations to shift their goals and basic ideas towards working for a more equitable distribution of wealth and power. Rappaport (1981) states that community psychologists have found that people were told to control their lives and if they were not they are proned to anxiety, depression and psycho-physiological disorders. Some eminent community psychologists like Joffer and Albee (1981) state that powerlessness form the foundation of the entire social problems and psychopathology.

Joffer and Albee state that there is no meaning in developing separate programmes for various small problem-groups like the child abuse, spouse abuse, elder abuse, women exploitation, minority groups, migrants, handicapped, the mentally ill and the mentally retarded when we see all these groups are powerless because of socio-economic conditions. Then the right approach is whether there can be an equitable distribution of power through redistribution of wealth in the community.

Community psychologists in a short span of thirty years (1965-95) time have brought out innumerable number of research papers, books and pamphlets in the field of community psychology. They have gone beyond the limits of Rappaport's paradigms out of enthusiasm to extent their services. Mainly they are interested in social change, social justice, political justice, economic and social systems. They consider that the paradigms of community psychology are helping professions. For a country like India it may be stated that one of the paradigms of community psychology is a social, economic and political reformation. All these three should be linked together. It will not be possible to implement any of the paradigms of community psychology particularly, the social and economic change without the political involvement. This is what Joffer and Albee state.

Therefore, in view of the above discussions community psychology may be defined as the action-oriented profession which attempts to bring about revolutionary changes in the society by eliminating the factors that are causing behavioural and social problems in the physical and social environments, using a variety of approaches to provide maximum opportunity to each person and to the members of the disadvantaged groups and sub-communities for an equitable share of the material and psychological resources for the development of human resources.

Thus the aim of community psychology is to approach human social and behavioural problems which are caused by the physical (environment) and social (community) environments and to make changes, both in the individual and in the physical and social environments and alleviate the problems by promoting harmonious relationship between the sub-communities and the environments or by fitting the individual person or groups to the environment or fitting the environment to the individual or groups. Community psychology aims for a change in the society in which there should be equitable distribution of material and psychological resources. Those who were deprived of their rights and liberty should have their right to choose and to reveal their potentialities in the respective areas.

Generally, community psychology is interested in the behaviour of those persons who do not adjust themselves with the society or in those who are rejected by the society. There may be a small group of people in every society who do not fit into the society or keep themselves away from the society. Such people are called marginal people. Community psychology is interested in making them to adjust themselves and to be harmonious with the greater society for which community psychology has formulated action oriented programmes. These programmes are mainly based upon promoting social changes wherever necessary and make the problem people to have the right of having the maximum share in those resources which were denied to them earlier. Further. community psychology is an area with trained professionals and directs them toward prevention and treats the problems of the persons or patients without removing them from their habitual situations.

4. COMMUNITY PSYCHOLOGY AND COMMUNITY MENTAL HEALTH

Community psychology was born out of community mental health and clinical psychology. In 1960s the time was ripe enough to have a new field of psychology which can deal with the behavioural and social environmental problems of the community. Further, community psychology integrates other social sciences and also involves political action. Mental health services are often provided outside the clinics and hospitals, in the schools, business centres, factories and in the person's/patient's own community situation. Though community psychology and community mental health are basically related they can be distinguished from each other.

Community Psychology is primarily interested in social action—on prevention—mostly primary and secondary preventions where there is no impairment of organic or organic system. Community psychology is concerned with the behaviour problems of individual persons and tries to alleviate them by altering social systems in the institution level and by creating different and better environment for the people to live in. It also reduces the forces that are causing maladoptive behaviour and promoting opportunities for the individual persons to realize their potentialities. Community psychology requires intervention with schools, humanitarian service organizations, courts, police and planning agencies. It requires more of political involvement for such works. It is least medical in service.

Community Psychology is interested in social systems change and inclined to be away from the traditional clinical services. Glidewell (1971) states that community psychologists who are opted to community mental health services should pay the highest place for cooperative, self-modifying social interventions to prevent disorders by making it easy, the achievement of the developmental tasks in children. It is universal that successful completion of one stage is pre-requisite for going to the next.

The successful completion of each stage is considered that it is determined by the environment. The view accepted is, that the failure to complete the developmental task is not due to illness, but the social system has failed to provide necessary resources. The responsibility is not resting on the individual persons but upon the socializing agents like the families, schools, police and the political, social and economic systems. This type of developmental problems are found at a high rate in many communities. Even if such programmes are implemented the expected changes will not take place immediately. It will take years and decades for the fruitful effects of the equity distribution of the material and psychological resources. Every year a survey should be made to find out what percentage of people are benefited by the social change programnes.

Community mental health, instead, is interested in providing care for the troubled and needy people who have been treated by the traditional mental health professionals inadequately. Community mental health movement delivers mental health services to the persons who are in need of services. Its services are often individualistic just like the traditional therapy in rooms. The community mental health personnel are psychiatrists, clinical psychologists and social workers who conduct both individual and group therapy in the centres. Community mental health aims to remove the deficits as they have been tested and found as not fit into the expected social norms. Community mental health seeks the individual person's adjustment to the demands of the society.

Community mental health programmes have been recommended by the Joint Commission which was an interdisciplinary body appointed by the American National Institute of Mental Health. The commission after making a survey of the mental health services presented a report called 'Action for Mental Health' (1961). According to this any mental health programme is required to solve three problems. They are (1) manpower, (2) facilities, and (3) cost. The community mental health programme should have sufficient number of *personnel* for delivering the services and they should be well qualified. Treatment depends upon the knowledge and the training possessed by the personnel. The non-medical mental health workers, volunteers, non-professionals, clergyman, physicians and educators may be accepted as members of the network service. But a medical supervision is important. Regarding the *facilities* for delivering the service, new buildings need not be built as far as possible. The schools, industries, and offices may be used wherever they are available. Service personnel should move in group and they can use van or any suitable vehicle. The service should not be made *costly.* Whatever the funds are available should be the estimation of the expenses of the services.

The mental health service personnel should make their services available to persons who are *emotionally disturbed,* in their local communities. Before the problem becomes serious or in early stage of mental illness, mental health personnel should intervene as a way of preventing the problem. An emergency care for serious cases of emotional disorder is very essential. In case of shortage of professional manpower, ways should be found to deliver the services to the patients. The services of community psychology and community mental health are equated as sometimes certain services seem to be overlapping. But still these two fields may be differentiated from the service points of view. Community psychology is mainly non-medical whereas community mental health is mainly medical. But, it has been observed in several instances that extreme emotional disorders have been the causes of certain fatal physical diseases like heart attacks.

Emotional Disorders, Coronary Heart Disease (CHD) and Mental Health

Almost at the same time one of the eminent community psychologists Charles Spielberger (1984) who was working on the consequences of extreme emotional disorders in connection with mental health problems came out with an interesting result after two decades of serious research work and declared that the important causes of Coronary heart diseases (CHD) are not the four physiological risk factors, but the seven deadly emotional psychological factors. He supported his stand with the results of many medical researches like the works of two pioneering Cardiologists, Meyer Friedman and Ray Rosenman. Friedman (1969) Rosenman *et al.* (1979) brought out promising evidences linking Coronary heart disease to psychological variables. Rosenman and Friedman (1964) have identified coronary prone behaviour pattern individuals as Type-A and those who were not prone as Type-B by means of structured interview.

The Type-A individuals were uncommonly ambitious, striving, highly competitive, hard-driving, hurried, sense of urgency for passing time, highly aggressive and hostile towards others, overcommitted to their work, cannot wait in lines, fast thinking, fast talking, too busy to notice surroundings. The Type-B individuals on the other hand are less driven and relatively free from such pressures. It was found that Type-A individuals suffer from heart attacks more than twice as Type-B individuals even when other physiological factors were controlled.

Spielberger states that after the World War II men in United States have become the world's more hard working and they were prone to more coronary epidemic diseases. In 1950 it was seen that 55 per cent of deaths were due to coronary heart disease (CHD) and the heart attacks were not due to physiological risk factors but due to the seven deadly emotional characteristics and two of the key elements that contributed to heart attacks were anger and hostility. Spielberger says that Friedman and Rosenman have opened the heart to scientific study of *non-physical* risk factors. They have noticed in their patients prior to heart attack, that they were often been unusually ambitious, striving, competitive, hard driving and hurried. They possessed all the A-Type characteristics. Spielberger wanted to show that how the extreme emotional states like anger causes not only mental illness, but also fatal physical diseases like the heart attacks. The Anger Expression Scale developed by Spielberger (1988) has shown high positive correlation between elevated blood pressure and the tendency to suppress anger. Community psychologists intervention strategies should also work for non-tensional and less stressful social environment.

The psychological factors such as stress and personality were found to be the causes of high blood pressure, which ultimately lead to coronary heart disease. Chesney *et al.* (1880) state that as early as 1910 the Canadian physician William Osler (1849-1919) has described the typical 'angina' patient, who was found to be vigorous in mind and body, keen and ambitious and whose heart was always set at full speed ahead. The studies of Jenkins (1971, 1976), Rahe and Lind (1971) provide more recent evidences for the relationship between CHD and stressors due to overload of work, chronic conflict and the life stressors, which were assessed by Social Readjustment Rating Scale (SRRS).

The psychophysiological disorder is a real disease, causing damage to the body. These disorders are caused by emotional factors. It has been observed that people die from psychologically produced high blood pressure or ulcers in the same manner, as the diseases produced by infection or physical disease. In psychophysiological disorders bodily tissues are damaged. Psychophysiological disorders are more common in industrialized communities. The American Psychiatric Association (1987) in its recent revision has viewed that all physical diseases are *potentially related to psychological stress.* The recent revision (1987) requires that first of all a diagnostic decision should be made on axis I which means, that the presence of a psychological factor is influencing a physical condition, and this physical condition is specifically identified in axis III.

All the physical diseases are potentially related to the psychological stress. This is a very recent innovation in both medical and psychological fields. That is the reason that the concept, 'stress' is associated with health, it is both physical health and mental health. It is defined in several ways. Stress mainly involves a transaction between the individual and the environment with which he/she interacts and cognizes as distressing to his/her well-being, Generally it refers to mental, emotional and physical strain. But psychologically it may be stated as the demands or pressures on the individual which put strain, exceeding his/her adjustive resources. According to Hans Selya (1907-1993)(1950) it is a general adaptation syndrome. He used this as a model to describe the biological reactions to sustained physical stress. The model has three phases. All the three phases of the model used to describe the biological reaction, all quite suitably applicable to human reactions to social and environmental stresses.

The organism faces the stress and it tries to resist the stress and if the stress is very powerful the organism put up resistance and tries to adapt to the stress through available coping mechanism. But if the stress is too strong and the stresser persists, the organism is unable to resist the stresser and the organism gets disorganized and suffers from irreparable loss. This is what happening in the life of human beings. Individuals differ in responding to stress. When an individual has failed with all his resources to cope with the stress physiological changes like rapid heartbeat, increase of blood pressure, secretion of stomach acid leading to ulcers are taking place. These psychophysiological disorders affect other systems. A healthy body can sustain this for some time, but not always. Repeated instances may result in emotional break down. Gardner Murphy (1964) quotes from Freeman, the 'Plimsoll mark', the point beyond which the individual may not be safely loaded with strain or violent stimulation, it is the point of break down, of disorganization.

Modern life is full of stressful events. Assault, pollution, cyclone, crowded surroundings, rape, bombings, terrorism, overwork, death of a spouse, illness, poverty, unemployment, separation, conflict, disregarded old age—are all stresses of the present world. The events are called stressors. When the stressors are severe they may produce severe physical and mental consequences. Feelings of helplessness, damage to self-esteem and inability to complete the assignments or tasks are also called stressors. The stressors are the causes and the stresses are the consequences. Various stressful conditions have been found to be playing the role in the etiology of hypertension and heart attacks. In the studies of Innes, *et al.*, (1959), Ruskin *et al.* (1948) and Ax (1953), it was found that stressful interviews, natural disasters, anger and anxiety have produced elevation in blood pressure. Kasl and Cobb (1970) studied the effects of loss of employment. They found that a group of workers who lost their jobs for two years had increased blood pressure. Stone and Hokanson (1967) found that blood pressure was associated highly with inhibition of aggression. Herburg *et al.* (1973) found that in areas where there was high stress crime rates were high. Therefore the psychological stresses seem to be the causes of many disorders in the community.

Spielberger states that the new findings made in the field of medical science, made it clear that anger is a major component of Type-A behaviour and he states that it is proved that Type-B people also suffer from heart attacks. According to him *anger and hostility* are the two important emotional components contributing to heart trouble.

5. INTERVENTION AND PREVENTIVE APPROACH

Community psychology's interests and commitments are to conceptualize human behavioural and social problems in terms of collective human behaviour and advancement of community mental health by means of preventive approach and to develop human potentialities. While thinking about the remedial measures to community problems the community psychologists confront the fact that the strategies for effecting a generalized and sustained social change in the community are more for the future generation than for the present community. Because a sustained social change as programmed by the community psychologists or by the community mental health scientists will not take place over night. It will take decades for identifying the community as the causative factor and also as a potential therapeutic agent. But a cardinal characteristic of community psychology and community mental health movement has been the emphasis on *interventions* that are sought for prevention rather than amelioration of mental illness. The concept, 'prevention' appears to be simple, but the concept as applied to community psychology and community mental health has a deep meaning with it.

In dealing with the problem of mental illness of a community there is a lack of manpower for the treatment, large number of people with mental illness are coming on and on and the manpower is not in a position to attend all of them. As a result of it the treatment is ineffective. In such case if a programme of prevention of mental illness was successful the number of cases of mental illness may be reduced considerably and the treatment by the few professional men may be also very effective. It is not giving treatment to cure mental illness, but preventing people from getting mental illness or any other disorders. Though this concept is borrowed from public health field it is very much self explanatory to community psychology and community mental health fields. This prevention programme has reduced the stress in the community and also among the professionals who treat and cure mental illness in mental hospitals and clinics.

The idea of preventing mental illness rather than providing treatment to the patients was first proposed by Adolph Meyer (1866-1956) in 1900s. Adolph Meyer was a most influential psychiatrist of twentieth century. Rappaport (1977) states that community psychology and community mental health field must owe very much to Meyer for originating the preventive ideology. Meyer was very keen in educating the general public regarding the nature and cause of mental illness with the view of preventing mental illness instead of treating mental illness. He was of the view that the activities of the mental hospitals should be extended into the community. He wants that the patient should enter into the community as smoothly as possible.

Meyer wishes to introduce the preventive approach into the community, many years before the community mental health movement was started. Somehow his ideas were not accepted in the early days. There was resistance for Meyer's preventive approach as the general medicine has failed to impress with the preventive approach. At the time when Meyer was advocating preventive approach in the first quarter of twentieth century, psychodynamics and psychoanalysis were getting into prominence, and Freudian techniques were received with the great glamour and young psychiatrists and psychoanalysts have shown much enthusiasm in them. Therefore Meyer's preventive movement ceased to exist from the mental health field till the end of 1950s.

Around 1940s Eric Lindemann (1944) spoke about preventive approach. Later on Gerland Caplan (1964) has applied this concept in mental health field and evolved three types of prevention. They are primary prevention, secondary prevention and tertiary prevention.

Primary Prevention

The primary prevention involves reducing the incidence of mental disorders of all types in the community and ultimate elimination of disorders by modifying the pathological components of the environment. Any new cases of mental illness are immediately attended to. It alters or eliminates the circumstances that cause disorders before they cause seriousness. Primary prevention is not dealing with specific individual case, but it tries to reduce the causative factors of mental illness for the whole population. The goal of primary prevention is to create an optimal living situation for all members of the population. It mainly finds out the environmental factors that are harmful and also the experimental forces that are helpful for fighting the adverse influences.

According to Caplan (1964) primary prevention may help us to understand the cause of mental disorders. By this means a person may have an idea about the environmental forces that predispose a person to particular type of mental illness and also he may know how to handle these forces for building up resistance against such mental illness. Caplan was aware of the incidence of the primary preventive programmes and also the successful efforts of the public health medicine long before the causes of the diseases were known. Smallpox was prevented by vaccinations. Caplan has designed a conceptual model of primary prevention as a guidance.

According to the conceptual model of Caplan's primary prevention every individual needs supplies to a particular stage of development to avoid mental disorder. He suggested three types of supplies according to this model, such as, physical, psychosocial and socio-cultural. He warns that if there is any deficiencies in quality or in quantity of the supplies then it can at once cause disorder. For example, there may be insufficient food or excess of wrong type of food which can cause malnutrition,

The physical supplies refer to food, adequate shelter, and other fundamental requirements necessary for bodily growth and for good physical condition.

The psycho-social supplies refer to social interaction and cognition and emotional stimulation. The interactions may be with other people, families and peer groups. Many needs are satisfied by the social interaction. Emotional disorders may be caused by the failure of enjoying the love and affection of other people. If the relationship is not healthy, harmonious and cordial there may be mental disturbances which may lead to mental disorders.

The socio-cultural supplies refer to the influences exerted by the culture. Socio-culture determine a person's way of life in a society. A person born in a disadvantaged society meets with many obstacles in his development of personality. In some cultures, an individual may find few chances and in some cultures it is also denied. This kind of negative attitude may affect an individual's mental health. The material and psychological resources are not equitably distributed in such communities.

Programmes of Primary Prevention

Primary preventive programmes according to Caplan are approached in two ways. One is social action and the other is interpersonal action.

Social Action

Social action requires producing changes in the community. The fundamental idea of social action is to make improvements in the community. It involves improvements in the material and psychological resources. The improvements are intended to satisfy the various needs like the physical, psycho-social and socio-cultural supplies. Social action also involves helping those who are facing crisis. Social change cannot be done without political involvement and the patronage of government. Therefore mental health consultations should be made with political leaders who are the legislators and also with government bureaucrats for making changes in the behaviour of the community people.

Interpersonal Action

The interpersonal action programmes involve making changes in the behaviour of the individuals who are facing crises. This programme tries to bring out the community mental health personnel to face-to-face contact with individuals and small groups or communities who are facing crises. Another important task facing the community mental health personnel is to educate or to explain the importance of community mental health services to the social or community leaders and to increase the chances of the basic supplies to the community.

Lindemann (1944) suggests that community mental health specialists must personally contact individuals who are facing critical situations in the communities and on finding that they are failing to adopt well, must be identified and assisted in taking them to clinics and hospitals.

Community psychologists apart from paying their attention on mentally ill cases, they are also concentrating other problem areas like overcrowding, poor housing, job discrimination, schools, children from broken homes, school lunches and meals on wheels. In Indian community the mid-day meals system or nutritious meals system in primary schools is receiving greater attention. Originally it was introduced in Tamil Nadu. This system has increased attendance in the rural primary schools. Now this is followed by other States also. But this programme is implemented by the State Government. Some humanitarian organizations from foreign countries make some financial assistance to this programme. The Indian Psychological Association is not showing any interest in such services. Since psychology is not popular in India and in many Indian Universities, particularly in south it will take decades for the psychologists in India to understand the values of community psychology and to organize preventive intervention works. There are many problem areas in India for the community psychologists to formulate programmes.

Secondary Prevention

The aims of secondary prevention is to take efforts to find out the problems of the persons early and to prevent them before they become serious and develop into chronic disabilities. It takes quick steps to reduce the duration of disorders that have already occurred. It is also altering the factors that lead to new cases. Generally secondary prevention emphasizes early diagnosis and treatment and lowering prevalence of specific disorders. *Prevalence,* here is referring to the rate of proved cases of disorder at a given time. Therefore reducing the prevalence of any disorder can be made by removing the causes of disorder and reduce the rate of new cases and lowering the old cases by treatment. Detecting the existing disorders rapidly is the essential function of secondary prevention. The community is the client for the community mental health personnel and therefore the diagnosis and treatment should be as rapidly as possible and make significant improvement in the mental health of the community.

Secondary prevention programmes, Zax and Cowen (1969) state should be often directed upon the elementary school students. Because it is they who demonstrate the maladaptive behaviour between early school and later life. It is believed that for the educational and personal growth, the schools should be a primary object for carrying out the programme to the maximum efficiency. Cowen et al. (1973) state that the primary mental health project uses techniques for quick identification of primary school students who are having educational and behavioural problems.

Caplan (1964) suggests that if a case of difficulty is suspected it must be referred to treatment as early as possible. Crises intervention works and emergency services at all twenty four-hours, are the important works of the secondary prevention programmes.

Tertiary Prevention

Tertiary prevention aims to minimize the severity of organic disorders, reduces long term or short term after effect of the disorders. It is mainly focussed on the individual who is suffering from mental disorder and is trying to make him to readjust to normal community life. Tertiary prevention is an attempt to diminish the residual effects of mental disorder and to strengthen his mental health to make him one with the community. Caplan (1964) states that it is better to have a programme of educating the public to get rid of mental illness. It is very difficult for a person after the treatment to readjust himself, when returns home, with family, at work and with other colleagues. Therefore programmes of public education as a rehabilitation may serve as a useful method. Zax and Cowen (1972) state that in tertiary prevention, the concept "prevention" is not really justified. Because it embodies many forms of treatment like psychological and psychiatric interventions including hospitalization, psychotherapy and pharmacotherapy. Therefore the term prevention may be restricted to primary and secondary interventions. Tertiary prevention's primary aim is rehabilitating the recovered mental patients and to fit them into the community.

Community Mental Health Service—Its Styles of Delivery

We have discussed in the preceding sections the location of community mental health and the levels of intervention. Community mental health is more concerned with the delivery of services than its conceptions of human behaviour, Therefore community mental health professionals receive their conceptions from individual psychology for their purpose. According to Rappaport and Chimsky (1974) community mental health is more an attitude for service than for a body of knowledge. The attitudes are prevention and new methods of treatment. The attitude to service is social and not a scientific movement.

From these broad areas of community mental health, community psychologists can draw any theoretical conceptions of human behaviour to suit their purpose from psychoanalysis to operate behaviourism. Rappaport and Chimsky (1974) state that what a community mental health professional does when one is going into the community for service is to propose a scheme for models of mental health service delivery. According to them every type of mental health service has two components, a conceptual component and a style of delivery component. The model refers to the combination of these two components and it is referring to mental health service. This is also called medical model.

The conceptual component refers to empirical data and the theoretical aspect of the model and therefore it is taken for granted for understanding human behaviour. It is considered as the theory of human behaviour. There were severe criticisms from Ullmann and Krasner (1969) and Cowen (1973) for calling it as medical model and it has been suggested to call both the components, as they are separated, as medical model or disease conceptual component.

The second component *'style of delivery'* determines how the service stated by the conceptual component, delivered to the community in need. It is the medical style of delivery, doctor-patient contact. This includes diagnosis and treatment by experts in the hospital. Since the expert waits for the client to find out him, the style of delivery is called as the *waiting mode.*

Another style of delivery is called *seeking mode.* This is operated by the community psychologists. This taking place outside of the hospital or in the expert's office. This style of delivery is offered directly by any person, community workers, or professional or para-professionals under the care of psychologists, psychiatrists and social workers. This seeking mode service is generally offered outside of the expert's office or clinics or hospitals. It is offered in schools, business offices and factories of the person's own community. The professionals assume the role of consultants or programme innovators. These services are normally primary prevention or early secondary prevention. The important aspect of seeking mode of service delivery is the non-traditional role of the professional in dealing with the problem of the community.

There are various other conceptualizations suggested by the critics. a few of them are a social learning conceptualization suggested by Albee (1968), Bandura (1967, 1969), Mischel (1968), a neurological conceptualization suggested by Reitan (1969), a socio-environmental conceptualization suggested by Sanders, Smith and Weinman (1967), a non-psychological conceptional components which include sociological approaches suggested by Scheff (1967). But any one of these conceptual components may be applied in the *waiting mode* style of delivery or in the *Seeking mode* style of delivery.

6. INDIAN COMMUNITY PROBLEMS IN NEED OF INTERVENTION

Community psychology is mainly concerned with interventions and actions as well as analysis. The first step of intervention work begins with the selection of difficult area, which also means defining the problem. Community agents help to set objectives that combine the personal interest and those of the community. Berck (1976) states that a plan is aimed at a problem definition. That is, who is not getting what and from whom. Where are the deficits in the society and how can they be most efficiently eradicated. Community psychologists conceptualize change as remediation and are designing *interventions* as reactions to the problems.

Intervention is a decisive or intrusive role of the community psychologists in order to modify events or their outcomes that disturb or hinder the course of action of the people and to protect their interests. This can be applied to any human calamities caused by human beings or natural resources. Therefore there can be strategies aimed at the individual intervention and the strategies aimed at the social intervention. Berck (1976) differentiates these two interventions. Most of the works of community psychology are the attempts to change the solutions to human difficulties which do not solve the difficulties. Change occurs as a function of action applied to the problem situation.

In Indian society there is a very wider scope for various strategies aiming at the individual intervention as well as social and community intervention. There are a number of community problems which are becoming like erosion eating away the equilibrium of the community. The responsibility is not only resting upon the community psychologists or community agents who work for the social change, but also upon every one who lives in a community and aspires for a healthy and wellbeing of the community. Time has come for those who are interested in this and to contribute their shares in whatever manner to the intervention works to eradicate or to reduce the severity of the problem the community is facing today.

There are quite a number of problems in Indian community which are in need of interventions. It will not be possible to enumerate and discuss all of them here. Therefore we can mention here only some of the problems, apart from the community mental health problem we have discussed above. They are:

1. Everyday many boys and girls run away from homes causing anxieties to the parents. In radio it is broadcasted and in the Television programmes it is announced with photographs. Not only boys and girls, even young men and women, adults and aged people go away and their whereabout are not known to their parents or to their guardians or caretakers. But at no time neither the Radio nor the Television had announced that the missing persons were traced. Since this was not done it may be taken for granted that they were lost once for all. It is true that some of them are not mentally sound. But what about the rest of them? They have serious problems somewhere which they themselves could not resolve them. As a result of it the only way of avoiding the problem is to go away from the problem situation. It is in one way escaping from the problem. It is a defensive mechanism. But this is not the solution to the problem. Where the problem arises? Whether it is at school or home in the case of school children? What are the problems of the run away young men and young women? The problems may be mainly emotional maladjustment or quarrel with adults at home, poverty or unemployment. In the case of adult men or women it may be unresolved difference of opinion, conflict or frustration. In the case of aged people it may be old age abnormality, but it is not always the cause. The main cause may be that no body is taking care of them. Therefore programmes to identify the problems of such

children, young men and women, adults and aged people, suffering from various types of maladjustments, conflict, frustration, insanity, old age illness and to find solutions to alleviate their difficulties.

2. Juvenile delinquency and criminal activities are increasing every day. The young offenders activities are published everyday in the newspapers. The nature of offences are such that it is taking an alarming shape and it is very difficult to curb them. In many cases they seem to be juvenile adventurous activities and they adapt the models from the motion pictures which are also seem to be teaching all sorts of tricks, pranks and intriguing tendencies to the young persons. There are quite a number of instances of young persons killing their parents and grandparents for the sake of money, and also playing dirty tricks to cheat them. Programmes and strategies to deal with such juvenile delinquency and criminal activities should be formulated both inside and outside the schools and arrangements should be made to deliver the interventions to correct them.

3. The magnitude of adult offences is becoming a very big field of social pathology in our country. The frequency of occurrence of the offences seem to be that they are normally accepted as everyday events in our country. The offences involve in daring day light and night robberies, snatching the chains from ladies in broad day light in the midst of many people at the point of dagger, snatching the purse, watch, ring and other personal properties and run away in fast moving motor bicycles or in hired autorickshaws. There are instances of breaking the locked houses in day light and moving the properties, waylaying on highways and robbing the properties of the people travelling in cars and buses and trains. The dacoits coming in groups in disguised forms at night times with deadly weapons and break open the doors, beat the people left and right, tie them up and carry away all the valuable properties, dacoits travelling in the same long journey night buses, forcibly stopping the buses, robbing the properties of the passengers at the point of knife and disappear in the darkness, in big cities and towns forcibly making regular collections from shop-keepers, hawkers, posing themselves as the big bullies of that area as if there is no government or authorities to check or prevent them from such activities and this sort of things are going on in many places everyday. Weak and helpless people have no other option except to submit. Any complaint to police may aggravate their position. Strategies to curb and prevent all these problems in collaboration with police, and court should be formulated for a long range programme of eradicating the offences.

The main reasons for the increasing and repetition of these criminal activities by the offenders are several. Unless there is political involvement any of these crimes cannot be checked by any other means. These offenders are normally not apprehended, even if they are apprehended the cases do not go to the courts. Rarely if it went to the court they are not punished and they escape from the punishment. Further in case of punishment it is not severe enough to cause fear to the culprit as not to repeat the same crime. After few months of imprisonment the offender commits the same crime on his way back to his home.

Therefore it becomes necessary to formulate suitable strategies at the national level to reduce such offences and to correct old offenders and also preventing from the emergence of new offenders.

4. Formulating intervention strategies to deal with the drug abusers and the application of therapeutic techniques for modification of their behaviour becomes the responsibilities of community psychologists. Further suitable intervention strategies should be formulated for preventing new rising drug abuses in the community.

5. There should be intervention strategies of broad-spectrum of behaviour therapies to reduce the illicit distillations and alcohol abuses.

6. Identifying persons who are socially and personally maladjusted or mentally ill and providing them *immediate guidance* as to what to do and take care of them, if necessary may be referred to mental health clinics or hospitals to make them socially well adjusted and mentally healthy persons.

7. Many aged people who are thoroughly neglected by their children and near relatives, become destitutes, no place to live in, and many suffer, more than the physical declining, from old age disorders like dementia and delirium, prevalence of general lack of regard for senior citizens in this country and many are facing emotional problems of some kind. They must be immediately attended to and assisted in time or must be taken to old age homes, if serious, to mental health clinics or hospitals. The magnitude of old age problems can be assessed from the number of *Old Age Homes* functioning. There are about 380 Old Age Homes in India, out of which 80 are in Tamil Nadu. In the Madras City alone there are 25 Old Age Homes for both men and women. Are they not without children and near relatives? There are. Yet, they prefer Old Age Homes and live there by paying their pensions to old age homes if pension holder; if not, pay from their earlier savings or from their properties still under their control. Community psychologists as

social agents should evolve intervention strategies in such a way as to reduce the admissions to the old age homes that children should take care of their parents. Some television plays are presented with such themes, but there were no positive effects. Young couples do not give importance to such problem.

8. The unemployed are becoming delinquents, they are involved in all kinds of anti-social activities, many unemployed errants are already involved in various kinds of anti-social activities, and they should be taken care of with the help of Police and the court and get them fixed in some suitable jobs.

9. The rapid increase of population is fastly becoming a serious social problem, psychological strategy may be formulated and the concerned or respective organizations should be persuaded to implement the programmes with all seriousness to reduce the birth rates in all communities disregarding whatever are their cultural or religious convictions and beliefs.

10. The devastating effects of poverty on the people of the nation, which is an offshoot of increased population, because the population outruns the available resources of the nation, malnutrition, frequent and continuous starvation and disorderliness become common occurrences—all need strong intervention strategies to fight out them.

11. The normal adolescent and youth groups are becoming, highly unethical in principles, demoralized in behaviour and tempted with extreme violence, eve teasing, becoming socially and sexually deviants, accept vulgarity and obscenity as a model and adventurous way of life, show utter disregard for elders, wisdom and knowledge. They find sources for all these pathological conditions in sex perverted themes and poor artistic vulgar imaginations of the present day motion pictures and Television plays. Valuable human life is considered as cheap and being wasted in the name of art and culture, pastime and amusement. Instead of providing refreshment for mind and body, tension, anxieties, uncertainties and uncontrollable wild animosities are created. This sort of behaviour disorders of the youth are leading towards irrevocable loss. Voices of protest raised now and then and there is no reaction on the positive side, political involvement is lacking, no serious thinking was given to this deforming problem at any circle and, therefore, it is time for the Indian social scientists to think of these problems seriously and to evolve strong intervention strategies for rescuing the youth of the nation from the disastrous consequences and to make them aware of their potentialities and to actualize themselves for a much creative

and healthy way of life and also to reform the mass media, the motion picture and the television by making them free from the obscene and vulgar themes and to make them to think of refined and cultured themes to educate the public of this developing nation and to revitalize the youth for creative imagination and activities.

12. Human race from time to time was put into untold miseries and mass death incidences due to highly infectious diseases. It is recorded in the history that diseases like plague, yellow fever, cholera, flue, tuberculosis, cancer—all had their shares in killing large number of people all over the world in the past. Just like new scientific inventions and discoveries, fatal diseases are also emerging at times. Tuberculosis is a bacterial infection that is diminishing today because of an intelligent policy or prevention is being persued and anti-biotics are employed.

The other dreadful and highly infectious disease that is spreading very fast all over the world after 1970s and threatening human race with dire consequences today is the *AIDS*. Unlike the tuberculosis and cancer the AIDS has puzzled and baffled the chemical and medical scientists and they are hard trying to find out suitable medicine and methods of treatment for this. It is a new disease created by men and women and the correct root cause of it yet to be traced. Information about this disease was available only from 1980s. But it was somewhat traced in 1979 in America from the Ugandian blood sample drawn in 1972.

Experts say that it is a Sexually Transmitted Disease (STD) and therefore it finds its origin in human sex. There is no correct information as to how this disease finds its origin in human sexual activities. The reliable information available is that AIDS is caused by a virus called Human-Immunodeficiency virus (HIV) and AIDS is an abridged form for Acquired-Immune-Deficiency Syndrome. Ho and his associates (1985) were the first to isolate and identify the HI virus from the cerebrospiral fluid and neural tissues. The HI virus is capable of crossing the brain-blood barrier which is considered to be the defence mechanism.

The human body has certain capacity to resist anything that is disagreeable or harmful that may cause some disease. The system is called immunity which protects the body. The HI virus gets into the body and destroys this immunity system and makes the body deficit. Since the HI virus should have come from outside through some source it is stated as 'Acquired'. When the immune system is fully destroyed by the HI virus the person becomes the victim of the AIDS.

The root cause of other infectious diseases can be traced in the environmental pollution, food poisoning and germs. But the root cause of the AIDS seem to be in human sexual activities and through the drugs human beings consume and in the intravenous injections by unhygienic ways.

The main reason for this has been that the AIDS was caused by human beings through abnormal sexual deviations and by drug dependence and drug abuses. Since it is Sexually Transmitted Disease (STD) it is rooted in the promiscuous sex activities of hetrosexual or homosexual in nature. One of the important reasons the psychologists state for the infection of the dreaded disease is the attitudinal changes in different age groups toward *premarital, permissive and promiscuous sexual relations*. There are experimental evidences that the amount of education at the school and college level is positively associated with permissive attitudes towards premarital sex relations. The premarital sexual behaviour among males and femaies was found to be almost the same and the level was much higher than the previous era. Investigations conducted by Glenn and Weaver (1979), Phillis and Gromko (1985), Clement *et al.* (1984) confirmed this. India is an AIDS infected nation and studies should be conducted on different age groups toward premarital permissive promiscuous sexual relations. More AIDS cases were traced in Maharashtra and Tamil Nadu. It is not a sudden emergence in some of the States in India. The ground in India particularly in Maharashtra and Tamil Nadu was already fully fertilized for the germination of the AIDS. Otherwise, how there could be thousands of AIDS cases in these States. We do not know exactly whether the premarital permissive and promiscuous sex themes of the movies of the past two decades had the influencing effect upon the youths' behaviour had created a fertile soil for the emergence of the AIDS or poverty and circumstances forced the young girls to go into the prostitutions where the girls had contacted the HI virus and transmitted to the males with whom they had sexual relations had caused the AIDS. The Indian adolescent boys and girls at school and college levels and the youth fight for premarital permissive and promiscuous sexual contacts. This will lead to the creation of more sex starved youth. The AIDS fighting awareness was not given any serious attention in India (Asha, 1991). They only pay more importance to the gratification of their emotional desires without foreseeing the consequences and get their education and career spoiled. Whatever the cause behind the emergence of the AIDS it has to be explored scientifically and preventive measures should be taken. Medical approach is to cure the disease and the psychological intervention strategies are for preventing the spread of the dreaded disease. Prevention is better than cure. Community psychology includes dealing with the AIDS as one of the intervention strategies in United States.

Any one of the preventive programmes formulated by Caplan may be applied or modified and applied according to the Indian conditions and to the nature and severity of the problem.

Community psychologists have not yet designed, developed and published any special tests or scales to study the various community problems that are widely prevalent in many countries. But whatever the tests and scales that are suitable among the available test materials can be used to study the problems. The researchers or investigators themselves may design and develop suitable test materials to the problem they choose to study.

EXPERIMENT 1

Assessing the Level of Prolonged Deprivation

1. INTRODUCTION

A group of psychologists, who revolted against the works of the clinical psychologists during the first and second quarters of 20th century have seriously thought of approaching the human mental health problems in a new way by which they could make their services more useful to the society at large instead of concentrating on a single individual vainly. As a result of it in a short span of ten years time, many research programmes were started in United States and elsewhere. Pamphlets, research papers, journals and books were published very rapidly and to-day lots of study materials are available in the market.

Emergence of Community Psychology

The main theme of this field of psychology is to make the services of psychology available to the common man facing problems without much difficulty. In identifying the problems of the community, service programmes were planned to deal with the problems and to reduce them to the maximum possible extent. The subject matters they sought to deal with are many and they are put under a field of psychology called community psychology. According to Rappaport (1977) community psychology has its origin in the attempts made by a group of psychologists to deal with those individuals who are not fitting into the society. It mainly deals with the marginal group. The individuals who reject the society or rejected by the society are the subjects of study for community psychology. This may take place due to various reasons. Historically community psychology finds its root in clinical psychology and psychiatry, a medical method designed to diagnose and to treat mental patients.

Community psychology basis its strategies on the current trends of the time and takes into confidence three elements such as service, human resource development and politics. Since it is interested in the society as a whole the combination of these three elements becomes essential for its successful implementation of the programmes.

One of the important social problems community psychologists had in mind was, the study of the effects of deprivation, in other words, the study of psychological consequences of various impoverished states. This may be attempted in several ways.

Deprivation

First of all, the concept must be defined and the area should be delineated. What is deprivation? What is poverty? Deprivation, in general, means that something essential is not available to the organism. It refers to impoverishment in general. In the case of human being, deprivation may be defined as a kind of life experience that a person meets within an environment in which he fulfils his needs inadequately and thereby loses certain comforts or pleasures of life. It is not in the absolute sense, but in relative sense. This type of condition may vary from person to person, from family to family, and from culture to culture.

The deprivation may be economic, social, educational, cultural, emotional or motivational. Whatever it is, the individual or the community is put into inadequacies of various sorts of life aspects. But deprivation is mainly referring to social aspects. Economic adequacy alone cannot fulfill all the needs of the people. Therefore deprivation is having strong social roots and explained through social status of the people. For example, an employee who has been classified as poor may be given 300 per cent increase in his salary, but he cannot make any improvement in his housing condition and home environment with this. He has to live in the same housing condition and locality. Therefore, economic deprivation or poverty is a socially improvished condition.

Man's biological and psychosocial needs are increasing every day as the consequences of rapid scientific and technological developments that were taking place after the World War II. Man seeks more comforts and happiness with least efforts. One big disadvantage is the rapid increase of population. As a result of this man is thrown into the highly competitive environment. When his basic needs are fulfilled without much difficulties there is no problem. If his needs are greater than his earnings then he faces many problems. If this condition continues for a longer period he will be stooping down to various kinds of deprivations. The loss of life comforts and happiness for a long period may cause some psychological consequences like frustration, aggression, violence and all sorts of psychological and psychosomatic problems. When man lost the comforts of his life he may be also tempted to indulge in all sorts of antisocial and criminal activities. If the deprivation of life comforts are prolonged then the immediate consequence may be frustration. Children born and brought up in such families may have the chances of becoming young delinquents. The adolescent period is often stated as storm and stress. Therefore, there is no surprise if the adolscents fall prey to all sorts of antisocial and delinquent activities.

Deprivation is an event that may take place in the life of an individual who is not having sound life economically, socially and emotionally. The word deprivation is derived from the Latin word 'Deprivare'. The word 'Deprivare' is a combination of two words 'de' and 'private' (De + private) which means to rob; to dispossess; to denote; to remove. This man is deprived of means that he is robbed. He lost his possessions or wealth or belongings. He is now lacking adequate, food, shelter, comfort, education etc. The deprived man might have also lost his office, dignity, benefits etc. Deprivation also may mean that the man is prevented from having properties and enjoying the life comforts. It is not the person himself giving it up, but some one removed it from him and made him to dispossess it. Dipossession of property may come in any form. The man might have been an extravagant, gone beyond the reasonable limits and spent excessively and thereby he became pauper. Such people are robbed by circumstances. A person or a group of people in this state is called deprived and if the state of affairs continued for a long period of time an adjective 'prolonged' is added to it and it is called 'prolonged deprivation'.

It is observed that scholars who study deprivation levels often explain and interpret the word too broadly. The origin and development of the concept mainly referred to the material possessions used for life comforts and enjoyment being removed. But modern authors use the concept, 'deprivation' to all human values like the feeling aspects, cultural and social aspects. The concept, deprivation was not only applied in psychological studies, but also in animal studies in laboratory situations. Thus the experimental animal may be deprived of its food, or water, or company, or mating chances. In the beginning when it was applied to man it was mainly referred to economic deprivation which included food, residence, education, position, wealth, land and other properties. It was also referred to social as social deprivation. When more and more studies were made it was used as an independent variable combining with social, cultural, affective, physical and psychological terms and also with the terms of all human values. Therefore, there were innumerable studies made in foreign countries and in India, employing the concept, prolonged deprivation as an independent variable.

Studies on Deprivation

In India the psychological studies that were made employing prolonged deprivation confined to mainly cognitive, perceptual and motivational processes and level of aspiration. But in many of the earlier studies, culture, social class and socio-economic status were used instead of deprivation. Davis (1948), Eels *et al.* (1951), Bernstein (1960), Jenson (1968), and many others have used social class and culture in their studies. They have related these variables to learning, intelligence and language spoken and written. Davis was of the view that culture of a particular social class determine the mental functions of the individuals.

As far as the studies of deprivation or prolonged deprivation are concerned it had its start in the laboratory situation and behaviourists like Watson (1914), Hull (1943), and Tolman (1932) were the forerunners of this venture. In the study of animal behaviour they made the animals to be deprived of food, water and mating in the laboratory situation. Later on it was extended to other fields and applied on human beings. The concept, deprivation was associated with social, cultural, racial, environmental, affective, educational, economic and other factors. In this way there were studies on social deprivation (Rankin, 1970), (Tulkin, 1972), cultural deprivation (Kogan, 1970), (Wright *et al.*, 1970), (Rath and Dash, 1972), racial and environmental deprivation (Whiteman and Deutch, 1968), affective deprivation (Gerwirtz, 1961), educational deprivation (Getzels, 1969), economic deprivation

(Symmonds, 1968). In all these studies the dependent variables were growth and development of human potentials.

A study was carried out by Misra and Tripathi (1978) on the cognitive processes and motivation in relation to prolonged deprivation. The important aspects of this study were the development of one prolonged deprivation scale (PDS) and the study of various levels of deprivation among the subjects. The scale development itself was a laborious and very difficult task. Their main aim was to study the psychological consequences of prolonged deprivation with special reference to cognitive processes and motivation among 645 subjects drawn from rural and urban areas of Eastern Uttar Pradesh. In order to have proper representation to all sections of the population the stratafied random sampling technique was followed in collecting data. The test materials were Koh's Block Design Test, Picturial Depth Perception Test, Status Perception Test, Self Perception Test, Time Perception Test, Perceptual Identification Test, Portable Rod and Frame Test, Concept Formation Test, Cattell Culture Fair Test of Intelligence (CFT) and Motivation Tests. These test materials were prepared in Hindi for the administration among the subjects.

The villages were selected and the research team visited the places and sought the cooperation of the villagers. The investigators were given suitable instruction with regard to the nature and purpose of the study. The subjects age ranged from 15 to 25 years. It took two to three sessions for the subjects to complete the tests. Correlation coefficients, the "t" test and two-tailed analysis of variance were some of the statistical analyses used in this study. The results show that prolonged deprivation was a determining factor of cognitive functions. The higher the deprivation level the higher was the restriction on the opportunities for growth of cognitive process.

Prolonged deprivation study was conducted among the 10th standard students in Tamil Nadu by Rajamanickam and Venkatammal (1984). The aim of the study was to assess the level of prolonged deprivation of the students studying in 10th standard. The prolonged deprivation scale developed by Misra and Tripathi (1978) was revalidated and administered along with a personal information questionnaire. The sample consisted of 259 students of 10th standard randomly drawn from ten high schools from five districts of Tamil Nadu. The results show that 10th standard students from five districts had greater amount of dissatisfaction with regard to motivational experience. The students of Chengalpattu district show high level of deprivation. The study also revealed that deprivation was inversely proportional to family income. The lower the income the higher the deprivation and the higher the income the lower the deprivation level. Number of children in the family increased the deprivation level among the students. The level of deprivation was found to be very high in the area of motivational experience and very low in the area of travel and recreation.

There are various levels of psychological functions in an individual as a result of the input he has experienced during his life time as a member of a particular community or social group which is not identical with his social group in all respects. In a social environment all social groups or communities do not have the same type of socio-cultural life. There are two extreme groups inspite of some indentical habituation. At one end certain social groups having their bio-genic needs are fulfilled while at the other end the same denied or deprived. The accumulated deprived state of affair in the social environment for a considerable length of period leaves a different type of output in the social group which we may state as the prolonged deprivation. The consequences of this state may be revealed in various ways. Apart from the hindrances and handicaps for the development and exercise of human potentialities, prolonged deprivation also may cause certain behavioural patterns which are biologically determined and socially induced which become potential threat to the structure and goals of the society and to its members.

The behaviour patterns of these are expressed in psycho-social and psycho-somatic problems. The economic deprivation may be also stated as poverty in other words. Psychologists consider that the state of poverty or the consequences of prolonged economic deprivation as a psycho-social condition is often having influence upon the mental and physical life of man and also causing anxieties and uncertainties. It is not a new phenomenon. It has been in existence right from the time of man's birth on earth. But the seriousness of the consequences was realized only at the present time.

Dorothy Wedderburn (1947) states that the apparent cause of poverty seem to be unemployment, low wages, unwise use of money, inadequate income for the family, too many children in the family, drought and floods. The poor may be defined as one who is struggling to obtain the necessities of his life. The poor are those whose earnings are considered as far below than the rest of the people amongst whom they live. Poverty is also assessed by relating one's immediate environment of community and to the contemporary standard of living.

The characteristics of poverty can be identified in home conditions, type of food people eat, dress they wear, number of family members, number of members employed and unemployed, type of treatment they get for the sick, type of recreations they have, place where they live, type of anti-social activities in which they are involved, mental defects etc. Pasamanick (1956) and others made a study on prenatal and paranatal factors in the development of childhood behaviour disorders. The study revealed that there was a relationship between prenatal nutritional deficiencies in mother and organic mental defects in their children, depression, apathy and lethargy resulting from inadequte diets and nutritional deficiencies.

Several studies were made on the poor people with special reference to factors such as unstable family environments (Miller, 1964) low expectation of success (Gurin and Gurin, 1970) deficit of social skills (Beiser, 1965), over dependency (Burgess, 1981), arrested psycho-social development (Hallowitz, 1970), chronic diseases (Graham *et al.*, 1972). Benjamin's (1953) study showed that there was correlation between bad social conditions and restricted physical growth of children both in height and weight. Brown *et al.* (1963) have observed that there was evidence of the downward drift of income and occupational status in relation to schizophrenia. Tarlok Singh (1983) has stated that poverty was found to be concentrating in tribal areas, hill areas, drought prone and desert areas and chronically flood affected areas. The city slum dwellers and villagers who do not find work regularly are prone to poverty.

Psychologists wanted to study these problems experimentally and reveal the consequences of them to find out remedial measures. Many of the physiological and psychological disorders were due to severe and prolonged deprivations of various types. These phenomena need to be studied experimentally.

EXPERIMENT

(a) Problem: The aim of the present experiment is to study the levels of prolonged deprivation of the subject in various areas.

2. METHOD

(a) Sample: Describe the subject with all his characteristics like age, class, parent's occupation, monthly salary, educational qualification, home town, district, value of immovable property, number of members in the family, etc.

(b) Materials: Prolonged deprivation scale (PDS), manual for PDS, scoring sheet.

(c) Description of the material: The prolonged deprivation scale (PDS) was developed by *Misra* and *Tripathi* (1978) of the University of Gorakhpur to measure the experiences derived from environment with respect to difficult aspects of life. The PDS consists of 96 items and there are 15 areas of deprivations. They are (1) housing condition, (2) home environment, (3) economic sufficiency, (4) food, (5) clothing, (6) educational experiences, (7) childhood experiences, (8) rearing experiences, (9) parental characteristics, (10) Interaction with parents, (11) Motivational experiences, (12) Emotional experiences, (13) Religious experiences, (14) Travel and recreation, and (15) Miscellaneous and cultural experiences. Every item is scored on a five point scale from 1 to 5, 1 indicating the lowest deprivation and 5 highest deprivation.

Procedure

The investigator or experimenter should make the subject to sit comfortably and talk to him nicely and establish good rapport and make him understand the value of this study. This can be used for individual testing and for group testing.

As soon as the subject is ready, the experimenter should give the following instructions:

> "Please look at this booklet. There are 96 statements in the form of questions. There are five types (a, b, c, d and e) of possible answers for them. You will have to choose any one of the five which is almost suitable to your life conditions. After determining the correct answer, put a check mark against the answer in the answer sheet. There are no right or wrong, or good or bad answers here. There is no time limit. But please see that you answer all the questions sincerely and frankly. This is the cooperation I seek from you in this matter. The replies given by you would be treated as highly confidential".

The experimenter should collect the answer sheet as soon as the subject has answered all the questions and allow him/her to go away.

Method of Scoring

The response categories a, b, c, d, and e were assigned with numeral values ranging from 1 to 5 respectively for all the statements except the statements 70, 74, 75 and 77. These statements were assigned with reverse value as 5 to 1 respectively for the categories a, b, c, d and e. In this system of scoring, the lowest score indicates low deprivation and the highest score high deprivation. The deprivation score for each area can be obtained by using the scoring formula for the respective area statements and a total deprivation score can be obtained by adding all the scores of the 15 areas.

3. RESULTS

The scores of all the 15 areas of deprivation scale should be presented in Table 1.1. Show the deprivation score of the individual for each area and also the total deprivation score of the individual. Collect the group data from other experimenters and present them in Table 1.2, showing score for each area and for all the areas of deprivation. Work out the mean for each area and for the whole scale.

Table 1.1 : Showing the individual score for the 15 areas in the test of prolonged eprivation

S.No.	*Areas of deprivation*	*Score*
1.	Housing condition	
2.	Home environment	
3.	Economic sufficiency	
4.	Food	
5.	Clothing	
6.	Formal educational experience	
7.	Childhood experience	
8.	Rearing experience	
9.	Characteristics of parents	
10.	Interaction with parents	
11.	Motivational experience	
12.	Emotional experience	
13.	Travel and recreation	
14.	Religious experience	
15.	Socio-cultural experience	
	Total Score for all areas	
	Mean Score	

Table 1.2 : Showing the group data on the test of prolonged deprivation

S. No.	Name	Areas															Mean Score
		1	2	3	4	5	6	7	8	9	10	11	12	13	14	15	
1.	R.G.																
2.	K.R.																
3.	B.V.																
4.	M.S.																
5.	T.V.																
6.	P.V.																
7.	R.M.																
8.	S.P.																
9.	S.R.																
10.	V.S.																
11.	A.L.																
12.	P.S.																
	Mean																

4. DISCUSSION

Discuss the individual's deprivation scores. In which area he/she scored high and where he/she scored low and find out the possible reason and state. Compare the individual with the group and discuss the results, comparing the various deprivation areas. What are the areas in which the group members consistently scored low and consistently scored high. Relate the personal information with high deprivation levels and state what type of factor were causing deprivation to the members of this group. Compare your results with that of the earlier studies and discuss.

5. CONCLUSIONS

State the highest and the lowest deprivation areas of your subjects and also whose score is the lowest and whose score is highest in the group. Compare these two levels with specific areas where both scores are high and low.

EXPERIMENT 2

Prediction of Violence

1. INTRODUCTION

The incidence of aggression and violence is an every day event that is taking place in some parts of this country which may vary from minor quarrel like verbal abuses to serious group clashes like mass killing. Newspapers every day publish some incidences of physical attacks, stabbing in the running train or bus, aggravated assaults, robbery, arson, gang fights, murders, forcible rape and all sorts of anti-social and criminal activities. These incidents are also broadcasted in radio and television programmes. Motion pictures now-a-days depict more scenes on aggression and violence with group rivalry more gang fightings and vulgar sex crimes. Participation in such anti-social activities is considered to be valiant act and it is the display of valour. The rural mass particularly the youth are very much attracted towards such displays which are exciting for them. But what sort of consequences such displays cause among the people, particularly among children and youth is a matter of serious concern.

Psychologists and other social scientists and those who are interested in the study of human behaviour have shown more concern over such consequences and have taken some steps to counteract them by propagating ethical and moral principles through mass media with a view of correcting them. But the effort of such interventions had very little effect, because the anti-social and criminal activities are increasing every day. Therefore, it has become an important subject matter and problem for social scientists to make empirical studies.

Aggression and violence

Violence is the outcome of aggression and studies on aggression and violence were made in U.S.A. and elsewhere. Gilula and Daniels (1969) describe aggression as the assertive, intensive and attacking behaviour. The form of aggression that concerns us most is violent which is a form of destructive act that involves physical damage on persons or property. Aggression is expressed in actions against others in its more violent and anti-social forms. Hostility, aggression and violence are mostly treated synonymously because of the damage caused by them in action. Dollard and others (1939) have formulated the aggression theory. According to them aggression is the reaction to frustration. When there is interference in the goal directed activity the organism gets frustrated and it leads to the sequence of behaviour which is injuring the person who is the cause of the frustration. There are instinctive theories and social learning theories. All justify man's aggressive tendencies. Freud (1917) says that the might of a community is the law and it is right. It is nothing else than violence. It is communal or group violence which occupies the major part of human social life. Anything a crowd or community has approved is right or law and it acts on it. The act naturally becomes violent riots, revolutions and wars—all may be stated as group violence or mob behaviour. All these result in killing and in injuring people destroying properties, and illegal appropriation of property.

Violence means the exercise of Physical force usually effecting or intended to effect injuries, destruction or devastating force. It is unjust, unwarranted and unlawful display of force such as to tend to overawe or intimidate. It is the physical force so as to inflict injury or damage to person or property.

Violence in a weakened sense refers to improper treatment or use of words wresting on perversion of meaning or application of unauthorised altercation of wording. It is undue constraint applied to some natural process, habit etc.

Violence is a forceful or powerful action or motion cannoting destructive force or capacity. It is the vehemence of personal feeling and action in excessive and extreme form of ardour or fervour. It may be also stated as the passionate conduct of language. It is having some qualities in such a degree as to produce very powerful effects, especially in the way of injury or discomfort.

Violence is always associated with aggression and hostility in psychological studies. Gilula and Daniels (1969) state that aggression in its expressed form is an attacking behaviour, overt and covert attacks, deformatory act, self-directed attack and dominance of behaviour such as forceful and determined attempts to master a task. The form of aggression in which we are concerned is violence which is a form of destructive aggression that involves causing physical damage on person or property. When aggression is expressed in actions against others it becomes more violent and anti-social. According to Heimstra and McDonald (1973) all violence imply characteristics of physical force, intense emotional excitement and unjust coercion.

Since violence is the manifest form of aggression these two phenomena are used synonymously in studies or in combined manner. Studies of violence were made on small children. It was found that the neonates show crying response to unpleasant changes in the immediate environment. It is not possible to predict whether their reactions are fear or anger. Bridges (1932) says that it is possible to differentiate fear from anger responses only at the age of six months. Boys at the age of three express more violent themes in their stories. Both the boys and girls of this stage report more themes involving death. But the themes of boys tend to be more violent and less friendly than those of girls. Interest in aggression and violence of the adolescents continued in adult years also.

The influence of culture on aggression and violence varies from mild form of unpleasant facial expression or look, scorn look, verbal abuses to physical attacks, lynching and extermination. In racial prejudices the influence of culture in aggression and violence is very turbulent. Violence in civilized societies may lie dormant and expressed in the form of extrication of the enemy from the scene slowly. But in primitive societies it is extermination once for all.

Urban societies have several social classes. The lower class groups often display more direct physical violence than the middle class groups. When inter-personal or inter-group differences are not resolved by social devices like discussion, conversation and negotiation the middle class people feel guilty and frustrated for hostile behaviour. It is because they wanted to avoid violence, whereas in the case of lower class groups social devices even though available for them they do not realize the value of them and often resort to impulsivity and let lose temper and often resulting in violence.

Garver (1968) states that violence can be studied under four dimensions. They are on the basis of personal or institutional and overt or covert. Thus we have overt personal violence, covert personal violence, overt institutional violence and covert institutional violence. The overt personal violence includes physical assault, rape, mugging, and so on. The covert personal violence includes threatening, black mailing rather than physical attack. The overt institutional violence comprises of mass riots, revolutions and wars. The covert institutional violence includes avoiding unliked people, hating people belonging to different social groups, racial prejudice and so on.

While discussing violence Ilfeld (1969) adds two more dimensions apart from being overt personal, it is also intentional. The intensity of the response caused by the violence also should be taken into account. He states that the violence may be intense, wilful cause of physical harm by an individual or by a group against himself or against another person or group. He differentiates good violence from bad violence. The good violence is approved by the society and justified on moral reasons. This kind of violence is used for self-defence. The self-defence may be with weapon or without weapon. The bad violence is not approved by the society. But some individuals or groups deprive of others legal rights and protection and act causing destruction to life and property.

Causes of Violence

The causes of rural aggression and violence is mainly based upon inter personal conflicts, social and group conflicts, riots, group revenge, group competitions, disputes over land possessions etc. These may generally lead to physical attacks on individual persons or on groups or communities, homicides, kidnapping of persons, burning houses and cattle. Most of the rural violences are having the sources in motion pictures of the present time.

Most of the motion pictures depict rural life with too much of rude and violent activities of various types. The rural youths are very much attracted by these violent activities and they try to imitate them in all possible means in the rural life situations and try to invent new methods to deal with their rivals. Therefore rural violences are increasing day by day and sometimes the whole village people might have been put into the grip of terror. Therefore violence may be defined as the overtly threatened or overtly accomplished application of force which results in injury or destruction of persons or property or reputation. The definition includes all anti-social and criminal activities such as homicides, aggravated assault, robbery, arson, suicide, forcible rape, gang fights, mob violence, lynching and extermination.

Biological Causes

Though there are several reasons for aggression and violence, whether it is rural or urban, based upon the situation or learning, the biological factors are also found to be the causes of violence. It has been experimentally verified that the causes of violence are rooted in genetic abnormalities or chromosome abnormalities. According to this study

(Morris, 1973) men will have an extra 'Y' chromosome (SYY). They are physically taller than the average men and are extremely aggressive. The extra 'Y' chromosome causes the adrenal glands to secrete large amount of male hormone. These persons reach sexual maturity earlier than the normal males and have abnormal sex drive and commit more sex crimes. They may be more violent and have high criminal tendencies. Further the factors are also associated with the damage of the central nervous system which also makes the individual susceptible towards violence.

Learned Response

We have discussed in the preceding section that most of the rural violences are having their sources in motion pictures which mean that they are learned responses. The rural youth try to follow or imitate their movie heroes or even learn to adapt the techniques used by the villains to become rich or get their desire fulfilled by violent means. The child rearing practices, the environmental situation, the individual's membership in a group—all contribute to violence. For example, the child understands that the application of force is a form of violence often used by the parents to discipline their children to a limited type of behaviour. Wolfgang (1970) states that it is permitted and encouraged in most of the cultures. Thus the child imitates the models of aggressive behaviour of the adults and learns to be aggressive and violent in his behaviour.

Quite a number of studies have been conducted on this problem that children learn to be aggressive and violent. The experiment conducted by Bandura and Walters (1963) showed that children who observed aggressive behaviour of adults were found to be aggressive themselves towards the plastic doll and imitated the behaviour of the adults sharply. The United States Surgeons General's Office (1972) has published their report that there is a possible link between TV violence and aggression. In modelling and imitation behaviour the role of violence portrayed in television and in movies had the impact. Violence has become a standard response in many situations through learning.

Situational Factors

The child first of all learns to be violent in the family situation and later on in the peer groups and then behave violently. Heimstra and

Donald (1973) state that situational causes of violence are complex and numerous. But most of the situations that arouse violence are based upon frustration of some type. Spiegel (1968) states that most of the sources of frustration are based upon the incompatability between democratic ideals and the authoritarian practices.

Studies on Violence

It is important to review some of the studies conducted on this area. Blackburn (1968) has tried in his study to see whether non-paranoid schinophrenics would be more violent than paranoid schizophrenic using the incidence murder and attempted murder. In one group there were 24 non-paranoids and in another there were 24 paranoid schizophrenic offenders. The author of this study also examined the history of persistent aggressiveness in both groups. He found that ten of the non-paranoid offenders and five of the paranoid offenders had a history of homicidal assaults. The difference between these two groups was significant at 0.05 level. In another analysis he found that there was inverse relationship between extreme assaultiveness and persistent aggression ($r = -0.56$) which is significant at 0.05 level, indicating a tendency for those patients who have committed offences of a homicidal in nature. Thus extreme violence was often found in well controlled persons and conversely the habitually aggressive or over controlled individuals tended not to commit the more extreme acts of violence.

Megargee and Mendalshon (1962) in one of their studies used the MMPI scale scores to study the violent behaviour of four groups. The first group consisted of 14 extremely assaultive men referred to a probation department clinic after conviction of homicide of assault with deadly weapon. The second group consisted of 25 moderately assaultive men referred to after conviction of battery. The third group consisted of 25 non-violent criminals referred to after other non-assaultive crimes. The fourth group consisted of 46 normals with no known criminal records. The MMPI scale scores discriminated the three criminal groups from the non-criminal group.

A study was conducted by Tutoo (1975) for determining the response patterns of youth belonging to varied socio-economic background on various aspects of violence. An opinion schedule was prepared on violence and it was administered on a student community of 46 members. The analysis of the data revealed that majority of the students' answers were either undecided or reserved in giving their opinion about most of the aspects of violence. The fact was that they considered violence as an uncivilized and unethical behaviour. Findings of Socio-economic background showed that the students of low income group were of the opinion that the primary causes of violence were ethical.

Studies made in India on aggression and violence revealed interesting results. Rajamanickam and Arumugam (1991) have conducted an investigation among the university students to study the level of aggression and violence. The sample consisted of 140 university students, studying at Annamalai University. Of these 56 were Arts and Science students and 66 were from Engineering and Agricultural sections. The aggression questionnaire developed by Pati, the Pd, Pa and Sc scales of the MMPI were used to determine aggressive tendencies and violent behaviour. The results showed that there was good association between the scores of aggression questionnaire and the scores of 3 of the MMPI scales. This means that those students who score high on aggression questionnaire also score high on the MMPI's violent scales.

Therefore it is known from this study that those who were aggressive were also violent in their behaviour patterns. This study also revealed that the non-professional (Arts and science) students were more aggressive and violent than the professional (Engineering and Agriculture) students. The lower socio-economic class students were the most aggressive and violent group. The middle social class students were moderately aggressive and violent and the upper social class students were the least aggressive and violent in their behaviour pattern. On the basis of age, the older students were more aggressive and violent than the other two younger groups.

EXPERIMENT

Problem: Predict the nature of violent behaviour pattern of a person and a small group of persons by using suitable test and compare the results with the previous studies.

2. METHOD

Participant: Describe the characteristics of the participant, such as age, sex, education, socio-economic status of the parents, etc.

Materials: Psychopathic deviate scale, paranoid scale and schozophrenic scale of MMPI. Scoring key and answer sheet.

Description of the Materials: The psychopathic deviate (Pd) scale consists of 50 statements, the paranoid (Pa) scale consists of 40 statements and the schozephrenic scale consists of 78 statements. All the three scales consists of 168 statements. The subject has to answer each statement by putting a circle around the responses True (T) or False (F). All these three scales are the measures of certain personality traits independently. But they jointly measure violent behaviour pattern of a person or a group.

These three scales are selected from Minnesota Multiphasic Personality Inventory. This Inventory was designed and developed by Hathaway and McKinley (1967) jointly to provide an objective assessment of some major personality characteristics that affect personal and social adjustments. Megargee (1962) says that violent behaviour can be analysed by using these three scales (Pd, Pa, Sc).

The Psychopathic is a personality trait and the person with this trait is supposed to be aggressive, hostile, unable to accept ethical and moral values. The person may be unprincipled business man, shyster lawyer, quack doctor, crooked politician, criminal, a typical lier, and may break the law impulsively and may be also ungrateful in his dealings. He is a burden on family and friends. The psychopathic often drifts into criminal activities. This scale has been used by many researchers to identify the criminals from non-criminals (Megargee and Mendulshon 1962).

The paranoid scale identifies the personality characteristics of a paranoid. The highly aggressive persons are more inclined towards the paranoid tendencies. The person is characterized by suspicion, rigidity, extremely jealous and stubbornness. The person of this type ascribe evil motives to others.

The schizophrenic scale identified the person with schizophrenic characteristics. The person of this type is seculsive, shy, avoids interpersonal relations and often day-dreams. He is also aggressive and hostile and eccentric in his behaviour.

Procedure: This test may be conducted as a group test or an individual test. The experimenter should make the subject to sit comfortably and should establish a rapport with him. Then the experimenter should first collect certain required personal information from the subject and then administer each test separately one by one.

The following instructions should be given before he hands over the test materials to the subject:

> "This scale (psychopathic deviate) consists of a number of numbered statements. Read each statement carefully and decide whether it is 'true' as applied to you or 'false' as applied to you. You are to mark your answers on the answer sheet supplied to you. If a statement is true or mostly true as applied to you write 'T' against the respective statement number on the answers sheet. If a statement does not apply to you or false write 'F' against the respective statement number on the answers sheet. If the statement does not apply to you or if it is something that you do not know about, make no mark on the answer sheet.
> Remember that you should give your own opinion about yourself. *Do no leave any statement unanswered.* While marking your answers on the answer sheet, see that you are marking on *the same number* of the statement number. Make your marks clear and legible."

When the subject has answered all the items of the 3 scales the experimenter should collect the answer sheet and the test booklet from the subject. The experimenter should check the answer sheet whether everything is answered correctly. The individual's score for all the three scales should be worked out with the help of the key.

Method of Scoring

All the three scales should be scored according to the scoring procedure of the author of the Inventory. The doubtful answers 'cannot say' or left unanswered statements should be omitted first. Then compare the subject's 'T' and 'F' answers with the key. Every answer given by the subject that agrees with the answer in the key will receive I mark, whether the answer is 'T' or 'F'. Then total the marks for each scale which is the individual's score. The high score indicates the high tendency in that personality trait and the low score indicates the low tendency. The total score of all the three scales is the indication of the individual's violent behaviour pattern. A high score indicates high tendency and a low score low tendency.

3. RESULTS

The individual's scores on the three scales should be given in Table 1.3. Analyse the individual's scores. What the high score in each scale indicates and what the low score indicates? State whether your subject is a violent person. State the level—whether high, moderate or low. Collect the group data from other experimenters and give them in Table 1.4. Work out the mean for the group. Treat the data with suitable statistical procedure.

Table 1.3 : Showing the individual's scores on the three violent behaviour scales and the total scores

Subject	*Pd. scale score*	*Pa. scale score*	*Sc. scale score*	*Total score*

Table 1.4 : Showing the group data of the violent test

S. No.	*Name*	*Pd Score*	*Pa Score*	*Sc Score*	*Total Score*
1.	P.V.				
2.	S.T.				
3.	B.V.				
4.	K.R.				
5.	M.S.				
6.	T.V.				
7.	K.P.				
8.	R.S.				
9.	E.R.				
10.	G.C.				
Total					
Mean					

4. DISCUSSION

Write the discussion part of the experiment in the light of the introduction and other studies made on violence. Compare your subject's violent score with the group mean and state where he stands on each area and in the violent behaviour pattern. Who is the most violent in the group and who is the least violent. State the reason for the same from the personal information collected from the subjects. Find out and discuss whether there is any difference between male and female subjects and also whether age is having any influence in the individual's scores in the violence test.

5. CONCLUSIONS

Draw the conclusion whether your subject is violent or not. If violent state whether it is most, or moderate or the least, who is the most violent subject in the group and who is the least. State the reason for the widely prevalent level of violent if any among the members of the group.

EXPERIMENT 3

Measuring Physiological Changes—Blood Pressure (Hypertension) and Pulse Rate

1. INTRODUCTION

Bodily Changes and Emotions

Human behaviour may be displayed in various forms at all the stages right from childhood through adolescence, adulthood and old age. Man in his display of his actions never fail to expresss one of the most or the most important component of his life, the emotion. The concept, emotion need not be mistaken only for the expression anger or rage. It includes many things. Candland (1968) states that emotion is an important attribute of all psychological processes. Emotions are also parts of happy occasions of our life. Emotions brighten our lives and also draken our days. Woodworth (1952) says that each emotion is accompanied by a feeling and an action. The emotion of fear is a set for escape, anger is a set for attack, mirth is a readiness for laugh and grief is for cry. Fear is an excited unpleasant state expresses unpleasant feelings and mirth or thrill is also an excited state, but expresses pleasant feelings. Both the emotions cause the body of the organism excited.

An emotion whether it is fear or mirth is an organic state. Organisms express these emotions in their bodily reactions in some manner. The heart and stomach and other internal organs of the body get disturbed in these emotional states. The excited or the stirred up state is common to both the emotions. Therefore, it is very difficult to identify which emotion has caused this excited state. This type of excited state is a general response of the whole person. Murphy (1964) states that we must take into consideration the person's whole body, not any specific part of the body, the whole consciousness, not any specific feeling or impulses, all are jointly involved in a unitary response and it is not local. According to Postman and Egan (1949) what we ordinarily call emotion involves a number of varied elements such as the nature of the stimulus situation, the verbal response to it, *series of internal bodily changes*, overt action and culturally determined responses.

According to Garrett (1961) the arousal of an emotion in an organism is marked by disturbance and confusion and the body is upset and agitated at the same time. The manifestations of the emotion are trembling, tension in the muscles of the body and face, dialation of the eyes, increased breathing and pulse rate, goose flush, erection of hairs and the man may even restlessly move about and shout. Are all these *physiological patterns of behaviours which are the characteristics of the said emotion measurable?* In studying physiological changes psychologists use various methods and instruments. The main purpose of measurement is to *relate physiological changes to emotional behaviours.* In some of the laboratory studies sophisticated instruments are used to measure the physiological changes caused by emotions. They record the breathing and pulse rate, *blood pressure and skin sensitivity.* The theoretical statements of Lange (1885) about the relationship between *emotional behaviour and blood pressure, blood volume, heart rate or the vascular system, changes in blood pressure* have often been reported *as the cause of emotional responses.*

Here, we are concerned with blood pressure and measurement of blood pressure and pulse rate in relation to emotional behaviour. Our knowledge in the study of measurement of blood pressure will be incomplete without knowing something about the functional anatomy of the vascular system.

Functional Anatomy of the Vascular System

The blood provides the cells of the body with oxygen, nutrients and other stimulating substances. The blood also removes the waste products and secretions from the surrounding regions of the cells. The blood is contained *within the vascular system.* The vascular system includes *heart and blood vessels.* The vascular system and the moving (circulation) of the blood within the vascular system constitutes the *circulatory system*. The *capillaries* are the smallest sub-divisions of the vascular system and exchange of materials between the blood and the tissue fluids occurs only through the walls of the capillaries (Easton, 1978).

Cardiac Activity

When there is more demand of energy in any given organ or organ system, blood supply must increase. Since the available blood supply is limited and constant, some other part of the body will be receiving blood less than what it was normally getting.

Blood is distributed throughout the body by *two principal mechanisms* which are supposed to be interacting, but sometimes may not act. *The first is the pumping activity of the heart*. It is also called cardiac activity. The amount of blood circulated varies with every change in the body's environment and with the activity of its organs. The physiological process that determines these circulatory variations is called *circulatory regulation*. Under normal conditions circulatory regulation is always a complex-reflex act in response to definite changes in the external environment and in the body. The activity of the heart usually is altered simultaneously with changes occurring in the blood vessels.

The amount of blood circulated per unit is a direct function of the rate and strength of the pumping action of the heart. When the heart muscle is expanded (diastolic function) blood enters into the heart from the venous drainage. The cardiac (heart) muscle is the important component of the heart. The cardiac muscle is found only in the heart. This muscle resemble both the smooth and striate muscles in certain respects, because of the conflicting demands made on the heart. Cardiac muscle shows high degree of automaticity. It is independent of nervous stimulation. It is beating regularly irrespective of what is going on the nervous system. The heart muscle must contract rapidly to provide rapid circulation of blood. It can contract rapidly so as to beat more than a hundred times a minute. The *contraction and relaxation of the heart muscle*, that is taking place alternatively, *is responsible for pumping of the blood* (Macey, 1973).

The amount of blood that is available for distribution during next contraction depends upon the duration of the subsequent expansion of the heart muscle. The *contractions of the heart muscle is called systole* and its relaxation or *expansion is called diastole*. The period of *a single contraction with following expansion of the heart muscle* is referred to as a *cardiac cycle.*

The heart is pumping the blood in a staggered manner. When the body is in complete rest the heart pumps blood into the aorta, the largest artery, about four to six litres for every minute. In the rest period the heart beats 70 times per minute. During each beat each side of the heart pumps about 70 milligram of blood. Therefore the amount of blood pumped each minute is 70 milligram per beat × 70 beats per minute. It is about five litres per minute (Harvey, 1931). But the number of beats per minute and the amount of blood pumped may vary according to nature and intensity of activity of the various organs and systems of the body. Therefore, the amount of blood pumped each minute may vary from 4 to 6 litres. The amount of blood pumped in each side of the heart during each minute is called *cardiac output.*

But, during the time of vigorous muscular work the cardiac output becomes faster and the blood output is increased to 20 to 35 litres per minute. In athletes on exercise or in action the output of blood per minute increases to 40 litres. Konradi, the Russian physiologist, states that this is caused by an increase of blood volume from 40 to 70 milligrams to 100 to 180 milligram per second pumped into the aorta during each systole. This also results in the heart rate from 60 to 70 beats to 180 to 240 beats per minute.

The second is the important role played by the autonomic nervous system in the cardiac output. The sysmpathetic nerve cells exert an influence on the heart and the stimulation of the *sympathetic fibres accelerates* the heart and makes it beat more forcefully. It follows that impulses running to heart along the sympathetic fibres act on the heart positively. The rate of heart beat and the strength of the beat are increased. But the other part of the autonomic nervous system, the *vagus parasympathetic preganglion nerve (X) fibres* carry the impulses to the heart and *reduce the heart rate* and decrease the cardiac output. Loewi (1955) has observed in his experiment that this slows down the rate of the beat and the strength of the beat. The heart is inhibited through excitation of the vagus. *The vagus nerve is the tenth (X) cranial nerve that contains many fibres of the autonomic nervous system.* The *fibres of the vagus which inhibit the heart* are always in a state of excitation which is not strong enough to stop the heart, but which is sufficient *to reduce the speed of the cardiac sound* to some extent. The continuous state of (increasing and decreasing alternatively) excitation of the neurons of the vagus which stimulate the heart is stated as *vagal tone*. When the rate of this pumping action is slow the circulatory exchange is at a minimum. When the heart rate is increased the blood flow also is increased.

Since the duration of the contraction (systolic) phases is too short, the output of blood per contraction also becomes so small that the amount of blood supply is decreased. The pumping action of the heart can be observed simply by increasing the sound that is generated. The rate of delivery of blood to the tissues depends upon the force of the heart beat. Like any other force the force of the contraction of the heart can be measured in terms of a weight that the force can balance. The force within the heart is distributed over the entire inside wall evenly. The physician's stethoscope can be used as a laboratory instrument that would amplify the heart beat and the beat can be heard over the ear aids.

Heart beat can be also read directly from a cardiochronograph which draws successive lines that the height of which are proportional to the duration of each complete cycle of the heart. Studies of this type has been made by Whitehorn *et al.* (1935), Whitehorn and Richter (1937), and Henry (1938). A more accurate means of recording the detailed activity of the heart is the electrocardiogram (ECG) which can provide a graphic record (electrocardiogram) of the activity of the heart muscle. This record may be obtained from electrodes attached to the arms or legs with one electrode on each side of the heart. The activity of the heart is controlled by sympathetic and the vagus parasympathetic nerve fibres of the autonomous nervous system. The heart rate may be used as an index of balance maintained by these two portions of the autonomic nervous system.

The heart receives the endings of sympathetic nerve fibres, the post-ganglionic fibres arising mainly from the stellate ganglion and through the three types of (superior, middle and inferior) cardiac nerves. The action of these sympathetic impulses in nourished by epinephrine and norepinephrine, the hormones secreted by the adrenal medulla whose effects imitate the arousal of sympathetic nervous system including an increase of heart rate. The heart is therefore subjected to change similar to the occurrence in emergency situations. In this way stimulation of sympathetic nerves accellerates and strengthens the heart beat and decreases the anteriovenous conduction time. The vagus *parasympathetic pregangelion (X) nerve fibres* exert an inhibitory effect on heart rate and increases the anteriovenous conduction time. These effects are mediated by the parasympathetic transmitted substance called acetycholine, which is a chemical transmitter substance *released at synapses by the synaptic knobs* of one neuron to excite other neurons. Thus with respect to the regulation of cardiac activity, the sympathetic and parasympathetic portion of the autonomic nervous system are mutually linked by the central regulatory mechanisms. Therefore the speed of the heart beat can be reduced either through the stimulation of the parasympthetic vagal impulses or by the inhibition of sympathetic system.

Vascular Functions

The vascular system and the blood moving within it constitute the circulatory system. The important function in the vascular system is the *exchange of materials between the blood and the tissue fluids* that occurs through the walls of the capillaries, which are the smallest sub-division of the vascular system.

The blood in its circuit through the body, moves from capillaries to veins, and back to the right side of the double pump of the heart. The blood at this stage is impure. The impure blood from here goes to the lungs where carbon dioxide (CO_2) is dropped and oxygen (O_2) is gained by the blood. This means that blood is purified in lungs. From lungs, the blood moves to the left side of the heart and is forced or pumped out to the body capillaries through the arteries. *The vessels that carry blood away from the heart to the tissues are called arteries* (Fig. 1.1), whereas *those that carry blood from the tissues to the heart are called veins* (Fig. 1.2). Blood in the arteries (arterial blood) is oxygenated, filled with rich oxygen and blood in veins (venous blood) is deoxygenated, very low level of oxygen. Thus, it should be known that oxygenated blood runs in the pulmonary veins (blood coming from lungs) and deoxygenated blood runs in the pulmonary arteries (going to lungs). The pumping system of the heart keeps the blood moving constantly. This activity is performed by heart.

As the activities of some organ or bodily parts change in varying degrees many tissues require more blood. There is a great change in the body during digestion and large supplies of blood are needed. There is an increased blood flow during sexual excitement in the sex organs. During strenous exercise and emotional states the skeletal muscle and heart muscle demand more blood. The heart will have to supply more blood through the vascular system. The extra demand of blood supply depends upon how fastly the heart pumps the blood. The faster beat will supply blood more rapidly to the tissues and the blood pressure

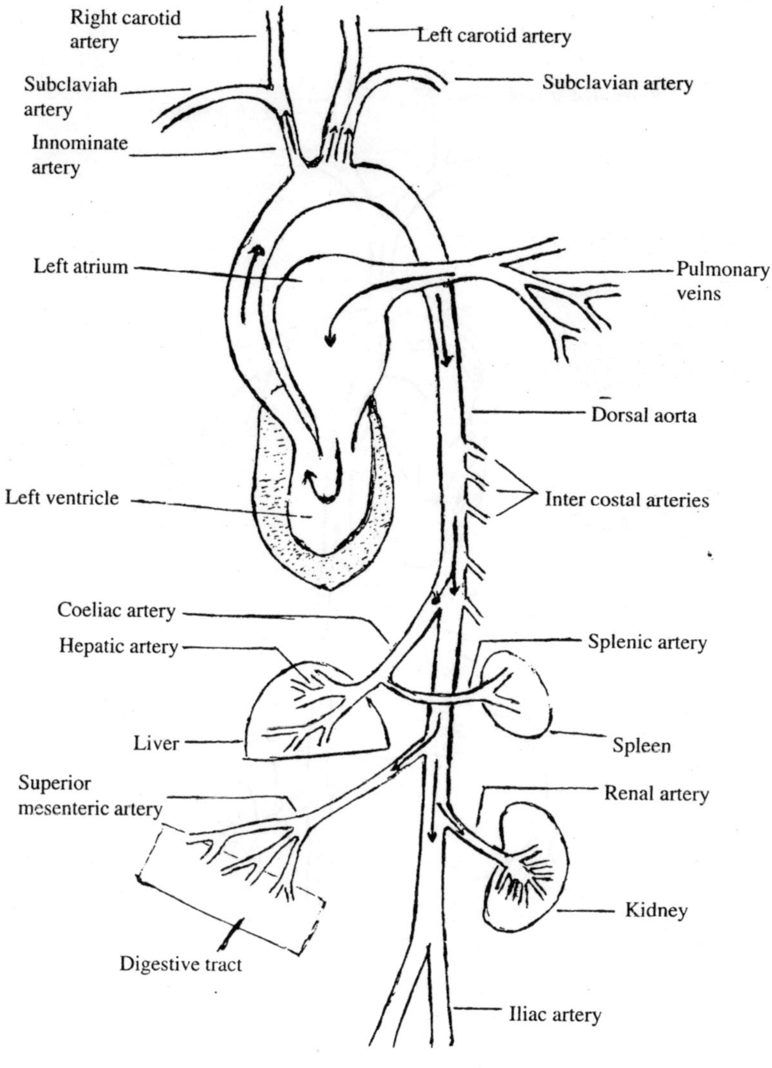

FIG. 1.1 : Left Heart and Blood circulation. Arrow in the Left atrium indicates oxygenated blood coming to the heart from Lungs and arrows in other parts indicate blood is being distributed throughout the body by the arteries. All the arteries carry blood away from the heart.

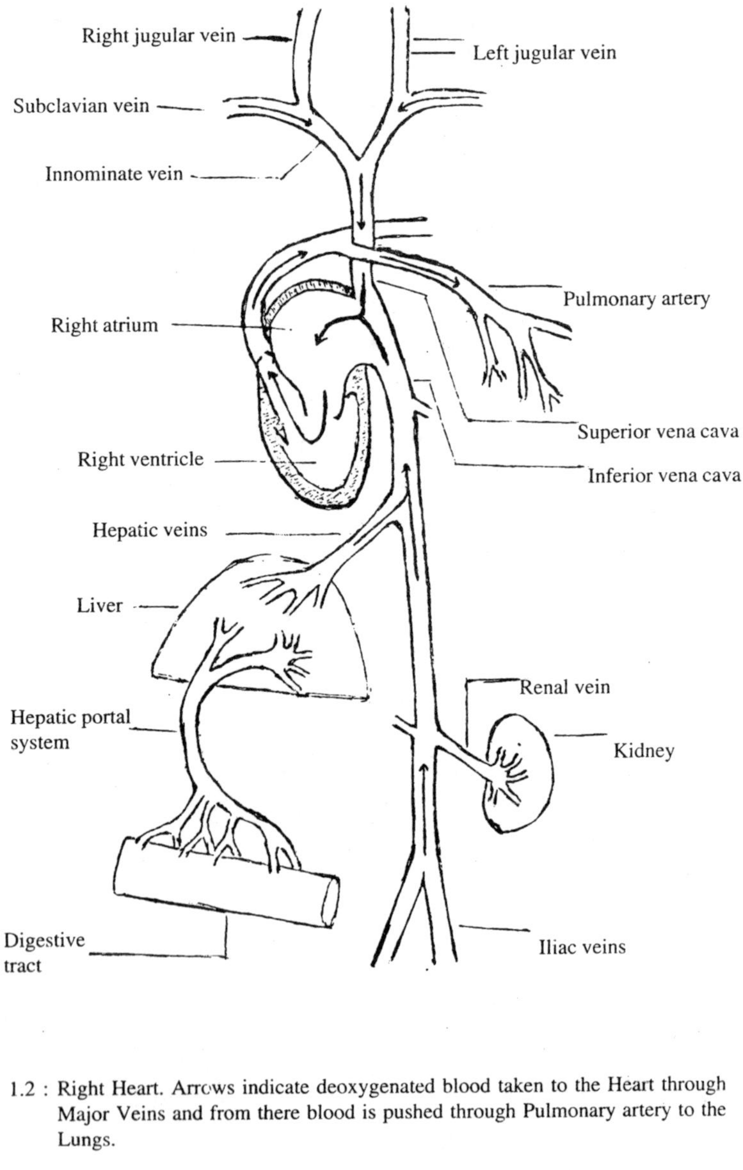

FIG. 1.2 : Right Heart. Arrows indicate deoxygenated blood taken to the Heart through Major Veins and from there blood is pushed through Pulmonary artery to the Lungs.

will be higher as the heart pumps blood into the arteries. But the moving of blood into the organs depends upon the *degree of access the blood has to the capillaries.* Blood enters into the capillaries through arterioles. The *arterioles are the terminal arteries* which act as valves and control the flow of blood into the capillaries. Therefore the flow of blood to particular regions depends upon the degree of *dilation of the arterioles in the vascular bed* of the particular organ. To meet this demand *the arterioles must* contract or *squeeze the inactive organs.* The walls of arterioles are made up of smooth muscles. These *arterioles offer resistance* to the body tissues to draw blood from the arteries *which are formed as blood reservoir.*

This blood reservoir is called *arterial reservoir* and this is pulsating moment to moment and this pulsation is caused by the heart beat. Every time the heart contracts, *it pumps blood into the arteries. This expands the arterial reservoir* and there is an increase of pressure. When the heart is relaxed or in a systolic state, *no blood enters the arteries, but some amount is left through the arterioles.* This makes the blood amount in the arterial reservoir reduced and the pressure is reduced. In this way for each contraction of the heart the pressure rises and at each relaxation of the heart the pressure reduces. In a normal healthy person the blood pressure rises to 120 mm Hg when the heart muscle contracts and falls to 80 mm Hg. when the heart relaxes. The actual pressure falls between the figures 120 and 80 mm Hg. This pulsation is felt on the body at many points. For example, it is felt in the wrist, ankle, temple, wherever the arteries are close to the surface. The average pressure is determined by the amount of blood in the arteries. The blood comes in from the heart and leaves through arterioles, which are very small narrow vessels. Because of their tiny size, they offer good deal of resistance in the blood passage. The walls of these arterioles are covered by smooth muscle. When the smooth muscle contracts the arterioles constrict and put up more resistance in the passage of blood.

Therefore we can see that two things are controlling the amount of blood in the arterial reservoir (arteries). As result of this there is average pressure in the arterial reservoirs. Firstly, the size of the arteriole passage can change and thus alter the resistance of the blood moving out of the arterial reservoir. Secondly, the cardiac output can also change, so that blood can flow into the arterial reservoir. During this function the amount of blood in the arteries (arterial reservoir) increases as there is increase in the cardiac output (increased outflow) and there is also an increase in arteriolar resistance (decreased outflow). But at the same time, if the cardiac output or the arteriolar resistance decreases the pressure also decreases. *The important function of the arteriolar resistance is to maintain average pressure in the arteries.* Macey (1973) explains this by a formula: Cardiac output × Arteriolar Resistance = Average Arterial Pressure.

We have discussed in the preceding section that the autonomic nervous system is having influence upon the muscles and the heart. The smooth muscles control the size of the arterioles. These smooth muscles are controlled by sympathetic nerves impulses. By increasing the frequency of these impulses further contraction is caused in the smooth muscles and the arterioles constrict. By decreasing the frequency of these impulses the muscles relax and the arterioles dilate. The products of metabolism such as acids and carbon dioxide also cause dilation of the blood vessels.

Metabolic Products

The metabolic products normally effect the blood flow. For example, a bandage is put very tightly around the arm that it stops off all the blood vessel lying under it. The blood flow to the arm is stopped completely. When the bandage is removed the blood flow is so fast that it exceeds the normal limit. The reason is that blood in the lower part of the arm is collected little more than the normal and when the bandage is removed it flows faster than the normal level.

The metabolic products on the anteriolar walls develop a mechanism to increase the blood flow through an active tissue. This takes place if only the blood pressure in the arteries is high. If the pressure is low the function ceases to take place.

Measuring Arterial Pressure: Systolic and Diastolic Pressures

The measurement of circulatory system is the measurement of blood pressure. This involves both the cardiac output and vasomotor activity. If blood is pumped through vascular then there is development of pressure gradiants (Grossman, 1967). The pressure *gradiants depend upon cardiac cycle.* The pressure gradiants vary according to the speed and strength of the heart beat. *The gradiants refer to the pressure or force per unit area of the vessels.* These are the functions by which the amount of blood is pumped by the heart for each beat and the size of the passage of the vessels through which the blood moves.

What we learn in physiology generally about blood pressure is that the pressure exerted by the blood on the walls of the blood vessels by the blood. *The pressure reaches its highest point during systole in the left ventricle. The systolic pressure* rises during activity and falls during sleep. *The diastolic blood pressure is the lowest point at which the pressure drops between beats.* This pressure sometimes becomes abnormally high, beyond the limit of normal condition, is stated as *high blood pressure or hypertension.* Though it is very difficult to state the normal blood pressure for any given age, for practical purpose the average systolic and diastolic pressures have been ascertained roughly in Table 1.5. High blood pressure offers resistance to free flow of blood from left ventricle which is the *major pumping chamber of the heart.* This state makes the heart to an excess of physical strain, leading to impaired functioning.

Heart disease by hypertension is the commonest form of disease today. In India it is estimated that one in every three cases is heart disease. A large number of deaths of high blood pressure among elderly persons is occurring every year.

In blood pressure, some chemical substance with pressure raising properties enters into the blood stream, circulates with blood and induces a sudden violent temporary activity or muscular contraction of the small blood vessels all over the body and raises the blood pressure (Easton, 1978). It has been observed that some of the important predisposing factors in the development of high blood pressure are mental tension, anxiety and rage. Spielberger (1984) states that some of the predisposing causes of heart attack are highly ambitious, striving, competitive hard driving and hurried. High blood pressure is a symptom-complex, underneath there are a variety of disorders like headache, giddiness, palpitation, tiredness and flushing. High blood pressure sometimes may impair the functioning of the heart and may result in heart failure.

Systolic and Diastolic Blood Pressure

During cardiac cycle the blood pressure in the arteries varies in two ways. The pressure rises to its maximum level in its first half of each systole and it lowers to a certain minimum in the second half or by the end of each diastole. Systole or maximum blood pressure takes place in the arteries for a short period of 0.1 to 0.12 second after the beginning of systole. The highest point is during this period only. In human beings in the large arteries this pressure constitutes 100 to 125 mm Hg.

The Diastolic or minimum blood pressure occurs towards the end of diastole. In human beings the diastolic value is normally between 45 and 80 mm Hg.

The pulse pressure or rate constitutes to difference between the values of the systolic and diastolic pressures. The variations in the systolic and diastolic pressures do not affect the value of the pulse pressure.

Determination of blood pressure

The blood pressure in human beings is usually *measured in the brachial artery*. It is by a bloodless method. *The brachial artery is the branch of subclavian artery.* At the arch of the dorsal aorta there are three arteries branching namely, innominate artery, left carotid artery and *left subclavian* artery. In the middle of the innominate artery at the junction the *right subclavian* artery is branching. The upper part of the innominate artery from where the subclavian artery branched is called right carotid artery. As the left *subclavian artery* runs into the arm, is successively called *the axillary and the brachial, and ulnar and radial, are the branches of brachial*, run into the lower arm. The *radial is close to the wrist* by which the *pulse rate is felt.*

The cuff of a sphygmomanometer is put around the upper arm of a person. By pumping the air, the cuff is inflated. The value of the external pressure is supposed to balance the blood pressure in the compressed brachial artery. The pressure in the cuff is transmitted to the muscles and vessels which pass through the upper arm and to the brachial artery in particular. When the brachial artery is fully compressed the pulse waves in the brachial arteries disappear. The disappearance of the ulnar or radial pulse corresponds to the pressure exerted by the cuff on the brachial artery, exceeds the maximum value of the blood pressure in the vessel. Then the pressure is lowered slowly deflating the cuff till the pulse reappears. This can be heard with the help of stethoscope. This is called *Systolic pressure*. On further lowering the pressure by inflating the cuff *till the sound becomes muffled*. The heart sound changes in its quality and intensity. This is the *diastolic pressure.* The *difference between the systolic and diastolic measures in the mercury level is the measure of pulse beat.* This can be checked by counting the pulse beat at the wrist by pressing the radial nerve. The normal blood pressure for individuals is 120/80 mm Hg.

Researchers are not satisfied with this type of technique since this is only an intermittent recording. Darrow (1937) and Steovkis (1938) tried with a technique by using systolic blood pressure continuously. Some investigators wanted to correlate with other variables. Sleep and relaxation have been viewed as complex circulatory changes by Shephard (1906, 1914), Landis (1925), Boas and Goldschmidt (1932) and Kleitman (1839), Berg and Beeba-Center (1941) have observed that a sudden loud noise stimulus makes an immediate increase in heart rate and blood pressure. Bodily exercises produce a rise in systolic pressure and a fall in diastolic pressure. Studies have been made correlating psychological stress and blood pressure by Landis and Gullette (1925), Landis (1926), Brown and Van Gelder (1938) and found that psychological stress increased the blood pressure and heart rate and induced vasoconstriction. The degree of anxiety had influence in the vasoconstriction was observed by Ackner (1958). Spielberger (1984) states that there are seven characteristics proved to be related to coronary heart disease (CHD). They are potential for hostility, irritability, impatient, explosive behaviour, vigorous response to interview questions, competitiveness, anger and some other symptoms. The emotion of anger is the underlying characteristics of high blood pressure and coronary heart disease.

The Better Method of Measuring Blood Pressure

The indirect method is better because the mercury manometer gives the most reliable readings. It is possible to measure blood pressure continuously in this unlike the aniroid and electronic blood pressure apparatuses. There are possibilities of error in the measurement if the instrument is not properly maintained or due to sheer carelessness or hasty on the part of the physicians. Various errors may creep in due to inappropriate level of the mercury reservoir, improper rise or loose application of the cuff or rapid deflation of the cuff. There can be also wrong readings if the patient is not properly relaxed. It is better that the patients relaxes for about 10 to 15 minutes on arrival at the clinic. Readings must be also taken by making the patient to lie down on his back (Supine), sitting and standing positions to note the effect of postures on the blood pressure.

Now-a-days blood pressure measuring instruments of self-assessments are available where even the stethoscope is not necessary. There is a small microphone fixed inside the cuff. Sounds, recorded are converted into audio-visual signals electrically. There are appearance of peeping sounds and the flashes of light indicating systolic and diastolic pressures. Therefore, one can measure his own blood pressure.

The physians who are hard of hearing can use an amplifying stethoscope which is available at present in the market. What are the diagnostic values of blood pressure measurement? The blood pressure values indicate the state of blood circulation, adequacy of perfusion of body tissues, strain on the heart, the effect of various factors like weather, humidity, emotional state, disease and drugs or other properties in circulation.

Blood pressure should be checked periodically or whenever a person suffers from some kind of disease. Normal individuals who have no strong family history of high blood pressure can have their blood pressure checked once in six months. In the case of cardiac patients it is better to have their blood pressure checked after every month.

EXPERIMENT 3

Measuring the Circulatory Changes Involving Blood Pressure (Hypertension) and Pulse Rate

Aim: Determination of blood pressure with systolic and diastolic pressures and the pulse rates of a person and comparing the same with normal measures.

2. METHOD

Participant: Choose a person of any age or gender and collect his/her personal information such as the type of ailments etc.
Apparatuses: Sphygmomanometer (mercury type) with cuff, stethoscope, and pulse monitor.

Description of the instruments

Sphygmomanometer: There are several type of instruments used for measuring blood pressure. They are mercury type, Aniroid type, Electronic type and Electronic printing type. The first will give the blood pressure rates. The other two are improved models. The last one will give blood pressure rates, pulse rate and respiratory rate. All these measures are displayed in the instrument and given in the printed form with date and time. For the electronic manometer the stethoscope is not necessary. But for the class room purpose to demonstrate the blood pressure measurement the mercury sphygmomanometer is very convenient. The rise and fall of mercury can be noticed by the experimenter.

The mercury manometer is packed in a rectangular metal case in a lying position. The metal case should be opened and the mercury tube should be raised. Mercury is stored in a cup at the bottom. The mercury cup is connected to one end of a rubber tube and the other end of the tube to the cuff. One rubber tube from the cuff is connected to the rubber bulb.

Stethoscope: The stethoscope is a Y shaped instrument having three ends. It consists of two ear aids at two ends connected with rubber tubes and at the other end there is a chest piece. It is a very sensitive instrument for sounds. There is some provision for adjustment in this instrument. There is also electronic stethoscope which is highly sensitive for sounds. Physicians who are hard of hearing can make use of this instrument. This is very much useful for training purposes.

Pulse monitor: It is a rectangular box type. It is operated electrically. One cable is connected to the main switch and at the end of another cable there is one electrode. This is connected to the thumb of the subject. There is a window to observe the reading. The window gives the reading of the pulse rate.

Procedure

Any medical test includes blood pressure measurement. Some physicians measure blood pressure in sitting position and lying position. But some take blood pressure in three positions, standing, sitting and lying to verify whether there is any change in the measurement. For experimental purpose it is better to have all the three positions and then take the average measure. First it is better to have the sitting position.

The subject is to be seated comfortably. Care should be taken that the subject is placed at ease and relaxed. Time should be given for recovery from some usual activities or exercises or meals. The subject's arm left or right should be completely bared so as to make certain that clothing does not constrict the blood vessels.

The subject may be given a brief instruction about the task the experimenter is going to perform. The blood pressure apparatus should be kept in correct position and it may be tested first by the experimenter whether the mercury level is right. The blood pressure should be taken first in sitting position. The subject's fore arm should be supported at heart level in a smooth surface. The cuff must be tied evenly and tightly around the arm, with the lower edge of the cuff approximately one inch above the elbow. Then the experimenter should hang the stethoscope in his neck and inflate the cuff by sqeezing the rubber bulb. As and when the bulb is squeezed the cuff is inflated and the mercury level is also increasing in the glass tube vertically. The glass tube is calibrated to read the pressure in millimeters of the mercury. The rubber bulb should be squeezed until the blood flow through the brachial artery is stopped. This will take place when the mercury level in the calibrated tube reach 180 or 200 mm. Then the stethoscope receiver is applied to the brachial artery firmly on the side of the elbow in the antecubital space. It should not make any contact with the cuff.

The experimenter, then slowly reduce the cuff pressure by means of a valve in the bulb until sounds heard in the stethoscope (korot koff sounds) indicating that the peak of the systolic pressure is just in excess of the cuff pressure (Cleary, 1977). Systolic blood pressure is the highest point at which successive dull sounds are heard. This is recorded as the systolic pressure.

The experimenter should continue the deflation of the cuff below the systolic pressure until the sound becomes muffled. The heart sounds undergo changes in intensity and quality. This is the best index of diastolic pressure. At this point the heart sounds completely cease.

These two points systolic and diastolic, should be noted down. After few minutes it can be verified in the same manner. The most important thing is that when the mercury level is at high level i.e. at 180-200 the experimenter should watch with the stethoscope the heart sound. When the air is released through the valve of the bulb the mercury level goes down, some sudden sound may be heard and when the mercury level still goes down another similar sound may be heard. These two sounds should be carefully observed. If it is not heard properly the procedure should be repeated by raising the mercury level once again to the highest point. After recording the systolic and diastolic pressures at sitting position the subject should be made to lay down on a bench or couch and the blood pressure should be measured in the same manner. Then the subject should be made to stand and the hand should be kept at the heart level and the measurement should be taken. In all the three positions the level should be verified with two times.

To test whether physical exercise is having any influence in the blood pressure levels, the subject may be given some exercise for 4 or 5 minutes by making him to sit and stand 10 or 15 times. One position is sufficient to test this. As soon as the exercise is over the sitting position may be used and the blood pressure should be measured.

The pulse rate of the subject should be measured by attaching the electrode to one of the thumbs of the subject and the pulse monitor should be operated. In the window of the monitor the numbers may run indicating the pulse rate. This should be noted down. It can be measured manually also by counting the pulse beats with a stop watch.

3. RESULTS

The recorded blood pressure measures for all the three positions, sitting, lying and standing should be given in Table 1.5. Check whether there is any difference between these three positions. Take the mean of these measures, and show also the B.P. taken after some exercise.

Compare your subject's blood pressure rate with the normal blood pressure rate of his age (from the Table 1.8) and give it in Table 1.6. Show also the pulse rate of your subject in comparison with that of his age.

Collect group data from other experimenters and present them in Table 1.7. Work out the mean B.P. rate and compare your subject's B.P. with other subjects B.P. in both conditions, before exercise and after exercise.

Table 1.5 : Showing blood pressure of the subject in 3 positions before exercise and after exercise

S. No.	*Position*	*Systolic in mm*	*Diastolic in mm*	*Difference in mm/Pulse rate*	*B.P. after exercise (sitting)*		
					Sys. mm	*Dias mm*	*Diff./ Pulse*
1.	Sitting						
2.	Lying						
3.	Standing						
	Mean						

Table 1.6 : Showing the comparative blood pressure rate and pulse rate of the subject with the normal B.P. and pulse rate (See Table 1.8 Showing Normal Range)

Group	*Systolic mm Hg*	*Diastolic mm Hg*	*Difference (Sys–Dias)*	*Pulse rate*
Exp. Subject				
Normal Subject				

Table 1.7 : Showing the blood pressure and pulse rate of the group before and after some exercise

S. No.	*Subject*	*Systolic mm Hg*	*Diastolic mm Hg*	*Difference (Sys–Dias) Pulse rate*	*After Exercise B.P.*		
					Sys. mm	*Dias. mm*	*Diff./Pulse*
1.	P.K.						
2.	T.P.						
3.	K.R.						
4.	E.K.						
5.	P.V.						
6.	M.S.						
7.	B.V.						
8.	A.R.						
9.	G.G.						
10.	R.V.						
	Mean						

Table 1.8 : Showing normal range, mean and lower limits of (Hypertension) blood pressure for both male and female subjects

Sex & Age	*Systolic*			*Diastolic*		
	Normal range	*Mean*	*Hypertension Lower limit*	*Normal range*	*Mean*	*Hypertension Lower limit*
Men						
16	105-135	118	145	60-86	73	90
17	105-135	121	145	60-86	74	90
18	105-135	120	145	60-86	74	90
19	105-140	122	150	60-88	75	95
20-24	105-140	123	150	62-88	76	95
25-29	108-140	125	150	65-90	78	96

Sex & Age	*Systolic*			*Diastolic*		
	Normal range	*Mean*	*Hypertension Lower limit*	*Normal range*	*Mean*	*Hypertension Lower limit*
30-34	110-150	126	155	67-92	79	98
35-39	110-145	127	160	68-92	80	100
40-44	110-150	129	165	70-94	81	100
45-49	110-155	130	170	70-96	82	104
50-54	115-160	135	175	70-98	83	106
55-59	115-165	138	180	70-98	84	108
60-64	115-170	142	190	70-100	85	110
Women						
16	100-130	116	140	60-85	72	90
17	100-130	116	140	60-85	72	90
18	100-130	116	140	60-85	72	90
19	100-130	116	140	60-85	71	90
20-24	100-130	116	140	60-85	72	90
25-29	102-130	117	140	60-86	74	92
30-34	102-135	120	145	60-88	75	95
35-39	105-140	124	150	65-90	78	98
40-44	105-150	127	165	65-92	80	100
45-49	105-155	131	175	65-96	82	105
50-54	110-165	137	180	70-100	84	108
55-59	110-170	139	185	70-100	84	108
60-64	115-175	144	190	70-100	85	110

4. DISCUSSION

Discuss your subject's B.P. rate in all the three positions. Compare it with the B.P. rate taken after the exercise. State the reason why there is change after exercise or no change. Discuss whether your subject's B.P. is normal or above normal or below normal. State the reason. What is the actual blood pressure (Systolic-Diastolic) of your subject. Compare it with the group mean and state where he/she stands. Find out the reason why your subject's B.P. is different from the group mean. Find out deformities if any with your subject or ailment and see whether it has any influence in the B.P. Discuss whether the exercise had any effect in the B.P. of the members of the group.

Discuss the pulse rate of your subject in relation to the normal subject. Compare it with other subjects and the group mean. State reason for the difference if any. Do you find any difference in the B.P. and in the Pulse rate due to age and sex.

5. CONCLUSIONS

What is the B.P. rate of your subject? Is it above or below the normal person (Table data)? Is it above the group mean or below? What is the pulse rate of your subject? Is it above the group mean or below? Had the exercise any effect in the B.P.? Had deformation of the subjects any effect in their B.P.? Is there any difference in the B.P. and Pulse rate due to age and sex.

2

HUMANISTIC PSYCHOLOGY

1. INTRODUCTION

The period around the first quarter of the twentieth century is a very remarkable period in the history of psychology from various points of view. This is the period in which the various schools of psychology have emerged as a sign of psychologists' concern over the variety of problems of human beings. Psychological studies began to touch almost every facet of human lives. Human society is becoming more rapidly multiplied and also becoming more complex. Problems of various types cause anxieties in the life of an individual. Various social groups often come to conflict when the adjustment problems are not resolved. Some of the individual and social problems are resolved easily, but many are not and are neglected. The mental health problems of the people were also receiving serious attention for a systematic approach. Therefore, it was felt that the study of human behaviour and mental processes should be given the scientific approach and every aspect of it should be experimentally analysed.

Just as there are different paths in all four sides to reach the hill top there are also different approaches to the study of psychology of man. Therefore, there are diverse view points. They are all called schools of thought and each one was founded by one eminent psychologist. The *structuralism* was founded by *Wilhelm Wundt* (1832-1920) around this period. Structuralism was originally based upon the conscious experience of man and it tried to discover the elements present in conscious experience. According to Wundt there are two categories of elements present in our experience. The first is sensation which comes to us from outside as a result of our contact with the environment and the second is feelings which form part of our internal experience. A few years after this a school of thought known as

Functionalism was founded by *Edward Titchner* (1867-1927) in America. Titchner was the student of Wundt. After taking up training under Wundt, Titchner went to America and started the systematic study on sensation at Cornell University. He preferred to call it as existentialism rather than structuralism. Since structuralism brought from Germany it underwent severe criticisms that how can the study of elements of experience constitute the study of mind. *John Dewey* (1859-1952) the American Philosopher and *James Angell*, an educationalist become the champions of this criticism. Titchner made more changes in the original system. Then the school of functionalism was born and several psychologists were responsible for the development of this school though it was founded by Titchner.

The school of *Associationism* was founded by *Edward Thorndike* (1874-1948) in America. This concept was evolved from the philosophy of Thomas Hobbes (1588-1679) and it is having a long history going back to Aristotle, the Greek Philosopher. But it was Thorndike who developed it into a system of psychology.

The school of *Psychoanalysis* was founded by *Sigmund Freud* (1856-1939) around 1900. Freud was an Austrian physician, based his theory on experimental analysis. Psychoanalysis primarily was a therapeutic technique that Freud was applying on neurotic and psychotic patients. But it had profound influence or psychological thinking. The basic assumption of Freud's theory is that man's behaviour largely is determined by the unconscious processes. Man is not aware of the wishes, thoughts and fears which are stored in the unconscious level that are greatly influencing his behaviour. Freud's theory of motivation, personality and the psychoanalytic method of treating the mental illnesses are having very much influence on psychological studies. Most of his important studies were published around 1990-1917.

While Freud was working on psychoanalysis in Europe, *John Watson* (1878-1958) was starting his *Behaviouristic school* in United States. Watson as early as 1900s advanced the idea that behaviour should be the sole subject matter of psychology. He rejected the method of introspection as a subjective observation. Watson's behaviourism has thoroughly changed the course of psychological studies during the first half of this century through its stimulus-response psychology and still it is strong in United States.

Around the period of the first quarter of this century, *William McDougall* founded a school called *Purposivism* (Woodworth, 1955) which was based upon his instinctive theory. Somehow this school of thought did not have many followers and since it is not based upon experimental evidences the school did not flourish.

In the first quarter of this century in America there were several schools of academic psychology functioning namely structuralism, functionalism, associationism and behaviourism. They were all working out using experimental methods and to qualify psychology as science. Enormous amount of facts were collected and interpreted. At this time a new theory called *Gestalt theory* has been developed in Germany in 1912 and *Max Wertheimer* has announced it in 1912 and subsequently *Wolfgang Kohler's* and *Kurt Koff's* books were published in English. This had great influence in the American learning theories. Though the Gestalts were primarily interested in perception, they have also extended their studies in learning and severely attacked the learning theories of Thorndike and Watson.

These various schools of psychology were studying different aspects of behaviour and mental processes. But they were not taking into consideration the problems of man as a person. The general principle did not deal with the certain specific problems of man. It was observed that the outcomes of the studies made by these systems psychology during the last sixty years did not reveal anything about man's capabilities. While reviewing the sixty years rigorous studies with all seriousness some shallowness and dissatisfaction were felt at some circles and a group of psychologists raised their voice around 1960s and started a new approach to study man, and the field is called humanistic psychology.

According to this approach an individual has to determine his actions and he is free to choose what he must do. Every one is responsible for his actions and he cannot blame his parents or the society or the environment. This conception was developed from the philosophical backgrounds, particularly from the existential philosophies of Kiergaard, Nietzohe and Sartre. These doctrines emphasized that man is different from animals in several respects, particularly by his free-will and self-actualization. The humanistic approach did not accept the views and methods that man is studied like a mechanism and his activities are often controlled by the external forces or stimuli and by his unconscious processes. Man is capable of controlling his own destiny and he changes the world around him. The individual's perception of the self and the world are more important subject matters for the study of psychology than his actions. But to know more about the conception of humanistic psychology and its themes and issues it is important that we must know also its philosophical roots.

2. THE PHILOSOPHICAL ROOTS OF HUMANISTIC PSYCHOLOGY

In Europe, during the period of renaissance, in 14th, 15th and 16th centuries several radical changes have taken place in art, science, culture, philosophy and religion. The period of renaissance was characterised by intensified classical scholarship, scientific inventions, discovery of new lands, assertion of active secularism, revolt against the orthodox church and a sense of individual potentialities. The Italian renaissance had brought out significant revival in painting, sculpture and architecture and had its influence in all the continental countries. After the end of renaissance during 17th, 18th and 19th centuries several conflicting philosophical doctrines have emerged and they all had profound influence in the political, social and religious life of the people all over the world. Scientific inventions and discoveries, educational policies and people's attitude to life all had new approaches.

Every philosophical doctrine had its own influence in certain areas. Thus the existing philosophies during this period were, the Rationalism of Rene Descartes (1596-1650), the Naturalism of Baruch Spinoza (1632-1677), the Materialism of Thomas Hobbes (1588-1679), the Scepticism of Emmanuel Kant (1724-1804), the Dualism of John Locke (1632-1704), the Idealism of George Berkeley (1685-1753), the Empiricism of John Dewey (1859-1952), the Positivism of August Comte (1798-1857), the Pragmatism of Charles Peirce (1839-1914) and the Existentialism of Friedrich Wilheim Nietzche (1844-1900). Strictly speaking each one of those systems is not cent-per-cent independent of the other. What is discussed in one system is also discussed in another system. These systems were not very rigid as every system yielded the arousal of another system from the critical views. In these systems there were references about the concept of man and the importance of his role and responsibilities. But some deficiencies in these doctrines were felt by some European philosophers. As a result of it during the second half of the nineteenth century two systems of philosophical movements were found to be emerging side by side stressing the importance of the personal experience and human efforts.

One school was called existentialism founded by *Kierkegaard* (1813-1855), a Danish philosopher and theologican. He rejected the organized Christianity and anticipated the existentialists in emphasizing man's moral responsibility and freedom of choice. His works included 'Either/Or' (1843), 'The Concept of Dread' (1847) and 'The Sickness into Death' (1849). According to him the individual is totally a free agent in a deterministic and seemingly meaningless universe, and what is demanded from him is the personal experience, and moral responsibility and he is responsible for his act. Kierkegaard's philosophy was mainly based on man's.personal experience, empirical as opposed to theoretical, concrete as opposed to abstract.

The other philosophy was the humanistic philosophy or humanism, which was founded by the British philosopher, F.C.S. Schiller (1864-1937). Schiller's humanism was an offshoot of pragmatism, a system of philosophy originated in the United States at the hands of the American Philosophers, Charles Peirce (1839-1914), William James (1842-1910), John Dewey (1859-1952) and Mead (1863-1931). Originally Peirce was the first to originate this idea and the other three were directly or indirectly influenced by Peirce.

Pragmatism as a philosophic doctrine has been interpreted in as many ways and so often also misinterpreted. This means that there were many kinds of pragmatism. Pragmatism is a form of empiricism and it has something in common with other form of empiricism—the positivism. Following the British philosophers John Locke (1632-1704) and George Berkeley (1685-1753) there aroused in the nineteenth century two related forms of empiricism called positivism and pragmatism, one positivism in France, the exponent of which was August Comte (1798-1857) and the other positivism in Austria in the last quarter of the nineteenth century founded by an Austrian philosopher, Ernst Mach (1838-1916) and at the same time Charles Peirce inaugurated pragmatism in the United States. Both Mach's positivism and Peirce's pragmatism were very much influenced by then flourishing empiricists' movements. Both the positivism and pragmatism were applied in numerous ways, specially in the recent history of sciences like psychology, sociology, anthropology, education and in the interpretation of religion.

The American pragmatism was functioning under two forms, one represented the views of William James and Schiller and the other represented the views of Peirce and Dewey. Originally James wanted to elaborate his views on the pragmatism of Peirce. But consciously or unconsciously it resulted in something quite differently. Schiller states that when we judge a belief whether it is true or false we are evaluating it. It is just like evaluating certain things as good and bad, pleasant and unpleasant, beautiful and ugly so also we evaluate things called propositions or beliefs as true and false. Therefore true is a form of value. Schiller defines true and false by stating that these are the terms which mean that a proposition is useful or useless. When an individual announces that a belief is true which means that the belief so far as his matter is concerned, it fits with the sum total of his interests. But some time an individual will declare a belief to be true and after some time withdraw this judgment. This means that during the course of time the belief has proved to be useless and therefore it is rejected. This is called false. This valuation is a *psychological act*. Schiller says, that this does not mean that the determination of true and false is an individual affair. What is to be accepted as truth is the result of social interaction. Truth is a social product since man is a social animal. Individual's truths and valuations are corrected by social interactions. The valuation made, should be of sustaining one. A truth entertained by a minority of one group cannot be a truth if it is left in that state. It must have social recognition.

The individual selects and uses the criterion for truth evaluation and constitutes by that means the objective truth which obtains social recognition. According to Schiller truth is the useful, efficient, workable to which our practical experience tends to restrict our truth valuations; if there is anything reverse of this claims to be true it is detected sooner or later and rejected. This is Schiller's pragmatism.

Schiller calls his Pragmatism as Humanism

According to him all the theories and beliefs are neither meaningful nor true unless they have some *human values* inherent in them. Schiller states that truth is useful primarily for any human end, ultimately for perfect harmony of our whole life which forms our final aspiration. Those beliefs which make for human happiness are true while those which make unhappiness are false.

The existentialism founded by Kierkegaard and the humanism founded by Schiller, though founded by different philosophers they have something in common. Schiller after discussing and explaining his pragmatic philosophy in detail, called it as humanism, Kierkegaard and Schiller put more emphasis on truth and the truth should have social recognition. According to Kierkegaard, an individual has necessity for commitment. The commitment is to see a particular truth, which may bring him happiness. Schiller also emphasizes the truth in the case of an individual as only truth can bring him happiness. Sartre (1946), a French Philosopher while discussing Kierkegaard's existentialism states that Existentialism is a Humanism. Though Kierkegaard, the founder of existentialism did not say anything directly about humanism the followers of existentialists like Sartre (1946), Heidegger (1947), Kaufmann (1956), Horner and Buhler (1969), May (1958), Lowrie (1938) were able to interpret critically his writings and state that Keirkegaard's existentialism is a humanism.

The first-half of the nineteenth century saw many existentialist philosophers in Germany and French. They all seemed to endorse Keirkegaard's existentialism. Those who were thinking about various types of existentialisms were Karl Jaspers (1883-1969) a German existentialist philosopher, and Martin Heidegger (1889-1976), a German Existentialist philosopher, who expounded his ontological system of philosophy in his work, *"Being and Time"*, in 1927. Later on in 1928, he published it under different title. The other was Jean-Paul Sartre (1905-1980), a French philosopher, novelist and dramatist. He was the chief exponent of *atheistic existentialism.* His works include the Philosophical easay, *"Being and Nothingness"* published in 1943 and his famous novel *"Nauses"* published in 1938. All these three existentialist philosophers were contemporaries lived after Kierkegaard (1813-1885), the founder of modern existentialism. All the existentialist philosophers emphasized man's individuality.

Kaufmann (1956) states that the modern existentialism is a system based upon the dissatisfaction of the traditional philosophy. According to him the traditional philosophical systems are superficial, academic and they are far away from real life of man. Kaufmann states that though the individuality is influenced by the early romantic movement which is characterised by an emphasis on feeling and comforts rather than order and form and free expression of the passions and individuality, the existentialism is free from self pitying anti-social attitudes of the classical romanticists, characterized by emotional restraint and conservatism. Kaufmann is of the view that romantic movement is an escapists movement which is quite similar to the present day hippi culture in this respect. Therefore he did not want to associate existentialism with the romantic movement of the eighteenth century.

Kierkegaard states that the objective fact or truth depends upon how man relates the meaning to it. A truth has no reality by itself. The truth always depends upon the reality of the relationship. What type of relationship one is having with an object. It is not referring to the remote or long past relationship. What type of relationship or contact one had with an object is the experience he had at that time. He quotes the existence of a tree and what type of meaning a man has with it. The tree gives different meanings to different persons. One person says that the tree is one which gives fruits, for another it provides shade, for a third person it is used as timber and for a fourth person it stands as obstacle on his way. But for all the four it is a tree and it has a meaning.

To Kierkegaard man is in a state of need and also he has commitment and therefore he requires freedom of choice and decision. And also man as a human has moral or ethical responsibilities. He can fulfil his moral responsibilities and commitment if only he has freedom of choice and decision. Buhler and Allen (1972) state that Heidegger (1947) rejects Kierkegaard's views on the ground that he was a religious writer and therefore he puts more emphasize on moral responsibilities and decision making. It is very unfortunate that Heidegger has seen only one aspect of Kierkegaard's existentialism. It may be true that he was very much influenced by Friedrich Nietzsche (1844-1900), a German philosopher, poet and critic, who was noted for his concept of the superman and he rejected the traditional Christian values. Jaspers as one of the founders of modern existentialism brought out his work in 1938.

With regard to the evolution of humanism there appears to be many difference of opinions. Who is the real founder of humanism? The origin of the concept humanism Buhler and Allen (1972) have attributed to *Nicholas V* (1397-1455), an Italian ecclesiastic pope, who advocated humanism in place of pious orthodox and traditional attitude towards ethics and religion. But Nicholas did not evolve a systematic philosophy on humanism. He only went against the rigid orthodox church and relaxed the ethical principles. Buhler and Allen also state that Petrarch (1304-1374) was the father of humanism and was the first person to use humanism. Petrarch was an Italian Iyric poet and scholar and was greatly influenced by the values of Renaissance. His collection of poems *'Canzoniere'* were inspired by his ideal love for Laura. His work *'Secretum'* (1342) a spiritual self analysis was his philosophical work. However, Petrarch did not evolve any systematic humanistic philosophy during his period. Nicholas V came after the death of Petrarch. Nicholas did not seem to have received any inspiration from Petrarch regarding 'humanism'.

But, it was Schiller, the British philosopher who with all seriousness declared that his pragmatism was humanism and has published his work under the title of *Truth in Humanism*. To Schiller, truth is an ultimate function of our intellectual activity and objects are evaluated or judged as true. Truth is manipulated on objects and established. The object is verified experimentally and found to be true. Truth is in perfect harmony with our life. Ultimately it makes for human happiness and therefore truth is the final aspiration. Similar views are also expressed by the existentialists. Therefore, Schiller was the first to formulate a systematic humanistic philosophy and it was evolved from pragmatism. Though William James and Schiller represented one form of pragmatism in the beginning, later on James tried to elaborate the pragmatism of Peirce. Schiller in his pragmatism put more emphasis on human values and rejected all other theories as either meaningless or useless if human values are not recognized and given importance.

In the preceding sections we have discussed how the two systems of philosophy, existentialism and humanism have given importance to man. These two systems recognize man and man's potentialities. Schiller in his 'humanism' protested strongly and rejected that any system which is devoid of human values in useless. Schiller's humanism was brought in half a century after Kierkegaard's existentialism. Secondly, Kierkegaard's existentialism did not say anything directly about humanism like Schiller's work. Therefore the influence of Schiller's humanism should have been greater on humanists than any other systems. But it appears that the founders of humanistic psychologists did not receive any inspiration or influence from Schiller's Humanism which has a better historical root than Kierkegaard's existentialism. Buhler and Allen (1972) in their 'Introduction to Humanistic Psychology' should have provided still much better valuable historical evidences for the evolution of humanistic psychology.

3. WHY THERE SHOULD BE A HUMANISTIC PSYCHOLOGY?

Every discipline or science that is taught and learned in the universities and colleges has background for its origin and development and a history of its own. No discipline or science was developed over a night or a day. Man is older than any of these sciences and through his every day life events accidentally or incidentally or intentionally he gains some experience and knowledge and the same has been passed on to the man of next generation. The man of next generation may add something new from his experience to the old and also may drop out something which was found to be useless. This was how knowledge in every field was accumulated and also preserved in all available means. The ancient man used stones in which he engraved his ideas in designs and letters and also inscribed in metal plates what were all he learned and accumulated. It appears that the ancient man had the foresight that by preserving his knowledge like this they might be known by the posterity and might be useful for them. Man is such an intelligent creature that he can continue the progress of his knowledge from the place where his ancesters have left. Otherwise man at every generation must begin everything from the stone age. This much progress what we see today in the world would not have taken place and man should live for ever in the state of nature. Apart from the material development and the expression of ideas that have been taking place from time to time there was also intellectual development and expressions that man has been making about in various ways. Ideally every phase of human experience and all the institutionalized activities of men should be examined if we are really interested in further development. Because they reveal a really comprehensive view of the world and also the destiny of man. The speculative system builders of every period had the great architechonic visions and they stand out as the intellectual expressions of an entire age in the form of some philosophy. The one philosopher who made this as his central task and examined all the phases of human experience in their historical development was G.W. Friedrich Hegel (1770-1831) a German philosopher. He created fundamentally an influential systematic thought. He viewed man's mind as the highest expression of the absolute. This he expounded in his work *'The phenomenology of Mind'* in 1807. According to Hegel man's most significant characteristic is his mind or the process of thinking, his striving to acquire ideas, and acquiring always new ideas by modifying older ones. Hegel has taken clue for his philosophy from the nature of man. According to Hegel human institutions are culminating in art, religion and philosophy and these are the highest manifestations of the mind.

To Hegel history is a collection of passage of events in which it could be noticed that man passes from the state of nature to the state of law and the founding of institutions was the manifestation of the law of nature. Since human nature is always acquiring new ideas by modifying older ones, this nature is found to be continuously acting when some existing idea is not in harmony with the passage of events or in line with the changing world. Or if the existing idea is not meeting with present day requirements change is sought always in some circle. If dissatisfaction is felt about the existing phenomena there is some tension or restlessness or some sort of pondering of the mind to find out new ways and means to deal with the current or changing the situations satisfactorily. This dissatisfaction was about to develop slowly at the end of second quarter of this century among some exponents of psychologists in the United States.

Some critical thinkers in the field of psychology began to review the outcomes of the work carried out on various areas during the past fifty years in dealing with human problem individually and also socially. Sigmund Freud's (1856-1939) psychoanalysis, which was found to be a suitable method of dealing with mental abnormalities during the first quarter of this century in Europe, by attracting great many people in United States, within a short span of twenty-five years, has began to dominate all the existing systems of psychology. The psychoanalytic method of dealing with the mental patients was highly fascinating for many young scientists and suitable modifications in psychoanalysis were also made. Freud evolved this method by combining hypnotic and free association methods. Freud in collaboration with Josef Breuer (1842-1925) was able to discover the clue of free association method during the years 1893-1895. Josef Breuer was an Austrian physician and physiologist whose collaboration with Freud was considered to be very important in the early development of psychoanalysis. He originated the Cathartic method. Breuer treated a young woman who was bedridden with a number of hysterial symptoms. Her two legs and the right arm were paralysed. Her sight and hearing were damaged and had difficulty in speaking. She often went into a dream like state and mumbled to herself. Breuer hyponotized her and repeated some of the words she mumbled. By this means he was able to make her to talk more freely about her earlier emotional disasters and release her emotional tension caused by previous events. Breuer called this cathartic method or talking cure method. The report of this case and other cases in 1895 became the basis for Freud's important later contributions including psychoanalysis. Most of the present day therapies were greatly influenced by Freud's psychoanalysis. Freud's method of psychoanalysis was a lengthy procedure. It was taking several weeks, months and sometimes years and the Therapist will have to spend several hours every week. Freud developed this method in his work while dealing with neurotic patients. While dealing with neurotic patients Freud observed that the patients often spoke about their dreams and therefore Freud felt that it is also important to study the dreams of the patient to find out the cause of the neurotic problem. Therefore after analysing one thousand dreams Freud published his famous work *'The Interpretation of Dreams'* in 1900 and his general introduction to psychoanalysis in 1917. They have drawn the attention of many young psychologists all over the world and they developed curiosity and interest to know more about these two phenomena. All other systems received only secondary importance. These have become the main thrust in the field of psychology. It had many offshoots like psychiatry, psychiatric medicine, clinical psychology and so on. There were many critical attacks on the psychoanalytic theory and on its limited range of effectiveness and its expensive treatment. But with all that psychoanalysis remained an important force in American psychological and allied areas. It is supposed to be the first force in the contemporary system of psychology. But around 1950s and 1960s in the clinical circle there were some controversial issues whether psychoanalysis and related therapies work successfully and effectively. Whether the cure is temporary or durable? If permanent cure why the patient goes to the clinic with the same complaint? Further some clinicians were very much perturbed with some of the concepts of psychoanalysis themselves such as unconscious, repression, insight etc. Sometimes the therapeutic results occur without a word from therapist. Abraham Maslow (1908-1970) was practicing psychoanalysis for some time. Once Maslow (1970) met with one interesting instance during his practice. This was what he had from his own personal experience. A college girl who came to his clinic wanted some advice about her personal problems. She spoke for an hour about her problem. At the end without even a single word from him she said that she had settled the problem to her own satisfaction and thanked gratefully for his advice and went away. Maslow says that many successful therapits were not trained. Willard Fricks (1971) says that many are disillusioned with the desired effects of psychoanalysis and get into the non-directive sleep inducing procedure which represents an undated inappropriate techniques of Rogers. Even though these are not sufficient causes to throw aside an important system of psychology, some dissatisfaction and urge aroused in some circle to evolve a system of psychology to be called as the third force.

The other force that was dominating the American Psychological world has been the *behaviourism* founded by J.B. Watson (1875-1958). Watson declared his behaviourism in 1913 and brought out a book *'Behaviourism: An Introduction to Comparative Psychology'* in 1914. '*Psychology from the Stand Point of Behaviourism*' in 1919 and another book *'Behaviourism'* in 1924.

These three works on behaviourism brought out radical changes in psychological studies in United States. Watson's behaviourism was based upon biological approach. Behaviourism had in common the conviction that psychology as a science must be based upon what is overtly observable, the physical stimuli, the muscular movements and the glandular secretions, the functions which they arouse and the environmental products that follow. Watson rejected the introspection as a scientific method of study. Behaviourists preferred experimentation on animals and infants. They claimed themselves as biologists and shown interest in how organisms behave under various experimental conditions. Watson in his 1914 work announced his new position and refuted Thorndike's law of effect and substituted it with his law of frequency and recency. In the case of animal learning the successful act was both most frequent and most recent.

Watson put great importance to Kinesthetic stimuli as integrators of the maze learning habits. The emphasis in Kinesthesis as the integrator of animal learning was useful for Watson when he perplexed about human thought processes. He said that thought was primarily an implicit speech activity. It is silently talking to oneself. Sensitive instruments would detect the tongue movements or other movements accompanying thinking activity. In Watson's behaviourism the key concepts were conditioned response and stimulus-response mechanism. Watson found that Pavlov's conditioned reflex was fitting to his theory and so he adopted it. Watson laid more stress on the details of physiology and anatomy and upon the experimental methods for the behavioural study of psychology and also made use of the conditioning principles.

When Watson was seriously working on his behaviourism in United States there were two other systems of psychology functioning. One of the systems of psychology was structuralism, founded by Wilhelm Wundt (1832-1920) in Germany and it was he who established the first psychological laboratory in Leipzig in the year 1879. Wundt tried to discover the elements present in conscious experience which he thought to fall under two categories. The first being that there are sensations which come to us from outside by our contact with the environment and secondly there are feelings which form part of our internal experience. Wundt strongly recognized the conscious experience as the starting point and analysed the elementary structure of experience thus it was known as Structuralism or Structural Psychology. But his student Edward Titchener (1867-1927) preferred to call it as existentialism. Titchener carried structuralism to America and set up a psychological laboratory at Cornell university and started systematic research on sensations. He used consciousness and also used introspection as a rigorous experimental method and provided strict training to introspectionists. John Dewey and James Angell have severely criticised structuralism. How could the study of the elements of sensations constitute the dynamic function of the mind. Since the American psychology reflected the same views, structuralism was rejected on the ground that Titchener was importing it from German laboratories. The American psychologists have revolted against a psychology of German origin. Therefore Titchener made several changes in the original structuralism and named it as 'functionalism'. John Dewey and others were already advocating a system similar to functionalism. Therefore, though Titchener was the founder of functionalism several prominent psychologists have contributed to it and it became an important school of psychology in the university of Columbia about 1900 and 1920.

The adherents of functionalism felt that the approach made by functionalism was incomplete to a problem of dynamic in nature. At the same time William James (1842-1910) wrote that consciousness is not a by-product of somatic casuality. Functionalism was holding the view that psychology was the science of consciousness. Animal laboratories were set up under the influence of functionalism. Watson himself was a functionalist in the beginning. But he revolted against the subjectively determining sensation, learning and other processes. He wanted to study everything objectively. Watson's behaviourism rejected the functionalists concepts like consciousness, introspection and the existence of the mind. He recognized only two kinds of behaviours called explicit and implicit. Many became the followers of Watson's behaviourism and behaviourism found the prominent place among the schools of psychology in the United States. But some of the Watson's followers later on gave different interpretations and there were several varied schools within behaviourism. Watson strongly rejected introspection, but Lashley one of the behaviourist believed that introspection has an important place in the study of psychology. There were also early behaviourists and later behaviourists. Guthrie

(1886-1959), Tolman (1886-1939), Hull (1882-1952) and Skinner (1904) were all behaviourists, but some of them were not followers of Watson though they were influenced by his behaviourism. Each one founded a behaviourism of his own.

Thus the two systems of psychology which dominated the American Psychological world were psychoanalysis and behaviourism. Psychoanalysis was mainly concentrating on clinical side and behaviourism on the experimental side. Information on psychology were received from the clinical laboratories and from animal experimental laboratories. The first one was mainly interested in the problems of the individuals who were mentally abnormal and the latter one was mainly interested in the study of animal behaviour and the results of same were attributed to human behaviour. These two trends were widely prevalent in the United States.

4. GROWING DISSATISFACTION AND FOUNDING NEW SCHOOL OF THOUGHT

Therefore there were widespread strong expressions of dissatisfaction about the outcomings of the studies of psychoanalysis and behaviourism around 1950s and continued in 1960s vigorously. Maslow (1935) himself has published papers on animal behaviour in his early days and later on human social behaviour. He became clinical psychologist and published papers and books till 1950s. The dissatisfaction against the existing forces was substantiated by Maslow by publishing his book motivation and personality in 1954. Maslow had the intention of establishing another rival school of psychology a third force as early as 1954 and to enlarge the conception of human personality by putting it into a higher level of human nature. He used the concept, self actualization to describe his higher level of human nature. Then in 1962 a group of American psychologists joined under the leadership of Abraham Maslow and founded a new association to represent a third force in psychology. This third force was the 'humanistic psychology' which was the stream of new psychological thought and an image of man that were different from those of both psychoanalysis and behaviourism.

The two dominant forces in the United States were the psycho-analytical and behaviouristic schools and against which contrasting opinions were expressed severely. The first one mainly concentrated on clinical side and became highly professional. The academic interests were slowly dying and even persons without serious professional training started to practice as professional. Persons with abnormal symptoms, different kinds of neuroses, various types of schizophrenias, parania, emotionally maladjusted, persons with severe conflicts, frustrations, sexual deviations, effective disorders, suicide, sociopathic disorders, delinquency, crime, alcoholism, drug addictions, psychosomatic disorders, organic brain syndromes, mental retardation, behaviour disorders of children and various other problems were the subject matter for them. It appears that the problems of this sort were multiplied and there are innumerable number of problems they are dealing with. Analysing the seriousness of these problems objectively without any discourteous view one will have to accept that these are all referring only abnormalities and nothing normal and therefore a separate field or school of study was sought. Psychoanalysis is not a school which emerged all of a sudden in America. What we see today is the culmination of hundred years work of hundreds of persons and it has grown into a science and an art and no area or school of study is having so much sources of information as the psychoanalysis is having.

But with all these, psychoanalysis is criticized, the defects are exaggerated, the services rendered by it have been derecognized, superficiality has been attributed to the professionals who practiced in clinical areas. The crux of the criticism is that psychoanalysis concentrates on a single individual for a long time and the normal person is attributed with schizophrenic and paranoid characteristics and the study of normal and healthy person is discarded. One of the reasons stated by the humanistic psychologists is that man rarely lives as a full human being and in harmony with his potentials. Man's own personal self is discarded and he is in a state of inability to relate his spirit and love with others mutually. Inter-personal relations are more loaded with hatred and unfriendliness. Alienation and dissatisfaction are becoming a way of life in personal and inter-personal relationships. Even when we are alone we have a feeling that we are living in the midst of strangers and enemies. Human touch in all our walks of life is becoming more and more extraneous. Man is becoming more and more slave to time and money. Corruption and dishonest way of life are justified. Loyalty and dutifulness are considered as the virtues of the slaves.

Social institutions appear to be in a state of transition, ethical and moral belief systems upon which they were built, now found to be no longer conceptionalized in that line. The individual's creative skills which form the basis of the individual's inherent wealth, personal recognition and sense of judgment have no chance for development and they have been suppressed and handled in an unsystematic way. Men are becoming slowly insensitive to the worldly affairs and are becoming as one of the components of the unchaste act of demoting of the ethical principles of the social institutions. Frick (1971) states that what we are experiencing today is the crisis of personal experience. According to him we are in a revolutionary period of history which puts emphasis on certain things and does not permit man to understand the validity of his inherent potentialities and his creative skills. Further, the individual is not able to understand the outer experience and also to know the reality and the meaning of the experience. Thus there is some sort of upset over the reality and the meaning of the experience. This state of affair need not be attributed to the emergence of any systems of psychology and to the manner in which they are functioning. But the culture and social institutions are putting certain limit over experience which Frick calls it as the intimidation of experience. According to him this intimidation of experience is going on at all levels of human interactions such as parent-child, husband-wife, teacher-student, master-follower and patient-therapist.

But what needed is the sharing of ones experience with that of another so that both may understand each other and develop a mutual respect and may bring out enlarged and enriched sense of awareness and reality. Children who are powerless must be told what they should experience. The relationships of most parent-child are based upon this intimidation until children become unfriendly from their own experience and rebel against the most intimate contacts with the parènts. Parents should allow themselves for change for reciprocal socialization. Possibly the most rigid form of intimidation of experience may be found in the field of education. from Kindergarten school to college level intimidation of experience is in existence as the essential aspect of educational system. Since the educational establishment should go smoothly it is encouraged. The examination system, the grade system, the conventional method of teaching all serve as the instrument of the expression of intimidation. The rigid-personal relationship which is built upon the expression of intimidation needs redefinition. The imposition of one person's experience upon another such as parent-child, child-adult, male-female, husband-wife, teacher-student, doctor-patient, patient-therapist, young-old, senior-junior, master-follower, white-collared all need to be free from rigid expression of intimidation. But this does not mean that one should reject and deny the human social structure and the authenticity of knowledge and wisdom. One should accept whatever is needed for expanding the awareness of the self.

Behaviourism in the United States under Watson has perspired very much to qualify itself to be called as a science and it became the foundation of modern psychology. Since behaviourism used mostly animals as its experimental subjects some critics began to look at it with a wall-eye and sour expression. This tendency slowly increased and was stated that it has only limited vision of man. Watson has explained every psychological concept through behaviouristic conceptions. Man is a complex machine, built upon graded stimulus response mechanism, resulting in predictable habit patterns. Behaviourists used *reinforcement* as the key concept for personality development. According to behaviourists man is not having anything inherently relating to revelation completely different from social influences. This is another point in which the critics raise a pertinent question, 'are we to accept such a philosophy which advocates that human personality has no determining influence within a society on man's perception of himself'. Whatever realities attributed to man, they were only from animal laboratories. The importance of man in laboratories as a subject matter was to a minimum level. On the whole man was not the centre of study.

In the competitive world man's role, his ambitions, aspirations, motives, values and his creative skills were not given direct expression in behaviourist studies.

In these, complex human problems described above, the schools of psychology that were dominant did not take any cognizance of it. They remained as passive observers. The interpersonal relationships, the expressions of intimidation, social and racial conflicts, the rigidity that prevailed on various walks of life, the unethical organizational structures, the suppression of creative skills of individuals under the pretext of institutional morale and various human dilemmas, all did not draw the attention of these schools.

They were showing interest in the concept of science. Psychologists have shown interest in measurable and quantifiable behavioural patterns and they were expressed in sophisticated statistical method which they considered important subject matter and worthy to be called as science. By showing more interest on scientific methodology of the subject matter modern psychology neglected important matters by paying more attention on trivial scientific matters. The data were given more sophisticated treatment. But they were all irrelevant to the problems prevailing in the actual life situations. The subject matters of research were highly professional and scholarly. But they were all insensitive to the human person, who is the subject matter. The long and continuous battle the psychologists fought brought respect and recognition to psychology and also gained the professional status. Some of the psychologists were highly science conscious and always defending for the status as scientists.

These psychologists were concerned mainly with research problems that were highly valued, easily controlled and solid. But with regard to man's experience they were out of context. Frick says that when we go closer and closer to man's experience, particularly his inner. experience and his creative imagination we seem to enter altogether into a different world, an unexplored world with different meanings, values and unusual perceptions. The individual person seems to represent a wider and deeper level of human personality.with most critical issues of life. Varied types of life's polarities are visible. For example, joys and sorrows, pain and pleasure, life and death, solution and confusion, revolution and conflict, stability and uncertainty, dominance and submission all seem to create a sense of tension and restlessness in the relationships. These areas of life problems were not taken into consideration by the behaviouristic psychologists and they prefer to deal with more simple and easily definable problems. All the approaches to study personality made by psychology and the experimental methods seem to be academic and far away from these personal and social changes and human problems.

The complete nature of man, his potentialities and resources, the current psychological theories yet to fully explore. What the information available to us in some psychological methods are not full revelations of human nature. With limited theoretical resources we see man and determine his potentialities and nature without going deep into his inner aspects of experience and personality. The existing theories, methods and approaches seem to be inadequate to see man's full nature and therefore it was felt by some psychologists that a revolutionary approach, completely different from the existing theories and methods should be made which they hope may throw such better light upon human nature and personality.

This type of revolutionary thinking by a group of psychologists has resulted in the emergence of a 'Third force' which they called, 'Humanistic Psychology'. Humanistic Psychology, Frick states, is the result of passionate expression of protest against the two major schools of psychology, the psychoanalysis and the behaviourism. It is believed that these two schools have limited scopes and therefore they have limited the images of man. Though they made important contributions, the studies they made on man have not exposed man's full nature and they remain incomplete.

Humanistic Psychology begins to explain its philosophical conception and positions about the nature of man and the nature and scope of scientific outlook to comprehend and acquire a more vivid and deeper understanding of man. The acquired subject matter in this way symbolizes a psychology with certain characteristics that are planned as to the nature of man. Thus humanistic psychology deals with the human person as a whole with broader and deeper perspective by combining science and philosophy. Man and his experience occupy the central position in humanistic psychology and it tries to formulate a theory of its own which can fully reveal man rather than accepting the model of man of some other theory. In dealing with significant human problems and man's full range of inner experience, humanistic psychology takes full liberty and enjoys unlimited freedom for expounding a third force in psychology, encompassing a philosophical view 'what is human life about' and 'what human life can be', if life is lived positively.

5. WHAT IS HUMANISTIC PSYCHOLOGY?

While discussing the various aspects related to humanistic psychology in the preceding section we have also mentioned some of the aims and scope of humanistic psychology. That is by way of providing additional information to the main theme of the section. Now, let us directly deal with humanistic psychology with all its definitions, concepts and methods. Humanistic psychology is in its infant stage now. Therefore it will not be fair on our part to expect too much from an infant science. The information available on this are very little and research studies yet to come up. Maslow, the founder of this school had many ambitions in his mind and before he put into action all those things he passed away in 1970, leaving the responsibilities to his colleagues and posterity. But in the case of the other two forces, the psychoanalysis and the behaviourism the founders had fully exposed their theoretical and experimental aspects of their schools and produced a great mass of followers and died. Therefore the responsibility of developing this school is left to Maslow's colleagues and his followers.

Humanistic Psychology may be defined as the science that studies human nature, man as a human person, his potentialities, experiences, decisions and acts in relation to his life lived positively and the personal philosophy of life. By defining humanistic psychology in this way we are including all the aspects of man into this and also the subject matter of study. There may be also other possible definitions. Charlotte Buhler and Melanie Allen (1972) state that humanistic psychology is to explore the behavioural characteristics and emotional dynamics of full and healthy human living. They have put it briefly. It is striving to study and understand the *person as a whole*. Buhler and Allen (1972) state that this was never done by either the structuralists nor the American behaviourists. The gestalts were only interested in the total activity behaviour. It was a total action perception which let to a subject speculation and not the total knowledge of the organism.

Kurt Goldstein (1939) has developed a new dynamic principle. This trend was in the direction of humanistic psychological thinking. According to him, the healthy individual's need is increasing for self-actualization which is the basic motive and the goal of life. This view is quite similar to Maslow's motivation theory and therefore Maslow has accepted it.

6. MAN AS A SINGLE WHOLE: METHODS

Humanistic Psychology tries to study man as a whole person or organism. The human person is the subject matter of study. Humanistic psychology put more faith in a healthy person for its study. The idea prevalent at this period was that every man is having some symptoms of schizophrenic or paranoid characteristics and no man is cent per cent free from these characteristics. According to this view we are studying persons only those who have problems of some kind. Humanistic psychology rejects this view. Then, who is healthy person? Who is the total person? How to find out him? Buhler and Allen have stated that attempts have been made to make out a total person from the experimental data and from the observations of some particular functions and behaviours and this was going on till recently. It was also viewed that since man is a social animal he was studied as a member of some group and to study man as a single organism is not the proper scientific study. In Germany, attempt was made by the educational psychologist, Edward Spranger, to bring out a method of understanding a man as a whole individual.

1. Wilhelm Dilthey (1961) and others formulated a method called *idiographic* which means study of individuals instead of finding out a

general principle for the study of groups by the method of nomothetic. According to Dilthey, understanding means the rediscovery of the self in the other person.

2. A method of study applicable to man and machine were discussed by Michael Polanyi (1958). He scientifically justified in his research, objectivity, which he called, personal knowledge or participating experience or personal participation which need not be mistaken for subjective experience. This is one way of 'comprehension' which has universal validity. Therefore in studying a person's problem successfully the objective data may be combined with Polanyi's personal knowledge. Maslow (1966) also asserts that *personal experience* has no substitute.

3. One of the exponents of humanistic psychology, Melanie Allen (1970) devised a method of study called *'the single or representative—case study'*. The method was demonstrated by her to the clinicians and to the humanistic psychologists with regard to its validity. But this was not accepted by the American Psychologists. Shontz (1965) and Duke (1965) have criticized this method and stated that such idiographic research method is having very small scope and it will not fit into the research world where individual is treated as a universe of responses. But however the method received appreciations from the critics. The method is stated in a statistical formula: $N = 1$ case study. The single case study $N = 1$ case is justified in several situations as the most suitable method.

4. Another method, *open-systems* theory has been formulated for the study of the person as a whole by Allen (1970). This system is based upon Bertalanffy's (1966) general systems theory. According to him the human organism is an open system. Allport (1897-1967) states that a system is any complex of elements in mutual interaction. According to Allport (1960) a closed system is one that does not admit any matter from outside and it has no transactions with its environment. The human organism itself is a system which may interact with various other systems. The open system supplies matter to the outer world and receives matter from outside. Thus there is a continuous exchange of matter. This, Bertalanffy calls the *steady-state*. Subsequently Bertalanffy (1966) revised his early theory and redefined the concept, steady-state as 'a distance from true equilibrium'. According to materialistic or biologistic proposition all organic matters have a tendency of energy system run down or disorganization. Bertalanffy states that this universal law is not applicable to human organism. Humanistic

psychologists say that man is striving always to go higher and higher in his life order and he even accepts certain temporary failures.

5. *The human life as a whole* taken together is considered as one of the methods conceived by the humanistic psychologists. The details involved in this method appear to be quite similar to biographical or case history method used in psychoanalysis. But there is difference between these two schools. In psychoanalysis or in psychiatric treatment the person's life events are with special reference to his life events of frustration or conflict or emotional maladjustment, the events that created unpleasant feelings are taken into consideration and sometimes even his dreams. But in humanistic psychology the method includes the person's whole life history, an account of his inner interests and attitudes and his responses to the events of his own life are all taken together to study the person. Buhler (1933) has brought out her biographical studies in which in addition to the sequence of life events of a person she related also the biological factors as the determinants of the events, experience and products. She also emphasised the interaction of the environment and the role of the individual in her studies.

In the preceding pages it has been discussed that humanistic psychology finds its basic philosophy in the two contemporary systems of philosophy, the existentialism and the humanism which was derived from pragmatism. Maslow had very much positive idea about man, his nature and his potentials. He is of the view that the individual human person is basically whole, sound, healthy and sole with innate drive for growth and self-actualization. According to him the human being by nature is active, resourceful, purposive and good. All human sufferings come to him when these basic resources are denied. Man or the human organism is not a collection of separate organs and functions. When the behaviour or an act of a person is studied we must know that it is an expression of the whole organism or person and not a separate existence. Maslow seems to have been influenced by the holistic theory of Gen. Smuts (1870-1950). According to Smuts (1926) every facet of life is an integral part of a synthetic object in the universe and it is moving towards an evolutionary development of a greater unity and to create a larger and integrated whole. Smuts also applied his holistic theory to personality. For Smuts the highest form of holistic integration is found in the development of personality. Personality, for Smuts, is the highest embodiment of holism in its individual and universal tendencies.

7. THEMES AND PROBLEMS GENERATED FOR A POSITIVE APPROACH TO HUMANISTIC PSYCHOLOGY

Humanistic Psychology was founded in 1962 by Abraham Maslow with a group of American Psychologists who were in need of a new thrust to combat with the growing social and cultural problems. Though it has met with severe criticism that it is vague and unscientific, humanistic psychology attracted many members from divergent discipline since its interests were encompassing the nature of man. Humanistic psychology has no specific and independent theoretical stand and it represents a general philosophical position with regard to nature of man. The interpretation of certain concepts from humanistic psychology may vary, but the concepts seem to be the same that we see in psychoanalysis and behaviourism and in other areas. Humanistic psychology yet to formulate and develop its own concepts and methods for its growth and development into a systematic and fully independent field of psychology. Though it has its historical root in the philosophies of John Dewey and William James now it has passed more than thirty years and humanistic psychology is still in the infant stage. After Maslow, the founder, there seems to be some stagnation in the thought process and development of humanistic psychology. However, we can discuss a few major themes on which the present humanistic psychology is being built. The themes to be discussed are (1) organization of personality, (2) Motivation, and (3) Self actualization. These are the major psychological processes on which the holistic principles were discussed by the exponents of humanistic psychology.

1. The Organisation of Personality

According to humanistic psychology, personality is an organized, dynamic and open system. Each dimension of personality, each facet or each identifiable part has a functional role in the development of the total organism. Each part or sub-system should be viewed basically in its relationship to a larger and more unified organization. This point of view we may call the holistic-dynamic point of view. Maslow (1970) states that the general point of issue set forth here to discuss personality is the holistic rather than atomistic. Therefore, Maslow has based his personality development on the holistic principles. The basic approach of holistic theory to personality study is to disclose the intrinsic features, inner dynamics which contribute to man's total functioning. That is the actualization of man's noble and creative potentiality.

The behaviour of an individual is always directed towards an integrated organized whole. There may be some isolated behaviour patterns which can be found at the outer end of the life. They are isolated as they are not important. They do not have anything to do with the main issues and goals of the organism. Science becomes closed circle and protective. Maslow wishes for a problem oriented science, involving open and creative process facilitating discovery. He is not for reductive analysis, but is more for a holistic and dynamic view. For Maslow the holistic-dynamic view is contrast to the general atomistic approach.

Maslow's holistic-dynamic view puts more emphasis on a syndrome concept of personality. According to him personality is a structured and organized complex appears to be having varied characteristic behaviour, thoughts, impulses for action and perception which are having a common quality of oneness, if each one studied carefully. Each characteristic (Maslow calls it a syndrome) is related behaviourally to the whole, an integrated personality. Each characteristic or trait is an expression of the whole. How can we study the whole organism? Maslow (1970) states that it depends upon the nature of the organization of the data to be analysed. According to him to know the nature of an organization of the data into personality the syndrome concept should be analysed. Maslow uses the concept, syndrome, which is borrowed from medicine, to indicate a complex of symptoms which were found together. Therefore, it refers to a group of symptoms and syndrome is a unifying name which he uses throughout his works.

The concept, syndrome is generally used to indicate disease and abnormal symptoms. But Maslow used it to indicate healthy and normal symptoms. For Maslow in a syndrome a group of feelings and behaviours with different names are included. The feelings and behaviours may be interdependent, one may extent over the other, if synonymous. Therefore these may be studied as parts specifically or study them together as a whole. For example, a house may have certain defects or inconveniences of having a small drawing room, small bath room, flimsy gratings for the windows, but large bed rooms, well furnished and pleasant painting. The house as a whole is good. Therefore the concept syndrome here is referred to the parts of the house. All the parts put together and organized into a whole—the house. In the case of human being syndrome refers to some disease symptoms.

In psychopathology syndrome may be used to indicate wheezing, coughing, sweating, hard breathing etc., all these mean asthma. Therefore a syndrome may be defined as a combination of diversities organized into a whole and all of which have the same psychological of meaning. Each symptom can be also individually stated as the symptom of asthma and all the symptoms together may be called a syndrome.

A syndrome may have several parts or symptoms and these parts are interchangeable in the dynamic process and one can substitute the other. But the change of a syndrome is only temporary. The syndromes have different levels as high, middle and low. This is the important variable of a syndrome. For example, a person may have high self-esteem but low in security. Syndrome levels may vary from high to low or from much to little.

Syndromes may also vary in quality. Maslow states that self-esteem or dominant may vary in quality of expression. For example, the syndrome of self-esteem in human beings can be differentiated in two qualities, on one side self-esteem may be indicated by strength and on the other side indicated by power. One person with high self-esteem may also show high level of security, self-confidence, cooperative and friendliness. Another person with high self esteem may be insecure, and uncooperative and unfriendly and not interested in helping the poor. Both the persons have high self esteem, but they are revealing it differently and vary in other syndromes. This depends upon the individual's characteristics.

With regard to the organization of the syndromes into personality there is some order of importance in grouping. Parts of undifferentiated syndrome may correlate closely with the whole. Any part of a syndrome may also correlate closely with the whole. There may be positive correlation between the level of one syndrome and another. There may be also relationship between the syndromes and overt behaviour of an individual. Each overt act is an expression of the whole integrated personality. Each act seems to be determined by each syndrome and all the personality syndromes.

According to Maslow (1970) behaviour is not always an index of character, as behaviour is determined by external situation and culture, character also is determined. When three forces (external situation, culture and character) act upon behaviour, the result is something midway of these three forces. Therefore we cannot say which one is perfect indicator of behaviour. But in certain situation by controlling the influence of culture and situation, behaviour may be good indicator of character. Because there is much higher correlation between impulsive behaviour and character. These impulses are parts of the syndrome. These impulses are free from external and cultural forces and controlled by overt acts. Maslow states that the behaviour we study is only the impulses to behaviour.

2. Motivation

Man is constantly put in the state of wanting something in some manner and when one is satisfied another need or want is in the foreground. After this a third need arises. Therefore, there is a necessity for studying the relationship of all motivational states with man. There is no one or two motives. There are multiplicity of human motives. When one motive is fulfilled there is a tendency for a new higher motive or need. Maslow (1962) rejects the concept of multiplicity of human motives as it is not sound from holistic point of view. The atomistic view of motives isolate one from the other and neglects the dynamic function of human behaviour. Therefore Maslow rejects the very definition of motivation based upon homeostasis or equilibrium or derive reduction and so on. Maslow postulates a theory of motivation from holistic principle which is called positive growth tendency. It may be also stated as growth motivation and deficiency motivation. According to him growth is seen not only in the gratification of basic needs like food and water, but above these basic needs it includes talents, capacity and creative tendencies and potentialities.

Human motivation, according to Maslow, is a function of hierarchical needs. These basic needs are in the order of strength. They are (1) the physiological needs, (2) the safety needs, (3) belongingness and love needs, (4) the esteem needs, (5) the need for self-actualization. When the basic physiological needs are satisfied the organism turns his attention to the safety needs. On fulfilling the safety needs he turns to the belongingness and love needs. Then he turns to esteem needs and finally to self-actualization. The gratification of each need is in the order of importance.

When this hierarchy of motives is in increasing degree than it represents the positive growth tendency. The organism gains strength for increasing degree of psychological health. It is for the fulfilment of the humanness and there is a change in the motivation. The organism progresses towards the ultimate value, self actualization or to become fully human.

The needs below the self-actualization are called deficiency motives. The organism meets with problems when the deficiency needs or motives are not gratified. The organism confronts conflict, frustration, anxiety and guilt at this stage. At the level of self-actualization the organism is free from the deficiency needs and struggle, so that he can satisfy the higher needs.

3. Self Actualization

The concept and the theme that is very widely discussed in humanistic psychology is the self-actualization. This is supposed to be the key theme in humanistic psychology and every one discusses it in the way in which he has perceived and comprehended. Though the concept was originated by Kurt Goldstein (1939) Maslow and Carl Rogers had made use of it in their studies to a greater extent and gave a new meaning to it. Christopher Monte (1977) states that the most pressing question that has truly humanized psychology is, 'What is man's true nature?' Erich Fromm (1968), tried to answer this question several times in his attempts to describe how society has forced the twisted shape of human character into the existence. Fromm (1947) rejected Freud's view that man's unalterable nature is his instinctual quality for sexuality and aggression and suggested that the most basic trait of human nature is a tendency toward self-actualization. According to Fromm, man's nature is not restricted by his biological instincts and self-actualization is a tendency to exercise his unique powers of reasoning and self- awareness completely. This is a force controlling man's existence and it is his need which can make him fully of himself. Fromm (1968) states that man has to fight not only against the danger of death and starvation but also against the danger of becoming insane and losing his mind.

Self-actualization in a single sense refers to man's desire for self fulfilment. Maslow (1970) states that it is a tendency of a man to become actualize which he is potentially capable of. It is also a desire to become more of abnormally reacting to everything what one is capable of. Maslow also states that self-actualization may be freely stated as the full use of talents, capacities and potentialities and exploiting them. People of this type fulfil themselves and would be doing the best that they are capable of doing. These are the people developing to the full level of their attainment. For Maslow, what a man is capable of he must be the same. This means that he must be true to his own nature. A man must strive hard to express his own nature in his achievements. He puts his personal self in all his actions and fulfils his desire. This is what Maslow calls, self-actualization. This will vary greatly from person to person. A person may desire to become a creative artist or a painter, another desire to become a scientist, or film actor or a politician or a sportsman. In all these great individual differences are there. But the arousal of these needs may take place only when he has fulfilled all other lower level of desires of the physiological, safety, belongingness and love, and esteem needs. Maslow used the concept self-actualization as one of the motives and also as constituent of personality.

Maslow's (1936) early training in psychology was in experimental psychology and secondly he turned to clinical field and conducted investigation on personality traits. In his later studies he combined what he experienced in animal kingdom and also in the clinical field—the dominance—feeling, confidence, self confidence, highly masculine, security-insecurity and so on. Therefore from his observations, interviews, test results, Maslow (1970) developed a schematic description of the self-actualizing personality. The self actualizing pattern consists of eighteen patterns, of which fifteen are positive and three are negative. They are (1) reality, which refers to an unusual ability to detect spurious and dishonest personality, (2) acceptance of self and others, which means accepting ones own nature, (3) spontaneity and simplicity, which refers to one's marked simplicity and naturalness, (4) problems centred, which refers to the task one must do of non-personal or unselfish, good of mankind in general, (5) quality of detachment, which refers to solititude and privacy, (6) autonomy, refers to independent of the culture, physical and social environments, (7) freshness of appreciation, refers to the ability to enjoy the basic good things in life, (8) peak (mystical) experience, refers to a sort of experience similar to mystical, characterised by feelings of limitless scope for the vision, having more powerful and more helpless feelings simultaneously, feeling of ecstasy, awe and wonder, loss of place and time, strong belief that something extremely valuable had happened, (9) Gemeirschaftsgefuhl, which refers to strong interest in others, genuine desire to help the human race, (10) interpersonal relations refers to strong interest in others welfare, strong and intimate friendship with few members, (11) democratic, which refers to friendly with anyone of suitable character irrespective of racial and social origins, (12) discrimination between means and ends, refers to the ability to differentiate between right and wrong, differentiate moral person from average, (13) unhostile sense of humour, which means one who does not enjoy jokes at the expense of others, (14) creativeness, refers to the ability to invent something new, a drive and a capacity having no relationship with rest of the personality, with which individuals seem to be born, (15) resistance to enculturation, means maintaining autonomous value of their culture, (16) imperfection of self actualizing people, which means that there are no perfect people, persons may appear good, but may be irritating, selfish and angry, (17) values and self actualization, refers to the extent of acceptance of the values by a person, (18) the resolution of dichotomies in self actualization, refers to the disappearance of (selfishness and unselfishness) dichotomies or polarities in healthy people. According to Maslow these are the characteristics of self actualizing persons.

Maslow (1971) states that an individual on reaching the stage of self-actualization enters a path called growth motivation. He is no longer engaged on the path of becoming self-actualized. He has already successfully gone through the process of achieving the hierarchy of basic needs. He is now entering on the growth processes of living to enhance his being, to expand his knowledge of the self and others. Therefore he develops Being-needs or B-Values. Apart from the needs said about, Maslow formulated further set of Being-needs that is emerging at the end point of self-actualization in the basic hierarchy. Maslow (1965) has assigned them as 'meta-motivation'. Self actualized people are not now motivated by the basic needs, they are meta-motivated by meta-needs or B-values. The individuals at this stage is in the peak-experiences in the most highly developed regions of self-actualization. All the values are inherently accompanying the emergence of meta-motivation and they are intrinsic in the structure of human nature. All the values are loaded in the intrinsic nature of man. In this context Maslow has revised his definition of self-actualizing personality. For him, the self-actualizing person is not only free from illness, sufficiently satisfied his basic needs and positively using his potentialities, but also he is motivated by some values for which he makes great efforts for the groups to which he is loyal.

Maslow's (1962) 'psychology of being' is a transpersonal psychology. From him, the values of self-actualizing persons are considered to be the expressions of higher and widespread needs. In the self-actualized person there is an intrinsic urge for self-actualization and on achieving this he is pressed towards good values like seranity, kindness, honesty, love, unselfishness and goodness. Beyond self-actualization man is meta-motivated by the meta-needs, the B-values (1963). Maslow (1962) lists the characteristics of B-values, as (1) truth, (2) goodness, (3) beauty, (4) wholeness, (4a) dichotomy transcendence, (5) aliveness, process, (6) uniqueness, (7) perfection, (7a) necessity, (8) completion, (9) justice, (9a) order, (10) Simplicity, (11) richness, (12) effortlessness, (13) playfulness, (14) self-sufficiency, (15) meaningfulness. According to Maslow (1964, 1967) the task of self-actualization and the meta-motivations are not culturally desired things. They are the organized parts of intrinsic human values and the moral and spiritual values are the components of spiritual life. The actualization of these values are needed to avoid illness and to achieve full humanness.

Carl Rogers (1902) the second theorist of humanistic psychology began his study of human nature on troubled personalities. Rogers (1942) desired in the therapeutic relationship a change in the personality of his patients and for which he explored the human potentialities. Rogers observed that when persons are prevented from getting what they are really it results in psychological disability. This was what Maslow also observed. According to Rogers (1963) any organism is active and progressively striving towards maintaining, enhancing and reproducing itself and this is the fundamental importance of life and this is the most important characteristic of human motivations. Rogers calls this as actualizing tendency—the central source of energy and the basic component of the actualizing tendency is expressed by the organism. It is the need to set up a wholeness of personality and to maintain a self consistency by keeping the self concept going well with experience. Roger is of the view that the most organic and basic strivings and needs of man are positive and constructive in nature and they are the natural expressions of the actualizing tendency.

Rogers (1959, 1963) while working at a healthy personality theory, introduced a second motivational tendency called the tendency toward self-actualization. The tendency of self-actualization is an additional expression of the organism manifesting itself in the development of the self-structure by actualizing those aspects of experience which represent as a part of the self. A hormonious relationship between these two basic tendencies (actualizing tendency and tendency toward self-actualization) leads to the function of a healthy and integrated personality. Rogers put more emphasis on *congruence*, which is a condition of personality when self-experiences are correctly represented and included in the self-concepts. Rogers (1959) viewed congruence and healthy personality synonymously. Therefore the development of a healthy personality is depending upon the development of the relative state of congruence.

The third important theorist of humanistic psychology is Gardner Murphy (1895) whose work on personality is a synthesis of all relevant personality theories and it is an integration of the biological and social determinants of personality. For Murphy (1947) traits are not individual parts, but aspects of a totality. But each trait has name and character. Murphy states that the achievement of a creative unity and wholeness is not made easily. Personality is passing through three important phases of hierarchy of organization and development. They are (1) an early and undifferentiated worldwide mass, (2) a period indicated by the appearance of the differentiation and emergence of parts and (3) development of an organization of the differential parts.

The *first phase* includes motor, sensory and effective dispositions, metabolism, various thresholds of response, and all the dispositions that characterizes the organism. The global qualities and the pervasive dispositions are expressed in every new response. In the *second phase* the differentiated parts reflect the aspects of its global heritage. In the *third phase* there is an emergence of congruence, an integration of the discrete aspects of personality and goal directed behaviour. Traits appearing in the second phase when integrated with others in the third phase, have membership character and they are not understood outside of this full personality contests. The wholeness is taking place when the second and third level traits become interdependent. Murphy's holistic personality interpretation goes beyond the internal organization and the processes of the organism and there is possibility of more supreme integration as man develops new relationships with his environment.

4. Humanistic Psychology and Therapy

A group of psychologists, in United States in 1960s who have felt that they have lost something great in human experience have closely united themselves with the younger generation of the nation have desperately attempted to regain what has been lost. They have decided to serve as friends, advisers, innovators and wanted to move into the community to turn such institution as the mental health clinics, the university, the public school and the prison in order that the old dated structures could be re-evaluated and replaced with better ones. They were calling themselves as humanistic psychologists. Sidney Jourard (1964) states that humanistic psychology recognizes and reacts to and with the spirit of states that a different image of man is being tried by humanistic psychologists and humanistic psychology is a goal and not a doctrine. According to him (1963) healthy personality is growing personality and not adjustment. Healthy personality is a way for a person to function in his world. Personal counsellors and psychotherapists help individuals who have reached a state of impasse.

James Bugental (1971) speaks of humanistic ethics. According to him every man is a responsible agent of his own life. This ethics insists that the man is not removed from being the one who can settle the influences of social or external pressures and also in determining how they are influencing his own life. The humanistic model of therapy holds the view that therapists should help people to go into their inner selves and true feelings and make them to express them. Carl Rogers (1942, 1951) has developed a humanistic therapy and he called it a client-centred approach. According to humanistic therapy the person is not called patient, but a client and he/she is more responsible for the success of the treatment. The therapists do not impose any goals on the clients. They only create conditions that could enable the clients to find out their basic natures and themselves make the judgments about what they need and how they can maintain themselves. According to the ethics of humanistic psychology the decisions arrived by the clients assumed to be good. The judgment of others may cause undue sensitivity to the client and also the denial of the individual's own nature may lead the client to pathological condition. People generally do not remain open to their experiences and they follow a negative attitude towards themselves. Therefore the client-centred-therapists use a procedure called *unconditional positive regard* as the basic tool in the therapeutic process. This is accepting the client's feelings and action completely without any hesitation. But the therapists should make skilful enquiry to make the client to uncover and express his deepest conflicts and frustration. By this process the client slowly learns to speak about himself more honestly and emotionally and gets entry into his basic healthy inner nature. Humanistic psychologists get into the feelings of the client. They do not thrust their techniques. Various psychotherapists applying humanistic ethics have developed various methods on this person-to-person relationship.

5. Humanistic Psychology and Education

Humanism emerged as a protest against the existing traditional approaches to psychology and education that man is conceived as machine, and an organism comparable to rats, cats, and monkeys. Man has viewed by the traditional psychologists as an analogue of everything but not what he is! a human person. To this effect an appeal also is made for adopting new attitudes, concepts and approaches in psychology and education. But humanistic authors like Irvin Child (1973) stated that since humanistic psychology emerged from a long tradition of psychology which centred only humanity and the same traditional term 'humanity' can be extended to humanistic psychology. Therefore the tradition of centering psychology on humanity is not incompatible with humanistic psychology.

Rogers (1951) described the theory in terms of three inclusive concepts, such as client-centred-therapy, phenomenology and humanism. Accordingly, a counsellor's role is no longer giving advice or solving problems of the clients. Secondly, the world is what the client perceives rather than as it appears to others. Thirdly, the development of human potential should be highly valued and the material goals attained to be not emphasised. All humans should strive toward self-actualization which is the expression of humanistic concerns. Rogers client-centred-therapy is compatible with the humanistic self-determination. This theory of Rogers has become part of humanistic psychology.

The emergence of humanistic movement in psychology has brought out considerable and corresponding changes in the field of education. As the humanistic psychotherapist, the humanistic educationalists were not interested in formulating techniques and advancing theories. They were only interested in the goal. All those discussed in relation to therapy are also in relation to education. George Leonard (1962) in his famous challenging work, 'Education and Ecstasy' states that these questions are from the issues of humanistic enquiries. The impact of humanistic movement in education resulted in evolving a variety of approaches to education, of which many of them were functioning under the pretence of free schools, open class rooms, and community-centred-education. The reason for the new methods of education is that they are based on the welfare of children and the approach is better. George Dennison (1969) in his book, *'The Lives of Children'*, has suggested an alternative approach, in which he has not only stated the beneficial effects on the lives of students, but also criticises the military discipline, the schedules, the punishment and rewards. Thus the movement in education is represented by various authors like Herbert Kohl (1969), Simon and Howe (1972), Gordon (1974), Postman and Weingartner (1971) and many others. They all suggested a variety of approaches to humanistic education.

The humanistic educationists suggest two important points. One is, humanistic education should not provide the teachers with lots of educational strategies and instructional tactics. The teacher's preparations should be in the area of attitudes and not methods. The humanistic educator should work towards a real care for persons, open and effective communication toward genuine empathy and warmth. The second point is that all schools should be concerned with the present and future welfare of students and all should recognize the worth and the rights of the individuals. Postman and Weingartner (1970) advocate for a Soft Revolution. They made a number of provocative suggestions for change emphasising greater freedom and creativity.

The other humanistic approaches are relating to the development of the self and the individual identity. The representatives of these approaches are Borton (1970), Satir (1972) and Purkey (1978) and they put more importance on books. Borton suggests a highly humanistic three-phase teaching model. These are to identify students. The students must be *reached, touched* as individuals and *taught* in a systematic way.

Gordon (1974) suggests a third main approach putting emphasis on communication. It is teacher effectiveness training (TET). The teacher should be taught with the principles and skills of effective human relations. Lastly the students be made to know themselves and to express themselves and to actualize themselves. Simon and Howe (1972) have suggested some specific strategies for classifying values in students. A revolutionary humanistic system of education which has gained greater attention was the one presented by Neill (1960) in Great Britain under the name of Summer Hills. This is a radical approach for child rearing. This was applied in Summer Hill schools. Neill wishes that children should be taught with fear and wished for a rehumanization of the culture through humanistic education.

8. TESTS AND MEASUREMENTS IN HUMANISTIC PSYCHOLOGY

Since the representatives of humanistic psychology were mainly interested in the growth and development of the third force and wanted to show to the world how this new thrust needed to combat the growing social and cultural crises that are rapidly affecting the human race, their efforts in other areas like development of psychological theories, tests materials and research method were not so much progressive as to fulfil the requirements in this field. Further, all the present exponents of humanistic psychology are from the field of psychoanalysis and behaviourism. Therefore it is not so easy for them to wither away all their wealth of knowledge and resources all of a sudden and to begin everything under a new garment. Many of them are of the view that the same test materials and research methods that are used in psychoanalysis and behaviourism could be also applied to humanistic psychology. Maslow (1970) had referred to the projective tests in many places, the merits of these tests. He referred to Murray's Thematic Apperception Test (TAT) and the Rorschach tests stating that these tests are unstructured and in taking up these tests the patient reports are primarily expressions of his way of looking at the world rather than purposive. Since the situations are primarily unstructured, the expressions of the patient permit the experimenter to make many deductions about the underlying character structure.

However, there are some methods and tests, developed by some of the representatives of humanistic psychology. Since the whole aim of humanistic psychology is to study the nature of man, man can be made to reveal some of his natural characteristics by means of some tests. In the preceding section we have discussed some methods of study designed by Dilthey, Polanyi, Allan, specially for humanistic psychology. They are tried by investigators in various situations. Jourard (1968) has developed a test called, 'A Questionnaire for Measuring Trust Between Subjects and Experimenters'. It is a test that would reveal what the individual is at a particular situation. Therefore this test is a 'Self Disclosure'. It is a two-way self-disclosure. Both the experimenter and the subject disclose their attitudes to each other. There are 52 items in this Questionnaire. Jourard states that more works are under way as the validity of this test yet to be made after conducting the test in various populations. Generally, every personality Questionnaire discloses some aspect of an individual's personality.

Maslow's (1970) Security-Insecurity test is supposed to disclose an individual's personality syndrome of security. Maslow states that his test was built on the basic assumption of picking out people who have psychological illness in general. An individual's some aspects of human nature can be brought out by any well standardized personality Inventory. Therefore test development is only secondary importance for the humanistic psychologists.

9. CONCLUSION

In conclusion it may be stated that humanistic psychological movement has attracted large number of persons from various fields. The humanistic approach in psychotherapy after Rogers' has yielded for various different approaches. It has facilitated certain improvements in therapeutic techniques. Similarly, in the field of education many educators thronged with their principles and concepts and wanted to renovate them through humanistic approach. This attitude has been the cause of bringing out several radical approaches not only in teaching methods and schooling but also in child rearing. But humanistic psychologists have not yet developed psychological and educational theories like the other two forces psychoanalysis and behaviourism. Buhler and Allen (1972) state that human civilization and culture face severe crisis. The socio-cultural situation is causing the continuance of the grave threat to the human race. At this juncture no human being can give up his responsibilities that he must owe to his society. But there are many who do not bother about their responsibilities and their societies.

Therefore one of the thrusts of humanistic psychology as an important force in social sciences is to make man to realize what he is and what he is capable of. But the immediate task that is laying before the humanistic psychologists is to evolve suitable theories for all psychological processes. The personality theory and the hierarchy of motivation and the emphasizing of self-actualization do not constitute into a school of psychology like psychoanalysis and behaviourism. All other schools such as structuralism, functionalism, Associationism and purposivism seem to have met with natural death since they did not evolve theories and methods and put them into experimentation for solving individual or social problems. Therefore the aims and scope of humanistic psychology are not completed by mere its scorching criticisms against the existing dominant schools and the valuable services they are rendering with their scientific outlook. A few instances should not be taken as the sufficient deciding factors for disqualifying a century old systems. All the systems of psychology can co-exist side by side, each one advocating its own valuable principles.

The important issues the humanistic psychologists stressing are that, there are no purposes in simply describing man's behaviour in terms of characteristics or traits and also attributing abnormal symptoms. The individual must know what he is and what his potentialities are. The view is that psychological studies must go deep into the human nature and bring out man's capabilities and man must be made to realize the self and work towards actualizing the self. This is what humanistic psychology aims to do.

Rogers (1959) state that the self as perceived by the person and his actual experience should go together harmoniously. It is through his experience that a person becomes aware of himself. Therefore a person's awareness is the symbol of his experience. Rogers says that this awareness is accepted and recognized as the aspect of the self and this self merges into a complex or larger or the structure of the whole self. This self is the individual self. Therefore, in the individual self several components or facets are merged or incorporated.

According to Rogers (1959) this *structure of the self* is gradually developing by the mutual support of the actualizing tendency and the tendency toward self-actualization. This process of self-actualization is normally taking place in every individual to the level of his potentialities and every one is also aware of it. It is not that these tendencies were totally absent and not revealed in the past.

All the scientific inventions and discoveries, the discoveries of new lands in the past, exploring unusual environments, landing in moon, living in space for months, the invention of computer equipments, life-saving medicines are all the outcomes of man's attempt to actualize the self. Therefore the awareness is already there in man. It appears that the humanistic psychologists refuse to reconcile with earlier or past achievements of man by way of self-actualization. In the history of human-kind there was no period without individual or group conflict, alienation, competition or rivalry, group clashes, revolutions and wars. Even within the family there is quarrel, misunderstanding and separation. How can we expect harmonious relationship between or among the millions of people of a nation or of the world? Man is a temperamental and emotional creature. Whatever type of tameness man experiences in the community his real nature prevails ultimately. The British political philosopher, Thomas Hobbas (1588-1679) in his greatest work Leviathan (1651), has given an excellent exposition of human nature.

According to Sigmund Freud (1856-1939) man is born with two basic instincts (motive), one is Eros (life) which is a motive force behind all his positive efforts and behaviour and also his desire to live long and, the other basic instinct is Thanatos (death) which is a motive force behind all his efforts for death and also for other destructions, hostility and aggression. Freud (1930) states that the aggressive instinct in human beings gradually accumulated and if it is not discharged in small amounts or in socially approved constructive ways it will be discharged finally in extremely destructive violence. In Freud's view this cannot be altered by any other means. This was what he also wrote to Albert Einstein (1879-1955) in his letter, 'Why war?' in 1939, stating that 'war cannot be stopped, it has to be fought'. As he stated the Second World War was fought. Freud's followers said that he is a prophet of the twentieth century. During the same time, the British philosopher, C.E.M. Joad also asked the nations if the best way to preserve peace is to prepare for war, why should all nations regard the armaments of other nations as a menace for peace. So there was a strategy maintained by the nations that war is the prelude to peace.

Maslow (1970) states that many members of the community with a profound despair and cynicism degenerate into corrosive malice and cruelty and they deny the possibility of improving human nature and society, discovering intrinsic human values and of being life-loving. Interpersonal relations are forged in hatred, in obligation, in guilt, in selfishness and exploitation. Alienation and disaffection has become, in fact, a way of life.

But we must also take into cognizance that somewhere in the world, wars between nations are going on all the times violating the United Nations Peace Policy. Terrorists create chaos everywhere. The terrorists of one nation are having link with the terrorists of other nations all over the world. Everyday we see some incidences like, the genocide, mass killing, dacoity, group violence, bomb blasts and all sorts of criminal activities are taking place in every community. In this context, where to begin with improving the human nature and the society? Humanistic psychologists are highly ambitious in this regard. There is no harm in having this ambition. We do not know what sort of new spirit humanistic psychology is going to inject in human kind to create a mentally healthy society? This will be known only after a half century of research studies.

EXPERIMENT 4

Study of Self-disclosure and Other Cathexis

1. INTRODUCTION

The critical thinking of modern psychologists of the recent times about the human problems has resulted in the evolution of a 'Third force' which sought to deal with the problems from different angle. They are of the view that the existing schools of psychology, the psychoanalysis and behaviourism expounded only a limited image of man and their contributions are not complete. A system of psychology should place the human person and his experience as the centre of attention. Under the leadership of Abraham Maslow (1972) a group of psychologists in 1962 assembled and founded an organization to bring out a third force in psychology.

Third Force

The third force in psychology is a diversified psychological thought, had varied images about man and differed radically from psycho-analysis and behaviourism. This third force is named as Humanistic Psychology. This has emerged as a school of psychology on the criticisms of the present way of life. Maslow (1971) states that social systems and the support of social institutions are out of touch with human experience, human longings, human needs and human nature. According to him the normal personality is actually a schizophrenic and every one shares this personality. Man is not in a position to relate his spirit of love to others mutually and interpersonal relation is getting hot and alienation, dissatisfaction, selfishness and exploitation are becoming a way of life.

Therefore humanistic psychology basis its origin in philosophical humanism (Frick, 1971). The philosophical position of humanistic psychology gives more importance to the human person and his experiences. It is interested in a theory that can more fully reveal man himself and is interested in closer harmony with man and his nature.

Buhler (1972) states that in a very short period humanistic psychology has spread rapidly all over the United States and many have been attracted towards it. Many research papers, books have been published. Experiments have been designed and conducted in psychological laboratories. One of the experiments in this field, Sidney

M. Jourad (1968) has designed is a Questionnaire, called 'Self disclosing the man to himself'.

Self Disclosure

Self-disclosure refers to the nature of personal information that one person is willing to disclose to another person. This we may consider as an index of close relationship and of the affection, love or trust that prevails between the two persons.

Generally we can state that self-disclosure and cathexis for the other person may have certain amount of correlation. Evidence to support this statement may come from both clinical observation and systematic research. Thus psychotherapists have long noted that when a person feels warm, trust and confidence in his therapist he discloses himself more freely and fully than when he perceives the therapist as a hostile person. Relationship between other cathexes and a self-disclosure is provided in the works of Journard and Lasakow (1958). They have found significant correlation between questionnaire measures of "Mother cathexis" and "Father cathexis" and the amount of disclosure of the subjects have made to their parents. Their study is a measure of the amount and content of self-disclosure to a selected "target person".

Self-disclosure refers to the process of making the self known to the other persons. The target persons are persons to whom information about the self is communicated. Journard (1959) had suggested that accurate disclosure of the self to other is a characteristic of a healthy personality, while neurosis is related to inability to know one's "self-real" and make it known to others. Journard states that what a person is going to disclose another person is the function of several variables. They may be the subject matter to be disclosed, nature of the person, the environment in which disclosure is to take place. The most important is the willingness of the person to disclose himself.

It is evident that contemporary social sciences are built upon self disclosure of respondents and the conditions and the dimensions of self-disclosure. From these we can conclude that systematic analysis of self-disclosure is holding information that is relevant to diverse area of theory and practice.

Therefore enquiries in this area are often directed into the (1) relationship between the person's relationship and the amount of personal information that he knows about other person, and (2) the extent to which the disclosure to others and the information about others could emit mutual relations between people.

One assumption is that a person who reveals himself much to another person may be also expected to receive much information about him and a person who knows great deal about another should be also relatively well known by him. Feeling of indifference or antipathy between the two persons may produce low disclosure to one another, and little knowledge about one another.

Generally, *Cathexis* for other person is determined by paired comparisons in terms of the criteria "liked best as a close friend". This procedure produced a rank order for preference for each subject. The best liked person receives the largest number of choices, and the least liked person receives lowest number of choices (Journard, 1959).

Dyad means a number, two. A group of two elements that has the combining power of the two units may be called a dyad. The relationship just established between self disclosure, cathexis, and knowledge about others suggest that the subjects tended to develop pairs of mutual closeness and intimacy. Dyadic effect is a tendency to develop pairs of mutual closeness and intimacy. It is stated that disclosure begets disclosure.

EXPERIMENT

Problem: The purpose of this experiment is to determine the nature of self-disclosure and other cathexes of the subject.

2. METHOD

(a) Participant: Choose a subject who has no knowledge about this experiment and get the personal information like age, class, sex, whether wearing eye glass, whether he/she had any illness physically, mentally.

(b) Material: Journard's 40 item self-disclosure questionnaire, answer sheet, score sheet and stop clock.

Description of the material: The self-disclosure questionnaire was designed and developed by Journard (1968) and it is consisted of 40 items. It attempts to assess the interpersonal truth. It has two categories of questions. One denotes the low intimacy questions, and the other denotes the high intimacy questions. There are 21 items in the first, and 19 items in the second. The low intimacy items are 1, 5, 7, 8, 9, 11, 15, 16, 19, 21, 23, 24, 25, 26, 28, 29, 30, 32, 34, 38 and 40. The high intimacy items are 2, 3, 4, 6, 10, 12, 13, 14, 17, 18, 20, 22, 27, 31, 33, 35, 36, 37 and 39.

(c) Procedure: The subject should be seated comfortably in the chair. The experimenter should give the printed instruction to the subject with questionnaire. And the following instructions should be given to the subject:

> "You are given a list of 40 questions. You are required to give your personal information about yourself in the answer sheet (The experimenter should point out). The answer sheet consists of two columns A and B. Column A is having the statement as "I have revealed information about these items to someone in my past". Column B has a statement as "willing to disclose information about this item to a same sex stranger on the first encounter".
>
> "You are requested to state how much information about each question you have told someone in your past and how much you would be willing to disclose to a stranger of the same sex you meet now".

1. "If you have never talked about the item to another person write zero (0) against the item under the column A. If you are not willing to disclose about that item to a same sex stranger write zero (0) against the item under the column B.
2. If you have talked generally about the item to another person but not in detail write one (1) against the item number under column A. If you are willing to talk about the item in general to the same sex stranger but not in detail write one (1) against the item under column B.
3. If you have talked in detail about test item to another person in the past write in a two (2) against the item under column A. If you are willing to talk about the item in detail to the same sex stranger write in a two (2) against the item under column B.

For example if you have not told any one how you feel about your overall appearance, you will have to write in a 0 in column A. If you have told someone that you are more or less satisfied about your appearance, but not in detail write in a 1 (one) in column A. But if you have talked in full detail about your overall appearance like this "My face looks very beautiful or My teeth is not giving me good look", you will have to write in a 2 (two) in column A. The same procedure should be followed for column B. This depends upon how you would be willing to disclose the same information at present to a same sex stranger."

The amount of time the subject has taken on the topics should be noted down in seconds.

Game of Invitation

The game of invitation involves the process of making one self known to other person and in turn getting to know who he is. By now you might have formulated some opinion about the person who will be your partner in playing the game.

Both the experimenter and partner receive a list of 40 questions of varying in their degree of personal intimacy. Before the game begins both experimenter and partner should fill up the score sheet each separately by indicating how much information each one is willing to disclose to each other. The following scoring procedure should be followed:

Write in a zero (0) for each question you would be unwilling to talk about with your partner.

Write in a one (1) for each item you would be willing to talk about in general but not in detail with your partner.

Write in a 2 for each item, you would be willing to talk about in detail with your partner.

Both the experimenter and his partner after answering the items should choose any 5 items to ask each other from the list. The rule in playing the game is that the experimenter may not ask his partner a question which he himself is not willing to answer. Write these 5 questions in the column 1 of the score sheet under "question I intend to ask my partner".

If your invitation to answer any of the five questions is refused by your partner mark it under column 2 (My invitation was refused by the other partner).

If your partner is willing to accept your invitation after he has answered your questions, you should also answer those questions. Similarly the partner should ask the experimenter the question he has chosen. The amount of time taken in this should be noted down. The scoring sheet should be collected from the partner and tabulation should be made.

3. RESULTS

1. The subject's score for high intimacy items and low intimacy items and also the total items score should be entered in Table 2.1.
2. The score for both categories that is for A (past) and for B (present) should be given in Table 2.2.
3. The score based on the difference between the number and the intimacy level of the topics the 'S' said, he would be willing to disclose to the same sex stranger and the number he indicated that he would be willing to disclose to the 'E'. That is called perceived risk score. Present this in Table 2.3.
4. The score for high intimacy questions is the number of high intimacy questions asked by the experimenter which the subject has answered. This is called the experimenter—Subject depth disclosure score. Present this in Table 2.4.
5. The score for the high intimacy value questions is the number of high intimacy questions asked by the subject and the experimenter answered. This is signifying his willingness to disclose this information himself. That is called S-E Depth disclosure score. Enter this in Table 2.4.
6. The cathexis for each person should be worked out. This score is obtained from the game of invitation for 40 items. (Liked best as a close friend). Determined the level of cathexis whether it is high, average or low. The number of items the experimenter is willing to disclose and refused. The number of items the subject is willing to disclose and refused should be entered in Table 2.5.
7. The dyadic effect, a tendency to develop pairs of mutual closeness or intimacy should be found out. This score is obtained from the 5 questions. Determine whether the dyadic effect is high, average or low. Enter this in Table 2.6.
8. Find out the number of items refused by the subjects (male or female) at each intimacy level and present the results in Table 2.7.
9. Determine the mean disclosure time in seconds of two levels and enter it in Table 2.8.

Table 2.1 : Showing the subject's level of self-disclosure with the same sex stranger on the first encounter in the test of Journard's self-disclosure questionnaire

Intimacy level	*No. of items disclosed*	*No. of items refused to disclose*
High		
Low		
Total		

Table 2.2 : Showing the number of items disclosed in the past and to the same sex stranger

Intimacy level	*Past A*		*Present B*	
	No. of items		*No. of items*	
	Disclosed	*Refused*	*Disclosed*	*Refused*
High				
Low				
Total items				

Table 2.3 : Showing the perceived risk score of the subject

Intimacy level	*No. of items willing to disclose to the same sex stranger*		*No. of items willing to disclose to the Experimenter*	
	Disclosed	*Refused*	*Disclosed*	*Refused*
High				
Low				
Total				

Table 2.4 : Showing the Experimenter-Subject Depth of Disclosure or Subject-Experimenter Depth of Disclosure

Nature of intimacy	*No. of high intimacy questions asked by the Experimenter, the Subject answered*		*No. of high intimacy questions asked by the Subject, the Experimenter answered*	
	Disclosed	*Refused*	*Disclosed*	*Refused*
High intimacy question				

Table 2.5 : Showing the level of cathexis for each person (liked best as a close friend: game of invitation) on the 40 items scale

'My willingness to disclose by the Experimenter' No. of items		*'My willingness to disclose by the subject' No. of items*	
Dislosed	*Refused*	*Disclosed*	*Refused*

Table 2.6 : Showing the Dyadic effect: a tendency to develop mutual closeness and intimacy: 5 questions the E and S intend to ask each other (game of invitation)

S. No.	*Questions Experimenter asked and subject answered*	*Accepted or declined or refused*	*Questions Subject asked and answered by the Experimenter*	*Accepted or declined or refused*
1				
2				
3				
4				
5				

NB : If 4 to 5 questions are accepted High Dyadic effect
3 questions are accepted average Dyadic effect
2 or less questions are accepted low Dyadic effect.

Table 2.7 : Showing the mean numbers of items refused at each intimacy level by the subjects (males and females)

S.No.	*Subjects*	*Intimacy level : No. of items refused*		*Total*
		High	*Low*	
1				
2				
3				
4				
5				
Mean (Males)				
1				
2				
3				
4				
5				
Mean (Females)				

Table 2.8 : Showing the mean disclosure time, in seconds, of Topics at two levels of intimacy

Intimacy level	*Mean Disclosure time in seconds*
Low High	

4. DISCUSSION

1. Find out whether your subject is scoring high in high intimacy question or low intimacy question.
2. State whether it is high disclosure or low disclosure.
3. Do subjects vary in the extent to which they disclose themselves to different target persons, target persons to whom information about the self is communicated.
4. Discuss the difference between the information disclosed under category A and E in your subject.
5. Discuss perceived risk score (Difference between the disclosure to the stranger and to the E).
6. Discuss the Experimenter—Subject Depth disclosure. This score is: the number of high intimacy questions asked by the E and answered by the S.
7. Discuss the score: the number of high intimacy value questions which the 'S' choose to ask the E, thereby signifying his willingness to disclose.
8. Discuss the cathexis: whether it is high, average or low (40 items).
9. Discuss the Dyadic effect: tendency to develop pairs mutual closeness and intimacy (5 questions), or high, average, low.

5. CONCLUSIONS

State the nature of self-disclosure and other cathexses of your subject.

EXPERIMENT 5

Rosenzweig Picture Frustration Study

1. INTRODUCTION

In our attempt to understand human motivation we must know whether the term motive refers to any inner condition of the organism that directs its behaviour towards a goal. Human being may develop unlimited specific motives, but there are certain basic needs that must be met if the individual is to function and survive in the society. These basic needs are both biological and psychological and the society in which the individual lives is having strong influence upon them. We know that the body apart from other needs should function to maintain its biological equilibrium and integration. The biological needs that are most important to human motivation and behaviour are the visceral needs, safety and avoidance of pain. need for stimulation and activity and the need for sexual gratification. The visceral needs are those for food, water, sleep, elimination of waste etc.

The psychological needs for healthy human development are influenced by learning and social processes. Though these needs are not so much identified as biological needs like food, water, sleep etc., still they are important for the individual to maintain personality integration and for effective function. Man is constantly in need of the psychological requirements like order and understanding, adequacy, competence, security, love and affiliation, self-esteem, power, prestige etc. Man's striving to fulfil these needs take different forms with different people. It depends upon his abilities and aptitudes, fortitude and self actualization or creative self-expression.

Human life becomes simple and happy if all the biological and psychological needs are fulfilled without any disturbance. But normally it never happens in the life of every human being always. There are many obstacles both internal and external that often interfere with need fulfilment. These obstacles put various types of stress on the individual. They are also called adjustive demands. They are usually called frustration, conflicts and pressure. We are now dealing with psychological process of frustration. The term is used to describe the blocking of goal achievement. It is a motivation without satisfaction. The psychological process, frustration need not be mistaken always for the abnormal characteristics. In our every day life we meet with several small and simple frustrations which may disappear very soon. But, when man experiences this frustration? Man experiences frustration whenever his needs or desires are thwarted. There may be some obstacles on the way of his most desired goal or some impediment on the way of his progress.

There may be wide range of internal and external obstacles that may lead to frustration. Some of them are heavy rains, floods, earthquakes, fires, wars, economic deprivation, social inequalities, marital and vocational dissatisfaction, disease, loss of loved ones, physical handicaps, personal failures, loss of property, serious frustrations like, failure to catch the train, car tyre bursts, slashing, a visitor breaking a vase, missing the notes on the examination day and so on.

The second psychological process is aggression. This is the reaction or response to frustration. Individuals seem to vary in their immediate reaction to frustration or failure. These variations of reaction seem to correlate with success or failure. In every culture children are exposed to three important conditions that influence their level of aggressive behaviour. They are their family, their peers and their socio-culture environment. Aggressions are of *three types*. They are *obstacle dominance, ego defence*, and *need persistence*. Obstacle dominance means that a person shows his frustration towards some inanimate object. Ego-defense means that the individual cannot show his frustration towards anything but he punishes or defends himself. Need-persistence means that the individual wants some need to overcome the frustration. It appears that the individuals who met with failure were inclined to blame the external world or others. There are three directions of aggression, such as *extrapunitive, intrapunitive* and impunitive. Extrapunitive is a type of reaction to frustration, which is directed towards others. Some people may blame themselves and they are called intrapunitives. The third type of reaction impunitive, is to blame none, but recalling successes rather than the failures. It is directed towards none.

It is possible to speculate all the three types of reactions of frustration. But in the case of extrapunitive there is a sign of revenge. The aggressive impulses were being preserved to express later on, on someone who was the cause of the frustration. In the case of intrapunitive the reaction is directed against the person's own self. The third one, impunitive type of reaction, entails a *conscious forgetting of the event* of frustration. It is an attempt to reconcile own self and others to the unpleasant situation that has taken place. The impunitive type of reaction may be stated in other words as *'forgive and forget'*. But the other two are not like the third. These three terms were employed previously. The recently designed terms are extraggressive, Interaggressive and imgressive. In combination of the three types of aggression with three directions it now becomes possible to provide a terminology as follows:

The three directions of ego-defensiveness are:

1. Extrapunitive, intrapunitive and impunitive.
2. The three directions of obstacle dominance are: extrapeditive, intrapeditive and impeditive.

3. The three directions of need-persistence are: extrapersistive, intrapersistive and impersistive.

On the basis of three psychological functions of the reactions to frustration, several theories of aggression have been formulated. They are (1) biological or instinctive theories of aggression, (2) the frustration-aggression theories, (3) Social learning and cultural theories.

1. The biological or instinctive theorists are of the view that man is a biological organism and a part of his nature is animal which has some destructive inclinations inherently. William McDougall (1923, 1926, 1933) was the first who made use of this concept very elaborately to describe the social behaviour of animals and human beings. According to him pugnacity was the fundamental instinct in mankind and it could be directed into constructive channel for a healthy effectiveness. But Sigmund Freud (1920) proposed two major driving forces in mankind, one erotic or life instinct and the other destructive or death instinct. Man's effort according to Freud is to take the instinct and redirect it into socially useful form. The aggressive impulse is dealt with through fantasy or imagination. According to Freud the way of dealing with aggression is thinking aggressive thoughts or day dreaming and expressing them through art, literature, sculpture and painting. By this means individual can reduce his inner aggression and it is likely that he would engage himself in constructive act openly.

2. Some investigators like Berkowitz (1962) do not agree with the instinct theory of aggression. They say that aggression is developing in response to some form of frustration. Therefore the frustration-aggression theorists state that the aggressive behaviour is a fundamental response of the individual to frustration of the goal seeking efforts. This view was expressed by John Dollard (1939) and his co-workers. It is a constitutional reaction to frustration that can be altered through learning.

3. The social learning theory was formulated by Miller and Dollard (1941). This theory places emphasis on the child's frequent imitation. The child may be observing this activity of his parents whom he may be admiring or may have a special appeal. Delinquent children often imitate their parent's criminal or aggressive behaviour.

Another social learning theorist Bandura (1969) states that a person may learn a response without direct reinforcement. Bandura (1965) says that it is sufficient if the model is observed and a response is performed. This itself is a reinforcement.

Aggression may cause damage to people or things. It may occur in several forms. Aggression can be expressed physically by assaults and verbally by abusing others or chastisement. The attacks can be direct or indirect. It is also expressed in the form of obstructing the work of another person, uncooperative attitude and withdrawal.

Aggression has been classified into two classes, one angry aggression and the other instrumental aggression. The first is aroused by only anger inducing events like, humility, teasing, insult, attack, appearance of the enemy. The instrumental aggression is aroused by competition or a most desired thing is being possessed by another person. Most of the aggressions are instrumental. Whenever there is competition for rewards the most powerful aggressor will achieve the reward. The property of aggression that leads to reward is stated as instrumental aggression. It is because the attacking response is instrumental in achieving the rewards.

The fact is that some motivation arouses a tendency towards aggression. This tendency may result in actual aggressive behaviour, but the nature depends upon several factors. But often the aggressive response if it is severe it results in some form of violence.

Aggression and violence are the complex forms of human behaviour. The parent's attitudes towards aggression may have a significant influence upon the child. Studies in this area conclude that violence is used as a means of resolving conflicts and young people who are exposed violent models often consider aggressive action as a part of their masculine behaviour (Heimstra and McDonald, 1973).

Studies on Picture-Frustrations

Quite a number of studies have been made on frustration—aggression and violence in United States and elsewhere. But in India there are very few studies on this area, particularly using the Rosenzweig Picture-Frustration Test. Any paper-pencil test with response categories would be easy for an experimenter to conduct an experiment or an investigation. The problem involves in Rosenzweig picture frustration test is that it is very cumbersome and complicated to score the responses and to treat the scores and to interpret the data. This test badly needs a simplified procedure for scoring the responses and to treat the data and to interpret them. The Indian adaptation should have been published with the revised version of the scoring method and interpretation of the data. But the Indian adaptation was not done like that and also was not published the test manual intelligibly. In each page of the test booklet there are four unclear pictures which do not correctly communicate the incidents. There should be only one picture in each page and subject should understand the incident correctly to give his reaction. Because of this many researchers and students do not choose this test for their studies. Most of the universities did not include this in their curriculum of the experimental psychology.

One study has been attempted by Khattri (1993) in India among the amputees and trainers. This study tried to assess the degree of frustration and the direction among the lower limb amputed patients. There were two kinds of amputed patients, one amputated recently and the other gait trainers who had been fitted with artificial limbs. The sample consisted of 20 male patients randomly selected among the patients whose lower limbs were amputated. They were drawn from Medical College, Lucknow. Their age ranged from 20 to 40 years. The income of their families was Rupees 500 and below per month. The Resenzweig Picture—Frustration Test was administered on them. The results showed that all the patients were highly frustrated with a dominant trend of extraggressiveness. Aggression against one's own self was negligible. There were few immgression cases offering solution to the problems. The ego-defense was extremely high. The recently amputated were found to be very extraggressive, least introggressive compared to the gait trainers. The gait trainees showed tendencies of extraggressive and ego-defense. They had regained their self concept and were active members of the society.

EXPERIMENT

Problem: The purpose of the experiment is to assess the nature and direction of aggressive responses to frustration of a person and compare the level of frustration with a small group of persons.

2. METHOD

Participant: Choose a subject who has no knowledge about this test. State the age, sex, class, socio-economic status etc., whether wearing eye glass, had any emotional disturbances etc.

Apparatus: Indian adaptation of Rosenzweig Picture Frustration Test adult form, Manual, Scoring sheet and stop clock. The test was Adapted to Indian Condition by Udai Pareek and R.S. Devi (1968).

Description of the Test: Rosenzweig Picture Frustration study consists of 24 pictures. Originally this test was developed by Rosenzweig (1948) to assess the American subject's reaction to frustration. The development of Rosenzweig Picture Frustration Study has long hostory as it was mainly based upon his research on frustration. Rosenzweig (1938) has first published his paper in the Journal '*Character and Personality*' stating that how frustration is an experimental problem. He has published it in two issues of the Journal. Later on in 1943, he has explained repression relating ego-defense reactions to frustration in the *Journal of experimental psychology*. Subsequently he published his frustration theory in Hant's (1944) edition of personality and behaviour disorders. In the same year Rosenzweig (1944) brought out his P.F. study under the title of *The Rosenzweig P.F. Study Form for Adults*. He has published the same in collaboration with Clarke and others in the *Journal of Psychology* with some changes in the 1946 version. Then Rosenzweig (1947) in collaboration with Fleming and Clarke has revised the scoring procedure of the test in his manual. Rosenzweig (1948) also has brought out the children Form of his test. In the year 1950 he once again revised his P.F. study of adult form. Therefore the final form varies very much from the first form. They are in cartoon forms. Each picture represents one Frustrating situation. In each picture there are two persons shown. They are either a male and a female or both males or females. One person in the picture is shown saying something to other person, which seems to cause frustration to the second person and he is saying something in response. What the second person could speak in that situation? This is what expected from the subject in this test. The original study was revised by Udai Pareek and R.S. Devi (1968) to suit Indian conditions and it was called Indian adaptation of Rosenzweig Picture Frustration Test Adult Form.

Procedure: The subject is to be seated comfortably in front of the experimenter and he is to be presented with a Rosenzweig Picture Frustration test booklet. The following instructions should be read out. The subject should listen to the experimenter and also should read out instruction himself.

> "In each of the pictures in this booklet two persons are shown talking to each other. The words spoken by one person are always given

> there. Imagine what the other person in the picture could answer and write it down against the item number in the blank sheet provided to you. The very first reply that comes in your mind should be written. Work out as fast as you can. Please do not omit any situation. Answer all of them in the same sequential order. Do not skip over any situation on the idea that you can answer it later on".

It is important that the subject should not be given any scope for the development of self critical attitude and he/she should be put more on the objective identification with the figures on the pictures. Therefore the subject should be made to project and reveal his/her own mind on the presented situation in some mode of response. The experimenter should domonstrate with the first picture or should show the way in which the response is to be made.

When the experimenter completed the instruction to the subject, the subject should be asked to open the test booklet and observe the first situation and write down in the scoring sheet the response he could think of on seeing the picture. The subject after giving the response to the first situation should be asked to go to the second picture, and respond in the same manner. Then he should be left on his own way.

In the administration of Picture-Frustration study it is important that the experimenter should see that the subject should respond to the pictures in the same order as they were presented in the test booklet. This should be explained to the subject, orally at the time of giving the instruction.

The amount of time taken by the subject in responding to all the 24 pictures should be recorded in the front page. Normally it should be 20 mimutes duration. If the test is administered on the individual subject then after completing the booklet he/she should be asked to read out loudly the responses he has written. The experimenter should note down if there is any significant change in the voice of the subject and should ask non-leading questions. If the answers were very brief, or strong or vague or ambiguous, the experimenter should make enquiries to supplement them for scoring. Then the test booklet should be collected from the subject and the responses should be scored very carefully according to the procedure. (See Appendix "A" for types of responses for all 24 items.)

Method of Scoring

The scoring procedure of this test is very cumbersome and complicated. Therefore the experimenter should read carefully the procedure described here and the models should be followed. The subject knowingly or unknowingly may project himself/herself and identify with the frustrating person in each situation given in the picture. He may project his own likes and dislikes in his replies. These types of bias responses are determined by assigning to each response the correct direction of aggression and type of the aggression. There are *three types of directions.* The first is *extraggression of E.A.* in which aggression is turned towards the object of frustration. It may be a person, object or some environment. The second is the *intraggression or I.A.* in which aggression is turned by the subject upon self. He/she blames himself or herself. The third is *imggression or M.A.* In this the aggression is minimised or avoided with a view of forgetting the event of frustration.

The *types of aggression are three* such as obstacle-dominance (O-D), ego defence (E-D), and need persistence (N-P). In the obstacle dominance (O-D), the obstacle causing frustration is revealed in the person's response. In the ego defence (E-D), the ego of the person prevails. The person justifies his stand that he is right. The need persistence (N-P) emphasises the importence of the motive and a solution to the frustration is stressed.

By the combination of *three types of direction and three types of aggression, 9 possible scoring patterns are evolved* for each item. For scoring purposes, the letters E, I and M are used to signify three directions as extraggressive, intraggressive and imggressive as responses of aggression respectively to any type of aggression.

1. The *obstacle dominance* is indicated by an apostrophe (′) and is to be written after the capital letters E, I or M with symbols like, E′, I′ and M′.

2. The *Ego-defence* types of aggressive responses are indicated by the capital letters E, I and M and they are used *without apostrophe.*

3. The *Need-Persistence* is indicated by the small letters e, i and m.

This point may be illustrated with an example. A response is required a score for *extraggressive obstacle-dominance (E′)* and *intragressive Eggo-defence (I)* is indicated by the factors E′/I. In the same way when one scoring pattern alone is required *imggressive need-persistence*, the score is written as //m. (See Appendix "B" for Method of Scoring of the responses.)

Brief definition of 9 scoring factors (keys)

I. *Obstacle Dominance:*

E′ for Extrapeditive or Extraggressive obstacle dominance

I′ for Intropeditive or Introggressive obstacle dominance
M′ for impeditive or Imggressive obstacle dominance

II. *Ego Defense:*
E for Extrapunitive or Extraggressive Ego-defense
I for Intrapunitive or Intraggressive Ego-defense
M for Impunitive or Imggressive Ego-defense

III. *Need Persistence:*
e for Extrapersistive or Extraggressive Need Persistence
i for Intrapersistive or Intraggressive Need Persistence
m for Impersistive or Imggressive Need Persistence.

As far as possible it is better to have only one factor or if unavoidable two factors for scoring most of the responses. If a score is assigned to more than one factors two different phrases should be used. It is better to avoid a third factor as there is some difficulty in differentiating the responses. There are 66 types of scoring responses according to the original authors of this study. For an experimenter who administers the test for some purpose it may take longer time to identify the subject's responses to the scoring responses. Therefore it is better to simplify it by identifying the subject's responses to the nearest scoring responses as far as possible without sacrificing the validity of the subject's responses.

Choice of O-D, E-D and N-P

The subject might have indicated in his response that he/she is blocked by the obstacle (O-D). Therefore he may go for attacking others or himself (E-D). He may sometimes take a different way of dealing with the situation to find out a solution to the problem (N-P).

For example in determining the scoring pattern for E′ and E the responses indicate the element of obstacle dominance in both. In this the ego-defense is ordinarily observed in the responses. In such cases O-D is preferred in scoring it and it should be entered in the column O-D. But if the response is having the *strong element of ego-defense,* E-D is preferred and E should be entered under the column E-D. There is every possibility of combining both factors E′ and E if two definite statements are found in the response to a situation.

Extraggressive Score (E-A)

In scoring the responses the factor E′ is employed if the statement indicates severe frustration or irritation rather than blame, guilt or solution. If the aggression is projected towards person without any guilt or inferiority E may be employed. It is important to distinguish between cases where the subject protests against inanimate object and situation in which aggression is directed towards other persons. In the case of the inanimate object E′ is scored and in the case of other person E is scored.

The factor e is employed when the speaker wants action on the part of another person for the solution to the problem. He may insist the solution of the problem in the way in which he wants. When the need for assistance is strong and explicit e should be employed. For example, in situation 6 the response "I know but I need all the 4 at a time" is scored with E′, while response "Please give me more than two" is scored with e because there is explicit request in the response.

Intraggressive Scores (I-A)

The factor I′ is employed in scoring a response that expresses the refusal of the presence of any frustration. The refusal may be in the form of ignoring the event. The speaker does not like that others should know his dealing. It may be for a need for punishment. For example, in situation one "Never mind. It is not a very serious matter. Go on" is scored with I′. When there is strong evidence of overt guilt feeling and also the element of I′ in the response it is the combination of responses. In such a case both I′ and I are scored.

The factor I is employed in scoring when the response involves speaker's sorrow, regret or guilt. If sorrow is followed by an offer to change the situation i alone is used. If there is any regret and an attempt to avoid the situation strongly more than the usual way both I and i are employed.

Imgressive Score (M-A)

The factor M′ is employed in scoring responses that have minimum level of frustration. It does not cause any feeling of untowards of the situation. The M is employed to score the response that explains the situation and m is used as the acceptance of the situation, and approving of it. If the approval is direct and without any condition m alone is used. For example, in situation 16, "Shall we settle this among ourselves." Here m is used alone. If the response expresses a request for satisfaction at present and a promising response later e is combined with m. For example, in situation 12, "I can do without these at present, but inform him please", this response can be scored with e and m (//e; m).

But if the approval is modified by some indication of some uneasiness then it is scored with E′ and m (E′//m). For example, in situation 6, "Okay, I will take two, though I need all of them".

The experimenter should note that in certain situations the frustration is not so much intense and the expressions may put more emphasize upon the need-persistence (N-P). In such situations the responses may be having the phrases like, Alright, Okay, Never mind, Very Well, these do not provide strong background for scoring them with the factor M. However it is the only factor that can be used for scoring responses in which the frustration is evaded and if the frustrating person is feeling free from guilt.

Super-Ego Scores (S-E)

There are situations in which the person who is an object of the frustrating situation may seek an excuse for himself/herself for having committed the original mistake. The person may also seek excuse for the other person's aggression directed towards him/her. In these cases factors I′ and I may be used. For certain responses E′, E and M′ may be used for scoring. The person may defend himself by denying the commission of the error and he may disown the blame for such behaviour. In these two instances the factors E and I may be used for scoring. A response that is expressing free from guilt is scored with M-A and I. In assessing super-ego pattern the factors E′, E, I′, I, E, I and M-A + I are all involved a some manner. The experimenter should carefully go through the definitions of the eleven scoring factors. Nine factors are evolved from the combination of type of aggression and type of direction and two are variants E and I.

Item Score and Group Confirmity Rating (GCR)

When Picture-Frustration booklet is answered with responses the booklet should be collected from the subject and the responses should be scored according to the procedure explained here (also refer to original Manual). The item scores should be entered in Table 2.9, for all the three directions O-D, E-D and N-P.

The scoring should be made in the score sheet. In completing the score sheet the steps should be followed carefully. In the item score sheet there are three columns and 24 rows as shown in Table 2.9. These 24 rows indicate 24 situations and the three columns three types of aggression. The score for each situation should be entered against its number. The factor of an item or situation may be entered into one or two columns of O-D, E-D, or N-P according to the nature of the responses. While marking the responses in the scoring sheet under O-D, E-D and N-P it should be noted that the responses should be entered on the left side as shown in Table 2.9.

Table 2.9 : Showing the Item Scores (24 items) of the individual in the Test of Rosenzweigh P-F Test

Score	*Item No.*	*Obstacle-Dominence (O-D) (C I)*	*Ego-Defence (E-D) (C I)*	*Need-Persistence (N-P) (C I)*
+	1		*E* *E : M*	
+	2	*I′*	*I*	
+	3	*E′* *E′*		
	4	*E′*		*i*
	5			*i* *i*
	6		*I*	
+	7		*E* *E*	
	8	*E′*	-	
+	9	*E′* *E′*	*E*	
+	10		*E* *E*	
	11	*E′*		*m*
	12			*i*
	13		*E*	*m*
	14	*E′*	*M*	
	15		*I*	
+	16		*I* *I*	
	17		*I*	*e*
	18		*M*	*e*
	19		*E* *I*	
+	20		*M* *M*	
+	21	*I′* *I′*		*i*
	22	*I′*		*m*
	23	*E′*	*M*	
+	24	*E′*	*M* *M*	

G.C.R.= 10.0 = 83% CI = Citerion item.

After scoring all the 24 items in the respective column, credit should be given to each factor. This is on the basis of full agreement and part agreement with key. Full agreement is entered as + and part as half (½). The full agreement will have one point and part will have ½ point. The total should be calculated and the percentage should be worked out on the basis of the total criterion items. Some responses may be unscorable. Such responses should be recorded as failure. They do not fall in line with criteria. For every item it is expected that the subject's response should meet the criterion scores. Therefore the experimenter can also use the criterion scores as given in Table 2.9 for any specific purpose. The assigned score for each item should be totalled at the bottom of the score sheet. This is called G.C.R.

The percentage should be calculated by using the formula:

$$\frac{\text{G.C.R. scores} \times 100}{\text{Number of criteria items in score sheet (12)}}$$

The G.C.R. percentage is also given in the Manual (*Appendix A*). The figure thus obtained is the percentage of G.C.R.

Profile and Deviation Pattern

The Profile and Deviation Pattern (Table 2.10) shows the types and direction of aggression. It is different from the scoring of G.C.R. All the entries made in the scoring sheet in all the three columns (O-D), (E-D) and (N-P) should be accounted for here. The first 12 situations are treated as first half and situations 13 to 24 treated as second half. A look at the scoring sheet will explain this idea. A situation's two factors in different columns should be scored proportionately. For example if a response has been scored as /I/i the item is scored as .5 to I and .5 to i. The maximum score or denominator for type and direction of aggression is 24 and therefore this is proportionately distributed in various cells. Each item is counted as a unit in the total score. For example, if any item is omitted or not scorable the denominator would be lower.

In the profile and deviation pattern under column O-D, there are four cells for E-A, four cells for I-A and four cells for M-A. Similarly under E-D and N-P columns, there are four cells for each direction. That is, E-A, I-A, and M-A. Therefore each square consists of 4 cells made up of two types of categories.

Table 2.10 : Showing the Deviation Pattern (Profile) of the Individual Scores in the Test of Rosenzweig P-F Test

Type of Aggression		*O–D*		*E–D*		*N–P*		*Total*		*Per-centage*
		1	2	1	2	1	2			
E–A	1	4.0		3		—	—	7.0	11.5	48
	2	—	1.5		1.5		1.5	4.5		
I–A	1	1	—	1	—	2.5	—	4.5	8.5	35.4
	2		1	—	2.5	—	0.5	4.0		
M–A	1	—	—	—	—	0.5	—	0.5	4.0	16.6
	2	—	—	—	2.5	—	1.0	3.5		
Total		5.0	2.5	4.0	6.5	3.0	3.0		24.0	100
		7.5		10.5		6.0				
Percentage		31.25		43.75		25.0		100		

NB :
- O–D : Obstacle-Dominance
- E–D : Ego-Defence
- N–P : Need-Persistence
- E–A : Extraggression
- I–A : Intraggression
- M–A : Imaggression

The total score for the first half items (1 to 12) should be entered in the left upper cell and the total of the second half (13-24) on the right lower cell of the square. In the same way the left upper cells and the right lower cell of the each square should be filled with totals. Then the total for all the 3 types (O-D, E-D and N-P) and the direction (E-A, I-A and M-A) should be worked out. The grand total of the type and directions should be 24. Then the percentage should be worked out and entered in the appropriate places.

Super-Ego Pattern (*S-E*)

The Super-Ego pattern is the measure of the person's defence of the self. The person is aggressively denying that he is responsible for the occurrence of the event ($\underline{E}$). The person is disowning the charge levelled against him. He admits his guilt as the situation is unavoidable ($\underline{I}$). These super-ego factors should be considered in relation to *E* and *I* and the direction of aggression, M.A. and the super-ego factor $\underline{I}$ implicate no guilt. It is neither blaming someone outside or oneself. Therefore it is better to consider all these factors in assessing the Super-Ego patterns. Thus we have here the frequencies of $\underline{E}$, $\underline{I}$, E, I and also *MA+I*.

By posting the frequencies of these factors according to the formula we have Table 2.11 with Super-Ego patterns.

Trends

There are five types of trends possible here. The final aspect of the scoring is the analysis of trends. The important analysis in Rosenzweig Picture Frustration study is *E-D column* that is the extrapunitiveness. The formula to work out the trend is $= \frac{a-b}{a+b}$. That is, 'a' refers to the amount of factor in the first half (1 to 12) of the test and 'b' is the amount of factor in the second half of the test 13 to 24). The above formula can be used to work out the Trends (or the Appendix B can be used to find out the trends for the value of a and b, if necessary).

Five types of trends are possible in this study, but all these depend upon the scores under each heading. But the two important trends are *4th* and *5th*. The minimum positive and negative values required for a significant trend is given in Table 2.10 of the manual. The value obtained from the formula can be identified with the values given in Table 2.10, of the manual and a positive (+) and negative (–) trends can be determined. (*If the trends are worked out according to the formula given here and the procedure is followed the Table of the Manual need not be used*).

3. RESULTS

Score the responses and present the scores, the subject's G.C.R. score and the percentage in Table 2.9.

From the profile and the deviation pattern (Table 2.10) indicate the percentage scores of the persons and also indicate the type of aggression and direction of aggression.

Table 2.11 :Showing the Super-Ego (S-E) Pattern of the Individual from the Test Scores

S. No.	*Type of Response*	*Score*	*Percentage (%)*
1	*E*	2	8.3
2	*I*	1	4.1
3	*E* + *I*	3	12.5
4	E – *E*	2.5 – 2.0 = 0.5	2.0
5	I – *I*	2.5 – 1.0 = 1.5	6.3
6	M – A + *I*	4.0 + 1.0 = 5.0	20.8
	Super-Ego Pattern Total %		54.0

Table 2.12 :Showing the Determination Trends of the Individual from the Test Scores

S. No.	*Trends*		$\left(\frac{a-b}{a+b}\right)$
1	E′ = .2 (+)	I′ = .5 (–)	M′ = 0 Within Column
2	E = .25 (+)	I = .5 (–)	M = 0 Within Column
3	e = 0	i = .5 (+)	m = .3 (–) Within Column
4	EA = .3 (+)	IA = .05 (+)	MA = .75 (–) Cross Trends
5	OD = .3 (+)	ED = .15 (–)	NP = 0 Cross Trends
	Total Pattern : E′ (8) > E (5) = M (5) > I (4) > I′ (3)		
Note : + Indicates Positive. – Indicates Negative			

State the Super-Ego pattern of the individual and state in which factor your subject has scored high and in which scored low. Also show whether all the factors having the characteristics of Super-Ego are involved with some frequencies.

State the trends in your subject. What type of trends, whether it is positive and negative.

Collect the group data for GCR, deviation pattern, Super-Ego pattern and total pattern of Trends and present them in Table 2.13. Work out the mean and interpret the results.

Model Interpretation of the Data

An individual's responses are scored and the scores are treated and presented in these Tables and interpreted *as a model.* The experimenter should read the responses written by the subject in the answer sheet carefully and find out the suitable scoring factors and write them in the columns under the three types of aggressions (O-D, E-D, N-P) on the left side against the item number in Table 2.9. All the response statements should be brought under any one of the *scoring factors* under the three types of aggression. The scoring factor must be either E′; or I′ or M′, or E, or I or M, or <u>E</u> or <u>I</u> or *e*, or *i*, or *m*. A model of scoring method is shown in Table 2.9. The credit is marked on the (left) first column. All responses entered in the Table are not scorable. All the unscorable responses are treated as failures. Because they do not fall in line with the criteria which are written on the right and of the columns of the three aggressions (*O-D, E-D, N-P*) using the same scoring factors. If a response is in full agreement with the criterion then a plus sign is made. But if it is part agreement half point is given. The total is made for all the 24 items and written at the bottom of the Table 2.9. Then the percentage is worked out on the basis of total criterion items.

This is called Group Conformity Rating (G.C.R.). This is obtained by using the formula $= \frac{\text{G.C.R. Score} \times 100}{12 \text{ (criteria)}} = \frac{10 \times 100}{12} = 83\%$. In this test the individual's total score is 10 and the G.C.R. is 83%. The score is considerably higher. From this score we can presume that the individual is more on the ego-defensive direction (Table 2.11). In five of the responses the individual is in line with the criterion factors E′ and *E* and in two items his responses are in line with I′. In two items he is in agreement with *M* and in one item with *I*. In all other items the subject's responses are in the form of combinations (Tables 2.10 and 2.12). The deviation pattern and the trends are worked out using the same formula $\frac{a-b}{a+b}$ for all the five trends. There are positive and negative trends. The person exhibited higher percentage (48%) of extraggressive and 35.4 percentage of intraggressive and 16.6 percentage of imggressive responses.

Table 2.13 : Showing the Group Data in the Rosenzweig Picture- Frustration Study

S. No.	*Name*	*GCR Score*		*Deviation Pattern (Profile)*						*Super-Ego pattern %*	Trends: Total pattern
		Score	*%*	*Type of Agg. %*			*Direction of Agg. %*				
				O.D. %	*E.D. %*	*N.P. %*	*E.A. %*	*I.A. %*	*M.A. %*		
1	P.K.	10.0	83%	31.25	43.75	25	48	35.4	16.6	54.0	E′ > E = M > I > I′ (B > 5 = 5 > 4 > 3)
2	S.V.										
3	M.S.										
4	G.C.										
5	R.S.										
6	V.L.										
7	B.V.										
8	K.R.										
9	P.V.										
10	T.P.										
11	S.L.										
12	A.R.										
Mean											

4. DISCUSSION

State your participant's position in the profile of aggression. Is he/she more aggressive or less aggressive. Discuss whether the G.C.R. value is high or low for the participant.

Discuss who are those having strong deviation in *O-D*, from mean and become obssessive by the barrier causing frustration. Also indicate the anxiety level.

State and discuss who are those have low *N-P, M-A* passive to frustration. Who are those having no effort to solve the problem and also state the reason if any.

Interpret the individual's data comparing the group mean of the G.C.R., percentage of Super-ego pattern, and total pattern of the trends. Where the individual stands in the group? How many of the individuals are above the group mean and below the group mean in GCR, in Super-ego pattern? State the significance of the same. Discuss the total trend pattern of the group.

Model Discussion

The data presented in Tables 2.9 to 2.12 are briefly discussed here.

The individual's GCR score is 10 and the percentage score is 83. This is a considerably high score. It appears that the individual is more on the ego defense direction. This assumption has been supported by the score he obtained in Super-Ego pattern which is more than fifty percent (54%). Further the individual is also having a tendency to find a solution to problem situation. The scores in the area of *E-D* and *N-P* seem to support this phenomenon.

The person's aggression is directed more on the side of ego-defense (43.75%) and secondly to obstacle dominance (31.75%) and thirdly need-persistence (25%). This shows that the person is more of ego-defensive. He aggressively denies the charge against him and that he is not responsible for it (Situation 10, $\underline{E}$).

The percentage of *super-ego trend is 54* for this person. This means that in frustrating situations he projects his aggression on others, finds fault with other persons and objects. The highest score for *M–A+I* is 20.8%, which means, the level of aggression is minimized, but the person strongly denies the guilt. The next highest score (12.5%) is for *E + I*, which is the expression of strong ego-defense. It is the extraggressive reaction of the person. This may be also stated that the person projects his aggressive feelings. The other psychological mechanisms in function are the reaction formation and compensation. The person puts the blames for his difficulties on others and also attributes his own stress to others. He also demands solution or explanation from others for the incidents occurred in his way of life.

In the case of this individual all the factors that are having the characteristics of ego-defense *E′*, *E*, *I′*, *I*, *E*, *I* and *M–A* + *I* are involved in his super ego pattern. The percentage of super-ego pattern of this individual is 54.

There are both positive and negative trends as revealed by the scores of the individual. Though the value of some trends are below the minimum the trends prevail. For example, in the case of the first trend for *E′* it is +0.2, the minimum Table value is +0.4, for *I′* it is –0.5 which is significant and for *M′* it is 0. This means, the individual's aggressive tendency is minimised and the individual thinks that it is not a very big matter and he does not seek any solution (Table 2.12).

The second trend also is having both positive (*E* = +0.25) and negative (*I* = –0.5) values and both are significant as the obtained values are above the minimum table values (*E* = +0.25, *I* = –0.4). This means that the person's extrapunitive aggressive tendency is higher and positive (*E* = +0.25) and his intrapunitive aggressive tendency (*I* = –0.5) is higher and negative. He is not directing his aggression towards himself. The aggressive impunitive (*M*) tendency is zero. It is quite clear from the values of positive extrapunitive and negative intrapunitive values that the person did not want to blame himself for the incident.

In the case of the third trend the individual did not seek any solution for the frustrating situation (*e* = 0) as the obtained value is zero. But at the same time the obtained values for *i* (+0.5) and for *m* (–0.3) are above the Table values. Therefore these two are highly significant. This means that the person has felt the sense of guilt and is ready to offer some solution to the problem and also hopes and expects the circumstances which can bring a solution to the problem.

The fourth trend also has both positive and negative values. Except the intraggressive (+0.05) the other two types extraggressive (+0.3) and imggressive (–0.75) aggressive tendencies have significantly higher values. They are higher than the Table values (*IA* =+0.25); (*MA* = –0.25). This shows that the person is having aggressive tendency without any feeling of guilt. Though the intraggression is having a positive obtained value (*IA* = +.05) it is not significant, whereas the imgression value (*MA* = –0.75) is very high (Table value for *MA* =

–0.25). This shows that the person is extrapunitive and hostile against the person or object. He did not want to minimize the frustrating situation or avoid.

In the fifth trend there is positive value (*OD* = +.3), one negative value (*ED* = –.15) and one zero value (*NP* = 0). The value of obstacle dominance (+.3) is higher than the Table value (*OD* = +.20), whereas the *E-D* value is less than the Table value (*ED* = –.20). This implies that the person is highly frustrated as he is blocked from reaching his goal. The ego of the person is dominating in the situation and he wanted to attack the object of his frustration. He may attack others or attack himself since the *E-D* is having the negative value. He did not want to go for any solution of the problem in this case as his *N-P* is zero.

Finally, the total pattern is determined on the basis of the occurrence of the factors. How frequently each factor has occurred in the record irrespective of the type and direction of aggression. They are entered in the order of frequency and each one is related to the other. Thus, we have in the model study, *E′* occurring 8 times. This is having the highest frequency in the scoring. Next *E*, and *M* have occurred 5 times each. This is next highest. The third is *I*, with 4 occurrences, the factor *I′* has occurred 3 times (Table 2.9). Therefore, the Total Pattern is :

$$8 > 5 = 5 > 4 > 3$$

$$E' > E = M > I > I'$$

It may be also stated like this:

$$E' \ (8) > E \ (5) = M \ (5) > I \ (4) > I' \ (3)$$

The individual aggressively point out the presence of the frustrating obstacle (*E′*). Because of it he is not able to achieve his goal. Therefore he blames the object of his frustration. He projects his hostility towards him or any object that frustrates him (*E*). But at the same time he thinks that the particular situation is unavoidable and minimizes his frustration and becomes obsessive (*M*). He directs the blame upon himself (*I*) and interprets that it is not frustrating. He thinks that it is strange, but in a way it is also good (*I′*) Table 2.12).

5. CONCLUSIONS

State the nature and direction of the aggressive response of your subject. Among the three directions in which direction he/she scored high and in which scored low. Among the three types of aggression which one identifies the individual. In the group who are those more aggressive persons and who are less aggressive person.

Model Conclusions

The individual whom we have discussed here is more an Ego-Defensive type of person. This is supported by the total Super-Ego-Pattern Scores (54%). This trend is further supported by the other scores also. The individual's aggression is firstly more of Ego-Defensive type (46%), secondly of Obstacle-Dominance (33%), and thirdly of Need-Persistence (21%). The highest score is for Ego-Defense and the lowest is for Need-Persistence. Therefore, the aggressive responses of this person determine him/her as the *Ego-Defensive type of person.*

Further, since the individual has scored the highest in extraggressive (48%) next high score in intraggressive (35.4%) and the lowest in imaggressive he/she is in the *Direction of Extraggression.*

APPENDIX A

Type of Answers given by One Person for all 24 Situations

1. Don't you see, the road is so broad that you could have avoided this dirty action.
2. I should not have done such costly loss to you.
3. It is very unfortunate that we have to sit behind this man!
4. Because of the tonga I missed the train. Now I must catch a bus.
5. Nothing is lost. You can take any watch.
6. I am sorry. I did not know the library rules.
7. Yes. It is true. I must be.
8. You studied together in school or college?
9. Wait? How can I wait till then?
10. It is not lie. Why should I speak lie?
11. This is not Ram's house. Enquire elsewhere.
12. I will try to find out him and get this exchanged.
13. You only gave me the appointment! Then when can I see the next?
14. What is wrong with her? Probably something unavoidable might have happened.
15. It is not your mistake, but it is mine.
16. I was on the wrong side. Sorry for the incident.
17. I was little careless. I must have kept it safely. Let us do something else now.
18. Does not matter. Keep one for me in the next arrival.
19. Don't you see I am pushing my cycle on the road as there is no light.

20. She must be having several problems?
21. Is it so. I am sorry. I will go and see her.
22. It is all right, not bad. I can walk.
23. Your aunt is coming to bless us! very good! But we should not miss the train.
24. Does not matter. Your child did not know the value of the newspaper.

APPENDIX B

Method of Scoring of the Responses

One person's responses for all 24 situations are given here and the Model of scoring for the responses are marked in Table 2.9.

1. In the first situation the answer given by the subject is hostile, blaming the person responsible for the incident. The aggression is turned against person who drove the vehicle. Therefore the response is scored with */E/.*

2. The second response expresses regret for the incident and she feels that she should not have incurred the displeasure of another person. Hence it is scored with *I'//.*

3. The response for the third situation shows the frustrated person's objections to the presence of the obstacle. This is to be scored with *E'//.*

4. In the fourth situation, the response is blaming the mode conveyance he had engaged to go to the station which resulted in missing the train (*E'*). The person wishes to solve the problem by some other means (*i*). Therefore this is scored with *E'//i.*

5. The response to the fifth situation is to make amendment for the mistake by asking the person to take some other way. Thereby the problem is solved. This is scored with *//i.*

6. The sixth situation is responded with denial of the essential fault, but accepted the guilt. The person still may argue that he/she has not committed any serious mistake. This is concerned with super-ego. Therefore, it is scored with */I.*

7. The response to the seventh situation refers to the aggression projected by the person towards the object of his frustration, the tailor, as he has not done the fitting correctly. The tailor is blamed. Hence it is scored with a factor. */E/.*

8. Situation eight was responded by the person with some irritation, expressing the severe frustration as he did not expect such statement

from him which deals with one's feeling aspect. Hence it is scored with *E'//.*

9. The response is the 9th situation is the expression of the frustrated person's aggression towards the object, the laundry man. The word 'wait!' with exclamation mark is the expression of severe irritation on the laundry man. Therefore it is scored with *E'//.*

10. Situation ten was answered by the subject with strong denial of the charge made against him. The person aggressively protest that he is not responsible for the offence. Hence it is scored with */E/.*

11. The response to the eleventh situation expresses pointing out the mistake made by the person and the inconveniences caused to him. The reply expresses the irritation. It is the projection of aggression against the object of frustration. This is scored with *E'//.*

12. Situation twelve was answered with a solution to the problem. The frustrated person himself offered a correction for his mistake. Hence it is scored with *//i.*

13. The response to thirteenth situation is a combination of projection of aggression towards the object and his frustration (*E*) and also wanted to bring about solution to the problem (*m*). The person who is responsible for the frustration is blamed, but since the mistake is made by the person himself by not making his presence promptly. Therefore, he himself offered a solution to the problem. This is scored with */E/m.*

14. Situation fourteen was received a response which is a combination of two factors. The person is blamed for causing the frustration (*E'*). But the blame for frustration is ignored as such situation is unavoidable (*M*). The aggression is minimized. Therefore it is scored with *E'/M/.*

15. The response to the situation fifteen is an expression of aggression towards himself (*I*). The person knows his mistake and therefore apologise for his mistake. Hence it is scored with */I/.*

16. The response of the other person in situation sixteen is an expression of his intrapunitive aggression, blaming himself for the mistake. Hence it is scored with */I/.*

17. In situation seventeen the response offered by the subject, is an expression of aggression against the the person who is responsible for the loss of the keys (*I*). But he offers a solution for the frustrating situation, a solution is anxiously expected by the other person. It is scored with */I/e.*

18. The response by the subject to situation eighteen is a combination of two factors. The person is disappointed and frustrated since the

article was already sold. But he did not blame person who is responsible for his frustration. The blame is evaded since such incidents are unavoidable (*M*). Therefore he offers a solution to the problem that he would get one from the next arrival (*e*). Therefore, it is scored with */M/e*.

19. Situation nineteen received a response from the subject which reveals that the person is aggressively denying that he is not responsible for the charge. He emphasises that he is right. Hence it is scored with */E/*.

20. The answer to the situation twenty given by the subject reveals impunitive aggressive response. Blaming the other person for the frustrating situation is evaded since such occurrences are possible and unavoidable. Hence the person who is responsible for the frustration is free from the guilt. Therefore it is scored with /M/.

21. The response to the situation twenty-one made by the subject exhibits the denial of the presence of any frustration. This denial is to make others not to know the person's involvement with the other person, though the need for punishment is there (*I′*). The speaker from her sense of guilt makes an amendment and offers a solution to the problem by saying that she will go and see her (*i*). Hence, it is scored with *I′//i*.

22. Situation twenty-two has been answered by the subject with response which expresses a combination of factors of intraggression (*I′*) and a solution to the problem (*m*). In the response there is a denial of frustration in such a way that others should not know his inner feeling. At the same time he offers a solution to the problem as if there is no problem. Therefore it is scored with *I′//m*.

23. The response to the situation twenty-three reveals the person's strong frustration. The person makes an irritative statement. "It is good. She is coming to see us!" But outwardly he does not blame her (*E′*). The blame is evaded. Because the incident of coming of her aunt cannot be avoided. Here the frustrating person is free from guilt. Hence it is scored with *E′/M/*.

24. The response to the situation twenty-four reveals the person's severe frustration, but the situation is explained as not frustrating (*E*). The blame for frustration is avoided and the person is free from guilt by justifying the child's action (*M*). Hence it is scored with *E′/M/*.

3

ENVIRONMENTAL PSYCHOLOGY

1. ENVIRONMENTAL PROBLEMS

Human behaviour is highly influenced by environmental factors and in return human behaviour changes environmental atmosphere. As citizens of a town or city or nation we are aware of the potential environmental hazards. Though environment provides all facilities for the survival of the organisms the way in which man manipulates the environment in the scientific age creates various problems which in return affects the very life of human beings and other organisms. The environmental pollutions we often hear in these days is the outcome of all badly handled consequences of the environment. Large segments of society do not accept that certain problems are inevitable and over which they have no control. Once they come to know then that becomes a serious problem and there would be widespread reaction not only of verbal expression but also in various forms of publication in mass media of communication and in radio and television programmes. It may also take the form of violent public demonstrations. When a problem became a public demand then something should be done for it.

People's demands are going on increasing every day, but solutions are lacking behind. The scientists are very sensitive to the real world problems and they can find out solution to such problems. For which considerable amount of research has to be conducted and much money also should spent on it. Just like all other scientists the psychologists also wanted to make contributions to alleviate the real world problems.

There are many problem areas. If one is asked to state the problem he faces he can make out a long list. Every one can make out a list of his own problems which may be personal or social or environmental. For example, there is no news in newspapers every day without some strikes, demonstrations, aggressions, violence, by individuals and groups in our society. Every day the crime rate increases abnormally. All sorts of criminal activities have become common occurrences. It has become unsafe for men and women to walk in the street of big cities. Women not only lose their jewels, but also their chastity. House breaks and lootings not only during night time, but also in broad daylight are happening deliberately. Cheating, forgery and misappropriation are justified. There are also other problems like alcoholism and drug abuses which are increasing rapidly in our country apart from smoking. Besides these we are constantly reminded of all sorts of disadvantages and dangers that our living environment is getting more and more into dangerous situation. If no serious thought was given at present, it would be too late for us to mend it later on. Many of these problems brought to our attention either by direct personal experience or through the nation's mass media of communication.

Science and technology, no doubt, brought more comforts to men. It has improved the ways of life of an individual in many ways. The individual completes his work in a short time, gets more money or wage and also gets more leisure time. Since he earns more money he buys more consumer goods and increases his comforts and luxury. Since he has more money at present than he had in the past his imagination runs riotously. He thinks of getting still more money. However, whether one is blue collar worker or white collar worker develops increasing dissatisfaction about the nature of his work and work environment. New technological changes brought changes in the nature of works and many of the workers will have to spend more time with their work environment. As a result of this many of the workers become dissatisfied with their environment. This becomes one of the important social problems.

The dissatisfaction, the individual has developed, does not stay within himself. He expresses it in various ways. Takes up his personal dissatisfaction to the society and makes it as an important social problem. Collects his co-workers, conducts meetings, organizes processions and demonstrations. When more people assemble it becomes a crowd and crowd behaviour normally may turn into aggression and violence. The aggressive crowd has no logic and whatever the crowd does is right. Damage to properties and life may also take place. Once the morale or order of the individual or crowd is disturbed then it is very difficult to rebuild it. Since psychology is a science that deals with the behaviour of human beings its contribution to various areas of human behaviour may provide solution to many real-world problems. Then what are the areas of psychology that are concerned with the solution of real world problems? The areas such as experimental, social, clinical or counselling, comparative, psychobiology, industrial, human factors, educational, legal and several others are specialized areas in dealing with real world problems.

Since the existing areas do not deal with some of the real world problems adequately some new areas also are developed. For example, the humanistic, community and environmental areas in psychology are recently developed to deal with certain specific real world problems. On observing the growing problems in the environment, psychologists have developed interests in studying the problems and helping to solve some of the problems of the environment. As a result of it new courses in environmental psychology were introduced in colleges and universities at graduate level and also at the research levels and a new field of applied psychology called environmental psychology had emerged.

Man is functioning only in the environment. The environment we speak of is not only the land in which we live. This includes the land, the water, and the space and the unusual environment. The unusual environments are not with normal atmosphere. There may be inadequate stimulation, excessive stimulation, reduced gravity and sensory deprivation. Human behaviour in all these environments may not be the same. Man's performance in unusual environment varies considerably.

When we refer environment, it normally means the home in which we live, family, society, temple or church or mosque, school, college, playground and so on. We are involved in our daily life with the total environment with many features like the buildings, bridges, dams, transports of various types and related communication. These things we can call as built environments. The other one is natural environment with a number of features. Both the environmental features are having impacts upon the daily life of human beings. These impacts may be good and also bad for us. The impact of the total environmental features on human behaviour in various situations become the prime interest for the environmental psychologists.

Several studies have been already made by some of the investigators relating environment. For example, man and the environment in which he works, man and transportation system man and machine system and so on. Kaplan (1972) states that since man is going along aimlessly increasing the population and deteriorating the environment, it is the bounden duty of the psychologists to understand the consequences of these disastrous tendencies. Environmental Psychologists, therefore, are interested in the natural environment as it is influenced by human behaviour and in return the way in which the environment influences human behaviour. But the effects of human behaviour on environment are becoming more and more hazardous and creating a number of problems.

The important problems are air pollution, water pollution, aimless design and construction of buildings, highway constructions, noise pollution, mining, moving heavily and creating noise, throwing garbages on the roads and in living areas, industrial smokes and so forth. The physical and biological scientists were already concerned with certain specific environmental problems, such as, cloud reading by meteorologists, pesticide by wild life and fish management organizations, fresh water production by microbiologists. But a specific field of study, named as environmental science is a very recent origin. The emergence of the environmental science had its origin in the unmerciful attitudes of the western culture towards the natural resources.

Heimstra and McDonald (1973) have stated that the basic philosophy of western culture is to exploit the environmental resources and they hope that some mysterious process will heal the wounds and make pure the rubbish produced by this exploitation. They say what man has done to the environment in the past is also doing in the present and he will be doing the same in future also. This has cause a sense of fear to the people all over the world. Pressure has been put on the rulers of nations and on scientists to study the problem at once and to take remedial measures for this. Hence environmental science and environmental psychology had their dawn on the public pressure and thus environmental problem is a social problem.

Environmental psychologists are of the view that human behaviour is a potent force in designing the physical environment and in reverse human behaviour is very much influenced by the physical environment. Therefore the inter-relationship between the two is perennial and unending process and the relationship can be distinguished. Environment puts certain restrictions upon human behaviour and man cannot act beyond his potentialities in the environment. Any violation of such restriction results causing punishment. For example, a man who does not know swimming should not jump in deep water nor can jump from a mountain top. Man's behaviour is restricted place to place and time to time. What he can do in one place cannot do the same in another place. So also what one can do at one time cannot do the same thing at all the times. Therefore, human behaviour is directed in certain characteristic way by the physical environment.

What Environmental Psychology is?

Therefore in the light of the preceding discussion let us now define, what environmental psychology is. Several definitions have been put forth. But a definition which does not relate human behaviour and environment is incomplete. Therefore any definition of environmental psychology must include a reciprocal relationship between human beings and the environment. Proshansky (1976) has defined environmental psychology taking into account one aspect of the environment. He states that it is the reciprocal relationships between behaviour and the built environment. This definition is correct, but it does not include the non-built environment or natural landscape. The American Psychological Associations' definition is: The effects of the environment on behaviour. This definition is like the behaviourists definition. It does include the effects of human behaviour on the environment. According to Kantowitz (1977) environmental psychology is the study of man in his physical setting. Heimstra and McFarling (1974) define environmental psychology as the discipline that is concerned with the relationships between human behaviour and man's physical environment. Bell, Fisher and Loomis (1978) define environmental psychology as the study of the inter-relationships between behaviour and the built and natural environment. While analysing the subject matter of environmental psychology these definitions seem to have some deficiency. It seems that something is lacking. Therefore a possible definition which could include all the important components and the processes yet to come.

Barker (1968) uses the terms ecological psychology, while others use environmental psychology in their works. According to Barker, ecological psychology is the study of the relationship between living organisms and their environment. It also may mean the set of relationships of a particular organism with its environment. When the study is specifically applied to human beings it is also stated as human ecology, which is the study of the relationships between human groups and their physical environment. Basically there is no difference between these two terms, ecology and environment.

Hence, a definition is attempted here, Environmental Psychology is the study of the effects of built and non-built or physical and natural environment on human behaviour and the consequent human behaviour towards the built and physical and natural environment. The effects of built environment on human beings may be different from the effects of non-built or natural environment. The human behaviour may reciprocate to the effects of the two types of environment in some cases and may be also repulsive in some cases. For example, heavy rains and floods in rivers may cause disastrous consequences to human beings. In such cases man's reaction is repulsive. He tries to control the floods by constructing dams or diverting the floods in some other direction as he does not want it. But in the case of seasonal or monsoon rains he favourably reciprocates it. However, the repulsive reaction also is a type of relationship man has with the environment. The disastrous consequences make him to react in different lines which in due course also may benefit him. Here man perceives the environmental stimulus more than a just stimulus. There may be several components in his perception. He perceives the landscape as a whole as a stimulus and relates it to his past and present experience and also what it is going to be in future. Therefore a definition of environmental psychology should include all the related components in it and a study of environmental psychology should be a unit of several components and there should not be any self contained components. Therefore, environmental psychology perceives the built and the natural environment as a whole and relates the components to human behaviour.

For example, the football matches for the World cup were played in Italy. Teams from all over the world participated in the matches. The whole stadium was packed with people to witness the matches. The witnessing audience were expressing their emotional reaction of thrill when their favoured Team, say team *A*, scored a goal against their opponents Team *B*. When Team *B* scored a goal against Team *A*, the audience who favoured Team *B* express their reaction of thrill still in louder manner. The stadium as a whole is responding to the event of scoring the goal. There may be also individual perception—the star players, the goal-keeper, one who makes fouls, the referees, the reaction of the Team Managers and the coaches. So, there are several environmental perceptual behaviour. Since these matches were broadcasted in television, millions of people all over the world enthusiastically witness the events. They too had expressed the same type of behaviour expressed by the audience in the stadium. There was also a news that some people who were witnessing the matches in the television had broken the television box on seeing their favoured Team was defeated and many literally wept for losing the game. The match is played elsewhere in Italy, the same type of behaviour was aroused among the people who were living millions of miles away. What sort of behaviour it is? We may call it as the social environmental perceptual behaviour. There were pleasant and unpleasant emotional reactions. The psychological reaction to the football matches all over the world is the same either pleasant or unpleasant behaviour pattern.

But the actual environmental behaviour may be different from the behaviour of the television audience behaviour to the football matches. In the actual environment there may be expression of aggression and violence by the affected party. In England once the football fans out of disappointment caused damage to properties and attacked people as their Team was defeated. The environmental stimulus is the football match, but the environmental behaviour of the fans is varied from the fans who were straightaway witnessing the matches, to cause damage to properties on the roads and shops and attacking people who were not concerned with the football match and the defeat. In this way the environmental perceptual behaviour is so wide and includes many components.

Environmental Psychology and Social Psychology

There are controversies between social psychologists and environmental psychologists with regard to their subject matter and the perception of environmental behaviour. Whatever pros and cons were presented by both the scholars, environmental psychology may be considered as one of the complementary areas of social psychology. Woodworth's (1952) formula for interaction may be stated here. The individual deals with the environment which is stated by the formula *W-O-W*, where *W* stands for the world or environment, *O* stands for the organism or the individual. The meaning of this formula is that the world or environment acts on the organism or the individual and the organism or the individual acts back on the world or environment. According to Woodworth this interaction goes on continuously back and forth so that the formula may be extended to an indefinite series of *Ws* and *Os*. This *W-O-W* formula provides answer to a broad question, how does an individual interact with the environment and how does it act on him.

The individual deals with his environment. Here dealing with means that the individual actively involved in give and take relations. It may be also stated that the individual is interacting with this environment.

Whether the individual is dealing with the environment or interacting with the environment depends upon the nature of the environment. Woodworth (1952) states that only in the *effective environment* that the individual can deal with or interact. He further adds that in the effective environment there are many kinds of things, many physical forces and conditions such as gravitational forces, heat, cold, sound, light, darkness, space and time, atmospheric forces like depression, storm and floods. The individual deals with all these conditions and forces and he is in constant interaction with the social environment. Dealing with environment refers to the external activities and is not referring to the individual's inner life of thought and feelings.

How is that the individual is reacting only to the effective environment? The action of the environment is such that he is influenced by it in many different ways. First of all the individual's growth and development mainly depend upon the adequate supplies of food, water, oxygen; heat and cold of environmental temperatures. He developes his skill and talents only in the environment. His attitudes towards other social groups and adjustments depend upon his participation in social situations. Of course, there are many things in the social environment and all of them do not have effect upon the individual as they do not stimulate him for any action. A greenish grass field is a barren environment for a hungry tiger. A small child does not find any interest in the philosophical discourses of the adults in a room. Therefore the effective environment is the one that could stimulate an individual and make him to react in some manner. This depends upon the individual's age, previous experience, his intellectual development, physical and social development, skill and talent. Thus, environmental psychology with all its ecological treatment seem to supplement to the field of social psychology. Since only in the social environment human behaviour can be studied, environmental psychology cannot claim to be completely an independent field of study.

However, environmental psychology has got its own unique characteristics. Some of them are discussed in the preceding section. Environmental psychology also differentiates between theoretical and applied research. The theoretical research mainly concentrates on acquiring knowledge about the subject matter. Studying the relationship between the cause and effect in the environmental situations and formulating theories and applying this knowledge to solve practical problems are the main functions of environmental psychology. But the applied research is intended only to solve practical world problems.

Unlike other areas of psychology, applied research in environmental psychology is conducted only in the actual field and not in the laboratory. Thereby all researches in environmental psychology are intended to solve some practical problems. For example, the effects of pollution on behaviour, changing the public opinion, designing the environment for healthy atmosphere could be studied only in the field.

Secondly, environmental psychology, by its holistic approach synthesizes other disciplines like, perception—perceiving the whole scene, work and landscape, architectural, urban planning, designing and building, pesticide and other chemical areas, geography, sociology and anthropology.

Thirdly, environmental psychologists put more attention on the real world problems. It is this that makes them different from other areas of psychology. There are more diversities in their methodology and they use some eclectic methods with innovative spirits.

2. METHODS OF ENVIRONMENTAL PSYCHOLOGY

Environmental psychologists almost use the same methods as other psychologists are using. The basic method are experimental methods, correlational methods and descriptive methods. But the research in environmental psychology is somewhat different from other areas of psychology. The physical environment is the prime concern in the environmental research. There is no distinction between experimental and control groups or variables in environmental research. For example, the crowd environment is a subject matter for the environmental psychologists. This crowd environment is not the same in all places. It varies in size and nature. Crowding in the street or road, in the home, in the school, in the shopping centre, in the dining hall, in the playground, in the stadium, in the industry, in the political meeting, in the aerodrome, in the bus terminus, all vary in density and behaviour. The room or the landscape size and the environmental stimulation are great concerns for the environmental psychologists and the levels of environmental situation affect the personality types.

In environmental psychology the multimethod research strategies are very often used. They choose the methods, because they must be appropriate to the problems and research. A single method may not be fully answering the questions, the experimenter uses for his research. For example, a study has been conducted by Aiello, Epstein and Karlin (1975) to measure the effects of high density dormitory on four different dimensions such as perceptual, observational, physiological and medically related measures. The longitudinal effects also studied in environmental psychology to see the reactions over time. Since environmental psychology goes beyond the boundary lines of some of the traditional disciplines it has involved the methods from other fields also. Therefore the methods used in environmental psychology are more of interdisciplinary type.

In environmental psychology, data are collected by employing two types of methods. One is obtrusive method and the other is unobtrusive method.

The Obtrusive Method

In this method the respondent knows that data are being collected. This method is easy and less costly. Since, the experimenter pushes his opinion on others (respondents) in an unwelcome way the responses may be affected. The respondents may try to favourably respond to the experimenter. In such cases the data may be incorrect and may not in accordance with the investigator's aim. The self-report procedure is used in this method. This mainly depends upon interview and questionnaire responses. Barker (1968) used this method to develop descriptive accounts of behaviour characteristics in different behaviour settings.

The Unobtrusive Method

The respondent is not aware of the data collection. Therefore there is certain degree of realistic approach. If one knows that he is being watched he may react differently. The means of observation is hided in this method. Bickman (1973) and others sent stamped addressed envelopes to dormitories of high and low densities. It is for studying the helping behaviour as a function of density by this method. They watched how many envelopes were mailed by the residents to the investigators. They found that those who were in greater density were less helpful consistently. They have also found that 58 per cent of the people from high density condition, 79 per cent of the people from medium density condition and 88 per cent from low density condition have mailed the envelopes. This means the lower the density the greater the helping tendency and the greater the density the lower the helping tendency. Cialdini (1977) used this method to predict votes in 1976 Presidential election.

Therefore the objectives of any ecological study should be to test an individual's degree of emotionality associated with the environmental issues.

It should be to test the tendency of a person to state things he/she is willing to do with regard to environmental issues.

It should also test whether a person actually has done and doing with regard to the environmental issues.

The objective should be also to test how much a person has actually known about the ecological issues and the social problems.

3. HUMAN BEHAVIOUR AND ENVIRONMENTAL STIMULATIONS

Psychology has been defined as the science of human behaviour. It studies human behaviour in a social setting or in an environment and compares one person with another and also the behaviour of one group with another group. Human behaviour is determined by several factors. In the study of various aspects of human behaviour and characteristics, several factors were found to be operating in the behaviour of human being and the factors are determining how a man is behaving in a particular situation. Man's sensory experiences, his perceptual processes, his intelligence, motives and emotions, ambitions and aspirations, his interests and aptitudes, likes and dislikes, attitudes and prejudices were studied in detail under various headings. While studying these phenomena psychologists have been using generally the environmental conditions. But environments, now-a-days viewed by psychologists in different ways. They state physical environment, natural environment, social environment, built-in environment or man-made environmental and so on.

The reason for different conception of environment has been that it has been observed that different types of environment is having different types of influence upon human behaviour. Further, man himself is changing the environment in various ways. In the ancient times the changes made by man in the natural environment was not so much realized. Since more changes have taken place from the beginning of this century and the changed environment was also found to be exerting a different type of influence upon human behaviour it has been felt that it is important to make a different type of study in view of the enormous amount of changes that have taken place all over the world. Man makes changes in the physical or social environment and the same environment is making changes in the life and behaviour of human beings.

The so called built-in environment or man-made environment is now-a-days overpowering the physical or natural environment in several ways. For example, the various types of designs and the construction of huge buildings everywhere, the roads, the huge and lengthy bridges, dams across the rivers, the long-break-walls in the seas, the harbours, walls in between countries to indicate boundary lines, the railway lines for thousands of miles at a stretch, the aerodromes, the application of electricity in all walks of life, the new type of agricultural techniques under the name of green revolution, man's migration to moon, under the sea, to the space, artic region all man-made environmental variables. There are many wonderful things like the tunnel railway line under the sea between France and England and man living in space for months were all man-made environments. In all these situations man cannot be as normal as he is on earth, but he has to learn to be in different manner. Man's style of life has to be thoroughly changed in all these man-made environmental conditions. Thus a different field of study in psychology has emerged under the heading of environmental psychology.

There are also other reasons for man to create the man-made environments. Fairweather (1972) states that man is facing very serious crisis in the present century. They are the rapid growth of population, fast degradation of the environment and inter-relationship between different races and nations. According to him, if man is to survive in a livable environment he has to solve all these problems. He must find out ways and means to aid the society and to find out some solutions for all these. It is felt that social change is the problem solving action. There is a great challenge to society. It is to make the changes immediately as required to solve the problem for survival. If man is to survive he has to make relevant changes in his life style, in his interpersonal relationships, in his physical and social environmental conditions.

Man has many things to do in his physical and social environmental conditions first. Otherwise he will have to face serious consequences not in the next generation, but in this generation. If he fails to make such changes needed, he is doing serious harms to his next generation, that is, to his sons and daughters and also to his grand-children. We must understand the conditions that improve our life style and how these conditions are spoiling the environment and more steps must be taken to improve and maintain the quality of life and mental health. The fast deteriorating life style due to the environmental pollutants should be improved by implementing ways and methods to prevent them from further destruction. Environmental psychology tries to investigate the effects of various types of pollutants like the littering environment, the effects of environmental pollution on behaviour, the effects of noise, temperature, heat and cold on behaviour, the effect of air pollution and so on. A number of psychologists, who are aware of the psychological consequences of environmental problems, are investigating them. The environmental problems are multidisciplined problems and therefore many discipline, such as, sociology, geography, planning, architecture, anthropology, economics, politics all must contribute to deal with the environmental problem. Craik (1973) has classified the topics of research, in which he has included environmental assessment as the area of research for psychologists. They must analyse the physical-spatial properties and the use of space, how people perceive the environment from personal and demographic point of view. It includes also making decision of environment regarding the planning of the physical environment, such as, residential area, institutional area, recreational area and so on.

Many investigators have started to examine the psychological consequences of environmental issues. These are organizations, public and private who are already aware of the potential environmental dangers. Various disciplines were asked to take steps to deal with the environmental issues. The psychologists attempt to deal with the environmental hazards resulted in the development of environmental psychology. How psychologists deal with the environmental hazards and what is that psychology has to offer? Psychology has plenty to offer with regard to a particular environmental issue. Particularly in the urban environment the most important matter to be considered is the air pollution. Air pollution in urban areas is taking place in various ways. The important one is the pollution of air, caused by the automobile transports. There are also transports not causing any air pollution. For example, the carts or chariots dragged by horses, bulls, donkeys, camels do not cause any pollution. But the automobile driven by oils, petrol or diesel which produce smoke cause air pollution. Sometimes some automobiles produce enormous amount of smoke for no cause but only to pollute the air. The people who walk on the roads have no other way except to breathe the smoke and spoil their health.

The other large organizations around every city are the industries, factories and workshops which are put into action round the clock producing or manufacturing materials and throwing enormous amount of wastages and smokes which are spoiling the residential areas with all sorts of dirty things and also polluting the air and also causing all sorts of unwanted noises and lights. People are made to live in the midst of wastages, excrements, noises, glaring lights, keeping all the time awake and suffer.

People, generally do not bother about the problems they are facing in the environmental situations till they personally get affected. When they find that many people fall prey to crises, they all of a sudden awake and try to find out remedy for it. Therefore it is the human behaviour that will most likely provide solution to the problems ultimately. But in our country people are ready to endure difficulties and hardships rather than try to find out a solution to the problem immediately. Various disciplines like developmental psychology, social psychology, abnormal psychology, community psychology, and physiological psychology generally help us to understand and explain the injurious and harmful effects of environmental pollution to human beings.

There are also disciplines, mainly industrial psychology, social psychology, the psychology of personality, attitude change, behaviour modification—all suggest ways and means of changing the behaviour of the people with the view of eliminating pollution in the environment. Another problem is environmental psychology that seriously views the designing of buildings or houses. In this problem several things should be considered. It is a residential place where individuals are going to live there for years. Therefore various aspects of the house should be taken into consideration. First of all, the matter of crowding. How many people are going to life in the building? Whether there is any privacy for those who live there. Whether the building or house can provide personal spacing to the individuals. This refers to the space around the individual. How the individual perceives the environment? Whether it is congenial for the individual in temperamental aspects. How the environment is designed? Whether it can fulfil his needs and also designed in such a way that one can live there comfortably without other inconveniences. It also depends upon further development in the environment.

The environmental design may be such that there may be lots of noises and the effects of noises may impair the sensory apparatus and the building or house may be radiating heat temperature or cold temperature which may have unhealthy effect upon the residents. Similarly the air ventilation and natural lighting conditions, the air ventilation should be such that there should be fresh air circulation to the whole house, so that the rooms do not get hot temperature. The natural light may facilitate for not having the artificial light all the twenty-four hours. Also the glaring of the artificial lights can be avoided. Therefore, the design of a house or building becomes very important. The house or the housing unit or the flat should provide all the comforts to the people whc occupy and live there. The residents of the house should have the joy of having social relations easily. A harmful social relations may be also caused to the occupants of the housing units. Therefore it is also important to see whether the occupants of the house or housing units are mainly concerned with the physical quality of the designed environment or the social quality of the other occupants of the housing units. If the neighbours are not friendly the occupants' social relationships would be strain which may even lead to quarrel, aggression and enmity. Therefore in the present day modern flat system it is better that like minded people occupy the housing units. Thus in such designed environmental situations there are possibilities that the environmental factors emit behaviour of the occupants and the behaviour of the people may change on the basis of the influence the environmental factors upon the people.

In this way environmental psychology is becoming a practical field of psychology and psychologists collect enormous amount of information both theoretically and practically. The study of the effects of environment upon human behaviour is not a recent in origin. The scientific study of psychology had its start in the end of nineteenth century when psychologists started to examine the human perception and sensation. All the psycho-physicists studied the influence of environmental stimuli like the light, sound, pressure upon the senses of human beings. Mainly they concentrated upon the sensory experiences exerted by the environmental stimuli. But when the behaviouristic school was started in the United States by Watson (1878-1948) in 1916 the study of the effects of environmental factors upon behaviour has received greater importance in United States and all over the world through his work, 'behaviourism' (1925). It has been viewed that the influence of environmental factors are mainly responsible for the development of personality, intelligence, motivation, emotion and so on. Subsequently around 1940's the industrial psychologists also started putting emphasis upon environmental factors upon human behaviour. In the field of human engineering the effects of environmental conditions like heat, light, sound, space upon human performance in the industrial work were studied with the view of making improvement in the performance and thereby increasing the industrial output.

Many researchers at the beginning of third quarter of this century paid more importance on various environmental factors which they believed having influence upon the performance of the workers. It is strongly believed that the built environments are having greater influence upon the behaviour of human beings in the respective setting. A collection of research works has been brought out by Proshansky, Ittalson, and Rivlin (1970) under the heading of 'Environmental Psychology: Man and his Physical Setting' is worth mentioning in this context. Proshansky states that if environmental psychology is to be called as 'science' there are several distinctive features for this. The features he described as a study of 'man-ordered' environment. Proshansky has made a critical remark that though environmental psychology is considered as a means by which the impact of the physical environment on people is studied it has ignored the person variable in urban planning and the architectural design. He states that the two broad classes of environmental psychology are (1) research on environmental quality and (2) the impact of architectural and spatial arrangements on people. But somehow Proshansky has missed the study made by Summer (1969). What Proshansky has stated as ignored, has been included in Summer's study. Summer has explained what is meant by the design of the built environment. He includes in the design of built environment, the furniture arrangements, the size of the rooms, the size of the windows and so on. According to him all these factors influence the behaviour of human beings in that setting.

The architectural design and the spatial arrangements are considered as ideal physical environments to obtain the required behavioural goals for planners and controller of organizations. Rappaport (1977) states that many of the environmental psychologists are working at descriptive level and not on direct action. Wholwill and Carson (1972) state that such descriptive research included in the formation of laws and regulations regarding the land usage and access of land, use of space and maintaining of environmental qualities. The action aspects of the empirical research include planning and redesign of buildings for residential, educational, recreational and mental health service. What is considered to be important for people should be given importance in the planning. For instance in a particular setting if social interaction is an important factor, planning and designing should be made in such a way that the buildings and rooms arrangements should be constructed to increase the social interactions. This is how the man-made environment should be planned.

On the basis of the problems discussed above several definitions of environmental psychology were formulated. But the important component in every definition must be environmental factors and human behaviour. There is always a reciprocal interaction between these two variables, environmental factors either built environment or natural physical environment and human behaviour. In the natural physical environment man is making some changes, whether the changes are made for his advantages or disadvantages, the changes have influenced upon human behaviour in return. Therefore environmental psychology may be defined as the science that studies the effects of built and non-built or natural physical environment. But the effects of built environmental factors on human beings may be different from the effects of non-built natural environmental factors.

Human behaviour towards the effects of natural environment may be reciprocative sometimes and repulsive sometimes. It is also possible to have the same type reactions with the effects of built environment if the building is not planned according to the needs of the occupants. A type of reaction to the effects of natural environment however repulsive, it is also a kind of reaction. For instance, the heavy rains may have both types of reactions, repulsive when there was destruction by the floods and reception when there was no water.

The scientists are of the view that events in the world are caused by other events in the world. It is possible to discover the causes of the events by scientific enquiries and the effects can be predicted. The same principle the environmental psychologists also can adopt in their studies. The basic assumption of environmental psychologists is that behaviour is determined by the environmental events and genetically generated events. The environmental events determine the behaviour of the people in that setting. For example, in a thickly populated urban areas the criminal behaviour of the people increases. The population density is the environmental factor and the crime rates in that area refer to human behaviour. If population density is very thin then the crime rates also may be low. Thus there is a positive correlation between the two variables. Environmental factors influence the behaviour of the people who live in that particular area. Whether the area is a natural environment or man-made or built environment or both combined, its effects are determining the type of behaviour needed to the situation. In return man also makes all sorts of changes and modifications in the natural environment. Constructing dam in rivers and directing the water in a different directions through canals and storing in big reservoirs for future use—all changing and modifying the environment.

Having done all such changes and modifications, human life or behaviour cannot be expected to be the same as it was previously. The new situation may exert a different type of force on human life and hence his behaviour changes. The relationship between environment and human behaviour in this way, is becoming reciprocal or mutual. Having studied this aspect-environment-behaviour relationship psychologists tried to provide some models and good theories about the relationship of environment and human behaviour. The Kaplan (1974) theories are restricted to environmental perception and therefore theories that could cover the whole area are inevitable.

The theories that can be applicable to the physical environment are discussed under various headings. Under (1) *physical environmental variables*, like the environmental pollution, noise, temperature (heat and cold), air pollution and wind are discussed. Under (2) *personal space* interpersonal contact, mainly the personal space, cultural and personal factors in interpersonal relationships, and territorial behaviour are dealt with. Thirdly, under (3) *Population density and the problem of overcrowding*, the effects of overcrowding, the behavioural consequences of high population density in humans are discussed. We are, therefore, discussing here mainly the effects of physical environmental components, noise, temperature and air pollution.

Stress

One approach of the study of environmental psychology is to study the various elements of environment and their effects on behaviour. Some of the important elements are noise, heat, cold and wind. These elements are causing stress and so they are called stressors. The stressors also are a kind of stimuli. But such stimuli are called aversive stimuli. Stress may be physical and mental. The stress is a kind of reaction to the aversive stimuli. Stress is a factor interfering in the middle of the work or interfere when some function is going on. It is a physiological component and also psychological component. Stress generally is a force or a system of forces producing deformation or strain physically. It also refers to mental strain or emotional strain. Therefore the reaction to the aversive elements may be stress and this stress may be physiological, behavioural and emotional. It is sometimes limited to some environmental situation. Thus stress is a reaction to the stimulus.

Any stumulus that causes the stress or strain may be called stressor. These stressors are the environmental components.

Several authors have studied this aspect. Seyle (1956) states that the reaction to aversive stimulus or stress causing stimulus is partly alarming. This takes place in the organism automatically. In this state there are also bodily changes like increased heart beat and pulse rate, secretion of more adrenaline and so on. There is also tendency to cope with the stressful situations and resistance to the stress. This also takes place automatically. The stressful situation is met by the organism by employing various skills. The stress caused by heat which met with sweating and if the extreme cold is the stressor the body shivers and the person puts on protective clothings. Selye (1956) states that all the stress causing stimuli are not aversive. The stress has also several cognitive components. Since all stressful stimuli are not aversive they do not produce automatic or alarming reactions and also builds up resistance to it. What is stressful to one person in a situation is not stressful to another person in the same situation. People living in tropical climatic conditions do not ordinarily develop aversive reaction to heat or feel sultry. But a person new to the place, probably for a person who came from a cold climatic conditions generally feels very hot or sultry for the stressor of heat. Lazarus (1966) states that the cognitive judgment of the individual such as knowledge about the stressor, past experience and motivation may have control over the stimulus. The more cognitive estimate a person has over the stressor, the more control he may have over the stressor or the individual can avoid the effects of the stressor. In the case of heat, cold, noise and other stress causing effects of the stressors can be controlled.

A stimulus may be a stressor and if the individual knows much about the effects of the stressor even if it is having threatening effect his cognitive judgment may play the role of rescuing the individual from the severity of the consequences. As stated by Selye, the alarming reaction and the automatic coping up mechanism as a resistance may cope up with the situation. The strategy may be anything like, accepting or finding out a remedy, escaping, facing the situation either by physical or verbal attack and a kind of settlement. Lazarus (1966) states that the cognitive coping process can be anything stated above and the coping process may be followed by a number of emotions like anger, fear, disgust, aggression and so on. But when all coping up strategies are failed, the individual get exhausted in dealing with stressor. But this is not the case always with stress situations. Something different also occurs. The aversive stimulus does not produce always the aversive reaction to the stress. The individual gradually learns to adapt to the stressful situation as the stress reaction is not becoming alarming and the coping up mechanism becomes weaker. Therefore a process called adaptation to the stress takes place. Another psychological process is that cognitive estimation of the stressor is not threatening. Hummel *et al.* (1973) have studied this aspect and found that people who visited environmentally polluted city had the fear in the beginning, the breathing difficulties, and expressed their anxiety about their health as they were exposing to the pollutions of the atmosphere. But after a few days they found that they were alive and not dead. This type of adaptation is becoming common occurrences in certain situations.

Many of man's life events cause fear or anxiety as they are full of risks and stresses. In the beginning the individual may find it difficult to deal with the stressors. But in due course he learns to handle the stress better and also feels confident of facing other stressors in the same manner. Thus it becomes beneficial for the individual to handle the stressor. It is not always easy for the individual to handle the stressor. It is both costly and beneficial. However, the stressors are simple or complex the individual has to spend more energy in dealing with them than the energy he spends in non-stressful situations. For example, in a mildly polluted environmental situation the individual may find it difficult to breathe freely. Therefore he will have to take precautious measures to have his breathing easy. If the environmental situation is filled with more humidity, persons who have asthmatic complaints or who have high eosinophilia counts in blood usually driven to hard breathing. To deal with such situations they will have to carry the medicine with them. Environmental stressors are not always causing harmful effects. Just like distractions in attention sometimes facilitate the performance, environmental stressors also are sometimes improving the performance. The reason is that the stress is associated with arousal if the stress is of mild form.

However an individual has learned to cope up with the stressor or learned to adapt to stressful situations, all his coping and adapting psychological mechanisms are only to certain extent. Sometimes the total stresses may exceed the capacity of the individual to cope with the stresses and they may also be of very severe type. In such situations some sort of breakdown, mental or physical may occur. The breakdown may result in psychosomatic illnesses, activity decrement, a sort of fatigue or weakness to have resistance to face other stresses. If this situation continued for longer period the individual may be put into an extremely stressful state. Another costly risk the individual faces is the overload of cognitive process. The load is beyond the capacity of the individual. Since the cognitive process is impaired due to overload the individual does not recognize other stresses. He ignores even important stimuli like other human beings, stimuli that facilitate his performance, even his health and safety. Thus the stress helps us to understand some of the consequences the individual faces in an environment and how he can cope up with them or adapt himself to the environmental hazards.

Arousal

In the preceding section while discussing about stresses we have also referred to a process called arousal. When stress is associated with arousal there is increased performance. When there is increased arousal there is increase in physiological activities. The human organism is aroused physiologically which results in increased heart beat, pulse rate, blood pressure, increased respiration rate, and also internal changes like increased secretion of hormones by the adrenal glands. The motor activity also is increased. It also accelerates the brain activity. Arousal is functioning as a mediator in several types of behaviour. Though arousal is associated with stress as one of the effects of stressor it can also function independently without any association with stress.

The human organism can be aroused not only while facing crisis, but also in pleasant situations mostly. A man may be aroused and excited on seeing an interesting event. Therefore unlike stress there is no threatening stimulus in arousal. The stimuli may be pleasant or attractive or the individual may like them. For example, an exciting sports events, the tennis match played by some internationally repute players, the world football matches, a thrilling ride, an amusement park, winning a prize of ten lakhs in a lottery, an attractive person of an opposite sex—all may arouse the individual for action. In all these, physiological changes, stated above, may take place. Arousal may have different levels of degree. It may be low or medium or high. Mehrabian and Russell (1974) state that there are three dimensions through which any environment can be described. According to them they are arousal, pleasure and dominance. In any environmental situations human behaviour can be explained and described with these three dimensions. These three dimensions vary in degrees depending upon the situation. What type of effect these may have on behaviour. For example, arousal may be at a higher level. When we experience, the effect of the environmental variable is severe, for example, the heat or cold, arousal reaction is very quick and at higher level. But most of the effects of stressors are moderate. In an environment the variable such as noise, glaring light and density of the people also may have the arousal effect.

The arousal function is a physiological response. It is felt by the individual and it is subjective and therefore it is very difficult to assess or estimate the level. Measuring the arousal level is one of the most difficult areas of research. It has to be inferred from certain evidences or will have to depend upon the concerned persons reports. Researchers in this area were able to observe certain responses and recorded many of them. The most clearly observed reactions are increased heart beat, pulse rate, breathing rate or respiration rate, increased blood-pressure, galvanic skin response, motor activity level, muscle tension, skin temperature, sweating, shivering and so on. The arousal levels also determine the activity or performance levels. At the beginning of the arousal, performance is slow, but increases when the arousal level reached the middle point or the intermediate level, the performance also increases to the maximum level. Then the arousal level may increase or fall, but the performance level also decreases. At the lower arousal level the environmental stress also is at a lower level and therefore activity level is at low. When the arousal level is at the other extreme the stress is very severe and it may reach even the breaking point. Therefore the activity level also is lowered. Berlyne (1960, 1972) in his studies has observed this phenomenon. Human beings always prefer the intermediate level of arousal or stimulation and they consider that either too high or low is wearisome or not liked.

Arousal may be increased due to various environmental stimulations which may improve the activity level or sometimes lower the activity level. This depends upon the level of responses of the person to the stimulations. The individual may have the least favourable condition or optimum level for a specific work. Broadbent (1971), Hebb (1972), Kahneman (1973) have studied this aspect. According to them low arousal is not favourable to maximum performance and also the extremely high arousal put too much stress on the person and he fails to pay a better attention on the work. Further, increased arousal may also cause aggression. Green and O'Neal (1969) have observed that if arousal is increased by noise it may also increase aggression. Therefore heightened arousal is the cause of aggression which may reduce the efficiency in work. Cervone (1977) and Lacay (1967) state that measurement of arousal is not uniform. One measurement indicates increased arousal in a situation. Other measurement shows decreased arousal. In such situations we do not know which measurement is to be taken as correct for the prediction of behaviour. But, however, arousal is providing some information and can be included for the study behaviour in the environment.

Excessive Environmental Stimulation

Environmental factors are supposed to be the stimulating variables of human behaviour. Except in cases where the individual himself has designed certain variables and work through them, in all other behaviour patterns the environment in various forms stimulate the organism for activity. Stimulations may be simple or complex, weak or strong puts pressure upon the organism. The organism behaves according to the level of pressure exerted by the environmental factors. The excessive stimulation exerted by the environment is also called environmental overload. Man has limited capacity to receive and process information. Anything beyond his capacity is a overload information. Cohen (1977) and Milgram (1970) state that the individual while responding to the environmental overload or excess information, the coping up strategy is unable to meet all the stimulus inputs.

The primary coping up strategy rejects or disregards the excess environmental load. Thus there is both positive and negative effects on the behaviour of the organism. Cohen (1977), had made a detailed analysis of the aspects of the environmental overload in behaviour. According to him there are four basic things to be taken for granted. The human organism has only a limited capacity to deal with the inputs and can put forth only a limited effort in processing the inputs on one occasion. Secondly, if the environmental inputs exceeded the capacity the organism disregards those excess estimate inputs. Thirdly, if there is greater and uncontrollable input there is greater adaptation and greater attention paid. Fourthly, after prolonged demands more amount of attention is made available to the organism temporarily and the availability is not constant.

Thus the excessive environmental load like the stress and arousal can predict many of the behavioural effects on the organism. The excessive stimulation may facilitate the performance and also reduce the performance in certain situations. Therefore from various studies we can understand that many environmental behaviour relationships are leading to undesirable behaviour and emotional consequences. This is because of the too much of environmental stimulation from too many sources.

Under-environmental Stimulation and Behaviour

All the environmental stimulations are not strong and strong enough to arouse behaviour in an organism. It has been observed that many of the environmental behaviour problems were due to too small or weak stimulation. Zubek (1969) has observed in his studies that individuals deprived of all their sensory stimulations were found to be suffering from severe anxiety and other psychological consequences. Schultz (1965) states that there are evidences that understimulation on the motivational development of young people had very harmful effects. In order to draw the individual's perception and acute excitement sometimes environmental stimulations are made more complex.

Investigators are of the view that in rural areas either there is no stimulation or little stimulation for behaviour. But at the same time in urban areas, particularly big cities there are constant over stimulations in social environments. Parr (1960) states that the mountains, forests and high seas have endless types of visual stimulations. No one can attend to all of them in a limited time. Similarly in the city streets there are equally sometimes more endless types of visual stimulations. The building constructions, in particular, the huge structure resembling same types and different types, the giant skyscrapers in rows in the city streets, the beautiful architectural bridges and overbridges across the roads and rivers all may have very little stimulation. All these do little stimulation for behaviour. In urban setting when individuals are not sufficiently stimulated for behaviour, persons succumb to delinquency and vandalism and many other such activities. The under-stimulations cause many problems. Wohlwill (1966) suggests a number of dimensions of stimulations such as intensity, novelty, complexity, temporal changes, surprisingness and incongruity. It is because of this under-stimulation many people from big cities go to natural environments.

Environmental Restriction and Behaviour

Environmental factors do not always act in a favourable manner for human behaviour. As there are excessive and under-environmental stimulations, which were causing harmful reactions in human behaviour, environmental forces themselves put restrictions and compulsions on behaviour. Such environmental forces all of us might have experienced in our life. For example, if you happened to swim in the river there might have been difficult places in the river and you might not have perceived it which might have taken you to a dangerous place. You are not having any control over the situation, as a result of it, you are facing very bad risk. Sometimes you might have been caught in a storm or in a whirl or in a desert like places where there are sands and there may be sand storms. The summer hot sun, in some places, is likely to cause sun strokes or extreme heat which no one can withstand. There is no chance of having any control over such environmental situations, similarly the lightning and thunder and heavy rains and floods. It is also not possible to predict what is going to take place in few minutes in the environment. We get news from various countries that the rain floods wash away towns and cities over which no control can be brought in. These are all loss of perception of the situations. When man is not having any control over the situations, naturally human behaviour is restricted and constrained. In many of the work situations in the fields and forests, ports and harbours behaviour is restricted due to loss of control. Seligman (1975) calls this as learned helplessness. All our repeated efforts have become useless to control the situation. After this stage we stop taking efforts to control the situation.

Conclusion

In conclusion, we can state what environment means according to environmental psychologists. This is not the environment which the experimental psychologists spoke to study the responses of an organism in the laboratory situation, nor what social psychologists spoke of social environment. The environmental factors or forces what the environmental psychologists speak are referring to the stimulating situations for human behaviour, whether it is in a rural or urban or big city situation, or the landscap situation, or man-made situation or natural physical situation, man is stimulated or forced for some type of behaviour. The psychological processes such as stress, arousal, over- stimulation, understimulation, restraint or constraint and other process are interpreted in different manner in human behaviour. Whether the organism is over stimulated or under stimulated or constraint, some kind of behaviour is there. It may result in the well-being of the organism or harmful to the organism, situational consequences cannot be avoided. Environmental psychology interested in all these aspects including the design of modern architecture and constructions of buildings to suit to the needs of the people or groups of people who are interested in social interactions. Social interaction should be facilitated by the man-made or built in environmental factors.

But modern architects, engineers and builders do not take into consideration the human factors. What type of architectural designs would provide free air, natural light and privacy to the residents of the building should be considered as the main factors. The overcrowding in a building may spoil the peaceful life as it would often cause friction among the residents. Therefore there should not be any chance for overcrowding in the building.

4. ENVIRONMENTAL EFFECTS ON BEHAVIOUR

Man is constantly put into interaction with his environment whether he is interacting positively or negatively. Man has to live in a physical or natural environment to find out his requirements. The primitive man had to live in a physical environment which was also natural environment. There were several natural forces with which he had to deal with to protect himself and his men. Till he learned to build up an abode or a living place he had been using the caves in hills and mountains as his abode. He has to find some shelter to protect him from the sun and the rains. He was living on fruits, roots, nuts and on some leaves. He used leaves and skin of the trees to cloth himself. In these physical and natural environment the primitive man learned to live and his behaviour was greatly influenced by these environmental conditions. Since natural calamities were often disturbing him with storm, heavy rains, thunder and lightning and floods, he slowly learned to adapt himself to all these disaster consequences. His behaviour was often determined by these natural forces and physical environmental conditions. He was reacting to each and every change that was taking place in the physical environment.

When his group has grown larger and larger, he found a social and cultural climatic condition and his social life was promoting him to make improvements in all his ways of life. At every stage he was influenced by his environmental factors and later on by his group members. Thus he found a social environment in which he has to react to the functions of his group. Slowly the ancient man has learned to build up houses, dams and bridges in the physical environment. Thus slowly the man-made environment came into existence. Whatever type of environment in which he lived he learned to adapt himself to the situation. In this way man has been experiencing the environmental stimulations in various ways. Some of the stimulations were simple and tolerable, but some of the environmental stimulations were too difficult and complex to deal with. They were causing harmful effects on his behaviour. Somehow man has to react to the environmental stimulations. There were both over stimulations and under-stimulations. Both were not favourable to his life situations. A medium environmental stimulation alone was agreeable for human behaviour. But man cannot alter the physical stimulations that were not useful to him. In certain situations he can do it to suit to his requirements.

The ancient man had his own environmental problems, but he adapted himself to the situation where he cannot do any change on natural environmental stimulations. Wohlwill (1974) used the 'adaptation level theory of sensation and perception' of Helson (1964) to discuss the environmental stimulation. Man's adaptation to the situation is based upon his sensation and perception. How we perceive a situation and what sort or sensation we develop? Though we are all human beings and sometimes become one among many in a crowd, Wohlwill states that on certain occasions human beings dislike crowds.

The crowd is collected in a physical environment. We like crowds on certain occasions, but not on all occasions. The likes and dislikes depends upon the situation. For example, when we go for some dinner or to attend a function, or shopping or to a picture house, if we find too much of crowds in the dinner hall, in the function hall, in the street, in the shopping centres it makes us disinterested to attend or to participate or to make shopping, and sometimes we even withdraw from such places without attending to anything. The Environmental crowds sometimes become very dense and people may find very difficult to move about or go forward pushing everybody. In such cases the crowd may suddenly get into stampede which may result even in death of some people. This type of situations are quite often occurring in many places now-a-days.

What is taking place in environmental situation, is the interaction between the physical world and human behaviours. Whether it was in ancient society or it is in modern society, among the urban or rural people, interaction between physical world and the behaviour of the people has been taking place on psychological world. If the physical environment is congenial then man does not find any problem, but if it is causing harmful situations, either man must learn to adapt himself to such situations or if possible he can modify the physical situation to his needs. This has been taking place in the life of man right from the ancient period. Adapting to the physical environmental world sometimes is easy, but many times it is difficult. Environmental psychologists who studied these aspects have formulated various theories of adaptation. These, we have discussed earlier.

Adaptive Behaviour to Environmental Stimulations

The environmental factors may have three characteristics. They may overstimulate, or understimulate, or may be an optimum level of stimulation. We are experiencing all these three stimulations in the physical environmental world. If we find the environmental stimulation within the range of optimum level we are reacting to it normally and we are not stressed nor disturbed by it. Our behaviour is not maladjusted. The organism maintains the homeostasis. We are responding to the call and we are quite familiar with such stimulations, as they are not stressful.

Sometimes the environmental stimulations may be too high or they may be outside of our optimum range. The stimulations may be more unfamiliar and undesirable in the environmental situations. They may be causing stress, resulting in arousal. Such stimulations are overloaded. To such environmental stimulations the reaction of humans is either ignoring them or learning to find out varieties of coping methods. When the coping methods to such situations are successful humans are free from the disturbing situations. They are free from the stress, or arousal or overloading conditions. The successful coping methods involve adjustment to the situations. Either man adjusts himself to the situation or he makes changes in stimulating environmental conditions, so that they become optimum level and not causing any stress. If either one is not possible, man withdraws himself from the situation to avoid the extreme stress. Withdrawing behaviour, according to Bell *et al.* (1978) is considered as socially undesirable behaviour. But from mental health point of view, though social withdrawal form of behaviour can get over the stress and overload, still it is viewed as undesirable form of behaviour. This withdrawal form of behaviour is also stated as maladaptive behaviour.

However, though the withdrawal behaviour is stated as maladaptive and undesirable form of behaviour, since it helps individual in the environmental situation to get over the stressful situation, it is viewed as successful coping method of behaviour. It reduces the tension, stress, overload and arousal. Since maladaptive behaviour like social withdrawal is considered as successful coping behaviour, modern mental health scientists are of the view that social withdrawal and psychotic and neurotic symptoms are also not abnormal behaviour patterns. They state that this type of social withdrawal is a normal behaviour pattern in an abnormal environmental situation. Therefore, it is concluded that though withdrawal behaviour is a maladaptive and undesirable form of behaviour it is considered as a part of adaptive behaviour. Any environmental stimulus that is having the probability of making the particular behaviour pattern to reoccur or to repeat is called reward or reinforcement. There are environmental stimuli that are having several types of rewards. These rewards may be in cash or in the form of fetching money, chances for improving personal qualities, recognition of one's skills and talents by the authorities, thrills and satisfaction.

Environmental stimulations that are very feeble may fail to arouse response in an organism. It may be very valuable stimulus but the organism ignores it as it is a very weak stimulus. We are also coming across in our life situations weak environmental stimuli that fail to arouse reaction in concerned persons. The same stimulus if repeated several times may draw the attention of the organisms or several weak stimuli together may have sufficient strength to arouse response in organisms. Environmental under-stimulations are not causing any harmful effect. There is no stress or overload. But the failure to respond to such stimulations sometimes may cause some kind of loss for us.

Human behaviour is much influenced by environmental situations, but it depends upon the strength of stimulations of the environmental factors. But the optimum or the desirable level of stimulation alone can establish environment-behaviour relationship. All stimulations are coming from the environmental situation and they attack our sensory apparatuses. If sensory apparatuses are not responding to the environmental stimulations, they have no value. Any environmental stimulus is having a value, if only our sensory apparatus is aroused to respond to it. But too high and too low sensory stimulations are harmful to the organism and also cannot arouse response and behaviour is an organism. Any environmental stimulus may be responded either by seeing, or hearing, or smelling or touching. Therefore all environmental stimulations are sensory stimulations. Only when we respond to a stimulus, the behaviour is aroused. Humans function successfully in an environment which is congenial and pleasant. Environments are not always congenial and pleasant to humans. The physical natural environment as it is, is not harmful. It is pleasant and healthy. So long as the natural or the physical environment is pleasant and healthy man is also happy to live in. But when the physical or natural environment loses its pleasantness and healthy atmosphere man also loses his happiness and health and becomes sick. What is the condition that spoils man's health and makes him sick? The condition may be stated as the environmental pollution.

Environmental Pollutants

What is environmental pollution? Pollution means making unclean and impure. Environmental pollution means making the environment unclean and impure. It is contaminating the environment with poisonous or harmful substances. The physical environment in which we are living normally is clean and pure. But man in various way destroys the purity of the environment and makes it dirty and unclean. In big and small cities we see everywhere collection of huge garbage dumpings. People throw all sorts of rubbish things on the roads or on the streets. There is also lots of wastages coming out from small places like the kitchens to big places like industries. The kitchen rubbish, the road and the street garbage are all collected by the Municipalities and Corporations. The Municipalities and Corporations do not remove the garbage and other rubbish things to far off places and recycle them. But they dump at some place in the city and on some road side. This is spread out by the cattle and pigs in search of food. People who are living in that area, however raise objections and make complaints, the concerned authorities do not take any action immediately. In such places mosquitoes are easily bred and cause malaria and other infectious diseases.

In certain town and city areas there are no storm water drainage and sewage systems. As result of it, the waste water in the streets is not drained down. Since there is no underground sewage system people use open latrines or use open places for their toilet purposes. All these things pollute the area and disease spreading insects breed very easily. People in these conditions are subjected to all sorts of infectious and epidemic diseases. The public health department escape from the responsibility by saying that they do not have sufficient workers to clear the garbage and other rubbish things. Municipalities and Corporations say that they do not have sufficient funds to employ men for public health services. Roads and streets are not kept clean. People have no other way except to live in the midst of impure and unclean areas, succumbing to all sorts of diseases. Their health is getting spoiled by breathing the polluted air. There is no chance for fresh air in these situations. Since the environment is fully polluted by all sorts of wastages and people also do not realize the consequences of throwing the rubbish things in and around their living areas, and as there is no chance for improvement in their sanitary conditions, their drinking water also get contaminated. Therefore people are infected with germs and virus and suffer from diseases like malaria, influenza, typhoid, cholera, plague and die. They die without knowing the real cause of their disease. The public health department run for recure only where large number of people die of infectious and epidemic diseases and also they do not remove the causes of such diseases and also do not provide protections to people permanently.

Industries, everywhere are growing very fast, and these industries are throwing various types of wastages in the environmental areas. In certain areas the major industries are cotton and textile mills. The other industries are the sugar mills, paper mills, chemical industries, fertilizers, leather industries, cement industries, rice mills and so on. All these industries throw some used waste products into the environments and some industries drainage the wastage into the rivers and contaminate the fresh water. The type of industries that pollute the environment most are the sugar industries. The molasses, a thick, dark syrup produced during the refining of sugar, stored in big area near the sugar mill. This causes strong stench in the surrounding areas and in the nearby lands the vegetation get spoiled. There is no means of making use of the molasses for some other purposes and remove it from the area at once without polluting the vegetative lands.

The same type of pollution is also caused by the paper mills. The wastage is channellized into the rivers and the river water is polluted. The pollution caused by the leather industries was such that it has much affected the vegetation of the nearby lands and farmers raised alarming voices and the Supreme Court has ordered to close about 120 leather industries in North Arcot district in Tamil Nadu. The cement industries throw dusts to the nearby areas and pollute the environment. People who are living in the surrounding areas have to breathe the dust-mixed air which may cause several health hazards. These industries do not make any provision for the wastages produced by the industries. The wastages must be protected in such a way that they do not pollute the environmental areas and also affect the health of the people. The chemical industries release toxic wastages which affect the health of the people and also pollute the surrounding areas and leave undesirable effect on the environment.

Baron and Bell (1975) state that new techniques to deal with the toxic wastages and making them harmless and ineffective are certainly essential at this juncture. This is possible if only the people, the Government and the industry decide that it is essential even though it appears costly. If the environment is to be kept clean and pure, techniques should be developed to recycle the wastages and convert them into some useful material. For example the garbage and the waste products can be converted into some kind of fertilizer instead of allowing them for polluting the environment. The industrial ashes, the coal dusts in the coal mine areas and in the railway station areas were thrown indiscriminately. The air of which spoil the health of the people of those who are not only working there, but also those who are living close to these areas.

Therefore it is essential that people must know the effects caused by the environmental pollutions. People must know what are the environmental pollutants. People throw everything that is unwanted for them. It may be pit of papers, cigarette and beedi pieces, empty tin boxes, poisonous metals, unwanted medicines, chemical substances, iron, lead, plastic bags, burning refuse, burned cloths, old dirty cloths, pillows, pillow and bed cottons, pouring washed dirty water on the road, throwing perished vegetables, animal bones and spoiled mutton pieces, birds' feathers, damaged vehicle parts, damaged vessels on the roads or streets—all cause environmental pollution.

People must be educated as to how environmental pollution is caused and how to avoid it. It is true that generally people would have developed indifferent attitude toward the environmental pollution. But if they know the real consequences of the environmental pollution, they accept the idea and avoid it. People who are living in urban areas feel that urban life is becoming very difficult due to continued exposure to tension ridden physical environment. For example, the traffic hazards, unclean water supply, unclean roads and streets with full of garbage and all sorts of wastages and dust filled air, all pollute the environment. The air is also mixed with the smoke of the transports which are throwing dark smoke indiscriminately on the roads. The pollution of physical environment often arouses our emotion of anger in numerous ways when we see that the river water is polluted and contaminated.

The urban areas are full of industrial dusts which pollute the air in the surrounding areas and people breathe the dust mixed air and succumb to lung diseases like asthma, tuberculosis and so on. The natural environment is clean and pure, but man encroaches into it and construct buildings, industries and various other constructions and spoil the natural beauties. These man-made environments often throw the wastages and pollutants like mercury, lead, poisoning the food and water by chemical substances which cause damage to kidney and brain, and also cause anemia, mental retardation and death. Therefore the Government set up a separate department called Environment Pollution Control Board to deal with all these aspects. In every state in India there are qualified personnel in the Department of Environment Pollution Control Board. This is only an advisory board, has no power to take action against the persons who pollute the environment.

Since environmental pollutions cause physically painful experiences to humans and affect their feeling aspects and also make life very sorrowful and unhappy it is important that everyone should know something about the causes and the consequences of the same.

The Environment Pollution Control Boards have been set up at various Metropolitan cities. At present they are creating a sense of awakening in the minds of the people all over India. The harmful consequences are illustrated in various ways. It is shown in television and also propagated in newspapers with the view of developing clean habits among the people. But what needed immediately is that the Public Health Department of the Corporations and Municipalities should keep the streets and the roads clean and unpolluted.

5. THE EFFECTS OF NOISE ON BEHAVIOUR

The physical environmental variables that are having effect on human behaviour are mainly the built-in environmental variables such as noise, temperature, and air pollution. The built-in environmental effects on behaviour were discussed in the previous section. We shall discuss here something about noise relating to the behaviour. Noise, sound, voice, may refer to the same thing. But we can make certain distinction among these three phenomena. Generally noise is a sound that is louder and disturbing. It is also loud shouting. Sound refers to a periodic disturbance. The concept of sound has several meanings other than noise, or a hearing stimulus. Sound is produced by a vibrating object. Sound is a sensation produced by anything that can be heard. Sound has volume or quality. Some information can be announced by sound. In all communication processes sound is involved. Voice refers to the sound made by the vibration of the vocal cords. Generally voice is the sound produced by human beings. All other sounds are not voice. The sounds produced by animals and birds are having different names. For example, the sound produced by a lion is called roaring. The lion is roaring, the dog is barking, the crow is crowing and so on. Therefore, voice is produced by human being.

But when we refer to noise it is an unwanted sound. This is simplest possible definition for noise. The machine is making some noise. When we do not like the advice of somebody we may say that he is making some noise, which means we do not like it. People who live by the side of railway station cannot avoid the sounds produced by the outgoing and incoming trains. But after some days or months they do not hear the sounds as disturbing as they become accustomed to them. A new comer to the house may hear the sounds but not the people who live there. So also people who live near the Aerodromes ignore the noises as they are used to it. These noises and sounds are man-made products of culture and technological developments. These noises and sounds do not occur in the natural environment.

We do not reject noises always unless they are extremely stimulating type. Extreme noises impair our sensory apparatus, the ear. Music whether it is vocal or instrumental is evolved only from sound. If it is within intermediate level of stimulation we enjoy it. But if it is transmitted through loud speakers very loudly we do not enjoy it. But there are people who want such louder transmission. Therefore it becomes subjective. What is music for one person is noise for another. It becomes noise and we do not want it. Therefore noises and sounds can be tolerated only to certain level of stimulation. Noise is a physical component and also a psychological component. The physical component of sound is perceived and evaluated by our ear and our brain structures, whether it is wanted or unwanted.

Unusual Environmental Stimulations

There may be also some unusual environment with stimulus deprivation. Some environments are unusual as they are with excessive stimulation. The excessive stimulating environment is of two kinds. One is involved in vibrations and the other is involved in noises.

The vibrating environment we are encountering in many situations of men-made surroundings. Vibration means causing movement back and forth rapidly or swinging, oscillating swiftly here and there. It is mainly used in physics to describe the periodic motion about an equilibrium position, such as the regular displacement of air in the propagation of sound. Vibration also may mean to send out a sound wave by movement. Vibration is also stated as the characteristic atmosphere felt to be emanating from objects or places. Generally the concept, vibration is used to describe the characteristics of sound. We say often that the sound is vibrating. We most often realise the movement of the heavy vehicle on the road causing louder vibrating sound even from a distance one kilometer. The movement of trains fastly running on the rails is felt by us even though we are 2 or 3 kilometers away. The sound vibration caused by the aeroplane in the air cannot be ignored. These kinds of vibrations are man-machine systems. Generally, in most types of heavy transports like lorries, buses, bulldozers, trailers on the roads, fast moving mail and express trains on the rails and the functioning of heavy industrial machineries like the metal and boiler industries, the grinding industries, aerodromes aerodynamics—all cause vibration of the sound, leaving harmful effect on humans or have influence in the behaviour.

The effects of sound vibrations have been studied by many researchers. Grether (1971) says that it is quite but natural to pay more concern over the harmful effects of such sound vibrations on humans that might occur. Sound vibration is commonly experienced in a repetitive or in a cyclic manner. The cyclic occurrence of sound vibration is defined in terms of frequency in cycles per second. But it is indicated with two letters as Hz. The Hz stands for Hertz. Hertz refers to the international unit of frequency, equal to one cycle per second. This was named after the German Physicist H.R. Hertz (1857-1894) who was the first to produce electromagnetic radiation resulting from the oscillations of electricity in a conductor. Therefore Hz is used in place of the cycles per second notation, the amplitude of the vibration and the direction of the motion, i.e., front or back, left or right up or down of the object.

But the effects of vibration should not be studied on human performance as it may cause physical damage. The effects of intense vibration on animals cause death. Studies of the effects of vibration on humans caused severe chest pains, gastrointestinal bleeding and so on. There are only few studies on vibration. Since experiments on humans are very difficult and cause harmful effect, what sensory aspects were damaged by these effects were not found out. But the vibration effects are experienced mostly in man-made environmental situations, particularly in man-machine systems of environment.

The other kind of environment involving vibration is the noise. Noise has been defined as the unwanted sound. This infers another ideas that there is also wanted sound. Therefore sound is not totally rejected at all levels. We live only in the noisy world. Sound is used to test many things. Whether a man is alive or dead is tested by testing the sound of his heart. Man by himself produces various types sounds. Man laughs, cries or weeps, or raises alarming voices, scolds, shouts, expresses scorn feelings—all by sounds. The sound, a man makes in an environmental situation also expresses the type of feeling he is experiencing. Generally, the sounds humans make are stated as voices. We say, there is a human voice or ask whose voice it is. Your voice is very sweet, quite nice, very good, not bad, not audible, horrible—all these are referring to human voice only.

Thus we come across generally, noise, sound and voice. Though all these three appear to be the same, they are not the same. There are differences in the characteristics of these three phenomena. Separate words or concepts are used to refer to various sounds raised by humans, animals, birds and insects. For example, we say that the lion roars, dog barks, woolf howls, baby cries, man speaks and so on. In all these some kind of sound is produced and each one is given a name. But only in the case of man the sound is called voice. All others are called sound and when a sound is unwanted or causes damages to our sensory apparatus is called noise.

Though there are sounds around us we do not want to hear all of them. We hear some sounds, but not all. We do not hear meaningless sounds or that are very loud. Therefore all those sounds that we do not want to hear either impair our senses or that are meaningless, are noises. Constantly hearing loud noises causes permanent loss of hearing. In the middle of eighteenth century there was worldwide use of steam boilers. The workers who were working in boiler plants have retired with permanent deafness. The type of works like hammering the metals, riveting the plates for joining, all cause horrible noises reverberating our senses. Modern industries and offices continue in producing noises. Every nation is fastly changing over from agricultural community to industrialization and urbanization. In all these there is an increase of unwanted sounds. However some of the modern industries tried to control noises by some means, the effects of noises are always there.

We do not disregard all the noises all the times, unless they are impairing our sense of hearing. We are required to raise our voice loudly or raise the pitch of the communicating instrument to a higher level when we wanted to communicate our message to a person or a group of people at a longer distance. It may be disturbing to the persons who are nearby, but it becomes necessity to send the message to a distance place. Music whether it is vocal or instrumental is evolved only from sounds. The vocal sound is always combined with several instrumental sounds. To a person, who does not know anything about vocal music or any music or instrumental play, is merely a sound. People, unless learned to enjoy music either by practice or habit, they consider it as only a noise.

What is music for one culture is a mere sound for another culture. Every culture whether it is a primitive or most primitive or civilized or quasi civilized have a music of its own by converting the plain and unwanted sounds into agreeable pleasant sound by producing the sound with different intensities, pitch or tone. Whether it is primitive culture or civilized, the people of that culture put some meaning in the sounds they produce, call it as music, whether it is vocal or instrumental, drum beatings or using pipes. Thus only sounds become music. This is not unwanted sound. But now-a-days a type of musical performance called chord music, in which three or four persons with a number of instruments simultaneously raising the pitch to a higher level and dance. They say that the more they shout and vigorously move about by running here and there, the more they arouse the emotions in themselves and also arouse emotions in others. Here the important characteristic is raising the sounds in pitch in consonant with fast movements. Thus sounds are the basic components of music of any type. As far as others are concerned if it is an intermediate level of stimulation they can also enjoy it. But when it is transmitted through loud speakers with very loud noise it becomes a nuisance and we hate it. The note that we can enjoy, can be also made to hate if it is beyond certain level. In this way it becomes a subjective taste, what is music for one is an unwanted noise for another. Therefore sounds and noises can be tolerated only to an optimum level. Noise or sound is generally considered as a physical component. Since it stimulate humans it is also a psychological component.

The Structure of Auditory System and Sound

While discussing about noise as a physical component it is also better that we must know something about the physical component of sound and the anatomy of auditory mechanism. Physics is the science that studies about sound components. The general principle is that any solid body will vibrate when struck. The vibrations of the solid body are regular, periodic and consistent. The sound waves have the characteristics of frequency and amplitude. Sound is produced by fastly changing pressure of air molecules at the eardrum. The air molecules are forced together create positive pressure. Instead if the air molecules pull apart then there is negative pressure. In a sound wave the pecks of the waves are positive pressures and the valleys are the negative pressures. The outer ear consists of three parts (1) the pinna, (2) the meatus or the canal leading to the ear drum, and (3) the ear drum. The sound waves reach the eardrum first by passing through meatus alternatively. The eardrum is a membrane that vibrates reacting to the pressure waves of the sound. The middle ear contains three bony livers which are vibrated by the rapid movement of the eardrum. It is these three parts of the middle ear, called ossicles that connect the eardrum with the oval window of the inner ear. The parts of the middle ear, the ossicles, is a liver system. These are (1) hammer (malleus), (2) the anvil (incus), and (3) the stirrup (stapes). This has a mechanical advantage. The three ossices of the middle ear receive vibrations from the eardrum and conduct them to the fluid-filled inner ear, the cochlea. These three bones are firmly connected and vibrate as a single unit. The third part of the middle ear, the stirrup (stapes) is fitted with the oval window of the fluid-filled inner ear.

The eardrum while vibrating, moves the three parts of the middle ear, the ossicles, first the hammer (malleus) which in turn vibrates the anvil (incus). The inner most bone of the middle ear, the stirrup (stapes) on receiving the vibration from the anvil transmits vibrations to the oval window of the inner ear. The important part of the inner ear are (1) cochlea, (2) vestibule and (3) the three semicircular canals. Sound waves entering the outer ear, strike the tymponic membrane or the eardrum and make it to vibrate. The vibrations are transmitted by the three bones (ossicles) of the middle ear to the cochlear fluid of the inner ear which stimulate the receptors.

The external or the outer ear and the middle ear are filled with air. The inner ear is filled with fluid. The coiled portion of the inner ear is called cochlea. This is very important part of the ear for hearing. The fluid-filled cochlea is divided into three major compartments by two flexible membranes. One of them is basilar membrane. The vibrations of the fluid in the cochlea cause to vibrate different parts to the membrane. These vibrations stimulate the nerve endings in the hair cells. These are the impulses which at last go to the temporal lobe of the brain and provide the auditory sensation (Fig. 3.1).

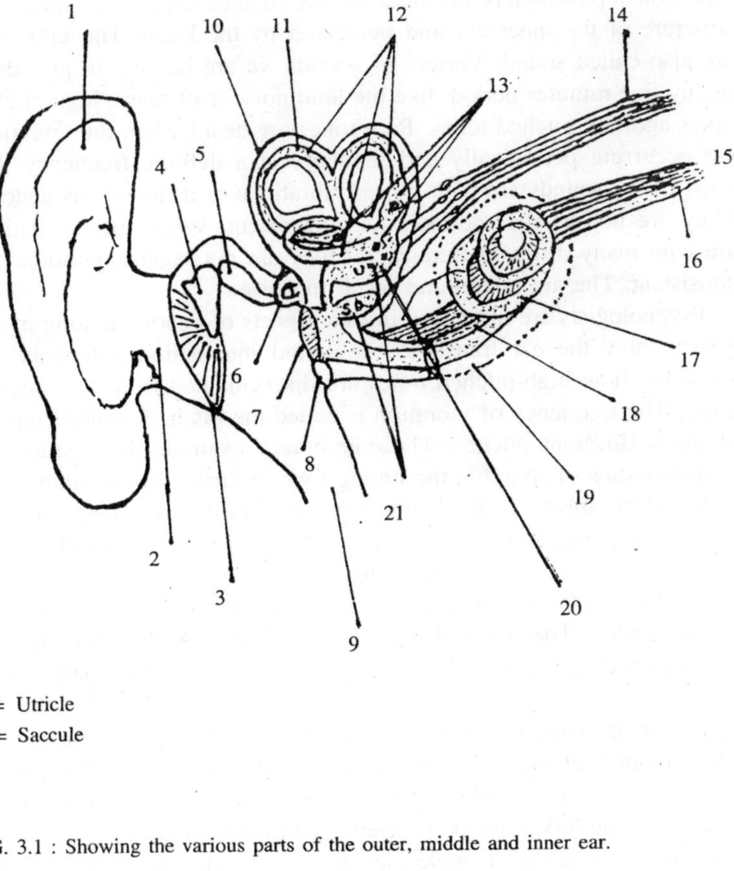

U = Utricle
S = Saccule

FIG. 3.1 : Showing the various parts of the outer, middle and inner ear.

1. Outer ear (Pinna), 2. Ear canal, 3. Tympanic Membrane (Ear drum), 4. Malleus (Hammer), 5. Incus (Anvil), 6. Stapes (Stirrup), 7. Oval window, 8. Round window, 9. Eustachian tube, 10. Perilymph, 11. Endolymph, 12. Semicircular canals, 13. Cupula in 3 Ampulas (in the semicircular canals), 14. Vestibule nerves, 15. Auditory nerves, 16. Cochlear nerves, 17. Cochlea, 18. Scala vestibuli, 19. Scala tympani, 20. Vestibule, 21. Utricle and Saccule

Characteristics of Sound

The word sound is used here referring to the sensations provided by the vibration (pulsation) of a solid material body when struck and the vibration or pulsation is transmitted to the cochlea, the coiled, fluid-filled structure of the inner ear and perceived by the brain. The vibrations are also called sound. Variety of sounds we are hearing in just about in any five minutes period, like the loud noise, soft noise, high pitched tones and low pitched tones. Pure tones are heard when the vibrations are occurring periodically and regularly at a definite frequency. But most of the sounds are with mixed vibrations of different frequencies. They are not regular, periodic and consistent. When the oscillations are with many different frequencies they are not regular, periodic and consistent. The are mixed and result in noise.

Psychologists are interested in two aspects of hearing among many. Firstly, how the ear translates the sound into action potentials and secondly, how high-pitched tones are discriminated from low pitched tones. The frequency of vibration is called the pitch. A sound consists of many different pitches. The commonest example to illustrate the characteristics of sound is the tuning fork. A strike on the tuning fork makes it to vibrate. In the beginning the vibrations are deep and they are slowly reduced. The regular movements of the tuning fork have a frequency rate and also amplitude. The motions of the tones of the tuning fork strike the molecules of air. The air pressure is determined by molecules. The air molecules collide with one another and are moving apart regularly and the waves of the air pressure change cause the sound.

The air pressure is the density of air molecules. The pressure at a given point will be above the normal first, then below the normal pressure. The tuning fork may be struck with varied intensities. How hard the tuning fork is struck, is determined by the amount of compression and rarefaction of the air molecules. It is to be also known how far the tunes of the fork vibrate back and forth to condense the air.

Amplitude: Amplitude is the limit of air pressure changes in a sound wave. Amplitude is the difference between the extreme limits of a vibration. In other words amplitude is the total amount of change of air pressure from condension (more tense) to rarefaction (less dense).

Frequency: There are tuning forks of varying vibrations. They vibrate at different rates. Each tuning fork is having a specific characteristic frequency of vibration. Frequency is the number of times the air pressure vibrations are taking place per second in a tone of a given frequency. Frequency rate or the rate of vibration is stated in cycles per second. It is normally indicated as CPS. A cycle is one vibration back and forth of the tuning fork. If the tuning fork is struck strongly then the vibrations are very rapid, resulting in high frequency. If struck mildly the vibrations are slow, with low frequency.

Wave length refers to the measured length of a complete cycle of change in a repeated phenomenon. In short wave lengths there will be rapid vibration or high frequency. In long wave length there will be low vibration or frequency. The amplitude is not changing for low or high frequency vibrations. Since sound waves travel at a fixed speed the relationship between frequency and wave length is constant. Sound travels in air at the rate of 1129 feet per second or 770 miles per hour. The fork is vibrating which means moving forward many times per second and producing many waves of compression which become the sound waves. The ear detects differences in frequency as differences in pitch. Sound waves travel at a high rate in a dense medium than in the air. For example in water sound travels at a higher rate as the molecules are very closely put together. Because of these, wave lengths are shorter and frequencies are higher. A motor boat under water produces high pitched sound, whereas in high altitude the molecules are farther apart and takes time to strike one another and this makes the transmission of sound slower and the frequencies also are lower.

Let us now put the membrane in the route of these sound waves. Each wave of compressed air hits the *Tympanic membrane*, the eardrum or tympanum and pushes it and stretches it. Every time the sound wave or wave of compressed air hits the ear drum the same thing takes place. The eardrum or membrane vibrates and initiates a series of events through the parts of the *middle ear* to the perception of sound. If the strength of vibration is increased in the membrane we hear loud sound. The pitch also becomes higher. When the vibration is decreased, the pitch is low and we hear low sound. It is possible for the human ear to hear between about 20 to 20,000 vibrations, cycles per second. It is generally indicated as Hz (hertz).

Disturbing Characteristics of Noise

The effects of noise are not pleasant. Noise is an environmental factor causing disturbance. The type of noise that is causing disturbance or irritation is unwanted one. Any disturbance caused by noise is psychological in nature. Because, the disturbance caused by the noise is arousing the emotional aspect. If the noise is of very much disturbing we get annoyed or we get angry or irritation. Therefore the problem caused by noise is psychological. It is true as stated by Kryter (1970), Glass and Singer (1972) that some noises are more disturbing than others. According to them noise has three important characteristics that cause annoyance. They are mainly (a) volume of the noise, (b) the predictability of the noise and (c) control of the noise.

(a) Noise is measured in terms of a unit, for measuring relative loudness of sound. The decibels (dB) are the basic units of sound. The loudness of a sound depends upon the amount of energy or pressure in the sound wave. The threshold, the smallest energy or pressure that can be detected by the normal human ear is about .0002 microbars or dynes per square centimeter. Dyne is a unit of pressure or energy. So decibel is the basic unit of measurement of noise intensity or loudness. Hence a scale of sound ranges from .0002 to 1000 dynes or microbars. The highest range 1000 dynes cause more pains than sound. How the volume of noise affects our behaviour? A volume of noise above 100 dB, a level of noise produced by a heavy lorry 60 feet away causes disturbing noise psychologically. If the same situation prevails continuously for ten hours it may cause physical damage to hearing. Louder noises may inhibit verbal communication and causes greater stress.

(b) The second characteristic is irregular noise, which is unpredictable. The unpredictable noise is more irritating than the predictable noise. A noise continuously produced without any break is called predictable noise. This is not so much of disturbing. If a noise is having intermittent breaks then it causes more disturbance. Unpredictable noises always cause severe stress. Unpredictable noises make us to put more efforts in our work.

(c) The noises which we cannot control may be more disturbing than the noises which we can control. Noises which we can stop may be less irritative than the noises we cannot stop. For example, a motorised machine is running in your work. When you find it highly disturbing you can stop it. But in the next building a high powered stone grinding machine is running with horrible noise. It is more disturbing and you are annoyed, but you cannot stop it. These three characteristics may be present in a situation in different degrees.

The Effects of Noise

If a born deaf person after twenty five years get his sense of hearing all of a sudden, then the first word he would certainly speak is what?

'The world is very noisy'. It is not a surprising statement. It is true that the world is noisy. We cannot avoid the noise, the unwanted sound wherever we go. Other than these noises, the noises made by the constantly moving various types transports, the non-stop industries, the flying aeroplanes, the crowds, the chord noises on the name of music, the loud speakers in high pitch on the streets are deafening the ears all the times. Therefore, the modern man cannot avoid the 'man-made' environmental noises in his life. But there is a range of sound intensity that man can tolerate and also a range he desires to hear. Hearing loss is a big loss for a man.

There are instances in which that man gets his sense of hearing damaged temporarily or permanently. In the middle of the eighteenth century there were steam-boilers widely used which caused the boiler makers deaf permanently. They were exposed to intense sounds of hammering metal plates. Modern industry is not free from sounds, causing damage to human ears. Damage in hearing occurs when the noise is heard above the normal amplitude (dB), for a person. The modern youth who are constantly exposed to the loud rock music lose their sense of hearing in early years. Labo and Oliphant (1968) have observed that the rock groups who play dance to the recorded music in clubs were exposed to 110 to 120 decibel (dB) sound music for one and a half hours of non-stop period, which resulted in serious loss of hearing.

The effects of noise on physical health has already been discussed. High level of noise causes stress which in turn causes hypertension, ulcers, heart rate, adrenaline secretion and so on. But some researchers state that evidences to pathogenic effect are not strong. Studies made by Cohen (1973) and Jansen (1973) conclude that exposure to high level of noise is related to cardiovascular disorders, allergic reactions, sore throat and digestive disorders. According to their studies, experienced workers learn to adapt to the higher noise levels but young and new workers seem to suffer from noises. Industrial managements do not control factors that are causing damage to health of the workers. In the stress causing works, pollutants in the work situation like smokes and dusts, the effects of noise on health should be guarded. Whether noise is having direct effect on physical health, has to be ascertained by further studies.

The effect of noise on mental health has been studied by Cohen *et al.* (1977). The studies made by Herridge and Low-Beer (1973) and Herridge (1974) state that the evidences are not stronger to support this idea. Mental illness was combined with physical health and stated that the effects of noise also cause mental diseases as some of the symptoms were of the mental disorders.

We have discussed so far that noise is having association with sense of hearing, physical and mental health problems. Another interest aroused is, the effects of noise on various kinds of *human performance*. There are conflicting views on this. Some are of the view that noise is not having any impairing effect on performance, some are of the view that noise is having impairing effect on performance and some are viewing that noise improves the efficiency. But experimental evidences show from the studies of Broadbent (1954) that sudden loud noise which is of unpredictable type, distracts individuals from the task and makes them to cause more errors. Corcoran (1962) has observed in his study that the arousal aspects of noise actually improves the performance. Glass and Singer (1972) in one of their studies have observed that the effects of noise on performance were to the minimum level and the individual even could ignore them.

The interference of noise in *communication* is one of the most important problems in commercial and industrial organizations. In the studies made by Mackanzie (1975) it was found that when a number of auditory signals are presented at the same time it was very difficult to distinguish and differentiate to the human ear. There was some difficulty to discriminate various kinds of sounds as there was masking. We will have to pay more attention to conversational noise in communication than non-conversational noise. Non-conversational noise requires less attention.

Another important factor that interfere in communication with noise is the *distance*. There is difficulty in hearing due to amplitude and frequency of the noise. But the distance between the communicator and the receiver is causing some problem to the receiver—one who receives the message.

The characteristics of noise that were interfering with our sense of hearing, physical health, mental health and performance also interfere with our social behaviour, particularly interpersonal relationships. According to Bell *et al.* (1978) there are three types of social intervention. They are attraction, altruison and aggression.

Attraction has some relationship with noise. Since noise is an unwanted sound, it keeps persons away at a distance. In personal attraction people come close together. The distance is reduced. It means noise is increased. Therefore attraction and noise is a test of physical distance between persons. For example, we sit close to people whom we like and keep away from those whom we do not like. Noise is an unwanted sound and so it is kept away. The distance between two persons is an indication of interpersonal attraction. If noise is decreased, then the inter-personal attraction is decreased and the distance also is increased.

Altruison determines social interaction. Altruism refers to the unselfish concerned for the welfare of others. The more unselfish one is, the more social relationships he develops. The more selfish one is the less social relationship one has. It is for the welfare of others that one works taking risk. Relating it to noise is not unselfish phenomenon. It is selfish. The more one is selfish the more noise he makes. The less noise one makes, the more unselfish he is. Since noise keeps persons away as it is unwanted, it is associated with selfishness.

Aggression can be related to noise. Aggression is the expression of dominance. It is a dominant response associated with arousal. Noise increases arousal and also increases aggression in individuals. We often see that when a person becomes aggressive he shouts and make noise. Aggressive people are always noisy. Or, the other way also is possible, noisy people are aggressive.

Under certain circumstances aggression is a dominant response in the behaviour hierarchy. Noise increases the arousal level in an individual and to that level it increases also aggression level. If the noise is controllable it is less aggressive. Glass and Singer (1972) in their studies have observed this. According to their studies unpredictable noise had more aggressive tendency than predictable noise, because unpredictable noise was found to be highly arousing and as a result of it the individual is led to increase aggression.

Experimental studies on Noise

Studies on the problem of noise are not available in plenty like other areas. Though there were some studies made earlier they were only in industrial situations with the view of reducing fatigue and increasing production. But studies on noise as a problem in general were few and also recent. Further, unlike other phenomenon noise is concerned with a number of variables. Studies have been made to see the consequences of prolonged exposure to loud noises. There were also studies to assess the effects of noise on human performance, the effect of noise on mood, and on emotions. But there are not studies to assess the effects of noise on personality traits. What type of people are easily annoyed for noise and what type of people not annoyed and what type of people welcome or seek noises has not been studied in detail.

The consequences of noise can be easily studied in the built in environmental situations, outside the laboratory. Particularly in the metal industries, boiler industries, textile industries, stone grinding industries and in generator workshops the effects of noise can be assessed and more information may be available from both the workers and the managements. The jet aircraft and heavy transportation sources also provide us information. The commonest form of effect can be the hearing loss, men from most of the metal industries retire as deaf. But to study the effect of noise by induced noise for experimental purposes is very difficult. Nobody would be willing to be a subject for such experiments in which they get their ears damaged. With some low and mild noises or sounds the effects cannot be fully assessed. Any experiment, if caused any decrement cannot be continued. As result of it the effect of higher or extreme higher level of noise cannot be examined.

The problem of noise on performance has been discussed by many researchers. Heimstra and McDonald (1973) state that noise and performance constitute complex affair with variables related to the task itself, with the subject and with noise. All these interact in determining that there is some change in the performance. Warner's (1969) investigation on the performance of the subjects throws some light on this problem. In this study the subjects have performed the assigned task under no noise, and under 80, 90 and 100 decibels of sound. The sound was produced intermittently by an on-off system. Warner had found that as he increased the intensity of the noise the number of errors made by the subjects were reduced. There were more errors significantly made by the subjects when there was no noise. Under 100 decibels condition the errors were less. Warner's experimental results show that noise increased the performance level.

In one of the studies made by Warner and Heimstra (1971, 1972) the performance of the subjects was tested in different noise situations. They had two levels, easy level and difficult level. In one condition they used 8 letters and in another condition they used 32 letters. The subjects were tested under four noise conditions such as zero noise, 30%, 70% and 100% in two difficult levels. It was found in their results that under 30% noise condition, the performance was increased whereas the 70% and 100% noise conditions decreased the performance. This study shows that if the noise is to the minimum level, it facilitates the performance.

Studies have been made whether noise is having any effect in the school students' performance. Cohen, Glass and Singer (1973) have studied urban noise in a school setting. The hypothesis was that urban noise may impair the educational development of school children if it is severe. The school was functioning in a high-rise apartment complex and the same was situated over a noisy highway in New York City. The researchers have found that the lower floors were exposed to more severe noise than the upper floors. The researchers have found that children in the lower floors who were exposed to severe noise had poorer hearing indiscrimination than the children in the upper floors. Secondly the hearing problems of the children on the lower floors had an influence in their reading ability. The children on the lower floors who were exposed to severe noises had poorer performance than those children who were on the upper floors and less exposed to noises.

Whether school children's performance was really affected by noise? This was tested by Bronzaft and McCarthy (1975) in a school, comparing the performance of the school children who were exposed to noise. The school building had two sides. One side of the class rooms of the building was quite close to the raised railway tracks. The other side of the class room building was free from the railway track noises and very much quiet. The investigators found that about 11 per cent of the teaching time was lost in the class rooms facing the noisy side of the railway tracks. The test was conducted on reading skills. The researchers have found that the reading skills of the children, on the other side of the railway track who were not influenced by the noise, were found to be much superior to the children who were on the noisy side. This means that the children who were facing the railway tracks were much influenced by the noises and as result of it their reading skills were much backward. Similar study was also made by Crook and Langdon (1974) with regard to the effects of aircraft noise in schools around London city and found the effects of noise had impaired the school performances.

Therefore, noise has been found to be having damaging effects on human performance, affecting the efficiency and decreasing the production. Though some laboratory experimental results show that noise had improved the performance and did not affect the work, the workers who were exposed to noise will have to put more efforts in their work to overcome the disturbance caused by the noise. Because of this, workers get fatigue soon after the work was started. Therefore, a noise free situation is pleasant for work which does not cause much fatigue to the workers for a long time.

There are various forms of environmental stressors which involve sudden and violent change, such as natural disasters like the floods, earthquakes and thunders. There may be also scientific and technological disasters like the dumping of garbage and waste toxic materials in the living areas. These are also unpleasant stressors. Noise is one of the sources of stress. The noise caused by the thunder is very much frightening. Thunder is a natural disaster, caused during the period of rainy seasons or when there is depression in the atmosphere. Thunder is a deep rumbling sound followed by a flash of lightning and on falling on the earth causes disastrous consequences of burning houses and killing the people. Important experiments have been conducted in environmental psychology on noises, which we have described in the preceding pages.

During some festival occasions people used to fire crackers. These crackers produce horrible noise of varying intensities. In some areas there may be firing of the crackers continuously for whole night. Some may tolerate these horrible sounds by saying that it is only for a day. But many could not tolerate and get annoyed by these continuous rumbling sounds. Every time when there are instances of fire accidents caused by the cracker-fires, destroying millions of rupees worth of properties. During the same festival time, in some places there may songs or rites relayed through loud speakers in high tones for the whole night which cause disturbances for the residents who wished peaceful sleep and calm living atmosphere. These are all some specific instances prevailing in India. Though these are undesirable, cause much disturbances, still they are unavoidable and people wanted such things. Thus noise is a both natural and man-made hazardous stressor.

6. THE EFFECTS OF SEASONS, WEATHER AND TEMPERATURE ON BEHAVIOUR

Nature and Characteristics of Temperature

Life exists only in a physical environmental condition which is surrounded by congenial atmosphere suitable for the bodily factures of the organisms. Atmosphere refers to the surrounding area of the earth which is enveloped by gases. The earth is surrounded by air which is the mixture of gases that forms the earth's atmosphere. At sea level exists dry air which is having high density. We often speak of weather condition and temperature. We also often hear weather forecast in the radio and in the television programmes. These media are communicating to us the weather conditions in advance, so that we can take precautious measures if it is going to be disadvantageous to us or cause any disaster consequences. Generally, weather refers to the day-to-day meteorological conditions especially temperature, cloudiness and rainfall affecting a specific place or area. We also sometimes enquire, how is the climatic condition of the place? What does it mean? It means, whether the weather condition, the temperature level is agreeable to us or not. Therefore we speak of weather and temperature.

Temperature means the degree of hotness of a body or substance, or medium, or a physical property related to the average kinetic energy of the atoms. It may be also stated as the measure of the degree of hotness indicated on a scale that has one or more fixed reference points. We may sometimes state informally that a body temperature is excess to the normal. Therefore the environmental component, the temperature has something to do with our body, surrounding area, the physical property related to our bodily temperature and so on. Temperature may be normal, abnormal and subnormal. There are different degrees in all these three levels. So long as the atmospheric temperature is normal there is no problem. But when the atmospheric weather condition or the temperature goes in excess to the normal or goes below the normal the condition affects the living organisms. Particularly, man is much affected both by the increase of normal atmospheric temperature and by the decrease of atmospheric temperature. At both levels man feels sick, as he is put into the most inconvenient condition.

The earth in which we live is going on changing the atmospheric conditions from extreme cold to extreme heat. In between there are several levels of climatic conditions and the seasons are going on changing in a cyclic manner. Living organisms, whether they are birds or animals change their reactions and behaviour according to the change of climatic conditions and temperature. Birds migrate to distant places, even flying thousands of miles for their survival and for procreation. Humans also change their living places according to the change of seasons and temperature. During the hot summers, people go in search of cool places on hills and mountains. They call such places a summer resorts. Similarly people who live in extreme cold places move to hot places. Those who could not change their places for the seasons, make artificial arrangement by cooling the living places with air conditioners and by heating with electric heaters. By these means they keep their body temperature at normal level.

Effects of Various Levels of Temperature and Atmosphere

In arctic regions of the earth it would be freezing cold, man cannot live there. But birds and animals live there as their bodily features can adapt to such situations. The human body temperature is 98.6°F or 37°C. It needs a moderate temperature between 115°F and 77°F. If the body temperature exceeds 115°F and goes down below 77°F, then the body get severely affected and death may cause. To any abnormal atmospheric changes the human body tries to adjust to the changes to some extent. But in the extremely hot temperature the human body gets much affected and physiological changes are taking place. The most serious consequence is that man gets sun strokes and dies. Similarly in the extreme cold climatic conditions, the adaptive mechanism fails to protect the human body in such situations and man dies of freezing cold. Therefore both the extreme hot temperature and the extreme cold conditions are environmental stressors on humans.

Man's behaviour is very much affected both by extreme heat and cold. The atmospheric condition may be also thick when there is heavy smoke. Adaptation becomes difficult. The weather or climatic condition varies from region to region, the type of life also varies according to the climatic conditions. The human body's core temperature should be always 98.6°F. This is measured by an instrument called thermometer. The skin of human body is very sensitive to the change of temperature. The receptors in the skin serve as psychological components. These receptors do not transmit the heat to the body. The difference in the temperature is felt between the skin and the environment. In the case of extreme temperatures the adaptive mechanism in the hypothalamus part of the brain fails to work.

Excessive Heat

In the atmosphere, heat and cold are the primary components. There is no life without these two, but they should exist at the optimum level. If the atmosphere is hot, hotter than the body temperature than the activating mechanism begins to work in the body. The important function of this mechanism during hot temperature is that it makes the body to give up the heat by some means. There is fast dialation in the blood vessels, particularly near the skin surface of the body. More blood is sent to the skin vessels from the heart and it also sends out the excess heat. Then the body sweats profusely. While sweating, the heat of the body is sent out. When there is more sweating in the body the heat from the body is sent out and the body gets cooled by the outside air. Thus the equilibrium of the body is maintained.

Further, there is another system functions in the body when there is heat wave or during the time of extreme heat. This takes place as an emergency measure in the body. On such emergency occasions more water is supplied for perspiration and when the perspiring water is evaporated, the body get cooled. This extra water is supplied for this emergency purpose by the process of reducing the urine formation in the body and by squeezing the tissues of the body for more water. But this condition should not continue for longer time. If these two mechanisms continued for longer period, the body gets dehydrated for want of water. The person feels very thirsty and tired and also feels weak. Therefore the body should be immediately refilled with sufficient water. This is the reason when we walk in hot sun we feel thirsty and tired. Players and sportsmen who take part in games and sports activities drink water often and also pour cool water on their bodies. This kind of adaptive mechanism takes place automatically in the hypothalamus part of the brain.

When this adaptive mechanism is not taking place then the body will get dehydrated and several physiological disorders may take place. Some of the physiological disorders are mainly heat stroke, increased blood pressure and heart attack. It may even cause coma and death. The body needs more blood for the cooling mechanism. The cardiovascular system is put into more strain and when there is more strain on this system then there is heart attack.

During hot seasons or summer period in urban areas the utility of air conditioning is increasing enormously in houses, offices and in industries. These air conditioners throw the temperature in the surrounding areas by 15 to 20^{0} F which make the urban areas always hot, hotter than the rural areas. This increased heat constantly attack when people come out of air conditioned room or attack those who have no such facilities. This type of atmospheric condition increases the rate of heart attacks in urban areas.

People who live is tropical areas often meet with environmental stresses such as temperature and weather conditions. The weather is always very hot, sultry and scorching. Generally, countries in the equatorial regions experience extreme heat since the sun's rays are falling straight away on the earth.

Excessive Cold

In arctic (northern) and antarctic (southern) regions there will be extreme cold. This is on the other side of extreme heat. But people do not go there. Explorers who make expeditions only sail into these areas. But the areas beyond the line of 'tropic of cancer', 23-1/2° on the north of equator and beyond the line of 'tropic of capricorn', 23-1/2° on the south of equator the climatic conditions would be very cold. If the surrounding area is very cold, then the body will have to maintain the adaptive mechanism and the body heat will have to be maintained. The heat of the body is maintained at 98.6^{o}F and the activating mechanism functions and maintains it.

When the body is experiencing extreme cold there are certain physiological changes like shivering of bodily parts. At this time there is vascular contraction in the blood vessels. Because of the vascular contractions, the blood vessels are made narrow. We find the hairs all over the body in the state of erection. This vasocontraction is opposite to vasodilation that takes place in extreme hot situation. This process of vasocontraction maintains the body temperature at 98.6^{o}F. This is by sending more blood to the internal organs. This increases the metabolism of the body and produces more heat. The skin surface is made thick to protect the body from the cold. In winter people put on heavy woollen clothes to protect their bodies. The temperature in the winter season sometimes goes down to even –5°C in most of the places in Himachal Pradesh and Kashmir. People who could not withstand the extreme cold sometimes collapse.

There are expeditions going to south pole and north pole to study the climatic conditions and the nature of atmosphere and also to find out whether there are animals and plants. It will take some more time for us to know more about all these informations. The effects of extreme cold on people depends upon the degree of intensity of cold. Humans can withstand the cold only to certain limit to the extent of the limit of the adaptive mechanism. Therefore human beings change their living places where they can find the optimum climatic conditions for their bodily adaptation.

Medium Temperature

The atmosphere of the earth is such that in some parts there is extreme heat, in some parts extreme cold and in some parts in between these two climatic conditions. There will be neither extreme heat nor extreme cold. This type of climatic conditions exists on the either side of the equatorial region or between the line of the tropic of cancer and the line of tropic of capricorn. People from extreme hot and cold climatic conditions may find much change in these areas and they could easily adapt to this climatic conditions. The bodies of the people from cold climatic conditions may sweat in these areas and within a short time they may be accustomed to this change of temperature. Similarly persons from hot climatic conditions when moved in these areas find it cold and they can adapt to this change of temperature. The climatic conditions where, people from hot and cold places can adapt to the situation is generally stated as the moderate climatic conditions. The adaptive mechanism is called acclimatization. Sometimes there may be high temperature or low temperature, but this type of high or low temperature will not cause any physiological changes or disorders, unlike extreme hot and cold temperatures.

People from extreme hot and cold places after staying in this moderate heat places may find that these places are quite suitable for them and they may even migrate to these moderate heat places and settled down there. This type of attitude prevails among people all over the world. Many people from India go to the United States either for study or for seeking employment and on completing their education or get a job settle down there as the climatic conditions there are somewhat similar to that of India. But they do not go to Canada as it is very cold country. Further a moderate climatic condition may motivate people for more work. Since the climatic condition is such that it does not cause much physical fatigue even if we do physical work for more number of hours. People work even for the whole day and also earn more. But in hot countries due to heat people become tired quickly after working for few hours. Physiological changes, in moderate climate, are not taking place as quickly as in hot climate.

Humidity

Another climatic condition is humidity. It is the state of being dampness, or slight wetness in the air. This refers to the amount of moisture in the air. It is of two types, absolute humidity and relative humidity. Absolute humidity is the atmosphere, which is expressed in terms of the amount of grams of water contained in one cubic metre of air. The relative humidity is the mass of water vapour present in the air which is expressed in terms of percentage of the moisture in the air to the highest amount possible at the temperature. Both the conditions are having almost the same effect in the body by causing certain physiological changes.

Generally, humidity is one of the primary environmental factors. This is a state in which mist is formed in the air. The air becomes wet. In hot climatic conditions the rate of humidity may be high. There is saturation or soaking of air with water vapour. Since the air is with full of moisture, the outside air is not absorbing the sweating water of the body. Normally the sweating water is absorbed by the outside air if it is dry. But in this state since the air is soaked with water vapour, body's sweating water is not absorbed. The sweating continues and not absorbed. Because of this man will have to perspire more than in the normal condition. Generally, in this state man is having more uncomfortable feelings.

This uncomfortable feeling may vary from person to person. Very healthy people, who have no respiratory problems may be very comfortable. But those who have respiratory problems, or those who have higher level of eosinophilia counts in the blood may feel very uncomfortable. These people in this state will have breathing difficulties. Generally during night time, people who are living nearer to the sea or mountainous areas may have very uncomfortable feelings, the hard breathing. Persons who are suffering from asthma may have accelerated hard breathing. There is an instrument called hygrometer to measure the level of humidity in the atmosphere.

In the atmospheric condition of 100^{0}F a person may not feel uncomfortable if the humidity level is as low as 30 or 35 per cent. But the same person at 100^{0}F may not feel comfortable if the humidity level is as high as 65 to 70 per cent. Sometimes the humidity level is as high as 75 or 80 per cent in the air in high mountains and certain sea areas. Whenever the humidity level is rised to the level of 60 to 65 per cent persons who are having respiratory problems will feel very uncomfortable. Therefore it is better that they should choose a place where the humidity does not rise more than 30 or 35 per cent. Such places may be 20 to 25 miles away from sea and mountainous areas and also away from big river beds. Thus, just like extreme hot and extreme cold climatic conditions the humidity conditions also are having influence in human behaviour. In moderate high temperature climatic situation it is important that the humidity level also should be taken into consideration as it is a more influencing primary environmental factor in human behaviour.

Atmospheric Influence on Behaviour

The atmospheric temperature is a natural physical component. This exists on the earth. Since the earth is moving, going round the sun on its orbit and also rotates itself, the atmospheric conditions are going on changing throughout the year. Because of this the seasons are going on changing one after the other in a cyclic manner. The season is one of the four equal periods into which the year is divided by the *equinoxes*, (the time when the sun crosses the equator, making night and day of equal length in all parts of the earth), and the *solstices*, (the time of the year when the sun reaches the point of farthest north), resulting from the apparent movement of the sun to north, and south of the equator, during the course of the earth's orbit around it. These periods are spring, summer, autumn, and winter. These have their characteristics weather conditions in different regions or parts of the world and occur at opposite times of the year in the North and South hemispheres.

The four seasons have varied climatic conditions and the temperature varies time to time. Cultivation of crops on the earth vary on the basis of the monsoon and the temperatures of the seasons. Every season has different climatic condition and temperature and cultivation on the earth is made according to these seasons. Since the temperature varies differently in these four seasons, peoples' life style and behaviour are also changing. Every season exerts different level of temperature and weather condition and people learn to adapt themselves to every season's temperature and weather. Cultivators and farmers who grow crops wait for the advent of the specific season to start their works.

The spring season comes between winter and summer. This is the first season of the year, fall between winter and summer. Astronomically this season is from the March equinox to the June solstice in the North hemisphere and from September equinox to the December solstice in the South hemisphere. Therefore, the spring season is not occurring at the same period in the North and South hemispheres. In the spring season the plants begin to grow and the trees begin to burst into leaves again.

The summer is the second season of the year which falls in between spring and autumn. The summer is the hottest season of the year. Astronomically summer season is from 21st June solstice to 22nd September equinox in the North hemisphere and at the opposite time of the year in the South hemisphere. But in the popular use, the period is from mid-May to mid-August in the northern hemisphere. During summer solstice the sun is at its northern-most point in the sky. The sun appearing in the southern most point in the Southern hemisphere at noon at its highest altitude above the horizon. This occurs in the Southern hemisphere in December 22. This is warmer half of the year in the southern hemisphere in contradistinction to winter.

Autumn is the third season of the year. The Autumn season is also called the fall. This is the season when leaves fall from the trees. It is also the season of fruit harvest. This season falls between summer and winter. Astronomically it is from September 21st equinox to the December 21st solstice in the Northern hemisphere and from March equinox to the June solstice in the southern hemisphere.

The season winter is the fourth and the coldest period of the year on the earth. It falls between autumn and spring. Astronomically winter begins from 22nd December solastice to the 20th March equinox in the Northern hemisphere and at the opposite time of the year in the Southern hemisphere. During winter solstice time the sun is at its southern most point in the sky appearing at noon at its lowest altitude above the horizon. This is the northern most point in the Southern hemisphere. It occurs in December 22. The period, coldest weather, is associated with the winter. Astronomically the point on the celestial (relating to sky) sphere is opposite of the summer solstice at which the ecliptic is farthest south from the celectial equator (C.E.D. 1984).

We can understand from the astronomical prediction that climatic conditions and the temperature are going on changing as the earth is constantly moving on its orbit and also rotating itself. The extreme heat we experience in the summer season and extreme cold in the winter and in between summer and winter we have autumn season and in between winter and summer, we have spring season. These two seasons, autumn and spring have moderate climatic conditions and the temperature in these two seasons is neither extremely hot nor extremely cold. Therefore the temperature in various parts on the earth varies due to the change of seasons and the change of seasons occur because of the movement of the earth on its orbit. The orbit is a curved path usually ecliptical on which the earth moves.

The temperature of these four seasons are having corresponding effect on the behaviour of the people. The life style of the people, the food habits, dressing manners, visiting places, the occupation, cultivation of lands, the sports activities, social interactions, expeditions and all other activities relating to human behaviour change. Since, change of season is associated with the change of climatic condition and temperature, human behaviour is much influenced by temperature. We can associate temperature, for example, heat and cold to all aspects of human behaviour. Apart from the general observation of the effects of heat and cold in the physical environmental situation, the effects of heat is also studied in controlled situations on human behaviour. Particularly the performance of people in various work situations and the performance of the participants in the laboratory situations were studied. Both hot and cold temperatures had some effect upon the performance of the people.

The Effect of Heat on Performance

The influence of high temperature of the surrounding environment on performance has been tested. The type of performances were reaction time, tracing, vigilance, memory and mathematical calculations. These performances were studied in a laboratory situation by Bell, Provins and Hiorns (1964), Griffiths and Boyce (1971), Pepler (1963), Poulton and Kerslake (1965), Provins (1966), Provins and Bell (1970). Some of these experimenters have observed that (1) heat did not have any influence upon performance. This was a very surprising result to those who believed that heat is having adverse effect on the performance. Some other experimenters found that (2) heat had detrimental effect on performance. But some experimenters have observed that (3) heat has improved the performance. In these three types of results of the laboratory experiments several factors seemed to be having some influencing effect upon performance.

The results of these studies varies because of the variables such as the level of temperature and type of task performed. The effect of temperature upto 90°F had facilitated performance on simple tasks. But the same levels of heat was having detrimental effect on complex tasks. This means, the nature of task seems to be an important variable in determining the performance. Another result brought out by Rohles (1974) and Wilkinson (1974) has been that performance varied person to person at the same temperature. The performance generally did not reach the maximum level for all the individuals in the same temperature.

Studies were also made in industries to see the effect of heat on performance. The industries were steel industries where the workers will have to work for eight hours in hot furnaces. It is observed that, generally, exposure to such heat, cause dehydration, loss of salt, muscular fatigue. Workers will have to take protective measures to meet with such problems. The workers have to intake more water and salt. Those exposed to intolerably hot situations for long time were taking protective measures of wearing certain clothings which do not radiate heat over the body. Crockford (1967) and Hill (1967) have studied these aspects. Pepler (1972) found in his studies that there was some effects of temperature on the students' performance in the class room.

Effects of Heat on Social Behaviour

What is applicable to the individual is also applicable to the members of the society. People who are exposed to extreme environmental temperature often feel very uncomfortable because of the intolerable heat. It is human nature that people get irritated when they are exposed to high heat situation for a long time. Heat generally may create unpleasant feeling in human beings and as a result of it they develop a sort of negative attitude to heat or high temperature. Studies have been made whether heat can increase attraction or decrease attraction. In Byrne's (1971) study it was observed that heat decreased the interpersonal attraction. Griffitt (1970) studied the effect of temperature in an experiment. The subjects were asked to evaluate the attitudes of others under different temperature conditions like 67.5°F and 90.6°F. The results show that high temperature decreased interpersonal attraction though the subjects had some degree of similarity of attitudes.

Heat has something to do with aggression. Aggression is stated as the long hot summer effect. It is found that riotous acts of violence increased by intolerable heat on aggression. In the studies made by Goranson and King (1970) it was observed that heat wave conditions were found to be associated with riotous activities.

Effects of Cold Temperature

Cold temperature is not without any adverse effects on human body and behaviour. If the surrounding atmospheric temperature goes down below the normal level then the body shivers and several physiological changes are taking place. The reaction to cold is opposite to the heat climatic conditions. If the temperature of the surrounding area goes below 70^{0} F then disaster consequences may take place. Human beings are taking all the protective measures when they work in cold climates. If protective clothes are not worn then it may result in serious illness or death. Wearing protective clothing may maintain the efficiency, though it would not reduce the efficiency. But the effect of cold in the efficiency of performance leads to reducing it. Studies on the effect of cold below the temperature of 55^{0}F to 65^{0}F (13^{0}C to 18^{0}C) were not made. Prolonged exposure to cold climates generally affect health.

The studies made by Landsberg (1969) brought out many interesting results. According to him prolonged exposure to cold causes two serious consequences. The first is the formation of ice crystals in the skin cells. This is called frostbite. When we expose to intense cold, injury to body is caused by such exposure. The tissues of the body get injured by the frozen dew or vapour which is called frostbite. But the Eskimos who live in arctic regions like Greenland and North America are not affected by this though they are exposed to extreme cold climatic conditions all the times. Those who are exposed to extreme cold climatic conditions can get rid of the disorders by wearing protective clothing and taking shelter. Prolonged exposure to extreme cold climate not only affect physical health like hypothermia, cardiovascular activity like increasing heart rate, blood pressure, but also mental health. Gunderson (1968) studied the health of the residents of antarctic stations and found that they were subjected to insomnia, anxiety, depression, and irritability. According to him these effects were more due to isolation and nature of work than cold climates.

Whether cold temperature is having any effect upon performance has been studied by many researchers. The results are of varied types, as some other factors, other than cold, interfered in the performance. In the studies made by Fox (1967), Poulton (1970), Provins and Clarke (1960) it was observed that temperature reduces efficiency to tasks like reaction time, muscular dexterity and tactile discrimination or touch sensitivity at 55^{0} F temperature. Any fall of temperature below 55^{0} F reduces the efficiency further. Due to extreme cold climatic condition the mechanism of the body is fully engaged in maintaining the core temperature and therefore there is no sufficient energy to attend to the physical and mental works. The hand and fingers are stiffen and any performance on dexterity type is much affected and the performance is reduced. Bell and Baron (1977) have observed that the surrounding extreme cold temperature affects the social behaviour of the people.

People often get irritated and as result of it interpersonal attraction is reduced and also develop aggression. A sort of negative feeling and attitudes toward cold are developed. Bell *et al.* (1978) state that severe winter and cold seem to increase helping tendency among people and the crime rates are also reduced.

Therefore, in conclusion, we may state that temperature, refers generally, to the level of heat in human body or to the climatic condition. If there is an increase of temperature in human body above 98.6^{o} F, then it is the indication of fever and we seek the help of a physician and take medicine to reduce it. Sometimes high temperature in the body means, high fever and it may result even in death. Therefore, we are often checking this from health point of view and maintain the normal level of temperature in our body. But if the climatic condition is hot, then the surrounding environment is getting hot. In such cases we seek protection from this in all possible ways. The environmental heat is revealed in bodily features by sweating profusely. Workers in the fields, in open industries, road works and in metal industries sweat more than on normal occasions. Generally workers in these places feel very much tired soon after the work was started and often wanted rest pauses more to the extent of getting relief from the fatigue they experienced due to the hot temperature. By working in such areas constantly the skin of the workers also get darken. Thus hot temperature of any kind is injurious to human body and therefore as far as possible humans avoid extreme temperatures.

As we have discussed earlier, temperature of the atmosphere varies according to the change of seasons. The four seasons that are changing one after the other emit varied temperatures. It varies from extreme cold to extreme hot. Both are unwanted temperatures for humans as they would affect not only the work performance, but also the health.

7. THE EFFECTS OF AIR POLLUTION AND WIND ON BEHAVIOUR

Nature of Air in the Atmosphere

Air is one of the environmental components that is very essential for living organisms on the earth. Air is more essential than food and water. Generally air is the mixture of gases that forms the earth's atmosphere. At sea level dry air has a density of 1.22 kilograms per square metre and it consists of 78.08 per cent nitrogen, 20.95 per cent oxygen, 0.93 per cent argon, 0.03 per cent carbon dioxide with smaller quantity of inert gases. Water vapour in air varies between 0 and 4 per cent. In industrial areas sulphur gases may be present in the air as pollutants. Air is filled in the atmosphere around the earth and above the earth in the space to certain distance.

The area which is filled with air, is called aerial space. There are several related variables to air, such as breeze, clean air, slight wind, wind, high wind, storm, cyclone, tempest hurricane—all referring to some type of atmospheric conditions related to air. Therefore the earth atmosphere is surrounded by some type of air. Life of any kind cannot exist in a vacuum, an atmosphere where there is no air and gas. Clean air keeps living organisms healthier. When this air is not clean or polluted then health is affected, man becomes sick and needs treatment. Therefore all human beings need clean or fresh air to live a healthy life. When air is polluted by some means, it causes several health hazards.

Psychologists have developed interest in the study of air pollution as it interferes with human behaviour. Human behaviour is much influenced by various types of air pollutions. Man lives in an atmosphere which is filled with air and gases. Psychologists began to pay more attention on the pollution of air only from 1960s onwards. This is one of the primary environmental problems that humans are facing at present. Living organisms, including man cannot survive in an oxygen deficiency area or atmosphere. It is a natural element. Oxygen is a colourless, odourless highly reactive gaseous element, that is present most abundantly on the earth's surface. Oxygen is also essential for aerobic respiration and oxygen is used widely in almost all combustion in industries. Persons who suffer from hard breathing are at once treated with oxygen.

Air Pollution and the Consequences

Air pollution is sometimes taking place due to natural calamities, like earthquakes and landslides. In such cases people suffer from the effects of air pollution. But such incidents are very rare. The most often occurring incidents are man-made air pollutions. On coming to know the consequences of air pollution, people become very much worried over it. Air pollution is not a local problem. It has become a world problem, because there is no city in the world that has managed to avoid the modern scourage of air pollution. Once there were cities in the world that were famous for pristine and clean air but now they are now constantly surrounded by air pollution in such a way that it can cause ill health to hospitalize and death, the otherwise healthy, as well as the sick and weak. For example, the cities like Beunos Aires, the capital of Argentina, Denver, the capital of Colorado, Madrid, the capital of Spain, Bonn, the capital of West Germany, and Rome, the capital of Italy were noted for their clean and uncontaminated airy atmosphere. These cities have lost their reputation at present. In India too, cities like Bhopal, Bangalore, Chandigarh were once stated as clean cities. But, now they are all highly air polluted cities by exhaust gases. At present there are few world famed clean cities, like Singapore and Koulalampur.

But what is meant by air pollution? Air pollution means that the air of the surrounding places is made unclean, impure and contaminated with poisonous and harmful substances, and also mixed with garbage, wastages, dusts, and exhaust gases causing bad odours, so as to spoil the health of people and make them sick and death. There are many poisonous and harmful substances people throw on the streets, on the roadside like the metal parts, lead, mercury, burnt materials, waste products, perished vegetables, spoiled mutton bones, birds' feathers, ashes, old cloths, cotton wastes and all sorts of garbage and so on. Besides these the sewage and drainage pipe breakages and leakages and flowing the waste products on the roads or streets cause both environmental and air pollutions. People living in such areas are put into hazardous or risky situations.

Studies have been made in United States on air pollutions. There were controversies on this problem. Those who were affected by air pollution wanted to clean up the environment. But on the other side, the industrialists claim that the matter is exaggerated and those who speak of air pollution are on the way of industrial productivity and economic prosperity. However, air pollution seems to affect the health of the people. In the study made by Blot *et al.* (1975) it was observed that there was connection between air pollution and physical and psychiatric health problems.

Therefore, there are cities and nations throughout the world began to deploy a wide range of strategies that can be successfully cope with air pollution. These attempts are ranging from banning the parkings and no-driving days to massive legally mandated programmes to instal advanced pollution controls on the power plants and big industries. Few of them seem to work well, but many of them sometimes escape the attention. The World Health Organization (WHO) estimated that above 70 per cent of the global urban people are breathing the air that is unhealthy atleast some of the time, while another 10 per cent of the people are breathing the air that is of marginal type. It is observed that air pollution affects children more than the adults. Poor children and those who are living in slum areas are exposed to more kinds of higher level of air pollution.

Studies have revealed that children who are living in cities with higher level of air pollution are having smaller lungs and abstained from school for more days, because of illness and hospitalization more often. Further smaller body weights of the children and the development of their bodily parts were put into greater risk. Since the infants have the habit of putting everything in their mouth and suck, they indiscriminately suck all available contaminated objects within their reach. Older children play on the streets or roads which are filled with exhaust gases or fumes from automobiles and lead exhaust.

Studies reveal interesting and alarming results in the field of air pollution. In the industrial city of Cubato of Brazil, it was reported that because of air pollution, 40 out of every 1000 children born in the city were stillborn (deadborn), another 40 for every one thousand mostly were deformed and died in the first week after birth. Further, in the same year, 1980 out of 80,000 of its population, the city of Cubato had about 10,000 emergency medical cases involving tuberculosis, pneumonia, bronchitis, emphysema, asthma and other respiratory ailments. These types of hazards of air pollution are highly alarming. In the metropolitan cities like Athens, the capital of Greece, it was estimated that the death rate found to be increased to 500 per cent on most polluted days. Air pollution causes damage even in remote industrial areas. Scientists report that in the rain forests of Africa, acid rains and the smog level were found to the level of the pollution of the central European cities, because of the burning of the vast grass lands regularly for clearing the lands for agricultural and industrial purposes. Therefore efforts are being taken throughout the world to curb the urban air pollution in large measures (S.J. Souvenir, 1995).

Air Pollutants

Air pollutions are caused in various ways. But air pollution policies have focussed for the control only on few most serious urban pollutants like the automobile gases and soot, hydrocarbons, sulphur dioxide, nitrogen oxide, ozone or photo-chemical smog, carbon monoxide and lead. Particularly, the carbon monoxide was found to be regularly reaching unhealthy levels in many of the cities in the world. This may result in decreased weight in unborn child, increased prenatal mortality and brain damage. All these are depending upon the duration of time the pregnant women are exposed to concentrated air pollution situations. This is what the World Health Organization has found in their world over observations.

The automobiles exhaust gases and the air borne particles from industrial works have been accounted mostly for all the carbon monoxide emitted in many urban areas. Nitrogen oxides pose multiple threats. Nitrogen oxide is a red brown poisonous irritating gas that exists in ordinary temperatures. This is produced when the heat of the combustion causes oxygen. Nitrogen is found in the air to combine with the gases of one another. Sulphur dioxide is a colourless soluble pungent gas produced by burning sulphur and it is used to produce sulphuric acid. When it is mixed in the air, the air may cause asthma attacks.

The smoke and soot are most obvious air pollutants, considered to be most dangerous matters. Lead is a silver gray metal. It is toxic in every form. Lead is an acute threat specially to children under six years of age, normally they ingest it. It is usually in the form of paint chips in walls of the houses and also in doors. If the metal is heavy it damages intelligence, affects the growth and affects the sensory apparatus of hearing. It reduces the ability of the child in language acquisition and spoils the child's concentration of attention.

All types of motor vehicles like the motor cars, buses, all lorries, all kinds of two wheelers run by petrol cause more air pollution than any other activity. It causes air pollution nearly half of human caused nitrogen oxides, two-thirds of carbon monoxide and about one half of the hydrocarbons in industrial areas. In most industrialized areas the use of power plants is accounted for two-thirds of sulphur dioxide emission and nearly one half of the total emissions of the most of the air pollutants.

Personal Air Pollution

Apart from these types of air pollutions, there is another form of air pollution called personal air pollution that has received much greater attention in recent times. It is smoking of all types. It may be cigarette smoking or beedi or cigar or smoking of any type. There is a risk of throat and lung cancer in smoking. It also causes emphysema, a kind of lungs disease often damage the elasticity of the lungs. Eiser (1983) has found in his studies that the evidences are well established relating smoking and the disease like lungs Cancer. Chassin *et al.* (1984) states that most people are aware of the damages, but still some argue that there is a positive effect in smoking like the reduction of tension, harmful stress, peer acceptance and weight reduction.

The consequences of smoking is not ending with throat and lungs cancer for the smokers, but the smoke they release by smoking pollute the air and persons who are non-smokers will have to breathe air and the smoke and get their health spoiled. This is called passive smoking. This is also having serious health hazard. A report appeared in *Washington Post* (1985) that even wives who are not smoking are affected by their heavily smoking husbands. They have high rate of lung cancer. Bleda and Sandman (1977) found that non-smokers dislike cigarette smokes and also develop negative attitude towards cigarette smokers and also they withdraw from such situations. The cigarette smoke is a burning smoke. It is burning tobacco and emitting the smoke. Tobacco is burned in various ways in the form of smoking. Whether it is cigarette or beedi, smoke is emitted. Smoke also is emitted in smoking of cigar and pipe. More tobacco is burned in cagars and pipes than in cigarettes and beedies. This kind of tobacco smokes mix in the air immediately and pollute the air. Some persons smoke marijuena. It is dried leaves and flowers of the hemp plant used for smoking in cigarettes, beedies and in pipes. It is supposed to have intoxicating effect. It is used as a narcotic drug. Cannabis is also called Indian hemp. The dried tops of the female of this hemp plant is used either by chewing or clearing or by smoking for their eruphoric effect. It is having very powerful effect and when the smoke is emitted, it is mixed in the air and pollute the air. These are all personal air pollutions, caused by individuals by releasing harmful smokes.

The individuals who use the tobacco or the products of the hemp plant face the risk of throat and lungs cancer. But their attitudes towards the positive effects of these pollutants make them to argue that they do not bother about what is going to take place after many years, but they say that at present they are free from tension and stress and have some kind of relaxation, a kind of pleasure, thrill and emotional excitement which they wanted for enjoying the life. They know that there were instances of death by throat and lungs cancer due to smoking and by using the narcotics. But still they are continuing the practice of tobacco smoking and the use of the hemp products. On one side World Health Organization (WHO) is propagating the evils or the risks of using cigarettes and narcotics, on the other side the tobacco companies and the cigarette companies put up counter argument that there is no harm in using tobacco in any form. Since there is no constitutional way of stopping this, the consequences of air pollution by smokes emitted by individuals cannot be checked in any country.

The personal air pollutions, caused by individuals by smoking, directly attack the non-smokers and smokers. But there are other forms of air pollutions caused through environmental pollutions. These pollutions are mainly caused by some of the industries which release enormous amount of wastages and other waste products in the environmental situations. They also release toxic materials. This is taking place in and around urban city areas. Modernization, industrial development and production of chemical substances are in fast progress and chemical substances are applied in modern industries in some form. The benefits, people are going to enjoy by these developments are highlighted by the industrial managements and the Governments. It is pleasant to listen to all such hopes and propaganda, but the consequences and risks they are going to face are not thought of either by the management or by the Government.

They promise that so many thousands people are going to be employed in these industries and benefited. People also feel happy when they are absorbed in such industries. But they do not know the risk they are going to face later on, the toxic effects in such situations. This was what had happened in the Bhopal Gas tragedy incident. Thousands of workers and the general public were much affected by inhailing the air in which the Bhopal industrial gas was mixed when there was leakage of the gas. Apart from casuality cases several thousand people were made incapacitated and disabled. The conditions of many of the workers and people are still very precarious. They were not given any compensation for the injuries they suffered and there was no proper rehabilitation for settling the families who were suffered seriously. Many of them who became victims of the gas are suffering from all sorts of lungs diseases by breathing the gas-polluted air. Neither the plant management nor the Government have shown any interest on these people.

There is every likelihood of leakage of gas at times in gas plants and the gas pollute the air and put people in all sorts of health hazards.

There are also factories like the tanneries where the animal skins are tanned. There are many tanneries in some towns. The chemical substances are used for tanning the animal skins and lots of waste products are drained down from these factories and they are channelized into rivers or stored in large areas. These wastages not only pollute the environment by spoil the vegetation in nearby areas and also the river water, but also cause very unpleasant stink (smell) which affect the health of the workers and the people who live by the side of such factories. Workers in these factories and those who live nearby are suffering from some kind of lungs diseases and also skin diseases. There is no means of escaping from such health hazardous situations. There was some agitation against this kind of air and environmental pollutions. But, the Tannery Managements are so rich that they were able to hush up the matter and continue the same thing. Particularly in Kanpur and in some towns of North Arcot district in Tamil Nadu the situation is becoming very bad. Court orders were not carried out. These factories at the time of establishing the factories must make arrangements to recycle the waste products or must convert it in some form so that they do not cause any air pollution and create health hazards. The government should insist upon such industries or factories to make provisions to the toxic waste products.

The sugar factories are also sending out lots of waste products called molasses, which cause very unpleasant odour, and humans cannot tolerate it. This also causes air pollution. Recently some technical device has been discovered to make use of the molasses in paper industries. This type of recycling of the waste products must be made in all industries. The industrial smokes and waste products consistently pollute the air in the atmosphere. This in turn affect not only the health of the people, but also cause damage to buildings. For example there are lots of complaints that the historical monument, Taj Mahal, is much affected by the pollutants of various types. Of which the polluted atmospheric air and smokes are very important.

The development of environmental psychology has brought to light many aspects of environmental conditions affecting human behaviour and health. For example, the persons who are planning the urban development and modernization, the architects, the builders and the engineers are perceiving everything in their own ways. Their intention is only to construct buildings and industries for modernization. They do not perceive the consequences of their acts in the near future. How much inconveniences and health hazards they are going to cause to the people who are going to live in the surrounding areas? They also do not realize whether the construction they are making are with proper air ventilation, or fresh air moving through the windows.

Environmental psychologists have observed many such constructions made without taking into consideration of the human aspects. Proshansky and others (1970) have observed two important areas of research in the field of environmental psychology such as the quality of the environment and the influence of architectural and spatial composition on people in the surrounding areas. The type of architectural designs and construction of buildings are either for residence or for office accommodations and also for the functioning of schools and colleges, hospitals, courts and prisons and they should suit to the needs and also provide conveniences to the concerned people. But on the name of modern designs, the buildings lack free ventilation and natural light. Since fresh air is a most important physical environmental component and also is having effect on life and health of the people, constructions should have free movement of fresh air in the area and in the buildings. High constructions prevent the fresh air passing from one area to other areas.

The flat system of constructions have several disadvantages from health point of view. People will have to live a stereotype way of life in flats. Life becomes highly mechanical and people lose interest to live in such buildings for longer duration. Further there is too much of crowding in the same building. Personal interaction or social interaction among these people depends upon several factors, which may not be prevailing there for want of like mindedness. There will be also more unwanted noises in such buildings, when several families are put together in one building in different flats. Therefore the architectural designs and constructions not taking into consideration of the physical environmental components, which are having influence upon human behaviour and health in the urban areas, cause much psychological dissatisfaction on the long run. The constructions should be free from mainly air and noise pollutions and the effects of crowding.

How Air Pollution is Perceived?

The atmospheric air in urban area is, generally, always hot, hotter than the rural air. The urban air with all its industrial and automobile smokes, the sewage and drainage smells are highly polluted and people will have to breathe the air mixed with all sorts of toxic substances. Humans breathe and smell all types of smokes and do not differentiate whether it is a bad smell or good smell or wanted smell or unwanted smell. We do not want to breathe and smell poisonous gases and smokes or the air mixed with chemical substances. But we enjoy the breeze by feeling and breathing and also the smells of flowers, smells of cosmetics, smells of the perfumes and scents. We breathe and smell the camphor, the sandal paste, and many things in temples. We feel that they are harmless smells and so we breathe. But even these smells when breathed cause allergy to some people and they avoid even these pleasant smell to breathe in. The nose is the specialized sensory apparatus which can differentiate any type of smell and can make us to accept or to reject. The olfactory membrane in the nose is very sensitive to odours. Whether the air is fit for breathing or not, is judged by the olfactory membrane of the nose. We breathe and smell only through our nose.

We breathe the air through our nose and also smell through our nose. Unlike seeing and hearing which are having separate sense organs the eyes, and the ears, breathing and smelling do not have separate sense organs. But in the nose the olfactory membrane is very sensitive to smells and when there is any stimulation in the olfactory receptors we realize the smell. The air is all the times is passing through the nose, but we do not realize any smell all the times. The olfactory receptors are located on the roof of the nasal passage (cavities). They are like the hair endings specialized in smelling. Generally, it is called olfactory epithelium. This is located on either side of the nasal cavity. This is smell sensitive area. At the end of each nasal passage located are, one olfactory bulb and the other is olfactory epithelium. If the breathing air is having any smell, it stimulates the olfactory area. Since the air passage is just below the olfactory area, sometimes we will have to take deep breath to smell something. But strong odours stimulate the olfactory area at once. Particularly polluted air, since mixed with strong odours, is smelt and perceived (Figs. 3.2 and 3.3). But certain odourless and colourless toxic substances pollute the air and we breathe without any sense of smell, often affect the health. For example, carbon monoxide which is odourless and colourless, is found to be highly poisonous gas. In urban areas where there is heavy automobile traffic carbon monoxide is having high concentration in the air.

Since air pollution is associated with smell or odour, people develop negative attitude toward the pollutants which cause air pollution. Bad smell in the air is disliked by people. It is not only in the air, but also in people. The Americans associate odour with human body. The

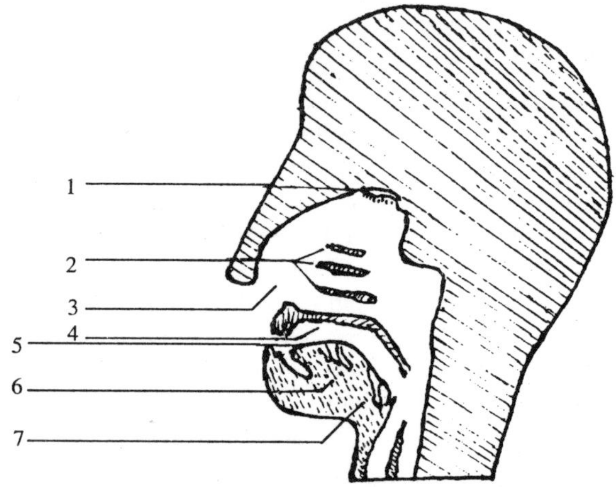

FIG.3.2 : Showing the parts of Olfaction

1. Olfactory nerve, 2. Turbinate bones, 3. Nasal cavity, 4. Hard palate (Palatine bones), 5. Tongue, 6. Lingual nerve, 7. Glosssopharyngeal nerve

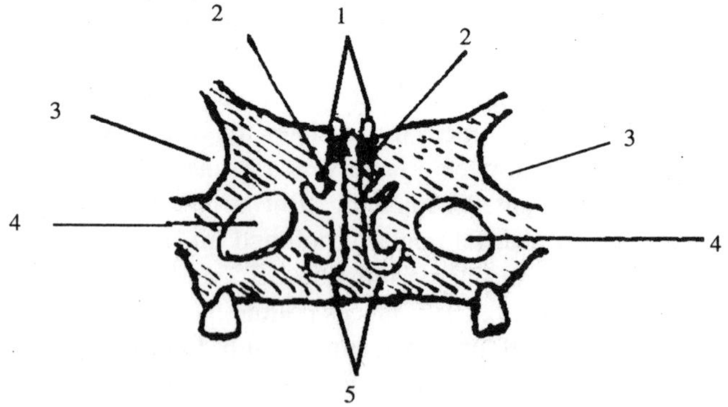

FIG. 3.3 : Showing the Frontal section of skull in the region of Olfactory Mucous.

1. Olfactory bulb, 2. Olfactory epitheliain, 3. Orbit, 4. Mazillary sinus, 5. Nasal passages

Europeans when they migrated to America, they brought the Negroes from South Africa as labourers to work in fields and plantations. They experienced some kind of odour in the body of the Negroes. Since they were black, dirty and unhealthy, the Americans associated body odour with the Negroes and with the people of different skin colours. This attitude become generalized among the American culture and they developed a negative attitude or prejudice toward people who have body odour or foul smell. This body odour or foul smell is also smelt in the bodies of the people of other races, even in the bodies of white people.

We could observe in any society that some people may sweat profusely which may cause some kind of unpleasant smell and we may hesitate to mix with such people. It is not due to unclean habits, but due to some racial stock or hereditary trait. In some experimental studies it was observed that if persons come to know that they are sharing the experience of unpleasant odour, they begin to develop more liking towards people experiencing similar smell (Bell *et al.* 1978). The social interaction among people is also based upon certain similar exposures. It may be experiencing bad odour or air pollution.

The Effect of Air Pollution and Wind on Performance

Air pollution is found to be having effect on human performance. Studies show that carbon monoxide with 25 to 125 concentration parts per million has been found in urban roads when there was heavy traffic. This much of concentration of carbon monoxide in air is very harmful. As the concentration of carbon monoxide is increased, even few minutes exposure to it is found to be causing impairment. Persons who breathe polluted air, were found to be having decrement in performance. Breisacher (1971) has stated that air pollution caused by carbon monoxide had unfavourable effects on performance like reaction time, manual dexterity and attention.

The effects of wind has been studied and found to be having adverse effects on human performance. Wind is air in motion. It is the strong current of air. A gale is a current air. Therefore wind is a current of air, sometimes it becomes a considerable force, moving horizontally from areas of high pressure to areas of low pressure. Sometimes it is also turning to be a sweeping and destructive force. These are the characteristics of the wind. Therefore when there is wind in an area it will not be possible for us to perform any work there. Generally on the sea shores wind may be forcibly blowing often. Wind may travel 80 mph to 100 mph. The area where rocky mountains meeting plains often subjected to torrent winds. The natural winds with speed and turbualence damage buildings and destroy properties, uproots trees in such areas, movements of any type are hampered, the trains are thrown off the rails, ships sink in sea water. Therefore the effects of wind are so dangerous that nothing can be done against it.

There is no correct means of perceiving the wind. Man is endowed with many sensory apparatuses with which he can perceive objects, sounds, tastes, smells, hard and smooth things, weights, hot and cold, but he has no any specialized sensory apparatus to perceive wind. He can feel only the pressure of the air or wind but no receptors to detect the wind. But man can hear the sound produced by the torrent wind and see the direction in which it is blowing. A scale has been devised to evaluate the wind by Sir Francis Beaufort (1774-1857), an English admiral in the first quarter of nineteenth century. The scale is named after his name Beaufort Scale. It is an international scale of wind velocities ranging from 0 (calm) to 12 hurricane force for practical purposes. This scale was devised for activities in high seas. But it can be also used in lands. Beaufort's scale is the earliest and most widely used indexes. Bell *et al.* (1978) state that there are also cases that elderly persons were killed by the blowing winds. Later on a scale has been designed on the model Beaufort by Penwarden (1973) to study the effects of wind on human beings. The scale can measure (index) the force of wind on the body.

There are not many studies, about the effects of wind on human performance, conducted in this field. These studies are not only difficult, but also complex. Several variances are involved in it. Whether the experiment should be conducted in the natural wind blowing situation or in an artificial wind blowing situation? If it is conducted in the artificial wind blowing situation, will the reaction be natural? But a study has been reported by Poulton, *et al.* (1975). The results of the study showed that wind had adverse effects on performances of the subjects.

Experiments on the Effects of Air Pollution and Wind

There are few experimental studies on the effects of air pollution. With regard to the perception of air pollution the studies made by Crowe (1968), Hummel *et al.* (1973) may be considered as worth discussing.

They used open-end question and they asked the subjects in simple question about air pollution. The subjects instead of answering to the question directly, they stated the effects of air pollution, caused by smoke and smog. They did not include factories and automobiles as the causes of pollution.

In the experiment conducted by Beard and Wertheimer (1967) the subjects, who volunteered, were exposed to carbon monoxide concentration, ranging from 50 ppm to 250 ppm for different periods of time. The task assigned to them was to make judgments about the time intervals. The experimenters have observed that when the subjects were exposed for 90 minutes to carbon monoxide at 50 ppm concentration there was considerable amount of performance decrement on the judgment of time intervals. When the concentration of carbon monoxide increased for similar impairment of work, they will have to expose for shorter times period. The experimenters also used rats in their study and they found that for the 100 ppm concentration of carbon monoxide, an exposure of 11 minutes had adverse effect on learning in rats in the operant conditioning position.

The effects of wind on behaviour has been studied by Poulton *et al.* (1975). The experimenters used female subjects in their experiment. They were exposed to the winds of 8 mph and 20 mph with different levels of turbulence. It was conducted in a wind tunnel. These wind conditions were designed just strong enough to cause slight discomfort to cause extremely uncomfortable state to have noticeable effect on performance. They altered the air temperature between 60° F and 70°F and the humidity varied from 70 to 85 per cent. The experimenters have observed several interesting results. The subjects were taking one side of the path instead of walking on straight path. They have taken more time to put on rain coat. The subjects' blinkings increased per minute for 12 to 18. They have taken more time to select words from a list. Their feelings of discomfort increased. These results of the experiment show that winds are having influence in performance and in the feelings of human beings.

Curbing Air Pollution

Since air pollutions and environmental pollutions have become international problems, Governments in India both at the centre and state levels have taken some steps to control the pollutions. The Pollution Control Boards are taking interest in controlling all sorts of pollutions.

Now, there are a number of technological devices developed to deal with the pollutions. They say that substantial reduction in the emissions of air pollutions has taken place. But the existing methods of dealing with air and environmental pollutions are not so much effective as expected. Therefore, new methods are being evolved to deal with the pollutions. This involves the operation of hydrogen. It is believed that the operation of hydrogen can achieve an emission of zero level or so close to it, but the difference cannot be measured by the existing instruments. Even in operating of natural gas these technologies can achieve zero emissions of some pollutants and near zero level in the case of others.

One of the recent technological developments is the use of combined-cycle turbines. The gas fired combined-cycle turbines are able to generate electricity that reduces air pollution to the level of 50 to 99 per cent compared to most of the coal burning power plants. There is also another technology in which the aircraft-derivative turbines are used. It has been observed that the aircraft-derivative turbines are able to curb air-pollution by 20 per cent to 90 per cent. A third device of technology is also used to curb the air pollution by operating fuel cells. The fuel cells devices are used for converting fuel into electricity chemically. This can achieve an efficiency of curbing the air pollution roughly about 40 per cent.

To speak of air pollution and inventing devices of curbing the air pollution appear to be a strange phenomenon. In the history of human kind it is unheard of in the past. But now we will have organize pollution control boards all over the world as it has become a serious human problem. The cause behind this growing problem is the inexorable growth of population and the growing amount of industrial smokes and gases, and the wastages and toxic materials released from the modern industries. Therefore it results in the profusion of new technologies to produce cars, power plants, and paints and other machines that could generate zero to near zero air pollution. The Pollution Control Boards at the State and Central levels should take steps to implement the policy of permitting only the vehicles that can emit only zero or near zero air pollution on the roads on a time bound programme.

The effects of air pollution and the wind, we have described in the earlier pages may be some use to those who are really interested in knowing something about air pollution and the disastrous consequences of wind. The effects of air pollution from psychological perspective is with regard to human performance and behaviour as a whole. The miseries caused by air pollution to human-kind are more often neglected by a section of people. So long as it is not affecting them directly they do not bother about it.

Man needs fresh air to breathe in for his healthy survival. It is true that no man is cent-per-cent healthy, but we do not want to be cent-per-cent unhealthy in this world. Therefore, a healthy atmosphere is needed for our healthy life. Many of us do not know what type of miseries we are facing when the air is polluted. Oxygen is abundant in the atmosphere and it is very much essential to life processes. What is taking place in man when he breaths in the polluted and oxygen deficient air? It becomes the cause of several respiratory ailments. The lungs are the breathing organs which have very much to do with the blood purification. If oxygen is deficit in lungs, in blood and in heart then the person has to struggle for breathing and at once artificial oxygen is supplied to the lungs and to the heart. Many heart trouble have their origin in oxygen deficiency. There are methods of producing oxygen artificially, but man cannot produce sufficient oxygen and supply to the atmosphere.

8. PERSONAL SPACE AND INTERPERSONAL CONTACT

Introduction

Though man is a social animal and makes out social environment of his own, he mainly depends upon the physical environment for his living. The physical environment affects his life in a number of ways. So long as the physical environments or our surroundings are not disturbing us and pleasant we are happy, but when they become unpleasant or disturbing, our life becomes miserable. Actually our physical environment and surroundings are more pleasant and exciting and we live our life happily. Psychological studies include the environmental aspects as one of the subjects of study in recent times since human behaviour is much influenced by many of the environmental factors. What sort of reaction man makes toward the positive and negative aspects of the environmental factors? Holahan (1986) states that environmental psychology deals with the interaction between the physical world and human behaviour. Sommer (1980) states that the goal of environmental psychology is to understand how the physical environmental affects human behaviour and also apply the knowledge to make changes and improvements in the environment. In the earlier sections we have dealt with various aspects of physical and social environments and also environmental stresses such as noise, temperature, air pollution and wind. Now we shall discuss personal space and territorial behaviour and the reaction to intrusions.

Personal Space

Every human being wishes to have a personal space of his own in the interacting environment. According to Sommer (1966) people interact with their environment in two ways, one is personal space and the other is territory. The personal space is referring to the invisible boundary line on all sides of us. It is limited to the individual's surrounding area. Others cannot easily encroach into the area. There is physical boundary line for this. It is not seen, it is invisible. This space is moving with every one of us. This personal space may enlarge in certain situations and also it may shrink in certain situations according to business or the type of interaction we make with persons and places. If there is any encroachment into this by others it may result in conflict or withdrawal.

Generally, territory refers to any tract of land, it is a geographical domain under the jurisdiction of a political unit. Or territory may refer to an area inhabited and defended by an individual or animal or a breeding pair of animals. Territory unlike personal space is fixed, permanent and stationary. It can be seen. The areas can be notified by an individual that it belongs to him. An individual can claim the ownership of the area. Territory is home centred. An man owning a physical space has a boundary line on all four directions and he claims that it is his territory. Physical spaces like the house, cultivating land, a forest area, a hill area, sea area, all have a territory.

Personal space is not a new concept. It has been used by early writers in their works. Psychologists have become more familiar with this concept only after 1960 when a field of psychology called environmental psychology has emerged. Personal space finds its root in other physical sciences, like biology, anthropology and architecture. The concept of personal space was first used by Katz (1937) in his work *'Animals and Men'*. Since 1960 the term has become very popular in the personal and scientific world. Bell *at al.* (1978) state that more than two hundred publications have been brought out in the field of environmental psychology in a short period of twenty years from 1960 to 1980.

Every man is maintaining an interpersonal distance between him and others. This is a universal practice. This becomes necessary from several points of view. If there is no certain distance between persons in the interpersonal relation, then it may sometimes lead to conflicts, aggression and even violence. There may be also pleasant experiences if only the interpersonal relation is between the opposite sexes. The interpersonal distance may also cause stress and tension. We may not like the olfactory stimulation, the smell of person which is caused at close proximity. The personal space between persons should be adequate to arouse response. Any inadequate personal space may cause under stimulation and hence there will not be any reaction from other members. Personal space which is too close may cause restriction in our behaviours. At close proximity there is no behavioural freedom for the individual. He loses his privacy. Sometimes there may be encroachment into another man's personal space. This may cause severe unpleasant experiences. Whether a person likes it or not there may be forcible encroachment into another person's personal space by some people, causing embarrassment and all sorts of inconveniences. In such cases the man is not maintaining any privacy or secrecy nor we may call this as intimacy.

In the physical environment we are facing certain problems created by the people around us. The social environment may be also stated as interpersonal environment. What sort of reaction we are having to the interpersonal environment is an important aspect of our everyday life. In the surroundings, we are moving about and each one of us is having a surrounding area. The area surrounding each of us is treated by us as an integral part of us. The area each one of us occupy in the space is considered to be one's personal space. This area is extended on all sides around us. But the area is very wider and larger in front of us than all other sides. The physical space one occupies in the surrounding environment is referred to as the personal space. This personal space is claimed by a person wherever he/she goes. Therefore one maintains an interpersonal distance. This is generally determined by the culture one belongs to. For example, when two people of different cultures meet, the interpersonal space is generally longer. They maintain an interpersonal distance. But when persons of the same culture meet, the interpersonal space is shorter. The interpersonal distance is closer.

Culture and Personal Factors in interpersonal Contact and Personal Space

Culture and Sex in Interpersonal Spacing

One's personal space in the interpersonal environment is limited. The individual is happy and comfortable in his/her personal space. But there may be intrusion in one's personal space by another person. This may be acceptable or may be aversive or intense dislike. But this depends upon the person who is intruding into one's personal space. The state of being the same culture of the intruder determine whether he/she is acceptable or not. Experiments have been conducted to test the effects of sex and culture. Ashton, Shaw and Worsham (1980) in one of their studies had two groups of subjects. One group consisted of pairs of friends and the other group, pairs of strangers. They were asked to stand at various distances and report what they have felt. The males and females of their subjects felt more comfortable when an opposite sex friend was close to them, but not comfortable when a stranger was there.

They have observed in their studies that females interacted more closely than the males. Females generally interact at a more closer distance with one another than the males do. Males usually maintain certain distance with one another. But in Rustamli's (1986) study the result was the opposite to this. Females keep more distance among themselves and with an opposite sex strangers than the males. With regard to invasion. Fisher and Byrne (1975) have observed that males were more inclined for invasion in the front than the females and females tend to be more negatively responding to invasion from the side. Hall (1966), an anthropologist originally was interested in the cross cultural studies, also has shown some interest in the study of the distance, people place between and among themselves in their interactions in various situations. According to the results of his studies people in North America, Great Britain, and Scandinavia like to have greater distance between one another, whereas people in the Middle East, France and Greece were not. The personal space with different standard often create many problems. Tourists who visit different countries who were not aware of such standards in the personal space get offended by these interpersonal spacing problems.

Age and Personal Distance

The socialization process, in every culture, is mainly responsible for this interpersonal spacing problems. Burgess (1981) states that young children while playing, move very closely and have very close distance, touch and hold each other. But when they advance in age to nine or ten years, children maintain spaces of greater distances among themselves. Their physical contact like touching and holding each other also getting reduced. Several investigators like Price and Dabbs (1974), Shea (1981) and others confirm this type of space distance. As they become adolescents and adults the distance is affected. Therefore age and culture determine the personal space between and among the persons. The personal space in the interpersonal environment in India is very much finding place in the social life of the people. In maintaining personal distance religion, caste and communities play an important role.

Situation and Personal Distance

The personal space is not the same everywhere. Personal space may be affected by the situation in which people are involved. In public meetings, in auditorium, in stadium, where football or tennis matches are played, and also in picture houses, personal distance is reduced considerably. In a crowd there is no personal space or distance. In certain situation there may be unintentional intrusions or invasions. Therefore personal space changes according to our needs and situations. Personal space also depends upon the nature of the people and business. According to Hall (1966) North Americans interact and maintain space in one of four of the distances such as (1) intimate distance, (2) personal distance, (3) social distance and (4) public distance. Hall states that the intimate distance is very close almost nil distance and it may vary upto one and a half feet distance. This distance in the interpersonal environment may be either in love making or in fight like wrestling or boxing. The personal distance may range from one and a half feet to four feet. This distance may take place with friends and also with strangers, and depending upon the nature of business.

The social distance may take place in certain business transactions, supervision works, in giving orders and so on. The distance may vary from four feet to twelve feet. The public distance is maintained mostly in political meetings, or similar meetings in which the person who speaks, keeps a distance from the audience. The public distance is also maintained in dramas where the actors are in the stage and the audience are away from the stage.

Interactions among people are taking place in all these four interpersonal environments. But what sort reaction people have and what type of effects are taking place in these various distances? We cannot say that interactions are comfortable at these distances and also had the desired effects. The more longer the distance between the communicator and the listener the more discomforts the listener finds and the effect also may be nil. Even in ordinary conversations the persons must be within an audible distance. Certain information people wanted to discuss at close range. People, generally, wish to talk private matters sitting close together.

Studies have been conducted by Albert and Dabbs (1970) among college students. The students were made to listen to some message communicated by an experimenter. It was a business type of interaction and the experimenter communicated the message by sitting at varied distances. He sat at two feet, five feet and fifteen feet away and communicated the message. According to Hall this type of information should be communicated from a distance of five feet. At the end it was verified with students to see which distance had better effect. It was found that the subjects were able to reproduce more information when they heard from a distance of five feet than the other two distances. It was observed that either more close and more far away distances were uncomfortable to the listener. Scott (1984) has observed in his recent study that people wish to sit more closer when they talk about private or sex matters with their intimate friends. Other matters they speak even at louder tone to communicate the matter to persons who are ten or fifteen feet away from them.

Culture and Interpersonal Contact and Personal Space

Experimental studies have been conducted to find out the determinants of personal space in various situations. Interaction or interpersonal reaction among various types of people takes place in society. The types of interpersonal reaction and the interpersonal space vary from culture to culture. Therefore we cannot say that the personal space in interpersonal reaction would be the same in all cultures as stated by Hall (1966) in his studies. Even in the case of intimate contact that takes place in sex and love the personal space varies. The personal space in the interpersonal contact in Indian culture varies very much from the European and American cultures. Even in the intimate contact like the sex and love the Indian culture maintain the traditional behaviour pattern. When a boy and girl love each other and wanted to marry, they cannot do this unless they belong to the same religion, same caste and sect. Even if everything is in agreement then, they cannot have free mixing until they are married. They must maintain certain personal distance. Otherwise it may create some social problem.

In some communities in India the boy and girl who are getting married will see each other only at the time of marriage. Parents and other elders make all arrangements and when they are satisfied, then the marriage is celebrated. The personal space even in the case of marriage is not close or very close. It is at a non-seeable distance. In some communities only at the time of betrothal the boy and girl can see each other sitting at a distance in the presence of everybody. This personal space may be ten to fifteen feet. This type of traditional pattern of behaviour in some educationally or socially advanced communities is getting changed.

The impact of western culture and the college and university education, the influence of the themes of motion pictures are making radical changes in the traditional patterns and in the interpersonal contacts and the personal spaces are getting shorter and shorter to the extent of having even premarital sexual contacts. The personal space that was maintained between boys and girls, earlier to 1950s was very long. In schools and colleges where boys and girls study in co-educational institutions, the boys and girls were made to sit separately, maintaining certain distance. In some educational institutions, at present, in 1990s free mixing of boys and girls is going on. These changes are taking place in Indian society due to several factors. The free mixing of boys and girls in some educational institutions is spreading out to other institutions and also to the adolescents and young adult groups which in many cases lead to love and sexual contacts and also marriages. The distance maintained between the boys and girls prior to 1950s gradually reduced in the interpersonal contacts and in personal space. This is the state of affair among socially advanced, economically well placed and educationally progressed communities in India.

But, on the other side, the socially backward, economically impoverished and educationally down-trodden communities in the interpersonal contacts, the personal space is maintained at much longer distance with other communities who are also well off in some respects. These people maintain longer distance with advanced communities in all sorts of communication. There is no chance for intimate contact or communication at a closer range between the down-trodden and the advanced communities. The distance maintained by them is still a 'traditional distance' which was maintained long long ago.

In some of the tribal groups and hill tribes in India the interpersonal contact and personal space vary from other community people. Among some of the tribal communities the male member should take the girls whom he is going to marry and live in his abode with her and produce one child in a specified time. Then only he is qualified to marry the girl. If he has not produced a child he is not competent to become a husband of a woman. This practice is also prevalent in some of the hill tribes. This type of contact is with regard to sex, love and marriage. The personal space of the male member with the female member is very close as it is intimate contact. The tribal customs permit this sort of interpersonal contacts. But the personal space between one tribal groups and another tribal group is very wide. They maintain longer distance in communication. Therefore, the determinants of personal space are not only the situations or nature of work or business, but also the cultural factors and traditions and the characteristics of the groups. Hence, experimental studies should be conducted among various groups and cultures to know the distance in the interpersonal contacts and the distance maintained in the personal space, between persons. The procedure applicable to one culture or group may not be applicable to another culture and group. Therefore, different methods should be devised to study the determinants of personal space. Knowles and Johnson (1974) state that there are various methods to measure personal space, but they have certain general association between various methods. They indicate only the same dimension. Therefore according to them there should be several measurement techniques instead of depending upon one single method.

Interpersonal Contact, Personal Space and Sex

There are several factors experimentally determined as the determinants of interpersonal contacts and personal space. They are mainly interpersonal attraction which is the effect of spatial behaviour, particularly with opposite sex, the interpersonal similarity due to various characteristics, particularly age, race, culture and community and the type of contact either in the individual situation or in a group situation, favourably or unfavourably.

The spatial effect on behaviour can be seen particularly, in sex and love. This occurs between individuals of opposite sex. The process involved in sex and love is between individuals. The process is attraction. This attraction between individuals of the opposite sex occurs among the individuals of the same age group. There cannot be interpersonal attraction between a young girl and an old man or between a young man and an old lady. In a spatial situation if there is any itnerpersonal attraction between a young man and young lady the more they look at each other, the greater the attraction exists between them, and the more they are physically closer, the shorter the distance between them. The personal space is physically reduced, leading to, intimate contact between them. Bell *et al.* (1978) state that the relationship between the feeling aspects and personal space is more complete in the case of sex. They state that their research results seem to agree with popular opinion.

In a situation if a male and a female interact, there is increased attraction and the physical space is shorter. This has been studied by Allegies and Byrne (1973), Byrne, Ervin and Lamberth (1970) and Edwards (1972). In these studies it was found that matched coupled liked each other and they stood close together than mismatched couples. The attraction—nearness relationship takes place, more in females than in males. The male moves closer as the female moves closer, thus both the male and the female move closer toward each other. Edwards (1972) found in his studies that there was smaller distance between the males and females if they were close friends and the females move closer toward the males. The females responded more to the attractions than the males in the spatial situation. In the movement of male and female toward each other there is mutual attraction between them, because of the nearness or proximity. Therefore the distance between the male and female is determined by the degree of mutual attraction. The more the mutual attraction prevails between the male and female friends, the shorter the distance exists between them.

Interpersonal Contact, Personal Space and Similarity

Similarity is one of the factors that determine the interpersonal attraction and the distance between such people is very short. Similarity may be in personality traits or characteristics, similarity in views or ideas, in political ideologies, in religious affiliation, nationality and so on. In India, people belonging to the same community develop interpersonal attraction. In the case of caste or community people forget all other dissimilarities in persons and develop interpersonal attraction and they move very close and the distance between them becomes very short. This is more effective among the persons of opposite sex of the same caste or community.

Researches have been conducted as to why should similarity leads to attraction and closer interpersonal distance. Byrne (1971) states that he has observed in his study how similarities in people function as a psychological process of attracting each other to closer interpersonal distance. People generally expect to have more interpersonal reaction with those who are liked by them because of certain similarities in them than those whom they disliked or in whom they do not find similarities. Byrne says that protection against some danger or threat is the cause of personal space. The personal willingness to interact closely with similar rather than dissimilar persons provides safety for each other. One can communicate information to liked persons, whom one chooses to be at closer distance because of interpersonal attraction.

The similarities, if greater in degree than, the interpersonal friendship also is greater and the distance is very close. Dosey and Meisels (1969), Rosenfeld (1965) studied the emotional states of the individuals in the interpersonal situations. They have observed that the negatively toned emotional states enlarged the personal space. The negative emotional situations created more distance in the interactions while a positive emotional situations created closer distances in the interactions.

Interpersonal Contact, Personal Space and Experience

Personal space is also determined by several other factors like individual differences, that is differences between individuals and differences between groups. Experiences of the individuals at various levels determine the personal space. Persons with the same level of experience maintain very close distance among them in the personal space. Persons with less experience maintain certain distance with more experienced persons in the personal space.

Occupation: Personal space also varies on the basis of occupational level. Persons of the same occupation maintain closer distance and persons of higher occupational level maintain certain longer distance with persons of lower occupational level.

Interpersonal Space and Age: Age also is another factor that determines the type of interpersonal reaction between individuals.

Persons of younger age maintain certain longer distance in the personal space with the persons of older age. Since there are several factors causing differences between young and old, the younger persons do not find congenial atmosphere with older people as the younger persons lack qualities to the level of the older people.

Race and Culture in Interpersonal Space: Apart from the personal characteristics of the individuals, there are also racial, cultural and national factors that determine the personal space. Persons belonging to different cultural and sub-cultural groups maintain longer distance with the persons belonging to different cultural groups of sub-cultural groups. The cultural norms and behaviour patterns vary from culture to culture. One who is not familiar with norms of other culture may find it difficult in the company of the people of other culture. When people of different cultures meet in a situation there is cross-cultural differences in the spatial behaviour pattern. People of different cultures show spatial differences in the interpersonal contacts. There will be considerable amount of distance between persons of different cultures. In the studies made by Hall (1966) it was observed that the Latin Americans, the French, the Greeks, and Arabs maintain intimate contact. Even in the case of smell and touch they maintained closer interpersonal distance than the Americans. In another study Sommer (1969) and Little (1968) have observed that the English, Swedish and the Swiss also maintain the distance in the interpersonal contact like the Americans. Willis (1966) found in his study that every cultural group members interact more closely only with the members of their own cultural group. They maintained certain distance in their interaction with the non-members of their group. But the distance maintained by the members of one cultural group was not consistant with the non-members of the group.

Socio-economic Status in Interpersonal Space

The distance maintained by the cultural groups in the interpersonal reaction was also maintained in the racial groups. For example, the white and black social group members have maintained a common distance. In the study made by Scherer (1974) it was found that the low-socio-economic status white children maintained certain distance in the interaction with middle-socio-economic status white children. The white middle class socio-economic status children also interact with greater distance with black children. It was also observed in these studies that the socio-economic status of the racial groups had better effect in maintaining distance in the interpersonal contact than the racial difference could maintain.

Among the various Indian communities though the communal hierarchy is there in maintaining distance in the interpersonal contacts, if the socio-economic status is better and equal, then the distance in the interpersonal contacts becomes shorter among various communities. The distance in the interpersonal contacts of the same socio-economic status of different communities may become so close sometimes that it may result even in marriage, if the members were of opposite sexes.

Likes and Dislikes in Interpersonal Space

Males and females show different spatial distance in their interpersonal contacts. There is more distance among strangers or disliked. But the distance is very shorter among the members liked. This distance in interpersonal contacts among females is very close among the liked members than among the strangers and disliked. Female pairs maintain closer distance than male pairs. This sort of closer distance can be observed right from childhood period, through adolescent stage to adult stage among female members. According to the studies made by Hartnett, Bailey and Gibson (1970) if the pair is of opposite sex (a male and a female) then the distance is very close than of the same sex.

Encroachment into one's Personal Space

Encroachment into one's personal space means close intrusion into personal space or invasion into one's space. Invasion has been generally used when a nation aggressively raid into another nation's territory. In the history of the world we come across many invasions of one nation into the another nation, mostly on the neighbouring nation. In the interpersonal contacts also invasion is used when one gets into another person's personal space. Invasion, intrusion, and encroachment convey the same meaning, which causes a negative experience. This is with respect to strangers of unknown persons. We are not willingly admitting a stranger to get into our personal space. Invaders aggressively get into the close distance with others. In such cases we develop negative experiences. But, the same intrusion made by one close friend or the lover arouses positive experience.

Studies have been conducted on the intrusions into the personal space. In the study made by Konecni and others (1975) the experimental subjects were standing, waiting on the road side to cross the road and there were the same sex associates, were also standing and waiting at one, two, five and ten feet away from the *E* subjects. It was observed that the closer the stranger stood to the subjects the faster they crossed the road. The rapidity of crossing the road varied with the distances the strangers stood from the *E* subjects. After few years, similar study was conducted by Smith and Knowles (1979). The same procedure was repeated. But in this study the experimental subjects were interviewed and they were asked to state the nature of behaviour they observed in strangers. The subjects have stated that the strangers who stood very close to them were more rude, aggressive and hostile than those who stood at greater distances. Another study was made in the crowded elevator situation by Syndstrom and Sundstrom (1977). They observed that if the intruder is not moving away, then there is a tendency to get rid of spatial intrusion either by avoiding the visual look or by moving away from that situation. Patterson (1973) also observed the same result in his study.

A stranger intruder, whether arouses a negative experience or positive experience or what sort of physiological arousal makes on the individual, depends upon the cognitive perceptual process the individual develops towards the intruder. It may be anger or friendship, happiness or unhappiness, love or hatred. Storms and Thomas (1977) used some male subject in their experiment. The subjects were asked to sit at a six inches distance or at thirty inches distance from male college students. It was found that half of the subjects were treated in a friendly manner, had positive experience. The other half of the subjects were treated in hostile manner and they had negative experience. The experimental subjects were both friendly and unfriendly with the male college students. The friends subjects liked best by them and least liked the unfriends subjects who interacted at six inches distances. In another similar study made by Cowen *et al.* (1982) among the children, it was observed that the children had reacted positively to the adult intruders who had helped them. Thus, in all these experimental studies it was observed that invasion leads to negative or positive experience. It was based upon the physiological changes due to cognitive experience the individual develops towards the intruder.

9. TERRITORIAL BEHAVIOUR

Characteristics of Territory

Personal space is invisible, flexible, body-centred boundary and it regulates how closely we interact with others. It is contrasted with territory. Territory refers to the geographical domain under the jurisdiction of a person or a nation or a political unit. An area whether it is small or larger owned by a person which is having a boundary line on all four sides. The boundary line drawn on all four sides is territory for the area or land. The concept territory applies not only to a piece of land owned by a person, but also a sovereign state or a nation ruled by a king or monarch or by a democratic or socialistic leaders. Any thing related to a land is having a territory. Territory is physical, visible, stationary and home-centered. Territory is maintained and regulated by someone who is responsible for it. Territory, since it is physical and having a boundary, and ownership, it is defended. Territorial behaviour can be stated as a type of behaviour and individual or a group of people stake and defend on the right of having the ownership of the physical space. Thus we can define human territory. Human beings use different approaches to indicate their territory by means of putting fences, signals and name boards.

Animals and birds also have their own territory. They indicate their territories by leaving their scent around the area as a mark by urination. The animals do not permit into their area other animals to trespass. The male animal, which is considered to be the leader of the group will fight with all its might to defend the area from intruders or invaders. Territorial behaviour both in humans and animals is the same type. Both defend and fight for the right. Though both are of the same type there are differences. Animals protect their territories for food resources, shelter, mating and nesting. They do not change their territories and use the territories constantly for a continuous period. Animals territorial behaviour is mainly determined by biological factors. In these respects humans differ. Humans use not one territorial area, but use a number of territories. Some of the territories are temporary and some may be permanent. Humans may leave certain territories for lease for certain period or even sell out once for all. Humans' territorial behaviour is largely determined by cultural and social factors.

There are quite number of definitions of territorial behaviour, formulated by various authors. Altman (1975) has enumerated both animal definitions and human definitions of territorial behaviour. Territorial behaviour is practised by animals and humans. The territorial behaviour of animals and humans serve some important needs and motives for the organism, indicating the area of occupation, controlling it and defending it. Altman (1975) states that territories provide two important functions for humans. Human privacy is facilitated by territories and they further help humans to control over the physical space.

Kind of Territories

Territories are of various kinds. Some tentative classifications have been made. Since animals and birds are also having their own territories the human territories are having some special significances. According to Altman, humans have three kinds of territories. Therefore human territorial behaviour is associated with these three kinds of territories. They are primary territory, secondary territory and public territories.

Primary Territory

Primary territory is owned by individuals or groups. Individuals and groups may claim ownership of this type of territories. For example, homes, apartments, offices, farms, fields are primary territories. People claim these as their own properties. They are more safe and comfortable. They are also more secured of their properties by the territories. They make use of these and own them for an extended period of time. The person or the group who owns them has complete control over the primary territory. The person who owns them makes them personalized and claims permanent ownership and also makes other to perceive them that they are belonging to the person. The owner of the primary territory puts his name boards, sign boards, puts fences around the territory, barricades, doormates and puts all sorts of precautions to assure his control. But sometimes there may be intrusion into the primary territory by some strangers who were not invited. This is a very serious matter and the owner is very much distressed when a primary territory is invaded by some strangers without any authorization. The owners of primary territories are more concerned about their privacy in their territories. They do not tolerate any invasion or encroachment into their territories and wanted to intercept the intruders. What is taking place in the individual ownership of the territories is also taking place in the group ownership territories and in safeguarding the national territories. The defense of territory is very high in the case of primary territory.

Secondary Territory

Secondary territory refers to a physical space which is used by a group of people regularly. Every individual shares with others in using the territory. The space need not be owned by the people who use it. The space may be owned by somebody else, but those who use it are different individuals, collected at this space for some business or purpose. For example, a classroom, in the beginning of the year when a student attends the class occupies a seat and finds it comfortable. Hence everyday whether he/she goes to the class early or late can occupy the same seat. So also in a church service people normally occupy the same seat which they preferred to occupy in the beginning. In Parliament, Assembly, Municipal Council and in other organizational meetings seats are specified for the members and ministers. They occupy only the allotted seats for them. This space or seat is not owned by the individual. It is claimed as his/her seat during the period of legitimate occupation. An outsider who has nothing to do with the institution or organization cannot go there and occupy a seat. Only the qualified persons are competent to use the seats. Though the individuals do not have legitimate right to claim that it is his/her seat there is certain mutual understanding that one should not occupy another person's seat. Therefore there is no chance for uninvited encroachment in the case of secondary territories. In secondary territory there is only moderate defense.

Public Territories

Public territories refer to places or the physical spaces used by quite a number of people at the same time. The utility is only for a short period. For example, the sea shore beach area, the public waiting rooms at the airport, waiting room in the railway stations, waiting places in bus terminals, public parks, play grounds where matches are played, are all public territories. Seats in these places are occupied temporarily only for a short period. Seats in these places or space to these places are occupied whoever goes there first. Seats are available on the basis of first come first served. The seats or spaces in these territories are not owned by individuals. So long as one occupies a seat or space is his/her seat. This claim exists only for a short period temporarily.

Werner and others (1981) state that with all these characteristics of the public territories there is also chance for defending the public territories. According to Werner and others, particularly, players in a game situation claim temporary ownership of a given instrument or machine by touching first, and avoid or prevent any intruder from claiming the same instrument. When some space is marked by some one for his/her books in libraries others do not intrude into the marked space. It is just like reserving a space by some one. In play grounds and libraries this sort of marking instruments or spaces is quite common.

Dominance on the Territory

In maintaining and controlling the territory, animals and humans exercise dominance over the invaders or strangers in their own territory. But there is difference between animals and humans in defending or protecting their territories. Generally, humans are not defending their territories very actively. If the intruders come to know the territorial claim of other person they avoid confrontation. Humans tend to be more liberal in using and maintaining their territories. In the case of humans they put written board with address that this area belongs to so and so, no trespassing and so on. They also indicate by drawing lines. The area beyond this line belongs to them and the area within this line belongs to us. This is how humans claim their territories and maintain dominance. These types of indentity and organizational function reduce the stress with regard to territories.

Birds and animals are not like humans, adjust to the situation and contexts. For example, birds like pigeons and fowls maintain a territory of their own. These birds peck strange birds and drive them away. They protect their case or nest from the strangers and any one who goes near the young ones they fight with all right that the area belongs to them. In critical situations the pigeons go into their nest and claim their territories. The crows, particularly when they are hatching their eggs in their nests in the trees they do not allow other birds or even other crows to go nearby the tree. They also attack humans when they go near the tree fearing that they would destroy the nest and kill their young ones. The male and female crows one after the other would be watching whether anybody is nearing their nest. Thus the territory is dominated by these birds. Similarly the hen will protect the area where her young chicken are. The hen will not spare even her mistress when she approaches the young chicks.

Animals like the lion, tiger, elephant and other animals maintain their territories and if there is any intrusion the leader of these animals become very aggressive and fight with the intruders and drive them away. Therefore dominance on the territory is maintained by all living organisms. Rajecki *et al.* (1981) call this residential effect or home field advantage. Martindale (1971) states that people make more successful efforts in their own setting than in the setting of others. Taylor and Lanni (1981) state that a person can ascertain himself in a conversation in his own place than in somebody's place. The territorial dominance is more established in sports and games activities mostly. The home team in games like football, basket ball, hockey, tennis, has certain advantages for winning over the visiting team. It is because of the territorial dominance. It is functioning not only in the players, but also among the audience who are witnessing the match. But there is contradictory views, prevailing with regard to the territorial dominance in games. Hirt and Kimble (1981) state that the home team is more often the winner, while Baumeister and Steinhilber (1984) state that home teams tend to perform below their actual ability in the home ground.

Humans do not become very aggressive, normally, while defending their territories like birds and animals. But humans also become aggressive sometimes in defending their territories, like the boundary of their houses or farms, if any encroachment by the neighbours. Though in such cases humans go to court to get the disputes decided, if they find that it is too unjust, they become violent and attack each other. In Indian society the land disputes and quarrels sometimes become so serious that even murders may take place.

Territorial disputes among neighbouring nations may continue for years and sometimes war between the nations takes place, and forcibly one nation may occupy the disputed area. India as a nation had several bitter experiences with China and Pakistan. India fought several wars with China and Pakistan on territorial disputes, and still the dispute is going between India and Pakistan. Defence of territory, humans make, not only in the case of land boundary lines, but also in the case of sea and air. A nation is not tolerating another nation's aeroplanes flying over her nation. Except the commercially and internationally accepted route areas, other areas are prohibited for the aeroplanes of other nations. If there is any intrusion or encroachment of an aeroplane of other nation it is considered as an aggression and invasion and at once action will be taken against it. Similarly in the sea, there is international water line and any violation into a nation's water area, is taken as an aggression and dispute on the territory may take place. Often we come across such information in newspapers about the violation of territories of the nations.

Consequences of Territorial Disputes

Territorial disputes arise when the ownership of the particular physical space is brought under questionable status. There is no chance for dispute if the territory is well established, that it is belonging to some one. But if the territory is not established or unestablished one, then there is scope for dispute over it. The disputed or unestablished territory may cause aggression, quarrel and violence. There is chance for more than one person to claim that the particular territory belongs to him. One may claim the ownership on several backgrounds. On disputed territory persons who make claims on it often thrown into aggression and violence and also leading to criminal activities. When territorial boundaries are not well defined or ambiguous, persons, who are having more manpower organize gangs and claim the territory by force or violence. Such gangsters even occupy the areas and claim ownership of the territory. In Indian communities this sort of claims made by aggressive groups, the areas under disputes or unestablished or an area not having any owner, are quite common. Among the nations it is common occurrence in Arab countries. There is continuous aggression between the Israelites and the Palestenians on territorial disputes. The territorial dispute on Jammu and Kashmir between India and Pakistan is becoming never ending territorial dispute. The territorial dispute over 'Ram Jenma Bhumi' has caused lots of aggression and violence. Already mention was made that territorial disputes caused, India, China and Pakistan, to fight several wars.

While humans fight when territories are unestablished and disputed, animals fight when the territories are well established. For animals, might is right. This happens in the case of some animals. This kind of things also happen among humans, particularly if the concerned person is weak or vulnerable. The manner in which others perceive territories cause fear of violence among individuals who could not protect themselves. This type of tendency prevails among aged and among women. Undisputed or established territories do not cause any aggression or violence. There is stability and confirmation in established boundaries of territories. There is no chance of aggression and hostility.

Disputes over territory may occur wherever different ethnic or racial or cultural groups live in close proximity. One ethnic group may be occupying wider area in a place and more number of people may be living there, whereas the other ethnic group may be occupying very smaller area and may be with minority members. The greater strength of one group may be always having some dominance over the minority group and naturally they may even encroach into the area of the minority group. This sort of encroachment is out of aggression. When the majority group intrude in the area of the minority ethnic group aggressively, there is no logic or reason for this. Might is right for them. For example, When Iraq's president Saddam Husain intruded into the Kuwait territory, there was no territorial dispute between these two nations. It is a plain aggression into the Kuwait's territory for economic reasons to capture the oil fields of Kuwait. But because of the United Nations and America, Kuwait was saved and the oil fields were restored. The territorial boundary lines are well defined between these nations, but still intrusion has taken place. Similar aggressive invasions have taken place on several instances in the world. China occupied Indian territory in the north-eastern area and Pakistan occupied a part of Jammu and Kashmir though the boundary lines are well defined. These are aggressive invasions into the well defined territory. Therefore India has to fight to get back the territories from China and Pakistan. What China and Pakistan did, were public territorial invasions.

Primary territory invaders are likely to arouse most intense aggression on the owners. Primary territories are important to the owner's life and therefore more intense feelings are associated with owners and threatening the invaders and deal with them more roughly. Geen and O'Neal (1976) state that the primary territorial invasion-aggression relationship became so intense that the owner of the house went to the extent of even killing the intruder and the local laws prosecuted the house owner on a charge of killing the intruder. Therefore the owners of house should put up boundary lines around the primary territories to prevent the intruders. In United States since there is no compound walls to indicate the territories of the houses the owners put marks for the territories like sign boards stating that this area is owned by so and so and no trespassing. Edney (1972) in his observation found that individual home owners who put up such display marks and erect territorial defenses had lived in their houses for longer period than those who did not put up territorial defenses.

In India, big and medium size houses have compound walls to indicate the territorial defenses. This does not arouse any dispute or invasion or aggression. But in rural and semi-urban areas invasions into the primary territories are taking place. Disputes and quarrels arise and sometimes go to the extent of murdering the intruders. Therefore in the case of primary territory invasion-aggression relationship is very intense. In India, intrusion into the agricultural lands are quite common and disputes and quarrels are arising quite often between neighbouring land owners. On these issues the owners go to the civil court and the case may prolong for years. Sometimes the disputes may become so intense as to cause even murdering the intruders. There are quite a number of such instances in India. Such is the consequence of intrusion into the primary territory of a person.

Areas not well marked as either primary territory or public territory are subjected to the occupation of nomads and those who claim to be the ruffians of such areas. An area either must be a primary territory or a public territory and should have a mark of it. The Government territories do not have any mark. As result of it many occupy such places and utilize for their own purpose till the Government officials find out this and penalize them. This is often happening in India.

10. POPULATION DENSITY AND THE PROBLEM OF OVERCROWDING

Population refers to all the people living in a space or country in a given time. Density means the degree to which something is filled or crowded or occupied. Hence population density means the degree or number of people occupying a particular space of a given or specified size. If population density is referring to the occupation of the specified space of a small size by a large number of people then it becomes a problem. A small space has been occupied by a large number of people is called overcrowded. Crowding may also means a large number of people gathered together or collected in a space of small area. Overcrowding refers to the crowding of people in a specified space more than its capacity. The space can hold only certain number of people to its capacity. But if people more than the required number of people are gathered in the space it is becoming overcrowded. The density of people is more intense than it should be. If the degree of density of the people is very intense in a given space then it is called overcrowded. Psychologically this becomes a problem. Because this overcrowding is affecting the behaviour of the people in the space.

Overcrowding may also occur in many places. For example, in a stadium where a football match between two nations is taking place, or a cricket match between two nations, the stadium may be fully packed with people who are interested in games. People may be densely packed together in the stadium. In a picture house people may be densely packed to the capacity. A stadium, or auditorium or picture house may permit people to assemble there only to the capacity. This, we may state as density. The actual number of seats are filled with people. The space is limited and numbered and so many people are permitted to gather there, which may be designated as density.

Density and Crowding

But, crowding or overcrowding refers to the people who are collected in a space more than its capacity. A crowding or an overcrowding is caused of too many people in a too little space. Hence crowding is the effect of many people in a too small space. There is unpleasant response in crowding. For example, in passenger trains or mails or in express trains there are certain carriages reserved and certain carriages are unreserved. In the reserved carriages the passengers are limited to the number of seats in the carriages. If all the seats are filled up in the carriage then it may be called as density, whereas in unreserved carriages there is no limiting of seats. Any number of passengers can get into it and find a place to sit. We might have observed in trains that there are four seated benches in which six or seven passengers are sitting neck to neck closely. And also passengers standing everywhere, wherever a small space is available to put their feet. It is also observed in some suburban trains, passengers travelling standing on the footboards. Instead of 64 passengers to the capacity of a carriage more than 120 passengers may be travelling in it. This may be stated as crowding or overcrowding. This type of conditions are occurring in buses plying within the city area in every metropolitan city. Some private service buses get into accidents or turn down causing death of the passengers. This type of overcrowding is often occurring in the country boats carrying passengers for crossing the river. In India such instances are often occurring, the mishap of boats in the rivers due to overload of passengers. These are the consequences of overcrowding. Therefore crowding can be differentiated from density.

Effects of Overcrowding on Animals

The effects of crowding can be experimentally demonstrated in animals. Calhoun (1962, 1971), Marsden (1972), Ng. Marsden, Colburn and Thoa (1973) have studied the effects of animal population when they were allowed to multiply without any check. The resulting effects were high density condition, considerable amount of diseases and leading to behaviour disorders. The environmental conditions, supply of food and other conditions were very normal. The result observed in the real experimental situation was high density behaviour. The experiments were conducted on rats. Calhoun was the first to conduct experiments on animals to demonstrate the consequences of overcrowding. There were negative responses. Calhoun's animals were provided with very good treatments. They were well fed, with lot of water and good physical environmental conditions. But these animals (rats) reacted negatively in a number of ways. These animals had physical illness, expressed aggression and eating its own kind.

There were some studies on the same type of experiment later on by Chapman, Masterpasqua and Lore (1976), Anderson *et al.* (1977), Massey and Vanderbergh (1980). These investigators have found the same results in their experimental animals. One of the early studies on animals was the naturalistic observation made by Dubos (1965). The experiment was conducted to assess the behaviour of the animals in real physical environmental settings. The density of the animals is made to vary naturally in the natural settings and animals were affected by their density variations. Dubos used Norwegian arctic short tail rats (lemmings) for his observation. He found when these animals were overcrowded by the increased population, they developed behaviour disorder due to malfunction of the brain and migrated to sea and many of them were drowned in the sea. This type of behaviour disorder and drowning was caused by overcrowding of the animals in the natural settings.

When we keep some animals, which can procreate fastly, in limited amount of space, the animals in due course of time increase their population density. After some time the population increasing process reach a stage of crowding. What we call overcrowded depends upon several factors. It will not be possible to describe everything accurately unless as attempt is made to conduct some research on the lower animals under certain experimental conditions and observe the effects of overcrowding on behaviour. Many studies have been conducted on animals of various types which increased their population rapidly and limiting the population by themselves. One classical study was made by Calhoun (1962) on rats to see the population density on the behaviour of the animals.

In the experiment conducted by Calhoun, a 10 × 14 feet room was used. The room was divided into four small enclosures or rooms. Each small room was made as a living room for the animals. The small enclosure consisted of a food hopper, drinking water spring, and a window staircase in an elevated position. The small rooms were partitioned by electrical partitions which had a sloping walk by which the animals (rats) would go from one enclosure to another. There were only three sloping walks between enclosures, between 1 and 2, between 2 and 4 and between 3 and 4. There was no sloping walk between 1 and 4. Therefore the rats were prevented from going 1 to 4 or from 4 to 1 enclosures.

There was s window in the ceiling of the room, through which the behaviour of the rats could be seen. Each experiment has taken considerable amount of time and several experiments were conducted. The number of rats was varied in every experiment, ranging from 32 to 56. But the population, the total of rats was not changed. It was always 80. This number was maintained by removing the infants and leaving the young rats in the enclosures. The old rats that were dead were replaced by young rats. Since the enclosures 2 and 3 had access from 1 and 4 as there were sloping walks on either side, enclosure 2 and 3 had the chance of increasing the population density more than enclosures 1 and 4. The population of female rats were equally distributed by themselves in all four enclosures by and by. But the population of male rats was increased in strength in the middle enclosures 2 and 3. The other two end enclosures 1 and 4, each one was having a dominant male rat who tolerated a few other male rats, who were submissive to the dominant male rat in each enclosure.

In these experiments Calhoun was observed that there was some eccentric behaviour among the female rats particularly in the middle enclosures 2 and 3, where the rats were crowded. The female rats in the density populated enclosures 2 and 3, were less skilful in building their nests properly and finally they gave up building nests totally. Further, they did not transport their beds from one place to another. They simply laid their young ones on the plain floor at different places in the enclosure. These female rats have developed stress in many ways. The causes of stress were mainly during the periods of heat, when they were constantly chased by a number of male rats for mating. There was a very high mortality rate among these female rats due to disorders, particularly during the period of pregnancy and delivery.

The aggressive dominant rats were behaving normally, but even these animals on certain occasions were behaved abnormally. On these occasions these dominant male rats were violently attacking female rats, young ones, and male rats not active, and biting their tails often. These are rare behaviour among the rats. The male rats that were not dominant become homosexuals and they were not able to discriminate between male and female sexual partners. They started having sexual union with males and female rats not ready for sexual activities and with young ones. These inactive male rats did not fight back with the dominant rats. The investigator has observed that there were a third type of male rats which were fully passive and moved through the enclosures. These rats have shown utter indifference to other rats and others also ignored them. They appeared to be healthy, but socially moving with other rats. The most strange behaviour was found among the rats lived always in the middle enclosures and they were hyperactive, hypersexual, always watchful for the female rats that were in heat. Calhoun called these animals 'probers'. These are the effects of crowding on the social behaviour and physiological responses of the rats. These results show how high density of population, caused behaviour disorders in animals.

From these we can understand that animals show negative behaviour effects in conditions of high density of population. There were also physiological changes. But, the same type of reaction was not found among humans. What was the reason for this? One possible answer according to Calhoun (1971) was that animals were biologically oriented to situations, the overcrowding. But humans were influenced by cognitive and social factors and avoid extremes in their contact with high density of population. Further humans find ways and means to escape the negative effects of overcrowding situation at least for few minutes, whereas in the case of animals it is not possible. Therefore let us analyse whether overcrowding will have the same effects upon humans.

Effects of Overcrowding on Humans

The effects of overcrowding on all animals uniformly will have only negative responses. The overcrowding situation for animals is aversive, but for humans it depends upon the situation in which they are involved. In certain situations humans welcome overcrowding for some purpose. In certain situation they do not tolerate overcrowding. Even if it is not unavoidable they try to accommodate themselves by some means. But if they find the overcrowding a disturbing factor they also avoid it. For example, if a political party is organizing a public meeting to explain its policy to the people, they expect very big crowd. There may be overcrowding to the extent of stampeding sometimes. The human overcrowding leading to stampeding sometimes takes place in many of the occasions. It sometimes even cause deaths. This means there might have been too many people in the space. The space has become too small for so many people that they even could not stand there. There may be waves of people pushing from behind and the people in the crowd could not hold their feet on the ground for standing comfortably.

The effects of high density in humans have been studied by many investigator experimentally in laboratory situation. The laboratory studies have several advantages, but the laboratory studies have also certain disadvantages. That is, to collect many people in a laboratory situation and studying the effects of high density is an artificial approach and the results cannot be generalized to natural situations. Further, we cannot hold for longer time the artificially created high density of population. The density can exist only for a short time, for a few minutes. Results obtained in such situations are not very reliable and transferable to other situations. Therefore, it is better to conduct researches in the real natural situations, by using field research techniques. The field research technique may provide a better realistic approach than the laboratory experiments. It is also possible to observe the effects of high density for a longer time.

But a technique that can be better relied upon for the effects of high density of population is the sociological correlational research. This technique has been used by sociologists. They have examined the association (correlation) between population density (number of people per square mile) and frequency of abnormal behaviour, or crime and physical and psychiatric illness. The experiment was conducted by Zlutnick and Altman (1972) in two situations. One is the study of effects of inside density of population. This is with reference to the number of people per room or residence put in for experimentation. The other is to study of effects of outside density of population. This is with reference to the number of people per acre or per square mile. It has been found in this study that there was a positive correlation between the density of population and social problems. But the results of this study were questionable with regard to their reliability. Because the variables such as income and education were not controlled in this study. The high density of population was also the lowest in the average income and also had the lowest level of education. Booth (1973) had the assumption that people who were economically and educationally backward also revealed the same social problems. According to him, crime and physical, and psychiatric illness may be intrinsically due to poverty and poor education rather than high density of population. Galle, Gove, and McPherson (1972) have also verified this in their studies and found that there was no relationship between high density of community size and social problems.

Sex and Effects of Density

The high density of population causes negative effects more in males than in females. The males reveal stronger negative feeling than the females. Several studies have been conducted to see whether sex could be a determining factor. Freedman, Levy, Buchanan, and Price (1972), Ross, Layton, Evicson, and Schopler (1973) have observed in their studies that in spatial conditions the males have shown more negative moods in high density of population than in low density of population. But in the case of females the reactions were the reverse of the males. The females have revealed a low level of negative moods in high spatial density conditions. This shows that females have more liking for crowds and interested in socialization. The males, at the same time, consider socialization as competitive and the crowd as a source of threat.

The Effects of High Density of Population on Physique

Since high density of population affects human feelings and moods it is assumed that it will have effects upon human physique also. It may cause physiological changes such a increased blood pressure and also may cause changes in cardiovascular system.

This hypotheses has been tested in an experiment conducted by Evans (1975). Evans used five males and five females as his experimental subjects. The subjects were put in a small room where there were high density of conditions and also in a large room where there were wider and spacious conditions. They were kept in the room for three and half hours for the study. The subjects' heart rate and blood pressure were measured before the experiment and after a period of three hours. It was found that the subject who were put in a high density smaller spatial conditions had higher heart rate and higher blood pressure readings than when they were in wider and spacious conditions.

These subjects had shown also other physiological indications like changes in the skin resistance in high density conditions, whereas in spacious conditions there were no such changes. Similar studies have been conducted by Saegert (1974), Aiello, Esptein, and Karlin (1975), by putting their subjects among large number of people. These investigators have found that there was more palm sweating in their subjects, which did not occur for them when they were alone outside.

The Effects of the Kinds of High Density of Population

Generally people have the tendency to react negatively to a crowd and to a small space. Where there is spatial restriction we hesitate to proceed further as it may cause physiological and psychological inconveniences. The space is restricted because it may accommodate only limited number of people and if there is more collection of people it may cause sultry, sweating, and some people even get dizzy sensation. There will not be any space for movement. Therefore spatial restrictions and overcrowding arouse the feeling of dizziness. Individuals, who are in crowded situations, are aroused and attribute the arousal to the spatial restrictions. This was tested by Worchal and Brown (1984) in their experimental studies. A film was screened to small groups of subjects where the seating arrangement was such that their interpersonal seating distances were suitably or unsuitably close. There were four different kinds of films which were arousing different emotions such as humorous, aggressive, sexual and one film was not arousing any emotion, and every one saw only one film. It was believed that the subjects sitting in an unsuitably closer distance condition should ascribe their arousal to the film, if it was due to any one of the arousals and they should not have felt the inconveniences of the crowded situation. Instead if the film was not an arousing one, the subjects should ascribe the effects to the crowded situation. The results of this study supported the hypothesis. The type of density was mainly responsible for effects of crowding. The subjects seem to have depended upon the perceived source of arousal, whether it was the film or the felt crowd. A general observation was that it was the kind of density of the population which had influence upon the effect of crowding or interpersonal conditions. Therefore it has become a necessity to differentiate between social density and spatial density.

Several authors tried to distinguish between these two densities. Baum and Valins (1977), Paulus (1980) have studied these aspects. The effect of social density was tested by increasing the number of people in a given space. It was studied in two situations. A certain number of people in an apartment in an ordinary evening was compared with an evening of a large party in the same apartment. The social density was more dense on the evening, when there was large party than the ordinary evening, when there was limited people in the same apartment. The spatial density was increased as the amount of space for a given number of people was decreased. This was tested in two situations. A large group of people were made to wait in an entrance of hall or a large building. Here the people did not feel the density of the crowd. But when the same group of people entered a small elevator, the crowd became very dense and each one felt the effect of the dense situation near the elevator. These two experiments show that a high social density and spatial density, generally cause negative effects on human behaviours. Ross *et al.* (1973) have observed in their experiments that social density had stronger negative effects among males than females.

Researchers in this field have observed that the effects of high density generally affect the social behaviour. We are not inclined to meet a stranger or known person in a crowded railway station platform or in an underground subway where every body was busy in finding out their way. We are not attracted by the people to meet and to talk to. Because the high density of the crowd cause decrement effect in our social meetings. Every one in such situations wishes to be confined to be free or if unavoidable, wishes to cut short the enquiries. Experimental studies have been made with regard to the type of social behaviour, elicited during high density of population. Baum and Greenberg (1975) have found that the effect of high density was disliked and also the high density was leading to lower attraction. Experiments have been conducted by Worchel and Teddlie (1976). It was short-term high density confinement. The subjects were, groups of eight males. They were put together for an hour. They have ascribed more friendliness to other group members under low spatial density conditions than under high spatial density conditions. Since the duration was very short they were able to maintain friendliness even in a small spatial area where the density was high.

The effects of long-term density confinement was also tested in a study. The study was a long-term density confinement in a hostel building, Baron and Bell (1976) conducted the experiment in a living triple room. Three students were put up in a room built for two. These students, since, will have to live there for the whole year they were less satisfied with the room mates and they found that they were less cooperative than the students living in double rooms with only two students. This shows that high spatial density causes low attraction. This low attraction in high density situation is more with males than females. Epistein and Karlin (1975) have conducted an experiment with male and female subjects. There were six subjects in each. There were both in high,and low density conditions in the experiment. The measures indicated that the males have shown more negative response to the group members in high spatial density situation than in low spatial density situation, whereas the females in high spatial density situation have shown positive response of liking the group members. In the same type of spatial density situation the males differed considerably from the females in their responses to the same sex members. What was disliking for males, was liking for females. Therefore sex is a determining level of the effects of density on the behaviour of human beings.

The experimenters have also observed another important result in their experiment. The males and females were made to experience the same type of effects of density. The social norms of the females was such that they endured the distress and shared with others in their group. It was this attitude that made them to like other members, and also there was group cohesion. But in the case of males the social norms did not permit them to endure the distress and share it. It was this that made them to have negative social attitude.

Aggression as the Effect of High Density

High density of population in a limited spatial area causes several psychological reactions. In this type of behaviour the males differ from the females. High density of population leads to negative and positive reactions, also leads to withdrawal tendency in humans. Dooley (1974) in his study has observed that the males were not willing to participate in another experimental situation after attending a high social density session and they were withdrawing themselves from the experiment, while the females were not. Man's helping tendency also varies. Weiner

(1976) and others have studied these aspects in urban and rural subjects. The effects of high density of population also leads one to aggression in a low spatial situation. Hutt and Vaizey (1966) have tested this assumption in their experiments. They have found that high spatial density to population arouses more aggression in humans. But, Loo (1972), who verified the results of Hutt and Vaizey provides the opposite result. That is, high density was not leading to aggressive behaviour. Loo states that high density affects the aggressive behaviour of children. Rohe and Patterson (1974) state that in high density conditions, competition over rare resources was an important determinant factor of aggression in children. Another type of research which verified the effects of high density on adult subjects, the arousal of aggression was there and the effects were consistent. The highly increased density of population in the low spatial conditions was leading to aggression in males, but it did not take place in females. Stokols, Pinner and Schopler (1973) have studied the aggressive tendency among eight males and eight females putting them in large and small rooms. It was found that the males were more aggressive in small room than in large room, while the females in small room did not show any aggressive tendency. In all these experimental situations there was sex difference in the social responses to high density of population and low spatial conditions. In high density situation males were expressing less liking for people and places, while the females were quite reverse of it. The same type of responses were prevailing in various experimental situations like, in participating in high density of population situation, the males were withdrawing, from it for want of large personal space, looking after the welfare of others and aggressive behaviour patterns.

Effects of High Density on Task

The effects of high density were also observed in impairing individual performance on complex tasks. Paulus, Aunis, Seta, Schkade, and Mathews (1976) have studied this aspect. They have found that high social density and high spatial density impaired the complex maze task performance. This type of work or task decrement due to high density of population and high spatial density can be observed mainly in schools, colleges, hostels and industries. But some of the earlier studies did not confirm this result. The reason for not confirming the result of Paulus and others study must have been that the earlier studies were on simple tasks. This has not caused any decrement in the performance due to high density of population. But all the studies conducted on complex task reported different conclusion—there was decrement in performance.

Effects of Long-term High Density

The laboratory studies explained above were all short-term effects of crowding. The subjects were exposed to crowding only for few hours. It is necessary to find out what happens over longer periods of time in a highly crowded situation. Individuals are often exposed to such situations in their everyday life. The settings for long-term conditions of crowdedness are homes, dormitories and hostels. The important facts creating stress is the number of bathrooms available in these conditions. Meer (1986) states that even in homes which are not crowded where there is only one bathroom, persons report more stress than those with more than two or more. Dormitories are another crowded setting where students live for longer period of time. Sometimes students, more than its capacity are packed in dormitories for want of space. Therefore dormitories are crowded always and there are more stronger effects of social density than spatial density of population.

Studies made by Baron, Mandal, Adams, and Griffin (1976), Gormley and Aiello (1982), report that three students living in rooms built for two were not fully satisfied with their room mates, as they were feeling more crowded in such rooms and they were greatly dissatisfied with their living situation than the students who were living in rooms built for two. Since these students will have to live there for years they perceive that a double room is too much crowded for three than a double room occupied by only two students. Karlin, Rosen and Epistein (1979) state that these students, three living in double room, also obtain lower grade points than those two live in double room.

Most of the Indian universities and colleges run hostels for the students who come from distant places for study. Students of the same place, town or city also study in the universities and colleges, living in their own homes. If their homes are close to the institutions they walk the distance, if little longer go by cycles or by scooters or similar two wheelers or by service buses. So these students have their problems at their homes. But the students who come from long distances have no other go except to get admission in the hostels. The Indian hostels have different types of rooms like, single rooms, double rooms, triple rooms and four and five rooms. Sometimes if there was rush for hostel admissions the double and triple rooms were also filled with more than twos and threes. Thus the double, triple, four rooms become crowded and students find it difficult to carry out their academic works. Every student in four rooms may have a visitor during the living hours. Hence the rooms will have always four or five persons more than its capacity. This causes more density in the room. Instead of social contacts there are chances for more friction among the students who live there. Since they have to live in the same rooms for one full year, they cannot fully avoid each other even though they wanted to avoid. This may also cause stress, tension and frustration and some students could not concentrate on their studies. The longer period they live in such hostel rooms the more they develop emotional maladjustments. The high density of population in a small room situation may lead to sometimes quarrels and also violence. In crowded college hostel room this type of behaviours are common occurrences. Therefore they have constant desire to avoid others. Because of the high social density they perform in their examinations poorly and not getting better grades and some even fail and have arrears in every semester. These conditions are mostly prevailing among the students of undergraduate courses, living in college and university hostels in India.

The effects of long-term crowding in dormitories in U.S.A. have been studied by Baum and Valins (1977). Those who were living in dormitories felt more crowded and wanted to avoid others. The social density was so high that there was no control over their social interaction. As the semester advanced the feeling of stress increased among the dormitory students and also they had the feelings of helplessness and other negative reactions. Some wanted to find out alternative arrangements for their living. These are the effects due to constant exposure to high social density or crowded situation.

Apart from homes, hostels and dormitories, the effects of crowding were also studied in prisons. The nature of crowding in prisons was such that it was considered as cruel and unusual punishment. The prison mates in the United States increased by 94 per cent during 1975 and 1980. There was increase in the total population and sentences for imprisonment. Many prisoners filed suit against the prison authorities that there was overcrowding in prisons which has become cruel and unusual punishment. Cox, Paulus, and McCain (1984) have collected data from prison records to know the actual effects of crowding in prisons. The general pattern prevailed in the institution was that as the population of prison increased, the death rate also increased, and also there was increase in the number of law breakers. According to their data, in one prison the population of the prisoners increased two times and the rate of law breakers increased six times and the suicide rate increased three times. It appears that the prison problems arise when the population density of the prisoners increased with high spatial density in prison rooms. In a small area more number of prisoners were packed, which caused, the increase of the number of law breakers and suicide cases.

Avoiding the Effects of Crowding and Negative Reactions

The effects of crowding are leading to negative reactions because of the high density of population and high density of space. People are crowded in a given space more than its capacity which causes several unpleasant events. People who were assembled in a small space do not find space to move about and there is negative reaction. Because of the high density of population, people are put into severe stress, tension, friction and find ways and means to get rid of the situation, if the situation exists for a short duration. But in a long-term crowding they meet with distress, as they cannot avoid it.

What must be the cause of overcrowding? One answer can be that it is due to the perception of loss of control. If that is the case, their perception can be modified. If the people are informed in advance with regard to the situation and what is expected there, then there is no chance for negative reactions. People in advance must know the consequences of the situation if they want to avert high density or overcrowding. One way of avoiding crowding and negative effects is to alter the environment. It need not be in a large measure. A simple change related to the problem situation can be also effective in avoiding crowding and causing negative effect.

In altering or modifying the environment we must take into account three important conditions such as identifying individual differences, situational conditions and social conditions, which have been noticed as affecting the reactions to high density. Fisher (1974) has studied this aspect. In the case of individual differences as variables, we must choose those individuals who are not sensitive to the restrictions of the limited space. For example, men are more sensitive to the effect of crowds than women. If the space is limited, it is better to choose female subjects for the situation to avoid experiencing the effects of the crowding. Secondly, in the case of situational conditions, we must have people on whom we can have control over the situation to avoid the effects of crowding and negative reactions. The subjects must withstand the effects of crowding or allow persons who had some training or experience in the crowded situations, so that they can share the space and protect their privacy. The effects of crowding thereby can be avoided.

Thirdly, in the case of social conditions, the effects of crowding and the negative reactions can be eliminated by creating a social climatic conditions. If there is more cohesion among the people of the crowd or high degree of friendship in the high density situation there may be high degree of social interaction which may eliminate friction among the people in the crowd. When people started liking each other they are ready to share the small space and accommodate themselves however crowded the situation is, and the effects of crowding are lost and there will not be any negative reactions. Instead, if the members of the crowd dislike each other and if they are strangers, then there is friction in the crowd and the effects are negative reactions.

But there are also certain thickly crowded situations in which people move about and adjust among themselves even if the space is very little. All of them are stranger and no one knows the other, who is by his side. But there seems to be no friction and negative reaction among them. This kind of situation often or even everyday are occurring in Indian Railway Trains and City Transports in many of the Indian Metropolitan cities. For example, one who had experienced in travelling in the city sub-urban trains in Bombay and Madras could have observed the behaviour of the crowd, in getting into the trains and in getting out of the train. Even in such thick crowds there is some understanding among the strangers and they help each other in getting into trains and getting out of the trains.

The behaviour of the crowded passengers, travelling in sub-urban trains particularly, in Bombay and Madras, during the busy hours is very exciting. The crowd, which is waiting for the arriving train, would simply push the people into the train as soon as the train is arrived on the platform. A wave of crowd is pushing you into the train and you need not walk. Similarly the passengers who are getting down are also pushed fast into the platform. Actually there is no pushing and pulling, but the movement is so fast that the crowd acts in such a way that each one gets a little space to stand there irrespective of the type of contact one is having with the other. Every one is in hurry to go to his/her work place or home as early as possible. There may be also vendors who carry their vegetables and other perishable materials to the city markets. All these people move very fast and also have learned to adjust themselves in the space available in the compartments though the crowd is very dense.

In this type of anxiety loaded crowd, there is no chance for any one to have negative reaction with any body. Since it has become an everyday incident, every one might have felt the problem of the other. As a result of it there is no chance for friction among these crowded passengers. This type of behaviour can be also observed among the people in city bus transports. There is no chance for friction among the people who are getting into the bus. But there may be some chances for pickpocketing and sometimes some people lose their money-purses.

Similar incidents can be observed also in the weekly fairs in Indian small towns and villages. The weekly fairs in small towns and villages are just like festival occasions and people in large number from the surrounding areas are collected there. That is the day for them to sell their products in the fair and buy all their requirements for the whole week. Particularly on important festival occasions these weekly rural fairs get more importance. All kinds of materials can be purchased and sold there including all sorts of livestock, like cows, bulls, camels, donkeys, goats, sheep, and also fowls. Every vendor carries his/her goods and finds a place where the fair is held.

However dense and crowded the fair is, every vendor finds his/her place in the fair in the same place, which was occupied by a vendor earlier. In occupying a little space for laying out the goods there is no conflict or friction among them. In fact there is mutual adjustment and co-operation among them in getting their things sold on the same day. There is also exchange of money transactions among them though they are strangers, and every one is from different villages. It is because, the rural people do not develop any egoistic tendency when they go out on any business. There is more of altruistic tendency among them, sharing the miseries of others in some way. In Indian rural areas the weekly fairs create some kind of cordiality among the men and women who meet there once a week. There is more of exchange of goods and friendly attitudes and there is no chance for friction and negative reactions among them.

EXPERIMENT 6

Measurement of Ecological Attitudes and Cognitive Aspect

1. INTRODUCTION

Psychologists have been studying the human behaviour as the subject matters come to them from the environment, and have been attributing the characteristic to human beings. They have also used these characteristics to classify people into various types. In the study of human behaviour the role of the environmental factors was also studied and later on experiments were conducted controlling the environmental conditions; and human behaviour was studied in controlled conditions and the same was compared with the behaviour studied in normal or natural conditions.

In the study of animal behaviour in the laboratory situations psychologists varied the surrounding situations and observed how the rats, cats, dogs and the monkeys learn as the result of the changes of the environmental factors. Similar studies also were conducted on human beings controlling environmental conditions. But it is felt that in such controlled experimental conditions the responses are not natural. Therefore some psychologists are of the view that some of the important problems in which they are interested cannot be solved by laboratory experimental methods.

Human behaviour should be studied in actual settings. Investigators must go out in the natural environment like the workshop, fields, shopping centres, schools, colleges, play grounds, streets, offices of the organisations, industries of various types, clubs and so on where the people conduct their everyday business in the complicated world.

Investigators like Sells (1966), Williams (1965) and Williams and Raush (1969) have done remarkable studies in this line. But shopping centres, schools, colleges and playgrounds are man-made environments and not natural environment and also people who go there may behave in a stereotyped manner and not naturally—this is one type of criticism levelled against the view of naturalistic psychologists.

Therefore, it needs some explanation. Naturalistic environment means, according to naturalistic psychologists, not uncultured or uncultivated, or primitive type environment. For them, natural environment means not influenced by experimental interventions, or subjected to specific culturally oriented environment or man-made man directing environment. It should be free from the influence of experimental or controlled conditions where people can have their reciprocal activities without any terms and conditions. For example, the college classrooms is a man-made environment. Even in this type of man-made environment a natural behaviour setting can be created. When the class start functioning the type of behaviour of the teacher and the students in the classroom is natural so long as some experimental conditions are not enforced there.

Environmental psychologists wish to see their subjects from the molar point of view. They wanted to study their subjects as whole system of environment and the behaviour is the reaction to the molar situation and not to the molecular. The molar environment is not an assembled body of many physical stimuli, but it is total integrated pattern where behaviour is supposed to be spontaneous or natural.

The concept environment is often used by psychologists in the sense that all the the surrounding conditions of the organism influence and modify the behaviour of the organism. Therefore it is not only referring to physical forces and conditions that surround the organism but also the society in which the organism lives and the cultural factors it adpats. It includes everything with which the organism encounters in its movements and in the every day life activities. According to Gump *et al.* (1957, 1963) the environment and the molar behaviour are having an orderly relationship. The type of relationship is so complicated that it cannot be adequately explain. Barker (1968) explains it with several examples like, a business meeting, watch repairshop, an auction sale. Epstein and Shontz (1971) explain it with a basketball game. The natural environment of the basketball game is meant many things. It includes, the ground where the play is held, the goal posts, the ball, stadium, players, the referees, the audience, the rules and regulations of the game, the defensive and offensive movements of the players, the encouragement from the audience, the television, camera, and transmissions to outside stations, the Television audience, their excitements and so on. This means all those connected with the basket ball game directly and indirectly influence the people and constitute environment.

A behaviour setting, according Barker, has both structural and dynamic characteristics. It means that it has an organized set-up for actions and objects and persons. The set-up is a force that can protect any descriptive forces which could interfere in the set-up and spoil the maintenance of the integrity of the arrangement.

For example, a football game is played in an organized set-up within the stadium which has protection from all sides for the game, audience, players and referees. Any disruptive force cannot easily spoil the organized set-up of the football game.

Secondly the behavioural setting of the environment is dynamic in natural. There is a type of relationship that holds the whole setting, the football stadium together as a single unit. The whole audience behave as a single unified group. Their interest is witnessing the game and enjoying it. There is a feeling of cohesiveness and a sense of belongingness that they belong to the particular spectators group. Each member of the group is contributing something to the group. Sometimes the interconnections and interrelationships may be such that behaviour of the group may be having the same characteristics as the milieu, a small social group environment.

Therefore, a behaviour setting is a part of the large environment and should possess the structural and dynamic characteristics. There must be proper relationship between the structural arrangement and the dynamic characteristics. For example, in the football ground some of the players simply run here and there at random and do not drive the ball to the goal and do not follow the principles and carry the ball outside the boundary line then their behaviour is not in agreement with the behaviour setting. If a correct and true behaviour setting is to function, then the structural or organized arrangement and the dynamic characteristics or the behaviour pattern should go together without any break or disruption. Since the behaviour setting is surrounded by the boundaries of space and time, behaviour setting beyond the boundaries does not exist. The behaviour boundaries according to Barker need not be only the physical or temporal or space and time, it can be also a person who does not know the rules and regulations of the game. A person who is ignorant of the rules and regulations stands outside the boundaries. Therefore, the environmental psychologists define the environment with all these characteristics.

The important point stressed by environmental psychologists is to determine the behavioural forms of biological adaptation of the organism in the natural environment. This is what the Ecologists do. Barker and his colleagues are ecological psychologists and they wanted to study the behaviour through social ecological approach.

If we state simply environment, it refers to the total environment. This total environment is very broad, not defined. Therefore it includes all interacting forces that influence us in a number of ways. Then it will not be possible for us to state which environmental force has influenced us. Therefore Heimstra and McDonald (1973) state that when we refer to environment we must have in our mind a specific aspect of the total environment such as home, family, social groups, occupational groups and so forth. The other features of the total environment are the buildings in which we live and work and other facilities, included in these, the social, religious and communal groups, the various types of transportation system and other things with which we are associated, all belong to build environment in contrast to natural environment according to Heimstra and McDonald. The built environment also forms an important part of the total environment. The total environment constitute innumerable amount of forces which are having influence upon us in various ways in our every day life either for good or for bad. Since these forces are having influences upon the behaviour of human beings they become a subject matter of study for the psychologists. As a result of this many psychologists started studying the total environmental influences upon human behaviour. Kaplan (1972) state that since man is going on increasing the population unmindfully and also refuse to deal with his hazardous environment it becomes the duty of the psychologists to try to understand what is going on behind these harmful attitudes of the present generation.

Human life, in the near future is going to be very difficult. Man, is unknowingly marching towards disastrous consequences by showing utter indifferent attitudes towards the rapid increase of population and thereby squeezing the environment smaller and smaller one. The environmental psychology has its origin at this juncture and it rapidly growing and warning the scientists with the dire consequences of their negligence to human life as a whole. In the recent years a number of programmes have been evolved to study the human behaviour in relation to man-ordered and man-defined environment in United States. This is to indicate the direction of the sub-field of study. But environmental psychologists are generally concerned with natural environment which influences the human behaviour and in turn how human behaviour influences the environment.

In whatever manner we define environment, whether it is built environment or natural environment, Heimstra and McDonald state that the basic assumption of this new discipline is that human behaviour is a potential force in shaping the physical environment and in reverse the physical environment has very deep influence in shaping human behaviour. Environment need not be referred to only land where only the multitude of people live. Man may migrate to arctic region, moon or space. Therefore, they also may be stated as environments. The sea, air and space are stated as unusual environment. Bevan (1967) states that an environment may be called as unusual environment from sensual point of view. Man in an unusual environment may fail to make use of his sensory apparatus efficiently. Man on earth functions on gravitational force. But man in outer space has to live in zero gravitation. But it is very rare for man to live in an unusual environment.

Environment psychologists apply several methods in their research. Investigators simply observe the behaviour of the people in some situation and record the events. Another way is to conduct interviews with the individuals on interested matters and collect information. But always the experimental method in psychology is considered to be more valuable for reliable data. The researchers can also make use of the independent and dependent variables.

Problem: Assess a person's ecological attitudes and the cognitive level about ecological problems, (b) test the person's degree of emotionality associated with environmental problems and test whether he/she has known of current social and ecological problems.

2. METHOD

Particinan

Choose a person who is having some interest in the ecological or environmental problems and collect relevant personal information such as age, sex, educational qualifications, occupation, family income, family size, whether he/she is from urban or rural area, type of house he/she is living, type of transport he/she often using, whether he/she lives in industrial or agricultural or metropolitan area.

Material

Ecological Attitude and Cognitive Scale, Manual, test booklet, key, scoring sheet.

Description of the Scale

The Ecological Attitude and Cognitive Scale was constructed and developed by Prof. M. Rajamanickam (1996). The scale consisted of two parts of 40 items. The first 30 items are with Right-Wrong answers. The second part has ten items with multiple choice with five alternative answers.

The present scale consists of four sub-scales. They are (1) Oral Obligation scale, (2) Real Obligation Scale, (3) Emotional Obligation Scale and (4) Cognitive Aspect Scale. This was developed on the same pattern of the Inventory of ecological attitude and knowledge designed by Maloney, Ward and Braucht (1975).

1. Oral Obligation Scale (OOB)

This sub-scale deals with the type of commitment of the individual. What the individual expresses about the ecological issues and problems? What he/she commits on the issues orally? Whether he/she is willing to do something about the ecological problems. This scale has ten statements which are, 1, 4, 7, 10, 13, 16, 19, 22, 25 and 28. These are answered with Right or Wrong answers.

2. Real Obligation Scale (RO)

This scale deals with the type of action in which the individual is actually involved. What he/she is doing relating to the ecological problems. What is the mode of action he/she is planning to do? The statements are: 2, 5, 8, 11, 14, 17, 20, 23, 26 and 29 and are answered with Right or Wrong.

3. Emotional Obligation Scale (EO)

This scale measures the type of feeling the individual reveals toward the ecological issues and problems. The sub-scale consists of ten statements and they are: 3, 6, 9, 12, 15, 18, 21, 24, 27 and 30 and are answered with right or wrong answers.

4. Cognitive Scale (CS)

This scale is intended to assess the level of knowledge the individual has gain about the ecological issues and problems. The ten statements included in this scale are 31, 32, 33, 34, 35, 36, 37, 38, 39 and 40 and they are answered with multiple choices of five alternatives.

Procedure

Keep your respondent seated comfortably in front of a table in a well illuminated room where there is no disturbance of any sort. Give one test booklet of the ecological attitude and cognitive scale in the hands of the respondent and give him the following directions.

"There are 40 statements in this booklet. They are dealing with various aspects of environmental issues. Read each statement carefully and answer them as directed. The first 30 statements should be answered with Right or Wrong answers. If the meaning of the statement is in agreement with your feeling underline the word 'Right'. If it is not agreeable with your feeling then underline the word 'Wrong'. Statements 31 to 39 have five alternative answers. Find out the correct answer and underline it. Statement No. 40, is having a blank space. Find out the correct answer from the five alternatives given below and fill up blank space with correct answer. There is no time limit. If you have any doubt you can ask me. Now, ready, go."

As soon as the respondent completed the questionnaire, the experimenter can collect it and allow him/her to go away. The experimenter should also make a note of the time he/she has taken to complete the questionnaire.

Method of Scoring

There are four sub-scales. For each scale there is a separate key. Each sub-scale should be scored separately. The experimenter should check the answers with the key. If the respondent's answer is in agreement with the key then one point is given. Otherwise no marks. In the key along with each number, letters A, B, C, D and E are given. The numbers refer to the statements and the letters refer to correct answers. The maximum score for each area is 10, and maximum score for the whole scale is 40. The minimum score may be even zero (0) for each scale or for the whole scale if the participant answered so. The high score indicates favourable attitude toward ecological issues and problems. The low score indicates unfavourable attitude toward ecological problems. Similarly a high score in the fourth sub-scale indicates better understanding or knowledge about ecological problems and low score indicates poor knowledge.

3. RESULTS

After scoring all the items according to the procedure find out the scores for all four sub-scales separately for the individual and present them in Table 3.1.

Table 3.1 : Showing the scores of the respondent on all four sub-scales

S.No.	*Sub-scales*	*Scores*
1	Oral Obligation (OO)	
2	Real Obligation (RO)	
3	Emotional Obligation (EO)	
4	Cognitive Aspects (CA)	
	Total scores	
	Mean scores	

State whether your respondent has scored consistently in the all four sub-scales. In which area he/she scored high and in which areas scored low. A high score in the oral binding scale indicates that the individual expresses his/her willingness to do something with the environmental issues. A low score indicates his/her indifferent attitude towards the issues. A high score in real binding scale shows that the individual is actually doing something with regard to the environmental issues. The high score in the emotionality scale indicates that the individual has expressed his/her high degree of feeling associated with environmental issues. This means that he/she is very much interested in the environmental problems. A low score indicates his/her disinterestedness in the issues. A high score in the sub-scale or cognitive aspect indicates that the individual actually knows about the ecological issues and problems. A low score means that he/she is not aware of the problems or has poor understanding.

In this section state where the individual scored high and where low and explain what the high score indicates and what the low score indicates. Work out the total score for all four areas and also the mean score for the individual in the whole scale.

Collect the group data and present them in Table 3.2, and work out the mean score for each area and state them. Work out also the mean score for all four areas for every individual. State whose mean score for the whole scale is high and whose score is low. How many are above the group mean and how many below the group mean.

Table 3.2 : Showing the group data on the Ecological Attitude and Cognitive scale

S.No.	*Respondents*	*Scores of Sub-scales*				*Total*	*Mean*
		OOB	*RO*	*EO*	*CA*		
1.	B.V.						
2.	M.S.						
3.	K.R.						
4.	M.R.						
5.	P.V.						
6.	S.V.						
7.	P.K.						
8.	T.V.						
9.	A.L.						
10.	R.V.						
	Mean						

4. DISCUSSION

Explain what this scale measures and how it is an important problem. State and discuss your respondent's attitude towards each area on the basis of the score he/she has obtained in the sub-scales. Whether he/she is having more favourable attitude toward each area or just favourable or having unfavourable attitude towards the issues. State the individuals cognitive aspect as revealed by the sub-scale. From the personal information find out the cause for his/her favourable or unfavourable attitude towards each issue, and for the better and poor knowledge of the problems.

Compare his/her attitude with the group mean score. State the mean score of the group in each area and state in which area the score is high and in which issue the score is low. How many of them scored more than the group mean and how many less than the group mean. From the personal information find out the reasons for more favourable or just favourable or unfavourable or more unfavourable towards the issues. Assess the cognitive aspect of the whole group. Whose cognitive score is high and whose cognitive score is low. What does it indicate? Discuss each issue separately on the basis of age, qualification, subject of their studies, sex and other information like owning and driving a vehicle, mode of their going to work place or college or university.

5. CONCLUSIONS

1. State whether your respondent is having favourable or unfavourable attitudes towards the issues. What is his/her cognitive level.
2. State what type of respondents in the group have more favourable attitudes towards the issues by scoring more than the mean and who are those scored less than the group mean.
3. What are the factors that are influencing the group for-favourable attitudes and for unfavourable attitudes towards the issues and problems.
4. State the cognitive level of the group. Whether the group is well informed or poorly informed about the issues or ignorant of the issues.

EXPERIMENT 7

Measurement of Attitude toward the Effects of Temperature

1. INTRODUCTION

Human behaviour is stimulated by various physical components and environmental conditions. The physical environment in many respects stimulate and direct human behaviour. Therefore we can state that the physical environment is a moderating force of human behaviour. The physical environment may be also stated as the natural source of motivating factor which may result either in acceptance or avoidance on the part of human beings. Thus, there can be influencing effect in the environmental conditions. The environmental conditions may influence man in numerous ways. The environmental influences may develop in man both favourable and unfavourable attitudes.

Generally human beings find pleasure and happiness in a pleasant physical environmental situation. The gentle stream, the flowing river, the mountain forests, the green plantations, the gentle breeze, the huge trees, the deep valleys—all are the physical environmental conditions we enjoy. Thus we develop a favourable attitude toward these physical environments. We do not like to cause any damage to all these. But if we see any one causing damage to any of these we do not tolerate. We do not tolerate a person polluting the fresh water of the stream or river, or throwing litters in the fresh water or setting fire to the forest plants. We may even get angry and try to prevent such activities. Thus we display our favourable attitude toward environment. But when we are constantly facing deleterious effects from certain environmental conditions we may develop negative feelings which in turn become negative attitude.

Physiological and Psychological Reaction to Temperature

The earth in which we live is enveloped and surrounded by the gases. The troposphere is the lowest atmosphere layer in which the air temperature decreases normally with height at about 6.5° C per km. The air or climate in a particular place is called atmosphere. The atmosphere may be also thick with smoke. Life can exist only in a normal atmosphere condition. Since the climatic conditions of the earth varies considerably from region to region, the nature of life also varies on the basis of the temperature of the area. Certain plants, animals and birds may live even in extreme cold area, in arctic regions, but man cannot make his abode in such regions and live there as his bodily make up is such that it requires moderate temperature between 115°F and 77°F. The human body temperature is 98.6°F or 37°C. If there is any change in the atmospheric condition either by increasing or decreasing, the body's core temperature is affected. The body temperature should be regulated to maintain the core temperature at 98.6°F. This is having survival value. Death may occur if the core temperature (98.6°F) increase above 115 and decrease below 77°F. Therefore there should be adaptive mechanism. The body gets over heated if it is exposed to high surrounding temperature for a long time and it get freezed or it becomes motionless if it is exposed to surrounding cold temperature for a long time. The body's adaptive mechanism is working in the hypothalamus part which is under the control of the brain.

Extreme Heat

The heat in the surrounding environment is the primary physical component. This heat is measured in terms Fahrenheit and Celsius scale. The internal temperature of the body is the psychological component. This is called core temperature and it is measured by thermometer and state in terms of Fahrenheit or Celsius. The skin of the body is sensitive to temperature and therefore the receptors in the skin are supposed to be the other psychological components. Gardner (1975) who studied this phenomenon states that the skin is sensitive to change of temperatures. The skin receptors do not transmit the heat to the body through the nerve impulse. The differences are felt between the skin and the environment. The human body perceives hot if the outside environment is hotter than the body and the body perceives cold if the outside environment is cooler than the body. It is because of this we perceive in extreme cold climate even the warm water as very hot. Similarly when the body is hot even ordinary cold water is perceived as very chill.

If the body temperature become too hot, above the core temperature (98.6°F) then there is activating mechanism in the body. This mechanism makes the body to lose the heat. At this time there will be something in the body, breathing takes place with some noise and also dialation in the blood vessels. This process is very fast in the vessels near the surface of the skin. Blood is sent more in quantity to the surface area from the central part (heart). Excess heat is sent through this blood from heart. This excess heat sent in the blood from the central area is eliminated by air and by sweating. Since there is dilation in blood vessels more sweating on the skin surface is taking place.

During the time of extreme heat or if there is any heat wave as an emergency measure the body supplies more water for evaporation. It is by reducing the urine formation and also by pressing the body tissues more water is supplied for evaporation. These two processes may lead to dehydration of the body and the person feels very thirsty. But the body should be again refilled with water supply. This is performed by the hypothalamus part of the brain. When the body is exposed to extreme hot climatic condition these adaptive mechanical processes are taking place automatically. But when the adaptive mechanism fails several physiological disorders are taking place in the body. These include heat exhaustion, heat stroke, heat anasthenia, increased blood pressure and heart attack and so on. But if there is heat stroke, then blood pressure may rise and then fall off which is the indication of coma and death.

The studies made by Folk (1974) bring out several interesting finding as a result of exposing body to prolonged heat stress. The body needs more blood for cooling mechanism, and makes excessive demands on the cardiovascular system. This results in heart attack. During summer months in big cities there are more deaths by heart attacks. The cooling systems of air conditioning throws much heat outside which increases the ambient temperature by 10 to 20° F. It is because of this that the surrounding temperature in the city areas is more than the temperature in agricultural areas. This is the reason that there are more deaths in big cities by heart attacks.

Moderate Heat

Another type of reaction or adaptive mechanism is *acclimatization.* The temperature sometimes may be moderately high and it will not cause any physiological disorders. The climate may be such that persons living the moderate climatic conditions find much change and they can easily adapt to the temperature. But persons from cool climatic places move into this moderately high temperature area also can adapt to such moderately high climatic conditions without much physiological changes. The bodies of such persons become accustomed to the change of temperature and begin to sweat as soon as they moved into the high temperature area. The tendency to adapt soon to certain moderately high temperature is called acclimatization.

Extreme Cold

The other side of extreme heat is the extreme cold climatic condition. If the surrounding area becomes too cold the body will have to react to it to maintain the equilibrium. The body heat should be maintained. The activating mechanism functions to retain the heat. This increases the metabolism rate. There are certain physiological changes like the shivering of the body, the walls of the blood vessels becoming narrow (vasoconstriction) and there is also erection of the hairs all over the body (pilo erection). The physiological change of vasoconstriction is the opposite of vasodilation. This maintains the temperature inside the body and away from surface temperature. The process of constriction facilitates the supply of more blood to the internal organs. This produces more heat by increasing metabolism. The erection of skin hair is followed by goose flesh which is thickening of the surface skin.

Humidity

Humidity is another primary environmental factor which may cause certain physiological changes. Humidity is the moist in the air. The air is wet. In hot environmental situation the humidity rate may be high. The air is saturated with water vapour. The air will not absorb the sweating water which was taking place normally. Since the atmospheric air itself is filled with water vapour the sweating water of the body remains unchanged. In this situation we will be more perspiring. We may feel uncomfortable. Persons who have high eosinophilia counts in the blood would be much affected by this high humidity. They find it difficult even to breathe in and breathe out. The atmospheric conditions with 100°F and 65 per cent humidity would put us in a more uncomfortable position, whereas 100°F and 30 per cent humidity may not cause any discomfort. The humidity level is measured by an instrument called Hygrometer. Therefore the primary environmental factors like the temperature and humidity are having influence in the behaviour of the individuals. A person can be put into very uncomfortable position if the humidity level is very high though he can adapt to moderately high temperature like 100°F.

The Effects of Temperature on Social Behaviour

Extreme heat was also found to be having effect on the social behaviour of the people. People who were exposed to extreme hot situation often develop unpleasant feeling and develop negative attitudes to temperature. Since people develop unpleasant feelings like irritation or anger they seem to avoid the company of other people in such situation and also they become aggressive. The interpersonal contact is not pleasant. Byrne (1971) and Griffitt (1971) have studied these aspects.

During the winter season there will be freezing cold in some places. Astronomically this season begins in December and continues till the end of March. Particularly, in some of the Northern states in India, the temperature sometimes goes down to even upto minus five (–5°C) degree Celsius. This type of atmospheric conditions are causing physiological changes. The body needs urgent protection from shiverings and other internal changes. The life style of the people is quite opposite to that of the summer season. People rarely go out for anything. In some of the regions people collect everything what they wanted in advance before the advent of the winter season. Since the consequences of winter seasons are the same for everybody the level of helping tendency among the people is increased considerably which was lacking in hot summer months. During the cold months, the severe winter brings people together to help each other. Bennett and Others

(1983) have observed in their studies that people develop a norm of helpfulness when the season is threatening them. People reduce their outside activities and confine with their homes. Some people also have the winter sports activities on snow or ice.

Normally if the temperature goes down to 75° F or 70° F then damaging effects are taking place. They need to take strong protective measures. Particularly workers in the fields or outside the buildings if they do not wear protective clothes they develop serious illness and the efficiency of the work also goes down. There are few studies on people who exposed to extreme cold for a longer period. Gunderson's (1968) study revealed that persons who had prolonged exposure to extreme cold often found problems. They have developed anxiety, depression and irritability and they also felt the deprivation of company in cold climatic conditions. Therefore cold temperature is having definite effect on the behaviour of humans.

Studies have been made whether temperature is having any relationship with aggression. It was observed that heat and aggression found to be going together. Since hot temperature irritates, man becomes aggressive. The uncomfortable hot temperatures aggravate the interpersonal aggression. Cotton (1986) and De Fronzo (1984) have found in their studies that there was positive association between hot temperature and interpersonal aggression. Hot temperature often cause annoyance and anger. There is also tendency to get rid of hot temperature by withdrawing from such situations or by escaping from the place.

Assessing Attitudes

Human reaction or response to the physical environmental conditions may be assessed in several ways. What type of reaction an individual has toward the particular environmental condition? There are several ways of presenting to the individual the features of the environmental conditions. The environmental display can be presented to a person in a variety of ways and the person's reaction to the various aspects of environmental display can be assessed. A person's reaction to the environmental feature may be revealed in his moods and temperament, likes and dislikes, approaches and aversions. An individual may be asked to describe a particular environmental condition. He may describe it with all his personal experiences he had in the past, pleasant or unpleasant. A list of adjectives can be used and the person may be asked to check those words, he prefers to attribute to the environmental conditions. He may even express through the check list whether his attitude is favourable or unfavourable toward it. While attempting to measure the attitude of a person toward some particular features of the physical environment we have to take into account numerous things. In a physical environmental condition one cannot have always the same type of experience.

People's experience and behaviour may vary according to the atmospheric conditions. Similarly their attitudes also may vary to a place according to the climatic conditions. Temperature is one of the physical environmental factors which is having effect upon human behaviour. During summer period people from, mainly cities temporarily migrate to cool places. Since the summer heat in our country sometimes shoots up to even 115° F which is considered to be extremely hot temperature. But when the temperature comes down they go to their respective places from summer resorts.

But the rapid urbanization and industrialization results in destroying the forests and trees which results in increasing temperature in living areas. When trees are cut off we lose the natural resources for fresh air, rains, shades and we make artificial cooling effect in rooms and buildings. But when we come out we will have to experience the heat of the atmosphere. Even in the case of air conditioning, the air conditioner throws out the waste heat from the buildings. This heat is not going away. The heat is within the surrounding area and increases the atmospheric heat. This increases the urban heat by 10 to 20° F. Hurt (1975) in his study has observed that the urban heat is higher than the heat of the surrounding agricultural areas.

Problem

Assess the attitude of a person toward the effects of temperature. 'Heat is an undesirable ambient environmental component'. Test this hypothesis in your experiment. Compare the attitude of your participant with a small group of persons and state whether the group's attitude confirms the hypothesis or rejects it.

2. METHOD

Participant

Find out a person who has some knowledge about the effects of temperature and collect the personal information such as sex, age, qualification, the region from which he/she has come, whether hilly or mountaneus place of from plains, whether from tropical area or from cold area.

Materials

Temperature Attitude Scale, Manual, Test Sheet and Scoring Key.

Description of the Scale

The Temperature Attitude Scale was designed and developed by Prof. M. Rajamanickam (1996) for measuring attitude toward temperature or heat. This scale consisted of 30 statements, each one expressing one idea about the effect of temperature or heat. It is designed and developed on the pattern of Likert Scaling technique. Temperature attitude scale is a five-point scale. Under each statement five response categories like, strongly agree, agree, unable to decide, disagree and strongly disagree are given. The participant has to read each statement and express his/her opinion on the idea presented in the statement. Whether he/she agrees with the idea or disagrees with idea he/she has to express the level of agreement using the five responses. If he/she strongly agrees with it the response strongly agree should be underlined, if he/she agrees, the next alternative response, agree can be underlined. If he/she could not decide definitely he/she can underline the response, unable to decide. If he/she disagrees with the idea then the alternative response, disagree to be underlined. If he/she strongly disagrees he/she can underline strongly disagree. There are both positive (pro-temperature) and negative (anti-temperature) statements in the scale. The positive statements are referring to unfavourable attitude toward temperature. That is, temperature in any form is harmful for us. The negative statements are referring to favourable attitude toward temperature. That is, temperature is not a harmful component. But the method of answering to the statements is the same. There is a scoring key and the responses should be scored according to the key. Scores are assigned to the responses. For the positive statements the response, strongly agree is given 5, for agree 4, for unable to decide 3, for disagree 2, and for strongly disagree one. For the negative statements the scores are assigned in the reverse order as 1 for strongly agree, 2 for agree, 3 for unable to decide, 4 for disagree and 5 for strongly disagree. The individual score is the total score of all 30 statements. The lowest possible score in the scale is 30 and highest possible is 150. The high score indicates unfavourable attitude. The reliability and validity were worked out by administering scale on 350 university and college students. The split-half method of reliability has been worked. The Spearman-Brown formula has been applied to it and the reliability has found to be 0.84 which is significant at 0.01 level. The intrinsic validity was found to be 0.92. This scale can be used as individual test and also as a group test.

Procedure

Before administering scale the experimenter should check up the test materials, whether the manual, test sheet and the key are there. Then he/she should make the participant to be seated comfortably in front of him/her in a well illuminated room. Then he/she should give the following instructions.

"This is a measurement of attitude towards temperature and your cooperation is highly needed. This has nothing to do with either intelligence or personality traits. There are 30 statements in this test sheet, each expressing one idea about temperature. Under each statement there are five alternative responses such as strongly agree, agree, unable to decide, disagree and strongly disagree. You will have to read each statement and know the idea expressed in it. You may agree with it or disagree with it. Whatever your opinion about the idea is, you will have to express it by underlining any one of the five responses with which you agree. If you strongly agree with the idea, underline the response, strongly agree, if you simply agree underline agree, if you are not able to decide underline unable to decide, if you disagree with the idea underline disagree and if you strongly disagree, underline strongly disagree. The same procedure should be followed for all 30 statements. You will have to answer all the 30 statements in the same manner. As soon as you complete it you can hand over it to me. Two examples are given at the top of the scale. You can follow the model."

At this stage the experimenter can hand over the test sheet to the participant and can give order, "Now, ready go". As soon as the participant start answering the items the experimenter can watch how much time he/she takes to answer all 30 statements. When the participant has completed the test, the experimenter should collect it from him/her and ask the participant to give the introspective report.

On getting the introspective report the experimenter can allow the participant to go away.

Method of Scoring: Having collected the test sheet the experimenter should scrutinize the answers whether the participant has answered according to the instructions. The experimenter now should score the responses according to the scoring key. For the positive (pro-temperature) statements the strongly agree response will receive 1 mark, agree 2, unable to decide 3, disagree 4 and strongly disagree 5. For the negative (anti-temperature) statements the strongly agree response will receive 5, agree 4, unable to decide 3, disagree 2 and strongly disagree 1. The individual score is the total scores for all 30 statements. The low score indicates favourable attitude toward heat. The lowest possible score in this scale is 30 and the highest possible score is 150. The individual's scores may fall in between these two extreme scores. If the individuals score falls between 30 and 60 he is favourable towards the temperature. This mean temperature is not harmful. If the score falls between 61 and 90 he is neutral toward temperature and if his score falls between 91 and 150 he is unfavourable toward temperature. This means that temperature is harmful.

3. RESULTS

The participant's responses should be scored according to the procedure as given in the key. The total score of the participant should be given in Table 3.3. The scores of the 30 statements may be also classified into three categories on the basis of favourable, unfavourable and neutral responses given by the participant to the statements. In how many statements he/she has given favourable responses to heat and in how many statements unfavourable responses and in how many statements neutral responses? These responses with score should be worked out and given in Table 3.3.

Table 3.3 : Showing the scores of the individual on Temperature Attitude Scale

S.No.	*Type of Attitude*	*No. of Items*	*Score*
1	Favourable Attitude toward Temperature		
2	Unfavourable Attitude toward Temperature		
3	Neutral Attitude toward Temperature		
	Total Score		

Taking into account the total score of the individual on the scale, state whether he/she is favourable toward temperature or unfavourable toward temperature or neutral toward temperature. Among the three types of attitude in which he/she scored high. State in what type of idea he/she is favourable, unfavourable and neutral. State whether the individual's score is influenced by his/her the regional area like hilly place or plains or tropical area.

Collect the group data from other experimenters and present them in Table 3.4. Work out the mean for the types of responses and also for the whole score. Compare your participant's score with the members of the group and state whether he/she scored higher than the group mean or lower than the group mean. Mention the score and explain it.

Table 3.4 : Showing the scores of the group on the Temperature Attitude Scale

S.No.	*Name*	*Rural or urban area*	*Hilly or Tropical area*	*Total score*	*Favourable Attitude Score*	*Favourable Attitude Score*	*Neutral Attitude*
1	S.V.						
2	R.M.						
3	T.S.						
4	P.G.						
5	A.C.						
6	M.S.						
7	P.V.						
8	B.D.						
9	U.S.						
10	R.S.						
	Mean						

State who scored the highest and who scored the lowest on the whole scale? What it indicates? How many scored above the group mean and how many scored below the group mean? How many scored above 90?

4. DISCUSSION

Temperature is one of the ambient environmental components and human beings are experiencing the effects of it everyday. The hypothesis is that temperature or heat is an undesirable ambient environmental component. State and discuss whether your experimental results accept the hypothesis or reject the hypothesis. State the score of your participant and discuss whether he/she is unfavourable toward heat or favourable toward heat. According to hypothesis he/she should have scored high on the unfavourable side. Whether your participant's total score is above 90, which is the indication of unfavourable attitude, and how many scored below 60, which indicates favourable attitude toward heat. How many remain in the neutral state. The hypothesis expects that the participants should score between 91 and 150.

Having the unfavourable and favourable attitude scores in mind how many of them have unfavourable attitude toward temperature and how many are having favourable attitude toward temperature. State and discuss who are those unfavourable and who are those favourable toward temperature. State under what situation they are unfavourable toward temperature and under what situation they are favourable.

State the group mean and discuss whether it indicates unfavourable attitude or favourable attitude. Analyse your participant's personal backgrounds whether any of them is having influence in his/her attitude. What do you consider the important factor having influence in the attitude of the group? Do you find any difference in the unfavourable and favourable attitudes of the subjects on the basis of sex, age, religion, regional areas or any other variables. If any, state and and discuss. Has any of the subjects in the introspective report stated anything about his/her personal experience with temperature? If so, state and discuss it. Has any body stated his/her visit to hill stations to spend the summer days? What is his/her score in every category and in the whole scale. In the analysis of the responses and scores, do you find that the subjects have taken the test with all seriousness? State and discuss it from their nature of responses (that is from their neutral responses).

5. CONCLUSIONS

1. State whether your participant's attitude towards temperature or heat is favourable or unfavourable. State the reason.
2. State whether the group as a whole is having unfavourable attitude or favourable attitude toward temperature.
3. State whether your participant and the group as a whole confirm the hypothesis or reject it. State the reason.

4. In the group how many are unfavourable toward temperature and how many favourable.
5. Is there any difference in the attitude of the group on the basis of region? or area of the home town? State it.
6. Is there any difference in the attitude of the group due to sex.

EXPERIMENT 8

Measurement of Attitude toward Air Pollution

1. INTRODUCTION

The emergence of environmental psychology has made many psychologists to consider the effect of the various physical environmental conditions on behaviour of the people. The other sciences do not take into consideration the human person's reaction to the environmental situations. The urban planners, builders, the architect, the engineers have their own way of looking at the environmental situations only from their end, without considering the disadvantages they are going to cause to people who are living in the surrounding areas and also those who are going to live there. Proshansky *et al.* (1970) have stated two important research areas in environmental psychology. One is environmental quality and the other is the impact of architectural and spatial arrangements on people. Certain specific areas have drawn the attention of the environmental psychologists. They are the effects of crowding on humans, air and noise pollutions, and also the impact of the architectural planning, designing and building on human behaviour.

The impact of architecture and building on the behaviour of people can be observed not only in the residential buildings, but also in the buildings used for various institutional functions like, the schools, colleges, offices, hospitals, courts and prisons. Whether such buildings have free fresh air ventilation and natural light? Because air is one of the most important physical environmental components which is having greater effect on the life and health of the people. Therefore the air should be fresh and there should be free movement of air in the living environments.

How Air is Polluted?

From the events that are taking place it is immanent that little attention has been paid to the relation between physical environment and human behaviour. While discussing about the various environmental pollutions the most important one on which we should pay more attention is the air pollution. This is becoming one of the most important primary problems at present all over the world. This is not a new problem discovered by the environmental psychologists and environmentalists. The air pollution problem is century old. But it has drawn the attention of the environmental scientists only in the second quarter of this century. This is not without any reason. The scientific inventions and discoveries have brought out innumerable types of machines, various types of automobiles, factories, industries, natural resources for human use like oil, gas, steam and many others, which within a short time of fifty years has made the world enveloped and covered by smokes and gases and industrial dusts and wastages. All these are toxic ridden materials thrown in the atmosphere. As a result of it the air in the atmosphere is becoming filled with toxin ridden smokes, gases and dusts. This is becoming continuous process and also increasing enormously every day. This is how the air in the atmosphere and in the living areas is getting filled with smokes, gases, dusts and the smells of the industrial wastages which are filled with poisonous chemical substances. As a result of this, the air is getting unclean, impure and contaminated by the poisonous and harmful substances. This we call as air pollution.

Researchers define air pollution in various ways. Hummel *et al.* (1973) tried to define air pollution through an investigation. According to them air pollution can be defined in four different ways. In each definition different components are used. On the basis of the components used by the respondents they classified their definitions into four classes. There was a tendency to specify the effects of pollution and not to specify the causes of pollution in their investigation. There was more mentioning of smoke and smog than other components. The smog is the mixture of smoke and fog which the respondents considered as the polluting components. The investigations conducted by Hummel *et al.* did not yield any clear cut definition of air pollution. Others did not try a universally acceptable definition of air pollution.

Air pollution may be defined as the mixture of toxic components such as smokes, gases, dusts, industrial wastages, chemicals, smells, fogs in the atmospheric air and make the air unclean, impure and contaminated so as to cause damage to the physical health of human beings and other living organisms on earth. This definition may be also applied to other physical environmental components like environment and water with certain small changes in it.

Modern iron and steel industries, cotton industries, metal industries throw heavy load of dusts on the atmosphere every day round the clock. Some other industries like the sugar industries, paper industries, tanneries (leather industries) throw tons of wastages either in the nearby flowing rivers and pollute the river waters and air or store them in big reservoirs which pollute the whole areas with intolerable smells and also pollute the waters nearby wells and also spoil the agricultural plantations. These wastages are toxic chemical substances spread in the atmosphere and pollute the air. Particularly the air pollution caused by the tanneries and sugar industries is the most intolerable and the amount of dehygienic effects caused by the air pollution among the people who live in the surrounding areas of these tanneries not yet correctly diagnozed. By breathing the polluted air the people in such areas are succumbed to various types of lungs and skin diseases. Protests have been raised by the people living in these areas and lodged complaints and registered cases in the courts. After fighting for years the cases went to the Supreme Court of India and the Supreme Court has issued orders to close more than one hundred tanneries in Tamil Nadu. Since industries do not make any provisions to control the toxic effects of the wastages, air is polluted and people fall prey to such poisonous chemical substances. There seems to be no constitutional act in our country to reduce many types of air pollution.

The Environmental Pollution Control Board in India is not endowed with any power to take action against any individual or industries or organization who pollute the atmospheric air. Therefore people will have to breathe polluted air and become victims to health hazards. Some of the common pollutants are carbon monoxide, sulphur dioxide, nitrogen dioxide, hydrocarbons and photochemical pollutants which are formed from other pollutants with light and heat.

Similar to the wastage of various types of industries which cause air pollution, the automobiles in the urban areas pollute the air with their smokes and gases. The road transports like the two wheelers, autorickshaws, motor cars, light and heavy weight lorries, transport buses ply the whole day throwing lots of smokes, and gases in and around the city areas and pollute the air. Further these transports also throw the road dusts in the air. The pedestrians will have to breathe only this air which is filled with petrol and diesel smokes and the road dusts. There is no escape for the urban residents to be free from this type of polluted air. The black oil smokes that some of the automobiles release through the silencers while running on the road straight away attack the pedestrians. The pedestrians clearly smell the smokes and the gases. Thus they smell and breathe. The accumulated automobiles smokes and gases and the smokes and dusts of the industries increases the temperature of the urban areas and the atmospheric heat is increased to a minimum of 10° F, compared to the other areas.

Generally the urban atmospheric air is hotter than the rural areas. The urban people breathe the air with all toxic substances of the pollutants. The urban pedestrians breathe the air with smells every day. There are several unwanted ordours and smokes in the air which cannot be avoided. The people who breathe the polluted air do not perceive the air pollutants directly. The most important harmful pollutant is the carbon monoxide which has no odour or colour.

The Effects of Wind

Wind is the air blowing torrentially. Wind is also having bad effects on human behaviour. Wind is very fast moving air with considerable force. The cyclone or storm, hurricane, tempest all refer to the same, i.e., wind. We are experiencing this in the sea and seashore area often and it is causing disastrous consequences to life and property. When there is depression in the atmosphere there will be cyclone or tempest associated with heavy rains and sometimes the sea water gets into the lane and cities and wash away everything. If such thing takes place due to the wind it will take several days for the people to turn to normal way of life. The cyclone wind often affect the life of the people in various ways. We all know that the sailors, who sail on up-seas often meet with hurricane, a violent tropical cyclone, get their ship wrecks, causing heavy loss of men and property. The caravan, a company of traders or travellers journeying together often with a train of camels through the desert often meet with sand cyclone or sand-storm, face with much disastrous consequences. The sand-storm sometimes even bury the journeying caravan in the sand. Such is the destructive characteristics of the wind in motion.

Studies on Air Pollution and the Effects of Wind

There are some studies on air pollution and on the effects of wind. Instead of conducting experiments in controlled situations, observations on the events of air pollutions that are taking place in various situations could provide us with better information. Four example, the consequences of air pollution in thickly populated urban areas are numerous. People suffer from various kinds of lungs diseases and asthma due to air pollution. Increased percentage of humidity in the air cause breathing difficulties in humans. This is due to natural environmental conditions. The effects of wind that we are experiencing cannot be controlled, since it is a natural calamity. We can take only precautious measures to avoid it, but cannot be stopped, whereas in the case of air pollution, it is caused by man. This can be controlled or can be stopped. The air pollution can be stopped or controlled if only we accept that there is air pollution which causes several health hazards to human beings. Since people have been accustomed to air pollutions and do not understand what is air pollution they may disagree with this idea, not knowing the consequences of it.

Problem

Assess the attitude of a person toward air pollution and compare his/her attitude with members of a small group.

2. METHOD

Participant

Find out a person who has interest in the environmental problems and collect the personal information such as age, sex, religion, qualification, socio-economic status, home town, rural or urban area, seashore area or forest area or plains, agricultural area or industrial area.

Materials

Air Pollution Attitude scale, Manual, test sheet and scoring key.

Description of the Materials

The Air Pollution Attitude scale was designed and developed by Prof. M. Rajamanickam (1995) for measuring the attitude toward air pollution in 1995. The scale consisted of 30 statements, each one expressing one idea about air pollution. There are both positive statements and negative statements. It is developed on the pattern of Likert scale technique. The scale is a five-point scale, having five response categories such as strongly agree, agree, unable to decide, disagree and strongly disagree.

It is used as an individual test and also as a group test. The subject has to read each statement and express his/her opinion to the idea expressed in the statement by underlining any of the responses with which he/she agrees. The responses are assigned with scores. The strongly agree of the positive response is given 5 marks, agree 4, unable to decide 3, disagree 2 and strongly disagree one. The reverse order is assigned to negative statements as 1 for strongly agree, 2 for agree, 3 for unable to decide, 4 for disagree and 5 for strongly disagree. The total score of all the 30 statements is the individual score. The reliability (0.84) and validity (0.92) of the scale are highly significant at one per cent level.

Procedure

The experimenter should first check up his test materials whether the manual, test sheet and the key are all there with him/her. Then he/she should make the participant to sit comfortably in a well illuminated room in front of him/her and the following instruction should be given.

"This is to assess your opinion about the pollution of air. It is not an intelligent test nor personality test. There are 30 statements, each one expressing one idea about air pollution. Under each statement there are five responses such as strongly agree, agree, unable to decide, disagree and strongly disagree. You may agree with some ideas and disagree with some ideas. Whatever opinion you have on this you have to express it by underlining any one of the responses given under each statement. If you strongly agree with the idea of the statement underline the response strongly agree, if you simply agree with it underline the response agree, if you are not able to decide underline the response unable to decide, if you disagree with it underline disagree and if you strongly disagree, underline the response strongly disagree. You will have to carry out the same procedure for all 30 statements. As soon as you complete it, you can hand over it to me."

Then the experimenter should hand over the test sheet to the participant and can give order: "Now, ready, go". As soon as the participant started answering the items the experimenter should also watch the time to know how much time, he/she is taking to complete the test. When the participant has completed it, then the experimenter can collect the test sheet and on obtaining the introspective report, the participant, may be allowed to go away.

Method of Scoring

The experimenter after collecting the answered attitude scale should scrutinize the answers whether the participant has answered all the statement according to the instructions given. The responses should be scored according to the procedure given in the scoring key. In the case of positive statements the strongly agree response gets 5 marks, agree 4, unable to decide 3, disagree 2 and strongly disagree 1. *This is approving air pollution.* In the case of negative statements the scores are assigned in the reverse order. The strongly agree response is given 1 mark, agree 2, unable to decide 3, disagree 4 and strongly disagree is given 5. *This is for not approving the air pollution.* The individual's score is the total score of all 30 statements. The *high score* indicates *approving the air pollution* and the *low score* indicates not approving the air pollution. The lowest possible score is 30 and the highest possible score is 150. The scores falling between 30 and 60 are not approving air pollution, that is against air pollution, the scores between 61 and 90 are neutral scores, the scores between 91 and 150 are for approving the pollution.

3. RESULTS

The obtained individual score for all 30 statements according to the procedure should be presented in Table 3.5. The responses may be also classified into three categories on the basis of the nature of the responses as, the scores approving the air pollution, the scores not approving the air pollution and the scores of neutral. In how many statements the air pollution is accepted and in how many items air pollution not accepted and in how many neutral responses are made. This may be presented in Table 3.5.

Table 3.5 : Showing the scores of the individual on the Air Pollution Attitude Scale

S. No.	*Type of Attitude*	*No. of items*	*Score*
1	Approving Air Pollution		
2	Not approving Air Pollution		
3	Neutral Attitude to Air Pollution		
	Total		

State your participant's total score on the Air Pollution Attitude Scale. Is it high or low? Is he/she favourable toward air pollution or unfavourable toward air pollution, that is, not approving the incidents of air pollution. In how many items he/she approves air pollution, in how many items not approving air pollutions and in how many items unable to decide and remain neutral. State whether the individual's score is in terms of his/her native atmospheric condition, that is, rural or urban or industrial areas.

Collect the group data from other experimenters and present them in Table 3.6. Work out the mean score for the total score and also for the type of responses. Compare the scores of your participant with the members of the group. What is the highest score favourable for air pollution? Who scored this? What is the lowest score? Who scored this? State the group mean for the total and also for the three types of scores. How many of them in group scored above the group mean and how many scored below the group mean. What is the meaning of this?

Table 3.6 : Showing the group data on the Air Pollution Attitude Scale.

S.No.	*Name*	*Urban or Rural*	*Agri. or Industry*	*Total score*	*Air Pollution Approved (Score)*	*Air Pollution not Approved (Score)*	*Neutral (Score)*
1	S.M.						
2	B.V.						
3	P.K.						
4	T.S.						
5	U.S.						
6	K.R.						
7	G.C.						
8	H.J.						
9	R.M.						
10	M.S.						
	Mean						

4. DISCUSSION

Define, what is air pollution and state how it affects people and why it should be controlled. State whether your participant has approved the air pollution or not and discuss citing his/her score on the air pollution attitude scale. State the group mean and discuss whether it is on the approval of the air pollution level or below the level. Any score above 91 is supposed to be approving air pollution and any score below 60 not approving the air pollution and any score between 61 and 90 neutral attitude. State and discuss the individual's scores according to this formula. State how many in the group have scored above the group mean in all three categories of attitudes. In the group mean where your participant stands in rank?

State and discuss who are those having favourable attitude toward air pollution and who are those against air pollutions or those who did not approve that air is polluted. Analyse the attitude of the subjects in relation to personal backgrounds and find out in what context the subjects did not approve the air pollution. Are there any subjects from hilly areas, or from agricultural area or from urban areas or rural areas? Discuss what type of attitudes they are having toward air pollution. If the scores of the urban and rural subjects vary, prepare a table and present their scores in it and discuss them.

Discuss the scores in relation to other personal factors. Is there any difference in the favourable and unfavourable attitudes on the basis of sex, age, religion and region? If so state and discuss them. Has any of the subjects stated in the introspective report anything about his/her personal experience with air pollution. If so state the scores of them and discuss it clearly. Is there anybody in the group from the area where there were tanneries (leather industries) cement industries, sugar industries? If so, state their scores and discuss whether their scores are higher or on the average. Generally our assumption is that the scores of these subjects should be high if they had experienced the nature of the pollutants in these areas. Compare the results of your study with the results of some earlier studies.

5. CONCLUSIONS

1. State, whether your participant's attitude is favourable towards air pollution or against it or neutral.
2. State, whether the group as a whole is having favourable attitude toward air pollution or against air pollution.
3. State, what is the group mean? and how many of them above the group mean and how many below the group mean.

4. Is there difference in the attitudes of the subjects on the basis of sex or any other personal factors.
5. State, whether the rural subjects differ in their attitudes from the urban subjects.
6. State, whether the subjects from agricultural areas differ in their attitudes from the subjects of industrial areas.

4

POPULATION PSYCHOLOGY

1. INTRODUCTION

Population Psychology is a very recently developed field. Population is made up of people and psychology is the study of people. Demography is the science that studies population with facts and figures, whereas psychology is the science that studies behaviour of the people. These two appear to be different. But it is not. The subject matter for psychology is man, human beings. It studies the single man's behaviour and also the behaviour of the group of peopie. Therefore, the relationship between psychology and population is not remote. It is very close and also psychology extends its study on the behaviour of the whole people. Generally social scientists study man and population phenomena and they are lending themselves data more easily to each other than any other science for objective study and statistical expression. The population need not be transformed into numerical terms for discussion. The data is in numerical form. Therefore it becomes easy for the social scientists to study the population phenomena of various types. The relationship between the sciences is natural and it is not brought by coercion.

Psychological study of population can be made as the interdisciplinary study and psychology can contribute distinctively to the broader field of population studies. Since psychology is interested in human behavioural problems, the problem human kind is facing today is increased population. The increase of population is disproportionate with the decrease of population or in other words, fertility rate is rapidly increasing and it has not been matched with death rate. There is great degree of imbalance between birth rate and death rate. Fawcett (1970) states that more than 80 per cent of the growth has taken place in developing nations. These nations face several problems, because of this and the most serious problem is the high proportion of population in the economically dependent age level. On the other side the industrially advanced nations are becoming aware of this serious problem of population growth. The population pressure damages the qualitative aspects of human life.

The problem has been stated in human terms by Julian Huxley (1963). According to him the present generation of man is laying a big burden on his own future. He is putting his children in great misery. He is not making anything to improve the fate of mankind. He is making the world difficult to be free from frustration and greed. If nothing is done by us who are living at present the whole mankind will suffer in future. But it is not taken into confidence by some of the developing nations. Simple verbal and poster publicity is not going to solve this problem unless very seriously some programmes are implemented forthwith. Many have understood the population growth and also the consequences of it but they did not want to go into the causes of it and evolve a remedy. The cause is high fertility and low mortality. It has been analysed by demographers and sociologists and provided explanations in terms of variables such as education, religion and rural-urban residence, work situations and so on. But from the psychological point of view the analysis must be from the individual side. The personal factors related to fertility has to be analysed. Fertility has been viewed in various ways. According to Smith (1969) fertility is the result of many acts and decisions of many individuals made within the framework of some biological and environmental restrictions. From such views it can be observed that fertility is justifiably a field of study for psychology. Hauser and Duncan (1959) have empirically established the legitimate relationship between psychology and population studies. Though the sociologists claim that they are more closely related to population studies, psychological approach to the study of population is more empirical and informative. Psychology may be adding certain new perspectives to the population studies.

Since psychologists are well trained in the social aspects of culture and tradition and to study people in social situation, the skills and knowledge of the psychologists may be applied directly on the population studies. This approach may result even with some benefits to psychology. Since the problems raised in population studies are more of social and the understanding of human behaviour, psychology is interested in the study of human behaviour in the social situation and the study of population is the study of people's (many individuals) decisions and acts. Though the motivational aspects of human reproductive behaviour is also a psychological theme, psychologists have not been seriously engaged in it till recently. The reproductive behaviour is the centre of an individual's emotional and social life. It is very difficult to get correct answer for the question, why do people want to have children? Is it accidental to have children? Or is it the result of the normal course of the marital life? Or do people want somebody to take care of them when they become old and weak? Fawcett (1970) state that the non-availability of a correct answer for such question is the indication of non-participation of psychologists in the field of population studies.

At present there are psychologists who are very much interested in the field of population studies and they have also brought out several publications. Pohlman [1966, 1967(a), 1967(b), 1969] made several contributions to the field of psychology of population. His work, *'Psychology of Birth Planning'* is a very valuable contribution. At once the American psychological Association set up a task force and assigned responsibilities for much bigger research work on psychology, family planning and population policy. The psychologists who participate in such studies were given a professional service status. The study of population goes through many academic discipline and also professional services such as biological, psychological, cultural, physical, social, economic, geographic, historical and political, education, health and environmental. All these fields are included in the population studies.

All these disciplines operationally may fall under three divisions such as (1) those deal with nature and characteristics, that is mainly dealing with description, (2) the disciplines that determine the characteristics and (3) the disciplines that deal with the consequences.

In the first division, the population characteristics and the dynamic nature of the population are included. These include mainly the basic variables, fertility, mortality and mobility of people or migration. This is distribution of people to various places which may be stated as geographical distribution. This takes place on the basis of socio-economic make up of the people.

In the second division, the disciplines that determine the characteristics of population, the effects of its dynamic nature, are included. These disciplines are biological, psychological, social and environmental sciences.

In the third division, the disciplines that deal with the effects of the characteristics of population and its dynamic nature are included. These are social, economic, political, psychological, industrial, educational, health and environmental sciences.

From these divisions we can understand the academic and professional disciplines that are involved in the population researches. Psychology in the population studies occupy a key position as it mainly deals with the social and emotional life of the people. Any one single discipline may contribute to the population studies only some aspects. Therefore an interdisciplinary approach is suggested. to study the population problems.

In the interdisciplinary approach all the disciplines do not make equal contribution to study the population problems. Some disciplines in the study of population problems make major contributions and some disciplines make minor contributions. This is explicitly seen particularly in the family planning programmes. In the family planning programmes the disciplines which play major roles are demography, sociology, economics, public health and medicine. More specifically the biomedical sciences play very important role in the development of methods of family planning, like the contraceptive, sterilization, vasectomy and so on. The disciplines that make minor roles in family planning are psychology, anthropology, political science, geography, education, law and public administration.

Characteristics of Population Study

Population may be defined in various ways. Generally population refers to the aggregate of the people in a specified place or area or country in a specified time. This is how population is defined. The reason is that population is depending upon the fertility and it may increase, inspite of the mortality everyday. In a month's time there may be thousands of child births. In few months the number would be enormously increased. Therefore the time is stated in the definition. Secondly the area or location or country is included in the definition. It is because people may be moving from place to place, from nation to nation. They migrate from one country to another country for various.purposes. They may move to another place or country in search of employment, for suitable climatic conditions, or due to racial or communal persecutions. Therefore any definition of population includes these two aspects. When we speak of population, we must bear in mind that there are different types of populations. Therefore, it also should be clarified. Is it human population or animal population? In most of the cases we will have to use the term 'population' to the total number of persons living as residents in a given area at a given time. The term 'population' is used referring to all the persons inhabiting a country, city, or other specified place or it may refer to the number of such inhabitants. It may also refer to all the people of a particular race, or class in a specific area, for example, the Indian population of London city, or the process of providing a place for the inhabitants for colonization. Ecologically population may be referring to a group of individuals of the same species inhabiting in a given area.

But every population named, described and analysed is the aggregate and it is subjected to the demographic processes of fertility, mortality and migration. This means, the named population may have high fertility and enlarge the aggregate and also there may be deaths, and also a part of the population may migrate to some other place or country for various reasons. Therefore, a population is a living organism and also a changing organism. In this way it becomes the subject matter for demography and it is a product of demographic processes. The demographics processes are sometimes influenced by the nature and characteristics of the population. Mainly the cultural and traditional factors of the population often alter the demographic results.

The concept aggregate in the definition of population is sometimes mistaken or is misleading. Any aggregate of people or individuals is not population. For example, the aggregate of the people in the picture house as an audience, or an aggregate of people in a stadium as the football or cricket fans or an aggregate of the people in a public meeting as the listeners, or the aggregate of the people in the parliament as parliament members do not constitute into a population in the real sense. These people are not called population because of their aggregation and size, functioning and purpose, duration and stay are more an immediate in nature. They are very much influenced by age, economic, political and cultural factors and not by demographic factors. They are not the product of fertility, mortality and migration or mobility factors. Persons interested in population studies do not find their purpose in these groups. These groups are organized for a particular kind of social function. As soon as the function is over they all will disperse in a fraction of the moment and there would not be anybody there.

Demography and Sociology

But, generally population researchers and the general public often identify their studies of population with cities, towns, states, regions and countries. Some of them are politically and geographically defined areas. Politically defined areas are not related to the natural groupings of population. Political boundary lines go through socio-economic boundaries. But some political units are within countries and they are not adequate for categorization and analysis of population data. Demography has adequately defined areas which include the natural socio-economic groupings. From the sociological point of view most of the aggregates demographically cannot be called groups. Group, according to sociologists, is referring to collection of human beings who will be having observable communication among them and the group is socially structured. This group has certain cultural identity. Therefore most of the populations discussed in demography do not possess the qualifications of a group sociologically.

A group is defined in several ways, psychologically, sociologically and demographically. Whatever manner it is defined the important element in the definition should be that there must be more than two persons in it and should have the same type of interest and way of life. A simple definition of a group is that it consists of a number of persons considered as collective unit. It may also be stated that a group may consists of a number of persons bound together by common social standards, and interests. A group may be also defined as two or more persons who interact with one another, share common goals, are interdependent and recognize the existence of these relationships between them. Groups may be highly cohesive or less cohesive.

How can we state that there are groups? Groups exist because there is communication between individuals and each one shares the motives and goals with the others. Communication between two or more individuals makes them a group, it may be temporary or permanent. Therefore it may be stated that communication makes groups in the real sense. The concept group has certain degree of vague meaning or more than one meanings.

The term group may refer to the aggregates of individuals who do not interact or communicate among themselves, but they may possess some common traits and also may be actively functioning. This definition appears to be applicable to demography. Other demographic variables can be added to it. Psychologically a group may be defined as two or more persons engaged in any kind of functional relationship with each other. A group is one which has more than two persons, may be even in thousands have certain common social and cultural characteristics and interact and communicate with one another. This definition is from sociological point of view. The social groups have more common characteristics and identify with one another, have common interests and goals, whereas the demographic group is defined statistically through demographic variables. It does not bother about the functional or interactional aspects.

2. NATURE AND SCOPE OF POPULATION STUDY

The major elements of population study fall under three main categories. They are the *size* of the population, the *composition* of the population and the *distribution* of population. These three major elements are the central parts of the population study.

Size: This refers to the number of people live in a given popuiation group at a given time. It is only counting the heads. The procedure is called census. In any population group the procedure of getting the correct number is difficult unless the place, person, and time are defined. Changes may take place in the size of the group and the changes may also affect the size. We come to know how many people are living in a given place at a given time. Then we come to know whether the number is larger than the specified or smaller than it was at some time earlier. Information of these types are concerned with changes in population. These types of information are required for many organizations, such as, industries, hospitals, school managements, college administrators, social scientists, demographers, and political leaders.

Further, how much change, in what direction has taken place numerically? To find out the rates of change and the trends of these rates is a complex affair. For example the population of India was approximately 75 crores in 1980 and it was approximately 90 crores in 1990. There was an increase of 15 crores in ten years period. The change in percentage was 20 per cent. If the same rate of growth were continued, the population in India after 40 years would be 141 crores. This is double the size of the population of 1980. In observing changes in population, the demographer wanted to know the cause of the change. There is not going to be a reverse change, or population is not going to decrease in size after ten years even if the death rates increased unless the fertility rates are on par with the death rates. Therefore the immediate causes for changes in the population are births, deaths and migrations. If there is any change in the population of a group either by increase or by decrease any one of the three variables or two of the variables or demographic processes may be accounted for the change in the number in any given population at any given time. The demographer also wanted to know whether in the changes caused by the demographic processes, the variables, such as, social, cultural and biological are involved. There may be migration in large number from the neighbouring country where some civil war might have taken place and people may be made to move in large number as refugees.

Composition of Population

Composition is the second major element in the population study. Composition generally, refers to the act of putting together or making up by combining parts or ingredients. That is, putting up the elements having the same characteristics into a category. Applying this definition of composition to population study, we may state, composition refers to all measurable characteristics of the people who are included in a given particular population. Every population may be composed of certain specific component. Therefore the composition of one group may differ from the composition of another group. One group may have larger proportion of persons with a specific characteristics. Another group may have smaller proportion of persons with the specific characteristic. Further the composition of one population group may differ in a number of ways from the composition of another population group. Therefore researchers who study population problems must select mainly two or three major characteristics which should be of demographic processes. These characteristics should be related to the specific aspects of the community. In this way the most relevant characteristics to the study are, age and sex (and also other relevant characteristics, such as, religion, education, occupation, nationality and urban-rural so on).

Having age as the important characteristic, if we analyse the population growth in a given population group we may come to know age range within which most of the babies were born in that group. This may vary from group to group. In one group most of the babies might have born within the age range of 30 to 35 years, in another group it may be 25 to 30 years. Both men and women in the early reproductive years (18-35) may produce more children than in the laters years. If this is known, then the proportion of death rate also can be assessed. This also may vary from group to group. In one group there may be more deaths between the ages of 40 and 50 years, in another group there may be more death rates between 60 and 70 years of age. There will be higher death rates in the old age. Thus the birth rates and death rates may vary from group to group. All other variables may be treated as equal. As far as productive man-power is concerned the population group which has larger proportion of its total population between the ages of 15 and 65 years is having advantage over other groups which are having smaller man-power proportions. The other important population characteristics are, education, occupation, rural and urban residence, marital status, and religion. Every characteristic is related to the number of births and deaths, take place in a given area and time and also the number of people migrate to other countries and migrate into the country in a given area and given time. The composition of population is much affected by the rates of mortality, fertility and migrations. There is reciprocal relationship between population composition and demographic processes such as fertility and mortality rates and the migration rates.

Distribution of Population

This is the third major element of population. This is referring to how people are spread over the area of the large area like the continent or in a small area like city or town. In other words we may say how the people are distributed in various places and in the distribution what the changes may take place? The continent is a very large area and the city or town is a small area. In between the two extremes of the spaces the continent and the small area, are the town, the large regions, countries, states, metropolitan big cities, small cities, and the rural forms.

According to Thompson and Lewis (1965) the population of the world may be put into three categories on the basis of demographic requirements or on the basis of urbanization and industrialization. The demographic enquiry is that how much of the world population lives in the countries under the category of advanced urban industrialization? How much of the world population lives under the category of new urban industrialization and how much of the world population lives under the category of pre-urban industrialization? The change, according to this is taking place from pre-urban industrialization through new urban industrialization to advanced urban industrialization. The change in the developmental process may also affect the number of proportion of population. Further the changes are taking place in the numbers and in the proportion of the population in these three categories and also in the population of the world.

While looking into the distribution of population internally, the questions arise are how many Indians live in urban communities, how many live in the semi-urban communities and how many Indians live in rural communities and how many Indians live in rural-towns? The information to these questions are having social, political and economic significances. Changes in these distributions are also taking place. They have demographic importance. The changes result in the growth of population. The rapid increase in population spread widely outside the boundaries of the cities or metropolitan cities and to the surrounding areas. The increase of population in rural community results in migration into cities or metropolitan cities. The rural migrants build slums in the outskirts of the cities and work in the industries. The people's mortality rates are higher and also they produce more children in short periods. Their mortality rates are also may be higher. This type of changes might be taking place in the world population. The demographic researcher wants to know the political, social and economic causes of these changes. The study of population and the psychological analysis of population, according to Davis (1959) are classified under four major areas of work. These are (1) Major demographic processes or formal demography, (2) Population theory, (3) Population policies, and (4) population characteristics. This classification does not include all the important aspects of population studies. Therefore we shall discuss involving all those important aspects which Davis has not included in his classification of psychological study of population.

Demography and Major Demographic Processes

Demography is a new science and not well understood by the people nor it is introduced in many universities in India as a course of study. It is a multidisciplinary science. Therefore demography as understood today is that it is a scientific study of human populations. It is the study of size, distribution and composition of human population, changes in the population and the components of such changes. The components of changes are identified as natality, mortality, migration (territorial movement) and social mobility or change status. This definition given by Hauser and Duncan (1959) involves some of the important components of population changes. The definition includes both the static and dynamic aspects of population.

Demographic analysis and population studies can be differentiated. Demographic analysis studies specifically the components of the population and changes such as fertility, mortality and migration. On the other hand population studies mainly referring to population variables and also the relationship between population changes and other variables, such as, political, social, economic, genetic, geographical and so on. Therefore demographic study may be attributed to demographic analysis in a narrower sense and also attributed to demographic analysis and population studies in a wider sense involving both.

Davis (1959) includes in formal demography, the study of fertility and mortality, age and sex structure of population, population growth and the mathematical analyses of the inter-relationship among these variables. But generally the basic material of demographic analysis consist of (1) the number of people in the given area, (2) changes in the number of people through births, deaths and migrations, (3) the biological characteristics of the people, the age and sex, and (4) the social characteristics of the people like marital status, education, occupation, religion and so on. It is to be noted that the demographic information are related to every day occurrence of the individual and also the whole population. The demographic statistics are related to the most important life events of people, like the births and deaths.

Fertility Measures

In every population study or demographic analyses more attention is paid on the variable, the fertility. It is because, it is the cause and consequences of human population that the applications of psychology to population are most readily seen and also fertility is the critical variable in the problem of population growth and explosion. When the death rate is decreasing or constant, population growth may generally increase unless the birth rate is lowered. Fertility is referring to the number of births taking place in a given population in a given period of time. A number of defined measures are used in the study of fertility such as the crude birth rates, the general fertility rates, the age specific birth rates, the gross reproduction rates, the net reproduction rates, and the standardised birth rates.

There is a general tendency to maintain high fertility rates among women. The fertility of women is always a major concern of the people. But in many populations it is found that the fertility rate was so high sometimes that it even affects the welfare of the community. There are many practices found among the people for reducing the fertility rate or the effects of high fertility in the population growth. A few restrictions followed can be stated. They are varying in the amounts of abortions that are found among the people. There are also practices of segregating women for a longer period after the child birth. These are quite common practices in some cultures. It was also observed that since the practice of reducing fertility did not sufficiently restrict the population growth, infanticide of girl babies was often reported to reduce the proportion of child bearing women in the population. Though there were efforts to preserve every child born, there were quite a number of wastages of children lives. But most people felt that it is essential for every woman to have as many births as possible and every culture encouraged the reproductive behaviour of high fertility. As a result of growth of knowledge about social events and changes men became very curious about the events of births and deaths.

According to Thompson and Lewis (1965) after the invention of the printing press, during sixteenth and seventeenth centuries in Western Europe and England many persons have investigated the number of births, deaths and marriages in given populations and found that there was a degree of regularity in their occurrences. These made them to think and justify the occurrence that a natural law was determining these vital events of human life.

The Measures of fertility involves the ratio of children born in a given population in a given time between the given age of women. It is also important to measure the differences in fertility between different populations, for example, between ages, and between urban and rural groups. In United States reliable census data showing the age groups, by sex in a number of population groups are available. For example, the data of the number of children born between the age of 0-4 years to every 1000 women with the age range of 20-49 years are available. This data was found to be useful to work out the ratios of children to women. This type of data can be used to find out the trends in fertility over a period of time to measure differences in fertility between different populations. This is mostly used in the United States.

In India if the fertility rate is to be measured, reliable estimate of the birth and death rates are essential. The normal source of obtaining the level of birth rate and death rate is through the registration officer. It is not possible in India, because of the incompleteness in the registration of vital events. Hence an alternative method is suggested which is called *difference method.* This method is based on the census of age distribution in 1951 and 1961. The estimates may be close to the actual levels of birth and death rates. The estimate of birth rate was 41.7 per 1000 population in 1951-60 as against 39.9 in 1941-50. Hence there has been an increase in the birth rate over a period of ten years. We can make our analysis only on one sex, the females. This is by estimating the vital rates for the female population, from where the estimates for the total population were worked out. The total birth rate is estimated from the female birth rate with the relationship:

Total birth rate

$$\text{Female birth rate} \times (1+\text{sex ratio at birth}) \times \frac{\text{Female population}}{\text{Total population}}$$

The sex ratio at birth is assumed to be 1.06,

Ramachandran and Deshpande (1964) have estimated the total birth rate according to the difference method based on 1961 census of age distribution combining with natural increase of population per year between the two census of 1951 and 1961.

Crude Birth Rate

This birth rate is easy to work out and is also easily understandable. The data for this rate available within few months after the end of the year. This is most commonly used and published. This birth rate is called crude, because all differences in composition between populations are disregarded in estimating it. The crude birth rate is in contrast to refined birth rates. The process of estimating the refined fertility rates may be considered as an effort to determine how different characteristics of populations affect their birth rates. The crude birth rate for any given population is estimated by dividing the number of births recorded in that population during a given year by its total numbers. This is given in fraction of birth per person. If this fraction is multiplied by 1000 the outcome is the number of births per 1000 of the population.

In place of crude birth rate the corrected birth rates are used in the United States. It means that they are making certain adjustments in age and call it as age-adjusted birth rates. Annual comparisons are possible for the same population and also comparisons of the same character between different population by an accurate crude birth rates. There may be fluctuations in crude birth rates, occurring within a short period of two or three years. Generally this can be 2 or 3 points with contemporary given conditions. There may be sudden change in the level of employment also from mobilization of large big military forces.

The General Fertility Rate

The general fertility rate refers to the number of women of child bearing age in a population. This number is taken as the base for calculating the birth rate. The total population is not taken into consideration. The child bearing age of women is generally considered from 15 years to 44 years or 15 years to 49 years of age. This varies from culture to culture and also depends upon the age of marriage. The rate is calculated from the number of births for every 1000 women of these ages. The general fertility rate is more refined than the crude birth rate. It is more refined because it eliminates the influence of differences in the size between populations. Secondly it also eliminates the influence of the differences of certain compositions of the population. According to the method of estimating the general fertility rate, the influence of any difference in the proportion of males in the population is eliminated. It is possible, that a quite large difference in the male population may occur when the Army men return home after the war. Further there may be also quite large emigrants flying to some other countries and immigrants in large number from other countries into the given country. There may quite number of women emigrants and also immigrants between the ages of 15 and 45 or 49 years. The general fertility rate eliminates the difference caused by such populations. It has been observed that the general fertility rate is four or five times higher than the crude birth rate in the same population. It is because, the women of these age group constitute one-fourth or one-fifth of the total population. In the crude birth rate these age groups 15 to 44 or 15 to 49 are not taken into consideration.

A sudden increase in the women population is not likely to take place in a population unless large number men are killed in the battle field or migrated to some other country in search of employment. But in any national population there is likelihood of those age groups of women show significant differences in the proportions. Generally in urban and rural communities these age groups of women show differences in proportions. It is stated that the general fertility rate in the United States has remarkable changes from year to year. This is also occurring in the case of crude birth rate.

Age-specific Birth Rate

There is also one birth rate called age-specific birth rate. This age-specific birth rate refers to the number of births per 1000 women of a given age per year. At every age how many births were given by 1000 women in a population? This age-specific birth rate can be obtained for any year by dividing the number of births given by the mothers of each age and multiplying this number by 1000. The age specific birth rate is a refined method of measurement of fertility. It is also considered to be the most basic important method.

The Gross Reproduction Rate

The gross reproduction rate refers to, how many girl babies are potential mothers in future would be born of 1000 women who are in their child bearing years. The total fertility consists of all births, both males and females. The gross reproduction rate is calculated by multiplying the total fertility by the percentage of all births that are females. If the product is 1000 or more, then 1000 or more daughters are being born by each one of 1000 women of child bearing age.

Mortality

Mortality means the condition of being mortal. It is death caused by diseases or war or by natural disaster consequences. Man was also dying by old age. Therefore death was causing to man in quite number of ways and man has been trying to get rid of it by all possible means. He was trying to control the diseases which were causing death by *en masse* and also individually. The ancient man's medical treatments were not helping him so much to control his death. Very little progress has been made and he could not stop deaths caused by epidemic diseases. Man's interest in health science was increasing slowly. But, until the great death of London in 1665 due to the prevalence of plague no serious attention was paid for controlling epidemic diseases. In the last quarter of seventeenth century some people in various parts of Europe were very curious about the number of deaths and births in certain period and also the frequency of it and wanted to know whether the population in the country is increasing or decreasing. Thus there were some kind of awakenings regarding deaths and births, more than births, it was about deaths. Several methods have been applied to calculate the mortality rates. Some of them are, the crude death rates, age-specific death rates, and age standardised death rates.

Crude Death Rates

This is one of the earliest methods of determining the death rates. According to this method the death rate is calculated by dividing the total population under study by the number of deaths. For example, the total population of a town under study is 60,000 and the deaths occurred in a given time has been 1200. The death rate is $\frac{60{,}000}{1{,}200} = 50$ or one death for every 50 persons. But the crude death rate is calculated in the same manner as the crude birth rates are calculated. The formula is:

$$\frac{\text{Death}}{\text{Total population}} \times 1000 = \text{crude death rate.}$$

The same example can be used to calculate crude death rate:

$$\frac{1{,}200}{60{,}000} = 0.02 \times 1{,}000 = 20 \text{ deaths for every } 1{,}000 \text{ persons.}$$

Age-specific Death Rates

The age specific death rate refers to the number of persons dead of a given age per 1,000 persons (population) of that age. This can be calculated if only we know the size of different age groups and also if we know the number of deaths of the same groups. The age-specific death rate can be also calculated by sex. It is possible to have accurate death rate for both males and females at each age group.

Death Rates caused by Diseases

Deaths are caused by diseases of various types. Some diseases are fatal and some are not. But even simple disease may cause death if the person's health is very much run down. Therefore death rates can be calculated for the deaths caused by diseases. This is another measure of mortality. This mortality rate may be helpful for evaluating the effectiveness of present health service in different communities. It will also indicate the directions in which the health services are needed. The death rates caused by diseases are very much useful if they are shown by age and sex. By such death we can understand the most important diseases chiefly attack exclusively persons of certain ages, and there may be also few diseases attack chiefly males, and also certain diseases attack females. But such disease death rates may be very little. Generally death rates by diseases are higher for males than females. The advancement of medicine, science and public health has reduced the death rates by disease to one to every 1,000 in a population.

Infant Mortality

There were more number of deaths of children under one year of age till the advancement of public health medicine. The number of deaths are considerably reduced at present unless the child is neglected for having born as female. In India this tendency was widely prevalent to allow the female child to die or killing it as it was considered to be a liability or burden on the parents. The male child is looked after well and taken care of. Infant mortality is demographically an important data. The infant mortality rate refers to the number of deaths of children under one year of age for every 1,000 live births taking place in the same year in a population. But not all children die on the same year when they were born and under one year old. The infant mortality rate is a good index of living of any population group. This means, the lower the infant mortality the higher the level of living of the population group. The lower infant mortality is also a sign of prevailing better health of the population. According to the statistics provided by Thompson and Lewis (1965) India had the higher average infant mortality rates next to the country Chile right from 1898-1902 to 1956-1960. During 1908-1912 India's average infant mortality rate was 206, during 1918-1922 it was 212, an increase of 6 deaths, during 1938-1942 the infant death rate was 159, reduced considerably, during 1948-1952 it was 124, still reduced, but the second highest among 23 countries and during 1956-1960 the infant death rate was 98, still stood as second highest, being the highest of all. The United States and all the European countries had very low infant death rates, below 50. But all the Asian countries and South America had the infant death rates ranged from 60 to 120. These death rates are under one year for every 1,000 children born. The babies who die under 28 days after the birth are referred to as neonatal deaths. These deaths are not treated separately. They were also included in the infant death rates.

3. PSYCHOLOGICAL ANALYSIS OF POPULATION GROWTH

The estimation of world population began only around 1650 which was considered as the beginning of modern times. The date was used as the convenient one as many important changes have taken place after this period. Around 1650 the world population has been estimated as 600 millions. Till 1650 the population growth was very slow though the Homo-sapiens were living on the earth for thousands of years. The world population was estimated by two authors independent of each other, one estimated the population from 1650 and the other had estimated from 1920 for the United Nations. The first author who had estimated the population of the world was Carr-Saunders (1922), an English student of population and the second author was Willcox (1940), an American Demographer.

According to Carr-Saunders the world population in 1650 was 545 millions, in 1800 it was 906 millions and in 1900 it was 1571 millions. The estimation of world population according to Willcox in 1650 was about 470 millions, in 1800 it was 919 millions and in 1900 it was about 1608 millions. The estimations of world population of these two authors varied at all three periods. The estimation of Willcox was smaller by 75 millions in 1650, 13 millions more in 1800 and 37 millions less in 1900.

It was estimated that in 1350 B.C. the population of India and China were 10 millions each before 1650. If India had a very low rate of increase in population atleast 2 births for every 1,000 for a year, it is an increase of 0.2 per cent. If this is calculated from 1350 B.C. to 1650 A.D. during these 30 centuries the population would have approximately risen to more than 4 billions or 4000 crores. This is seven times larger than the estimation made by Carr-Saunders of the world population in 1650. But the Indian population from 1350 B.C. did not rise even 0.2 per cent in its population. If there was an increase of 0.2 per cent by 1650 Indian population should 4000 crores. The same proportion applies to China also. Therefore the population in India or in China or in the world did not rise not even 0.2 per cent from 1350 B.C. Several reasons might have been for this. Since the birth rates and death rates are not available before 1650 A.D. It will not be possible to assess the rise of population.

It is believed that in these populations the potential fertility of the average women was low. some women, married and lived with their husbands did not give birth to any children. But there was also on the other extreme. Most probably in those days due to lack of nutrition, the potential fertility also might have seen very low and it might have varied from race to race, from nation to nation, and from class to class within any society. This potential fertility might have changed with time. Further it also depends upon people's food habits, nature of work, and living conditions. Giving birth to children varied from women to women and also fertility varied from culture to culture. Therefore in population growth either in the past or in the present times fertility must be considered as the constant factor that determine the possible upper limit of the human reproduction. It was also possible that a society's full potential fertility was not realized by its cultural pattern of behaviour and the fertility was restricted in some respects. Some of the restrictions were the practice of abortion prevailing among all people, in many societies, specifically in tribal communities, the most prevalent practice was segregating women for a longer period after a child birth, little care in the case of female child resulted in reducing the female population in some societies. In some of the ancient communities the practice of polyandry reduced the child bearing. Polygamy and concubinage since widely practised in such communities many young men in the most fertile ages were deprived of having wives and to give birth to children. The marriage customs in many ancient cultures extended the time of the system of constitution of family life for many years after puberty. All these cultural patterns of behaviour of the societies reduced the chances of human reproduction. But the birth rate in agricultural societies was relatively high inspite of reduction in fertility. The tribal people who were living on hunting and fishing, collecting fruits, roots, nuts, vegetables for their food had low birth rates.

Famine and Starvation

In the pre-agricultural and pre-industrial societies people were always suffering from lack of adequate food. The death rate was considerably increased because of this. This has been a constant potential check on population growth in the pre-agricultural and pre-industrial societies. The people of these periods have no means of storing their food for future. Whatever available at a time were used by them and when there was any lack of rains or any other disaster consequences they had not only failed to get their food by hunting, fishing, collecting fruits, roots and nuts but also succumbed to natural consequences like rains, floods, storms, and so on. They had no means of production.

However people who have learned to live on cultivated crops often faced crises in storing their food for future. Several causes have been attributed for this. They often faced with too much of rains and floods, unable to make harvest in time, resulting in heavy losses, and also the nuisances of grasshoppers, locusts and insects, and plant diseases. They have no means of controlling all these calamities. All these caused scarcity of food leading to starvation and death.

Those who were depending for their livelihood upon hunting and fishing, upon collecting on wild crops, upon their flocks and herds had the same fate, because of the failure of season, disease of the cattle, severe drought which affected very much the collection and supply of food of hunters and others, and the failure of crops of the agriculturists, all had more effect upon their death rates. Shortage of food has been the most difficult and constant hardship of mankind right from ancient time onwards. But still mankind could not get rid of this problem. Even now there are many countries in the world having severe food shortage. India is often faced with both kinds of food shortages, the chronic shortage and acute shortage.

The Chronic Shortage of Food

This is considered to be the most dangerous to mankind. The chronic food shortage will not kill people entirely, directly, but it is mainly responsible for untold millions of men's premature deaths indirectly. This also includes chronic under non-nourishment. These people who were suffering from under nourishment already very much weakened by inadequate diet and they die of premature death. If there were any epidemic diseases they were the first to succumb to death.

Famine or Acute Shortage of Food

Famine means, generally, severe shortage of food as if there were crops failure or overpopulation. It also means acute shortage of food or anything. It also refers to violent hunger. Therefore, famine may be described as an acute or severe shortage of food. This is in contrast to a chronic shortage or food values or shortage of vitamins. In the history of many countries there were instances of famine frequently occurring and lots of people died of starvation. Walford (1878) has given a list of 350 famines occurred in the world. Of the 350, 201 famines occurred in British Isles between 10 A.D. and 1846 A.D. In other parts of Europe there were 70 famines. In India there were 31 famines occurred between 1769 and 1878 and 17 famines occurred in Mediterranean sea areas. The other 30 famines occurred in other parts of world, particularly in India or China before 1769.

Mallory (1926) states that there were 1828 famines in China between 108 B.C. and 1911 A.D. Some of these famines were great, affecting a large territory of great populations, and some were small, affecting more the local people. Reliable evidences are not available about famines in India. But there were 31 famines in India between 1769 and 1878 as stated by Wilford. Since the rainfall in India often resulted in the failure of monsoons, famines were unavoidable. Therefore India had many hundreds of famines during the past 2000 years and that untold millions of people were died of starvation by famines. Following the increased death rates due to famine and starvation there was also depleted vitality which also had reduced the fertility rates.

China, in the past century, had met with the worst famines as the result of severe drought in the years of 1876 to 1879 in the north-west area. The drought had severely affected an area of 3,00,000 square miles. It had been established that about 9 to 13 million people were perished out of hunger and starvation and out of disease. The prolonged hunger and famine also caused violence and many died of violence. Mallory (1926) has stated that about one-fifth of the people in those areas were died. During the first quarter of this century around 1920 about 20 million people in the north-west provinces of China have become destitutes as the crops have failed. It is believed that about 5,00,000 people were died for want of food. The newspaper report from China during 1929 and 1930 was that million were died of famine, hunger, starvation and diseases. Some reports have stated that the death rate was as high as four millions. Although there were relief works from the United States the death of hunger were many.

Mallory (1926) states that the incidence of deaths due to famine, hunger and starvation was the same in case of India as it was in China. Droughts and famine were common occurrences and every, year some province in India suffered from severe shortage of food. Morison (1918) stated that there was very severe famine in Bengal from 1769 to 1770 and this famine was said to have killed one-third of the total population or about 10 million people in Bengal alone. There was also other great famines in the years of 1803 and 1804 and in 1837 and 1838. Though the correct figure of victims of these famines were not available the death numbers might have been in millions. The famine occurred in 1937 and 1938 was described as the great Indian famine virtually spread out almost in all parts of India. Theodore Morison (1918) quotes from the report of one of the officials, Gindlstone, who was on the spot and observed the events of the famine personally. According to him the great famine of India of 1937 to 1938 was the last of the great dislocating famines of this period of time. The Deccan plateau covering large area and in upper India the famine loosened the bonds of society. There were bad harvests successively since 1932 which has caused acute food shortage and disaster in various areas. The 1937 summer came with terrible drought. The monsoon failed and there was no rains and severe famine occurred. The agriculturists did not come forward to produce grains even at an exorbitant payments. They were also starving and people practically became wanderers. There were huge immigrants from Marwar and Hariana and other western provinces into the upper India. Violence broke out everywhere. The lower class people justified their violent activities and they looted all store houses and the public roads became dangerous for the travellers. The villages formerly filled with 300 to 400 farmers were now occupied by a half a dozen starving beggars. There were also untold miseries occurred in many of the provinces in upper India.

Russia was not exempted from the consequences of famines. Before the Russian Revolution there were three severe famines in 1891, 1906 and in 1911. At all the times, there were close connections between famines and epidemic diseases. The great famine of 1918-1922 was the most significant one in USSR. Though the American Relief Administration (ARA) fed more than 10 million famine affected people in 1922 there were about 5 million people perished of famine and hunger. Again there was another famine in Russia in 1934 and 1935 in which millions were killed. Thus the consequences of hunger and famine killed millions of people all over the world till 1935. As a result of it population growth was made very slow in most of the countries and it was not in line with any statistical calculation.

Diseases and Epidemics

Man as a living creature, often falls prey to diseases of all types. However careful he is, he contacts infectious germs, and viruses which make him inactive and helpless and bed-ridden. People's health may be deteriorating due to lack nutritious food and vitamin deficiency. Therefore man, in order to keep himself fit for work should take nutritious food and vitamins. Certain diseases are caused by vitamin deficiencies. Any disease sometimes may become fatal. Death comes to man in various ways, of which the diseases are the main causes.

Infectious Diseases

Since the medical sciences have developed to a significant level, man makes use of them to protect himself from the infectious diseases. Infectious diseases are preventable. But when neglected it will cause disastrous consequences by taking heavy tolls of human life. Right from the ancient time, man has recognized the infectious diseases. But he could not control it by inventing suitable medicines and methods. Since people in ancient times were living in small tribal groups or in villages and they were using the same water and food whatever were available for them. There was no hygiene, no clean water, any infectitious disease may rapidly spread out among the local groups of people. There was no means of sudden treatment or controlling the disease. As a result of it people easily get infected by the germs or the virus and die after few days of suffering.

Due to shortage of food or famine there may be migration of people from place to place and they also carry with them the germs, insects and viruses which cause epidemic diseases. The migrants also carry with them diseases like typhoid, smallpox, pneumonia, tuberculosis, and so on. In many areas the incident of malaria causing deaths and also making man to suffer a great deal and die at last. Diseases cause infant mortality higher. A study made in Sweden (1930) states that one-third of the babies died before they completed one year. Due to children's disease, before completing 5 years, great number of children die. Generally they die of measles, fever, typhoid, smallpox, in some areas yellow fever, typhus, plague and also due to respiratory ailments.

Epidemics and the Black Diseases

Epidemic diseases are those diseases which are occasional, but also they are unusual. The spread of such diseases would kill most people in that area and generally very deadliest when it occurs. Epidemic diseases may attack many persons simultaneously in a community or area. Epidemic is a widespread occurrence of a disease. An influenza is an epidemic, the other severe epidemic is cholera. Cholera, is an acute intestinal infection characterised by severe diarrhoea, generally caused by water food contamination. Cholera is of various types such as asiatic cholera, epidemic cholera and Indian cholera. Unlike infectious diseases epidemic diseases do not have much effect on population growth. Their visits are very rare. But the infectious diseases are always present in the community and take away many lives often, for example, tuberculosis, smallpox, respiratory and intestinal diseases.

The black death in Europe was often heard during the middle ages. Hecker (1944) has given an account of deaths caused by black death. Black death is a form of bubonic plague pandemic in Europe and Asia during 14th century and killed more than 50 million people. The European cities had very high death tolls. According to Hecker, London had lost 1,00,000 people, Venice lost 1,00,000 people, Florance and Paris each lost more than 50,000 people. It appears that in these cities nearly half of the population was perished. Italy was said to have lost half of its population. The whole of the continent of Europe, it was believed to have lost 25 to 35 million people and one-third of the population perished due to this epidemic disease.

Influenza

Another great disaster consequence was taken place due to influenza in 1918 and 1919 in the United States and in India. It was a terrible savage of influenza that even the industrialized country like the United States had been seriously affected. The number of deaths estimated was about 4,50,000 people. Though this was only 0.5 per cent of the total population, nearly half a million people dying of the epidemic disease of influenza, was a very big loss to the nation. Similar consequence was also caused by the influenza in India. According to Thompson's (1938) estimation there must be more than 15 million people died of influenza. Such deaths may occur only in famine stricken areas of a country. But an epidemic disease like influenza had the toll of more than 15 millions.

War

During the pre-industrial era the population growth was very much slow due to the effects of wars. This was, particularly to the greatest extent, in the tribal societies, because the tribal people were living in groups and each tribal group had its own identity and cultural variations. Since societies were not well organized into institutions, rivalries and conflicts between tribal groups were quite common and also to establish the superiority of one tribe over the other they fought wars constantly collecting their men. As a result of it the growth among them was much lowered. Sometimes the tribal wars continues for years and generations. Each tribal group had its own area or territory for hunting, fishing and for food collection. They have also developed crude method of cultivation. In the tribal wars they take away the properties and wives of the other tribal groups. The constant wars among the tribal groups resulted also destroying the crops and food of the rival groups and this led to food shortage and famine among some groups. There were also epidemic and infectious diseases spreading over the areas where the tribal groups were living. All these incidents have contributed to slow growth of population.

Right from ancient times onwards wars were fought between nations continuously. The Greeks and Romans, the Egyptians and the Babylonians have fought many wars. The Arabs and Turks, the Afghans and the Mongols were fighting for years. In India there were many wars faught by the kings and chieftains. In India right from the time of invasion of Alexander the Great wars were fought. In the great Kalinga battle fought by Emperor Asoka millions were killed. The Mogul periods were full of only battles. Much blood were shed in the soil of the upper India and the Deccan plateau. The great Marattas faught with the Moguls and the British many battles. Many millions of soldiers and others died in these battles. Similarly in south, wars were fought against the Mogul Kings and the British and also among the small kingdoms there were many wars. The Britishers and the French who were empire builders, fought several wars in India till the British set up their rule in India.

In Europe, during the period of renaissance there were many wars among the nations of England, France, Spain, Germany and Italy. Also there were many civil wars in France and England. Then, later on, in the first and second quarters of 20th century the World War I fought during 1914-18, mainly in Europe and the Middle East in which the allied nations principally France, Russia, Britain and Italy after 1915, and the U.S.A. after 1917. They defeated the central powers, Germany, Austria, Hungary and Turkey. The war was precipitated by the assassination of Austria's crown prince, Ferdinand at Sarajevo, on June

28, 1914 and swiftly developed its major front in Eastern France where millions died in static trench warfare. Then the World War II fought during 1939-45 in which the Allied Nations, Britain and France declared war on Germany on 3rd Sept. 1939 as a result of the German invásion of Poland on Sept. 1, 1939. Italy entered the war on the side of Germany forming Axis on June 10, 1940 shortly before the collapse of France. On June 22, 1941 the Axis powers attacked the Soviet Union and on December 7, 1941. The Japanese attacked U.S. at Pearl Harbour on September 8, 1943. Italy surrendered the war in Europe, ending on May 1945 with the unconditional surrender of the Germans. The Japanese capitulated on August 14, 1945 as a direct result of atom bombs dropped by the Americans on Hiroshima and Nagasaki, killing millions of people.

Thus in all these wars millions of soldiers and civilians were killed and all these made the population growth to a low level.

But modern industrial development and the progress made in science and technology and also in medicine within a short span of 50 years infant mortality was very much reduced, fertility rate increased and human longevity increased to a great extent, resulting rapid growth of population all over the world. The public health improvement, anti-malaria precautions, control of tuberculosis, invention of new medicines and medical treatments, control of infectious diseases, improved agricultural farming and production of more food, healthy food habits all to some extent contributed to rapid growth of population all over the world. All these developments have taken place only after the World War II.

The growth of population after the World War II was such that it is stated as population explosion. The growth seems to be more than what is required in the world today. Thompson and Lewis (1965) state that a rapid change in population has taken place in the developing countries which could not afford to meet the sudden increase. The increase of population in some of the western countries, U.S.A., Canada looks like a temporary increase with a modest decline in death rate. But in developing countries the death rate is entirely declined and birth rate increased with all its resources. It makes us to think that the medical-chemical research was soon made available the miracle drugs to fight the infectious diseases and the World War II provided opportunities to make the new discoveries on a large scale and to demonstrate in controlling the death rate.

From the demographic point of view the population growth between 1950 and 1960 is considered to be the most important as the growth resulted in several problems. The crude birth rate, in the developing countries were found to be well above 40 per 1000. But at the same time in Europe it was 20 per 1000. In United States Canada, Russia it was 24 or 25 per 1000. Though the death rates in the developing countries were high still there was no decline in the population rate.

The decline of birth rate in modern times is becoming very difficult. Until man reaches his declining years and die of old age there is no chance for him to die. Therefore the number is not reducing on any account. This is existing in all societies. There is a desire for man to enjoy the high level of life and maintain the standard. But this desire cannot be fulfilled unless there is reduction in the birth rates. Particularly, when the people of developing nations are going to realize that they must reduce their birth rates if they want to live a higher standard of life and prepare their children to suit to the modern scientific world! It appears that no developing country seems to have given a serious thinking to this issue. Although France is less industrially developed nation compared to England, the people of France came forward to have voluntary control of the birth rate as early as at the end of 18th century. But in England there was no significant decline in the birth rate until the end of 19th century. In the United States, in northern states there was considerable decline in birth rates in the early 19th century. Japan, particularly after the World War II is not having faith in the decline of population. Japan feels that it is too early for her to adopt any method to decline her birth rates as she suffered the worst consequences by the Atom bombs explosion by the Americans. But however Japan is preparing the way for rapid reduction of birth rate. They adapt abortion as a quick birth control method for stabilizing the size of the families. Abortions were made by expert physicians in hospitals openly and this method is made available easily. The Japanese were the most cultured and educated people in the world and they could easily understand the post-war policies and of the economic distress of the nation and its relation to the population position. The Japanese death rate was reduced rapidly and their birth rate was higher between 1946 and 1949. Japan's commerce and industry were practically destroyed by the war and the people of Japan were aware of it. Understanding the ensuing consequences the leaders of Japan were making constant statements in newspapers and through radio and other mass media that "if you want to provide better opportunities for your children, you should reduce the birth rate and you should adapt birth control practices." It was a great surprise. Thomson and Lewis (1965) state that these appeals had tremendous effect within a short time in Japan.

In many of the developing countries the traditional cultures were strongly prevailed with regard to the issue of lowering the birth rate. They felt that it is necessary to have high birth rate for maintaining the social and economic institutions, and the culture's reproductive behaviour for high birth rate was encouraged, because it was felt that it was essential for their survival. Therefore, it takes much longer time to educate the people in developing countries that if they were to control the death rate it is essential to hold the birth rate at a lower level. For example, India is the biggest developing nation and since its independence in 1947 the family planning and birth control and contraceptive methods were encouraged. But there was no evidence of its reduction in birth rates. It is rapidly increasing. The same situation is prevailing in communist China as the efforts of contraception was poorly effected.

Problems

Experts in the field of population studies are very much worried over the problems that are going to rise out of a higher rate of population growth. It is assumed that the world population is likely to increase about 2 per cent every year. This may continue for few decades, thinking that the supply of food would be available for all and there is no per capita or supply of food to each person decline in their food supplies. The most urgent problem is that if the population is increased at the same rate for 40 years what alternative arrangement is made if the food supplies is not met with. There will be heavy pressure from the population for food supplies. Unless sufficient food supplies are not produced the pressure will be increasing day by day. For example, the Indian population today (1995) is 92 crores. An increase of 2 per cent in the present population if continued for 40 years (4 decades) then the total population of India approximately would be 207 crores in 2035 A.D. the increase of population is by 120 per cent. The per capita consumption of the necessities of life also should increase by 120 per cent and if there is no rise above its present low level in India and in the world, most of the people in India and in the world would have inadequate food, and India and other developing nations will not achieve the low level of death rate. There will be shortage of food which may result in famine, starvation and death.

The real problem we are now concerned is the rapid increase of population in India and in other developing nations, which has become basically a serious national problem. It has not become a world problem. Because the world is not politically and economically organized in such a way that a country's food product, after the domestic consumption, if found surplus, can be transported to countries which are facing deficit product. Any surplus product whether food or other materials are the properties of the concerned country. No country can be forced by any body to transfer its surplus products to any of the developing nations which are not able to produce for their domestic purpose. But the deficit countries can purchase on certain agreement from surplus nations on the international money value. Therefore the production of food or any other product and consumption is a national problem as long as every nation remains within its own political, economic, social and territorial ideologies and having the national pride. There are groups of people living in different regions of the world with their own national pride and antagonistic attitudes to other nations inspite of the pressing needs of the overpopulation of those countries.

Therefore it is the responsibility of every nation to increase its own food supply and other necessities of life through its own production resources or through trade and commerce with the same speed as its population is likely to grow at the rate of 2 per cent or more. There are nations producing food and other subsistences more than their domestic consumption and also supplying to other deficit nations on payment or on exchange programmes. India was exporting textile goods and iron to various countries and in return it was getting wheat and other commodities. It was because of the population pressure that India has to buy food from other countries. If we want to stop this and stand on our own every Indian family should strictly adopt family planning and birth control with real national spirit like what the Japanese did.

4. DEMOGRAPHIC GROUPS AND POPULATION CHARACTERISTICS

The demographers who study population include several factors in their studies. The development of science and technology, commerce and industry, produce a number of societies and communities within the larger societies. This resulted in several complexities and a number of attributes have been used to clarify the society. Particularly in urban areas a number of industrial populations have emerged, such as small society, slowly changing society, isolated society, and so on. The industrial urban society is so complex that there are very few demographical characteristics in them. Researchers who study population deal with aggregates of people and not with individuals or small social or cultural groups. They use the variable to describe the populations mainly the traits which the individuals have. These characteristics have demographic relationships. The population characteristics, the demographers used in their studies fall under two categories such as social characteristics and economic characteristics. These particulars collected under the heading of social and economic characteristics are the information, enumerated in the census every where. *The social variables* are age, sex, religion, religious denomination, community/caste, place of residence, rural or urban, how long time he/she is living in the present place?, place of birth, nationality, mother tongue, educational qualification, married or single, relationship to the head of the house, number of children, number of male children, number of female children, total number of members in the family, any death of epidemic disease and other diseases.

The economic variables are employed or unemployed. If employed, name of the occupation, is it government or private organization? monthly salary, other income to the family from other sources, means of transportation to the work place, is he/she owing any vehicle?

These particulars mainly includes the individual's all personal information, social, educational, economic, occupational, income, religious and communal, residential, nationality, family size, health, and so on. All these are called *demographic variables* or characteristics. On the basis of these variables the demographers analyse the population and evolve statistics. These statistical information provided by the demographers, may be used for various purposes in various disciplines.

Communities in India have demographic differences particularly in the characteristics of sex, age, religion and castes. In certain communities the males may be the dominant in the population and in certain communities the females may be dominant in the population. There cannot be always equal proportion of the sexes. Similarly in certain communities the particular age group may be dominant. Religion as a demographic variable is used to find out the dominant religious group in a region or nation. There are nations consisting of people of only certain particular religious denominations. For example, in the

Arab countries the Mohammadans are dominant, other religious people would be very few by nationality, the rest of the people belonging to other religious denominations, may be migrants or moving population. In the European countries most of the people are belonging to Christianity. There may be certain low percentage of people belonging to Islam. There may be also negligible percentage of people belonging to Hinduism and Buddhism. In India the dominant religion is Hinduism. It has several sects, but all are called only Hindus. The next religious community with considerable percentage is the Mohammadans. The other religious community people are the Christians. There are also other minority religious communities like the Buddhists, the Jains, the Sikhs, the Parsees or Zoroastrian. These people (Parsees) were driven out of Persia, by the Muslims in the eighth century A.D. and they settled in India, mostly in the Western India. In China, Japan and in other south-eastern countries except Indonesia, the people are mostly belonging to Buddhism. If other religious people are there, they must be migrants and settled there temporarily.

Regarding age, demographers classify the people into certain age categories, and determine at which age-category the population is higher. It is interesting to know from the demographic classification that very few people are between 25 and 40 years of age. It is of both sexes. This age composition of population may change. This figure will not be permanent for ever. Because of the low mortality rates at higher age level any age composition is subjected to change.

Society and Status

Every society is interested in engaging people who are fit for some jobs or works. Work of a person, is viewed by sociologists, determines the status or position. Unless people are adequately trained there would not be any motivation for work. The status requires adequately trained and highly motivated persons. Status means a social or professional position, condition, or standing to which varying degrees of responsibility, privilege and esteem are attached. Therefore the concept status is more significant in a society when a person is occupying a position which has certain prestige. For example, the professional like an engineer, a doctor, a lawyer, a professor, a secretary, an administrator, a teacher—all occupy certain position. Therefore, we can see that society works through the members of the society. These are all occupational status that men have been occupying.

Apart from these occupational statuses, which bring to the occupants a sense of pride and prestige in the society, there are also other statuses which may be called social, held by the people of various categories. For example, a man, woman, boy, girl, father, mother, grand-father, grand-mother, political leader, social worker, student, are also maintaining statuses. There are certain duties and responsibilities encompassing every status. They also command certain amount of respect in the society.

But there are certain differences among the statuses. Ralph Linton (1936) an outstanding American anthropologist has classified the statuses into two kinds, as *ascribed statuses* and *achieved statuses.* According to him ascribed statuses are occupied by the individuals who possess certain specific characteristics. They cannot disown those characteristics. The characteristics are with them. For example, male, female, adult, Eskimo, white people, black people, are all ascribed statuses. They cannot change their qualities. The achieved statuses are left to the individual's desire or choice. The individual enjoys certain privilege and prestige because of the achieved status. In every country, importance is given to achieved status. The individual by his efforts and talents achieves a status which is considered as a respectable status. For example, a doctor, an engineer, a lawyer, an administrator, a judge, the ministers in a state cabinet are all achieved statuses. By virtue of one's qualification, talents, and hard work he achieves the status. He cannot lend his qualifications to others. Only he can enjoy the status and he cannot pass it on to others on his choice on his retirement or death. For example, if one becomes a millionaire by virtue of his wealth, he enjoys the status of a richman. This is achieved status. On his death the property goes to his next generation, his sons and daughters. They also in due course enjoy the status of the richmen. Therefore only in the case richness, achieved status can be passed on to others, but not in the case of other things. Here status is represented by wealth.

In certain countries like India, there is a caste system among the Hindus. The so called higher caste people by virtue of being born in higher castes enjoy a status in the society. They have certain ascribed ways of life, prestige, self esteem and also command over other lower castes. The caste system also established a caste hierarchy and higher caste people by virtue of their caste were able to control more men and became even leaders or chieftains in the ancient times. This type of statuses based upon caste system are ascribed statuses. This system is slowly dying down because of the social and political awakenings in the societies. Veblen (1899) states that the Kwakiutl Red Indian chiefs of North America used to destroy huge amount of wealth to establish their status and prestige. Franz Boas (1858-1942) an American anthropologist, born in Germany made a major contribution to the cultural and linguistic anthropology of the Kwakiutl Red Indians of North America in his studies. Quoting from Boas's study, Gardner Murphy (1964) states that among the Kwakiutl Indians, life was a continuous struggle between the chieftains for prestige and status. Prestige and status in Kwakiutl Indian society were represented by wealth. Wealth was tossed and destroyed frantically with unremitting effort for asserting the superiority of one chieftain over others. Therefore in every society, status and prestige were held by people by some means. But the nature of status varies from culture to culture and society to society. In pre-industrial society the ascribed status worked best in stable manner and it was slowly changing in societies. The achieved status is the result of the utilization of individual's talents. This also makes adjustment to rapid social changes. But the disadvantage of achieved status is that it leaves certain statuses unfulfilled for want of adequately qualified and talented persons. But, the other statuses are being filled by individuals who are not psychologically prepared. In the United States the native born white males have certain ascribed statuses which are very difficult for the Negroes, females and foreign borns to have them.

These two categories of status have no scientific basis. Other societies do not recognize these categorizations. Thompson and Lewis (1965) state that physical facts do not determine behaviour but physical facts can determine the limits of human behaviour. That is, a nation cannot have the whole total population as its labour force. It can have only the able bodied people as the country's labour force, eliminating children under 15 years of age and the senior citizens above 65 years of age and the women. There may be also categorization for the elimination on the basis of family and types of works.

Sex and Age

Sex and age are groups, supposed to be basic for all demographical studies and analyses, because they are the important physiological variables. These two variables have social and cultural importance. The effect of sex and age in population composition is very much and also on the fertility and mortality rates. Every society uses, the attributes of sex and age for classifying its population into various groups. Classifying people according to sex and age and assigning duties and responsibilities varies from culture to culture. Certain jobs require more physical strength than other jobs. Therefore both males and females cannot be considered as suitable for them. In Russia, public vehicles are driven by women and most of the physicians are women, whereas in America most of the physicians are all males. In India till very recently in the academic studies, engineering and agriculture were opened to only men, but now, all branches of engineering and all branches of agricultural sciences are opened to both sexes and there are quite a number of women students in both areas come out with distinction.

At the occupational level, females are competing with males in all areas. The competitive examinations conducted by the Union Public Service Commission for the group I services, particularly IAS, IFS, IPS and other Class I Central services, both men and women compete and several women candidates come out successfully in all these services. As a result of it we could see everywhere women IAS and IPS officers in keen competition with men. Many women candidates are found in many foreign embassies. Apart from top administrative and executive lines, women are recruited to lower level of jobs also in India. There are women police constables, women pilots, women drivers, conductors in many places in India. Half of the countries population, the women folk who were rejected for many jobs all these years on the ground that they were physically unfit, are now found physically and mentally fit for every job and now they compete with men in all areas. And also there are many women scientists in every branch of scientific research stations. Even in sports the women were not lacking behind men in almost all the fields. Therefore sex is not a barrier for achievement and for achieved status. The categorization of statuses made by American anthropologists, Ralph Linton (1936) has become outmoded. It is now found that the behaviour requirements can be assigned to both sexes.

The behaviour requirements of age by the societies also have demographic significances. Generally jobs or works are not assigned to persons below 15 years of age and above 65 years of age. But this norm is not followed in India and in many of the countries. There is strong protests against the child labour. Children below 15 years should not be engaged in any work. But in India thousands of children are found in work places doing various kinds of works. They are working in the fields in cultivation work, in cotton industries, weaving industries, factories, sewing factories and many other small factories. Further they are also engaged for all sorts of household works, firewood collection, fetching water, masonry works, digging trenches and in road works. In these types of works there is no sex differences, both male and female children are employed. In some states in India, children are mortgaged with landlords for doing farm works on taking some money from them for certain years. In America there is no retirement age. People can continue their works as long as they are fit to do a job.

Regarding the marriage age of women there is no standard age. It is said that women are not ready for marriage and procreation until the age of 20 years. But there are babies born to women under 20 years of age. In India there is child marriage, still prevalent widely in many states. A girl before attaining the age of 20 gives birth to two or three babies. Though there is prescription of minimum age for marriage in every society but individuals in societies do not carry out it. The age of marriage varies from culture to culture. However, the physical variables of sex and age are most important demographical characteristics for the study of population.

5. RACIAL AND ETHNIC POPULATIONS

Race is a subject matter for study for sociologists, psychologists, demographers and anthropologists. Racial study also is a study of human behaviour and group behaviour. Generally, race means a group of people of common ancestry, distinguished from others by physical characteristic such as hair type, colour of the eyes and skin, structure and so on. The principal races, in the world are the Caucasoid, Mongoloid and Negroid. The concept race may be also referring to the whole human race, human beings collectively. Race may be also used to indicate a group of people sharing the same interests, characteristics etc. Race is also referring to a group of animals or plants having common characteristics that distinguish them from other members of the same species, generally, forming a geographically isolated groups, which are the sub-species. Thus the definition can be evolved for race.

The concept race is a phenomenon as it involves lots controversy for the past many years. This has become a problem when the Negroes were taken to North America, as labourer and then treated as slaves. When the population of the Negroes increased in United States and when they claimed for equal rights the Negro-American problem has emerged in larger measure. Similarly the racial problem has emerged in Europe when the Jews were persecuted and when German Nazis claimed their racial superiority over other races. But race has been always a controversial issue bringing conflict, tension, aggression and violence between racial groups. Thompson and Lewis (1965) state that race is a most ambiguous and explosive concept all over the world.

Biological Aspects of Race

Race is similar to sex and age. A person's race is physically identified and therefore it is a physical fact and it cannot be altered either by the individual or by the society. Racial characteristics are biologically inherited. Just like sex and age, racial identity is visually observed. There is no chance for the individual to conceal his race. Therefore race is a fully biological variable. This is true only in the case of the Negro and White races in America. But in Europe there is no biological variations between the Europeans and the Jews as the Jews were treated as a separate racial group. Therefore the concept is both a biological concept and also a social concept. When an individual is biologically identified as belonging to different race there may be justifications from his physical characteristics. But when one is socially identified that he belongs to a particular racial group there may not be sufficient physical characteristics to justify the statement. Therefore sometimes the racial identity may lead to confusion. There is no difference between a Jew and a German biologically. Sometimes a German or a French may be mistaken for a Jew, because there are no specific physical characteristic to identify a Jew and a German or French. Therefore biologists and anthropologists use biologically inherited characteristics to identify and classify the human species. They mainly use the skin colour, hair type, and colour of the eyes as physical traits of the stocks to classify the peoples into races. Thus there are three races which are generally accepted. The Caucasoid or the white race, the Mongoloid or the yellow race, and the Negroid or the black race.

The Caucasoid is belonging to the light complexioned racial group of mankind, originally inhabitants of Caucasia and now they are spread all over the world. They are described as having white skin, also ranging from very fair to brown, having hairs all over the body and wavy hair on the head. The other race, the Mongoloid, or the yellow, race, described as having mostly yellow skin colour and also ranging from light brown to brown, having slight amount of hair or no hair on the body, black and straight hair on the head and having small slanting eyes, short nose, and scanty facial hair. The Negroid or the black race are described as having slight brown and black skin, crisp or woolly hair, a broad flat nose and thick lips and slight amount of hair or no hair on the body. But with regard to the physique no specific description can be given, as the heights, there is no much differences between the Caucasoids and the Negroids. The Mongoloids' physical heights underwent radical changes during this century though they were short in the beginning. Further the racial migrations has caused intermixture of the races which resulted in having the same biological characteristics in both the races.

Thompson and Lewis (1965) state that still some racial stocks are not yet adequately described and classified. Particularly the Polynasians and the Australian aborigines. The people are not included in any of the racial classifications. However, the biologists and anthropoligists have classified the human races into three divisions on the basis of the biologically inherited traits. But the biologically inherited traits, and the races, have not got any relationships with the languages they speak, the religious denominations, the culture and the nationality. The racial classifications cut across all these demographic variables. Juan Comas (1961) states that national, religious, geographical, linguistic and cultural groups do not necessarily go with racial groups. The cultural traits of those groups do not show any connection with racial traits.

Social Aspects of Race

We have stated earlier that the concept, race is a highly controversial one. Biologists and anthropologists made the classification on the basis of biologically inherited traits. But Mack (1965) states that race has no biologically caused consequences. Race has only social consequences. That is what men believe. Generally most of the people's discussions about race are based upon their beliefs and not on biological traits and also most of the actions of men about race are based upon what they have been taught about race and not on what the scientists' physical attributes of race.

The racial identity of the groups is found to be varying time to time and from society to society. The biologically inherited traits such as skin colour, type of hair, colour of the eyes found in a group of people in one generation are not found in the next generation of people, since due to migration and due to intermixtures of racial stocks changes .are taking place. Therefore what is biological trait at one time is not found next time. It is because of this that there are many Negroes are light skinned, tall and fair. Therefore some use non-biological traits such as religion, language, nationality, dress and food to identify the race. It is generally found that some people use religion, language, nationality, and cultural variables as the racial traits. For example, they consider that the Germans, Italians, English, Pakistanis, Indians, the Jains are belonging different racial groups. They mix language nationality and religion for indicating racial stocks.

Bryce (1910) states that the definition given by the Americans for race and Negro is different from that held in the rest of the American continent. In Latin America (part of the western Hemisphere south of U.S. in which the Spanish, the Portuguese and the French are the official languages) whoever is not black is white whereas in teutonic America, where the German language is official language, whoever is not white is black. In British colonies and dominions, mainly in South Africa, the hybrids are considered as a group different from both the whites and Negroes. In United States many hybrids of Indian and white blood origin are considered as whites. In India the people of the English and the Indian mixture are regarded as a separate racial stock called Anglo-Indians, and the French admixtures are called the Franco-Indians. Therefore, the definition of Negro race is a social and sanctioned by the customs and traditions and it is a biological one. But in modern biological and anthropological researchers, race as a biological and scientific concept has lost its meaning and the term is now disappearing.

Arnold Rose (1956) states that race as a scientific concept is totally inapplicable in scientific literature of modern times. Persons, those who lack knowledge about race and racial discriminations alone talk about different races as Negro race, Anglo-Saxon race, German race and so on. Rose states that scientists now speak of unity of mankind and a common belief that races can be classified as higher and lower in the revolutionary process is totally disregarded. The expert opinion at present is that human beings belong to the species of Homosapiens. This is evolved only once and the differences we see now between men are due to geographical conditions. Arnold Rose (1956) states, both the Negroes and the white men have the traits of the ape. In the case of Negro, only the dark skin and broad nose are slightly similar to the apes, whereas in the case of white man the thin lips and the straight hair are much nearer to the traits of the apes. Even in the case of white skin, if the ape's hairs are fully shaven its skin is white nearer to the white man's skin.

Therefore, the white man possesses more traits of an ape than the Negro who has only two traits similar to an ape. Therefore, the conception of Negro race is scientifically not accurate. Race is the basis of social caste system. It is because of the visibility and knowledge acquired from the parents that individuals find these social consequences in United States.

The American definition of race is based on colour. They do not give importance to other variables. The definition of race is commonly accepted by the general population. It does not refer to biological stock. For them there are three major racial groups, the white race, the Negro race and other races. The Americans use skin colour to discriminate the race. On the basis of colour they divide the population into two groups as whites and non-whites. The classification made by the American has no biological validity, but has social reality. The Americans follow their classification on the classification made by the Census Bureau.

Ethnic Minorities

The concept race is also associated with ethnic and national. Only in countries where the Europeans, Americans and the Negroes live the concept race is used to identify people. In countries where there are no whites and Negroes the concept race is not used, instead they use the concept nationality to identify people into categories. In India people are classified using the concept 'nationality' and not race. In this context the concept ethnic is also widely prevalent. Ethnic is a basic division of mankind, distinguished by customs, language and religion. Ethnic refers to a member of a minority or nationality group that is part of a larger community. Ethnic is also referring to a human group having racial religious linguistic and certain other traits in common, it is relating to the classification of mankind into groups, especially on the basis of racial characteristics. Therefore an ethnic or an ethnic group may be referred to a member of a group or a group of people belonging to different racial, religious, linguistic, cultural and national group living in a country in a small number. These people are called ethnic minorities. They are racially, religiously, linguistically, culturally and socially different from the people of the country where they live. Further they may differ in the manner of dressing, cooking, eating and social manners from the natives. This type of ethnic minorities are found in every big and small country.

For example, in England there are Indians, Pakistanis, Sri Lankans, Arabs, Japanese. All these people are sticking to their own religious practices, speak their own language among themselves, live according to their own cultural practices, even in dressing and eating they live according to their cultural behavioural pattern. Similarly in United States there are many ethnic minority groups living with their racial and cultural identity. In United States there are more number of ethnic minorities living with their own racial or cultural identity. There are quite a number of Indian families, Pakistanis, Sri Lankans, Jews, Japanese, Chinese, French, Germans, Russians, African, Australians and also people from other European countries. These people are following their own racial, cultural and national patterns of life, though in certain routine works they follow the Americans. All these groups of people are called ethnic minorities. Since there is no much difference in their racial stocks, they may rightly be called ethnic minorities and not racial minorities. Since they all belong to different countries and follow their own national characteristics, they may be also called national minorities.

The natives are politically, economically and socially dominant society. They regard these ethnic minorities, who are racially and culturally different, as subordinates. They discriminate these people in all living conditions. If these ethnic or cultural minorities are discriminated in educational institutions, in industrial organisations and in labour market then the discrimination will have effects on their fertility and mortality rates. This may result in the increase of the population of the minority groups. The increase of population of the ethnic minorities may bring some changes in the economic conditions and social aspects of the larger society. When the population of the ethnic minorities is increased, their economic position improves and social status also changes. At this stage certain major and minor differences between the ethnic minorities and the larger native society are reduced.

If the functions of the ethnic minority groups differ from that of the dominant society and if the behaviour of the minority group is required to have effects upon the fertility and mortality rates, and upon migrations and occupations, then such ethnic minority groups must be taken into account for demographic purposes. It is observed that the differences between the ethnic minority groups and the native dominant society may be dissolved within two or three generations, whereas the populations produced by the racial or ethnic minorities which are racially different from the dominant society will not lose the racial or cultural identity. It is observed that in the United States many of the ethnic minority groups who migrated from many of the European countries have already lost their cultural identity, whereas the Negroes who came to United States centuries ago still retain their identity as they cannot change their biological inheritance. The Negroes' nationality has been accepted and they are also called Americans nationally and culturally but they retain their racial segments as Negroes or blacks. The same case exists with the Japanese. The Japanese are culturally Americans but their biological inheritances make them to be kept apart as ethnic minorities.

Thompson and Lewis (1965) state that many of the ethnic minority groups in the United States work hard to dissolve their cultural identity from the native Americans and if there are any objections or hindrances on the way of their attempt they resist them strongly. But in European countries different types of situations prevail. Many of the ethnic and national groups who settled in European countries find it a pleasure and pride to maintain their cultural and national identities. If there is any pressure to eliminate their cultural identities, the people strongly protest such pressures. During World War II many of the culturally different groups were forced to leave the country. Except such instances in the Central Europe, in other countries including Great Britain there are quite a large number of people who maintain their cultural and ethnic identities by speaking their own languages, which are different from the languages of the dominant society. In fact they were found to be more loyal and patriotic to the nation in which they live than the native citizens.

There are instances that the Indians who migrated to Malaysia and Singapore and settled there two generations ago even took part in political activities in competition with the native dominant groups there and also became rulers (Ministers) in Malaysia and Singapore, and many occupy key positions in the Governments retaining their ethnic and cultural identities. Indians in South Africa, it seems are given importance in political spheres and also occupy high positions without dissolving their cultural identities. In these contexts stated above, the people of different origin who migrated to various countries with their population proportions, after many years either dissolve their ethnic and cultural identities or retain and survive and share roles with dominant native societies, become a matter of great importance for the demographers.

There are demographic differences among racial and ethnic minority groups in the American census data. In this, the problem arises with regard to the demographic differences of the racial and ethnic groups, whether these differences have any biological evidences. This problem arises because race in United States is defined socially. The dominant native citizen of United States mostly have a belief that the differences between the dominant groups and the racial and ethnic groups are mainly in mortality rates, education and in other variables which are biologically oriented. The biologists and anthropologists may say that these differences are due to innate variations. People also believe that there is biological or innate physical and intellectual evidences for the differences between the dominant groups and other racial and ethnic minority groups. But Thompson and Lewis (1965) believe that the differences among the racial and ethnic minority groups are relevant from social point of view. These differences facilitate for the division of labour at present.

These authors believe that these differences between the racial and ethnic minority groups and the dominant groups are due to the result of unequal distribution of job opportunities and educational opportunities. These divisions are made on the racial and ethnic basis and equal opportunities are denied to the minority groups. The racially and ethnically and culturally different minority groups are not given equal opportunities to share the environmental resources of the dominant native citizens. According to these authors racial meanings are given to the differences in occupational and intelligence tests scores. The differences in the occupational and in intelligence are not really caused by racial and ethnic differences. These racial, ethnic and cultural differences are prevalent all over the world wherever the racial and ethnic minority groups are living. Though this racial and ethnic problems are caused in Great Britain, South Africa, and Germany, the United States is having the racial, ethnic and cultural problems more than any other nation. The United States since needed more labourers for development programmes, in the beginning they invited many racial and cultural groups for their purposes. As a result of it people who were racially and culturally different from all over the world migrated to United States freely.

The racial and cultural problem did not strain the United States so much by the European migrants. They occupied certain areas and confined to the areas and lived with their cultural identities peacefully. But the problem much strained the United States was from the Negroes who were taken as labourers and slaves. They have also migrated to United States in large number. Because of the racial and ethnic differences there were much discrimination and segregation of the Negroes in the United States. This difference and discrimination also increased the population rates among the Negroes. The whole population of the United States was divided into mainly two categories as Whites and Negroes (black). As and when the Negro population increased there aroused more racial problems. The Negroes were mainly sent to southern States, leaving a negligible number in other areas. There were differences, discriminations, and segregations of the Negroes or the blacks from the whites. This resulted in conflict, tension, aggression, violence and persecution and in many places there were instances of lynching of the Negroes by a group of whites. These problems aggravated day by day and the Negroes demanded equal rights in every thing. This tensional and aggressive behaviour pattern has been called as 'Racial Prejudices.' But this racial prejudice had no clear-cut biological bases.

Researches and various types of studies were made in the United States and elsewhere on racial prejudices. Psychologists, sociologists, anthropologists, biologists, demographers, statisticians and political scholars were keenly interested in studying the racial prejudices and published enormous amount of research papers, monographs and books on prejudice, and on various themes relating to prejudice. Most of the Americans agree that racial prejudice is a worst national problem. The elimination of this prejudice was sought. The attempts to eliminate racial prejudice in the United States resulted that racial prejudice is a subject matter for study and people must be made to understand it correctly. Therefore innumerable number of books, propagating pamphlets have come out on the theme Racial Prejudice. These have become sources of information for many of the novels and dramas published in the United States. Organized efforts were sought from political, labour, religious, educational and cultural groups. Hence racial prejudice has become the American Governments' official matter.

Racial prejudice has been described as the myth that threatens America. It has been pathologically viewed as a disease of hatred. Alarming statements have been issued by men and women who thought about racial prejudice in the United States. Racial prejudice is not only a dark ghost covering the whole of coloured and the black races, but also it is a ghost's shadow following every American. Baruah (1946) has stated that some day the world will close down on the Americans, if the race prejudice results in dividing the Americans. All such views have motivated many Americans to think and act toward the elimination of the racial prejudice. Racial prejudice, thus, became a serious subject matter of not only the uneducated and educated citizen of America but also of the racial scientists.

Racial prejudice has become a more concentrated subject matter of study for social psychologists and sociologists than any other theme of social behaviour. As a result of it, we have large amount of information on racial prejudice from observational, clinical, experimental and psychometric fields.

Racial prejudice has been defined by quite a number of psychologists and sociologists. Prejudice may be defined as an opinion formed before hand especially an unfavourable one based on inadequate facts. The Handbook of Social Psychology defined prejudice as an unfavourable ethnic attitude (1954). According Ackerman and Jahoda (1950) prejudice is a pattern of hostility in interpersonal relations which is directed against the whole group or against a member of a group fulfilling a specific irrational function for its bearer. According to Allport (1954) prejudice is an antipathy based upon faulty and streaming generalization.

The unsophisticated white man's mind is working in its own way. The white man can say that his beliefs are based upon close personal experience and strong facts. Many white persons sometimes find it as a source for their private interest to extend their biased beliefs, in the direction of more unfavourable toward the Negro. Arnold Rose (1956) says that practically no white man honestly examines his belief critically. His views carried on for generations without being subjected to verification. If the white Americans believes that the Negro Americans are of biologically lower species than the Americans, then the Americans find sufficient reason to maintain their racial purity. The Americans' belief in the biological inferiority of the Negroes finds another support in the system of discriminations and segregations of the Negroes. The Americans find as many evidences as possible to prove the Negroes' biological inferiority. There are many things prevailing on the colour distinction. The Americans use some statements to justify the biological inferiority of the Negroes.

Some of the statements widely prevalent among the white Americans are that the Negro people are belonging to a separate race among the human beings. The Negro race has fully different ancestral heritage. The Negro race is inferior in many of the capacities. The Negro race has a biological plan between the white man and the anthropoid apes. The individual persons in the Negro race are quite similar to one another than one white man to another white man. This is the theory held by the white Americans about the Negro race. These views of the white Americans in the South are more strong than the American whites in the North.

Attempts have been made for changing the beliefs of the white Americans. How to change? New information are needed to shape views into the desired form. The information or materials must be from the white man's experiences with the Negroes. How the Negro people behave? The existing myths, legends and stereotypes that exist in American culture also should be taken into consideration. With the view of reducing the bias views of the white person's racial beliefs about the Negroes we must first draw some conclusion. This conclusion can be partly executed by improving the status of the Negroes, their behaviour and characteristics. Since the white Americans beliefs arc stronger and actively functioning in keeping the Negroes at lower level, the task becomes very difficult. The next point in this line of thinking is that the ordinary white man's conclusions about the Negro behaviour should be corrected and he should be informed of the error he is committing in attributing to them collectively, the inborn racial characteristics. People must be well informed and be honest. The false generalization should be eliminated.

6. DEMOGRAPHIC CHARACTERISTICS OF NEGROES

The early American Negro people's ancestry was Africans. Many of the present American Negroes were the intermixture of the American Red Indians and whites. Great majority of the Negroes brought as slaves directly to United States were from the West Coast of Africa. Therefore they were mainly belonging to the racial stock called the true Negroes. There has been admixture of white and Red Indian blood into the American Negro population. There has been changes in the American Negro population stock which makes it different from the present African Negroes or from the stock they were brought to United States.

The Africans who were taken to United States as slaves were only a selection from the African Negroes. These Negroes after going to the United States, there was some change in their physical composition. It is because of the different racial reproductivity and also by mutation. The slaves who were brought to the United States were not belonging pure Negro races. The original Negro race had an admixture of Caucasoid genes with the Mediterranean people. During the slave trade more white genes were added into the Negro races. The slave traders themselves were having promiscuous sexual intercourse with their female slaves. The Negroes who came to America during the slave trade and later on from the West Indies also had white and Indians blood mixture. The miscegenation in the United States took place right from the very beginning. Along with slave trade, the plantation system also was started and this has more strongly established the Negro-White sex relations in the early eighteenth century. This is the next stage of White-Negro relationship.

Lovis Wirth and Herbert Goldhamer (1944) state that no good looking Negro girl or Negro-White born mulatto girl was left unmolested by the whilte males and very few young men grew up virtually, and their loss of virtue was rarely attributed to the life with white women. Contemporary observers made such statements and this led to the assumption of well-to-do white men families that inter-racial sexual relations were normal incidents. But what proportions of Negro women were involved in the inter-racial sexual relation is not known. The inter-racial sexual relation was a pattern of life in the southern rural plantations. Authors who studied this problem agree that the interracial sexual relations during this period were more in Southern and also in the Northern States. There was another period of incidence, during which the Negro-White sex relations were common. That was during the American civil war and its unpleasant after effect. The Northern army, after the war, left a considerable number of yankee offsprings in the Southern Negro people. The Negro population gradually increased and they settled down at status levels. The slavery state has been substituted. The sexual contacts continued between the Negro-White as it was before the civil war. But there was a decrease in the number of offsprings out of the sexual intermixture of races. This shows that there was decrease in the sexual relations. There was also decrease in the more stable types sexual relationships such as marriage and concubinage. But there was an increase in the rate of prostitution and casual sex relations. Then there was an indication that there was a decline in the rate of white offsprings in the Negro population.

The American classification of people in the United States was that all hybrids are Negroes. The Americans caste rule was that there should not any Negro blood get into the American white population. But there were some Negroes with extremely light skin colour, more white than the Negro ancestry, leave the Negro racial group and become whites. Herskovits (1930) has made an extensive study of the American Negro. The sample of his study consisted of 1551 Negroes and 71.7 per cent of this sample had the ancestry of white and 27.2 per cent were the Indian ancestry. Herskovits sample consisted of too many upper class Negroes who were known to have the white ancestry. Herskovits wanted to know whether the American Negro population is really a mixed population group? He wanted to ascertain by making a direct study on this and find out the actual composition of the Negro population group. His findings had more psychological and demographic significances.

The miscegenation between the American Negroes and whites is said to be generally reduced. The children of White-Negro unions have become rare, because of the adoption of contraceptive method. Internal miscegenation within the Negro groups between individuals of different levels of white ancestry is a continuous process. The Negro immigrants from the West Indies and from South America by their racial intermixture there was change in the genetic composition of the Negro people in the United States. Rose (1956) stated that there was a complete intermixture between the Whites and Negroes with certain period, then certain proportion of the very light skinned mulattoes, who made the bridge between the white and Negro population, might have gradually decreased by marriages with darker Negroes.

There is no physical difference between the average American white and the average American Negro in skin colour. There is no quantitative measurement or research conducted on this to ascertain the facts. A comparative analysis between the average white man and an average Negro at present can be brought out and is found to be having the following physical traits. The head of a Negro is slightly longer and narrower, cranial capacity is slightly less, the interpupillary distance is greater, the nose is broader, lips thicker, outer ear shorter, nasal depth greater, nose shorter, arms and legs longer, pelvis narrower and smaller, stature shorter, skin more of black pigment, hair wavy, curly or woolly, wider distribution of hair and more sweat glands. Most of the Negroes have brown eyes, black hair. These traits vary greatly among different groups of Negroes. Certain physical traits are modified because of the environmental changes. In most of the traits the Negroes differ from the whites only at a very small level. Some of the traits are overlapping. The average person is not aware of all these differences. But some of the traits in some average Negroes are very much easily visible though these differences are not found in most of the Negroes. The socially visible and identifiable characteristics in Negroes are mainly the dark skin colour, woolly hair, broad nose, thick lips and the projection of the jaw beyond the upper face. These differences the white men are aware of in the Negroes. But some white men too much exaggerate these traits. It is noticed that the certain traits are prevalent only among the people as belief, but there are no evidences for them. There is also a belief that the Negroes origin was earlier than the Caucasoids. Several reasons are produced for this. One reason is, the appearance of hair over the body skin. The more older a race is, the less hairs the people have over the body skin. Races of later origin have more hairs spread all over the body. There are certain strong beliefs that are not scientifically verified, that is, all male Negroes have extraordinarily longer sex organs and also all Negroes have a peculiar smell. Anthropologists are of the view that the traits of pure Negroes are found to be changing to the context of the racial intermixture of white race. The American Negroes are found to be of the averable individuals. The American Negroes most of them are mulattoes, the white-Negro offsprings. Hence the traits described above mostly of the mulatto-Negroes.

Arnold Rose (1956) states that there is a type of physical trait susceptible to various diseases. It was also once believed that, there were differences in the particular disease rates, which were due to the differences in the biological make up. The large amount of deaths of the Negroes in the United States, once, was though attributed to environmental forces, some investigators felt that the mode of their life such as segregation, overcrowding and ignorance were found to be facilitating for a higher disease rates. This condition did not prevail among the white people. The American Negroes death rate is higher, because their biological make is more susceptible to diseases. The diseases common among the negroes are pellagra, syphilis, nephritis, tuberculosis and pneumonia.

There is no evidence that some of these diseases were due to poor diet. But studies have not provided any evidence that these diseases were caused by hereditary, susceptibility, nor there were environmental causes. The indirect causes attributed to these diseases were mainly malnutrition, overcrowding and lack of attention and nursing. Were the Negroes having any susceptibility to mental disease? It is very difficult to determine, even more difficult than the physical diseases.

The American whites and Negroes problem was now and then taking a serious turn which had drawn the attention of various private and public organization in the United States. The problems was considered individually and collectively for many years. But the real situation all over the country was not scientifically studied and remedial measures were offered. The idea of studying the Negro problem in America was first originated in the mind of Newton D. Baker, the then Secretary of War in Wilson's Cabinet and the Carnegie Corporation, one of the two largest philanthrophic foundations functioning under the Presidentship of Frederich P. Kappel who undertook the responsibility of making a comprehensive study of the Negro in the United States. According to his idea and plan, the study of the American Negro should be done wholly objectively and dispassionately as a social phenomenon. Kappel was looking out for social scientists who should hold the leadership of this study from a foreign country of non-imperialistic and without having any background of domination of one race over another. He should be one who could appreciate this task with a fresh mind and without having any influence of the traditional attitudes. He was having free hand in appointing and organizing the staff of his own choice in the United States and also can utilize the experiences of other scholars and experts, and the report presented to the public should represent his own decisions. On this basis Gunner Myrdal from Sweden was invited, and appointed in September 1938 to carry out the work. One Richard Sterner, who was in the Royal Social Board of Sweden was taken as the co-worker by Myrdal. Myrdal and Sterner have made extensive field trips all over the United States to draw up details for the study. Myrdal invited criticisms, comments and suggestions from the American experts in various fields related to the Negro problems. While the programme was going on Myrdal has asked the American experts to prepare research papers and monographs on Negro problems for his study. Myrdal had in his study group six top staff members, thirty-one independent workers, thirty-six assistants to the staff members, and outside collaborators and a group of secretaries and typists.

When the first phase of work was over in 1940 Germany invaded Denmark and Norway in April 1940. Gunner Myrdal felt that it was his duty to be in Sweden to do his service to the nation. The work was left under the direction of Samuel A. Stauffer, Professor of Sociology at the University of Chicago. Myrdal returned to America in March 1941 and continued the work. At that time the manuscript consisted of fifteen thousand typed pages. At the end of 1941, Arnold

Rose also joined the study and assisted Myrdal (1944) along with Sterner and the work was completed and published in 1944 under the title of '*An American Dilemma*', which consisted of about two thousand printed pages. This book is an extensive and comprehensive report of the American Negro problem. Since it was very voluminous and costly for an ordinary reader who is interested in the problem, Arnold Rose has published a summary of the American Dilemma in about three hundred pages through Beacon Press, under the title of '*The Negro in America*', to make it available to any reader.

This comprehensive study, '*An American Dilemma*' has become a source book for any one who is interested in doing research on the Negro problems in America. There are enormous amount of information available for demographic studies. Psychologists who are interested in racial and ethnic prejudices, group tensions, origin and development of races may find relevant information in Myrdal's *American Dilemma*. Though the Negro problem in America is more of a psychological theme, the problem was studied by a group of sociologists under the leadership of Myrdal, the sociological and demographical approaches of this study provide plenty of information and scope for psychological analyses.

7. PSYCHOLOGICAL ANALYSIS OF POPULATION THEORIES : CAUSES AND CONSEQUENCES

The studies over years on the changes in population provided scope for evolving two important aspects of population. One is the *population theories* and the other is the *population policies*. Population theories mainly deal with the causes and consequences of size, structure and distribution of a population and also the dynamics of changes. Population policies are indented to make changes in a population. Population policies are mainly concerned with altering and controlling of some selected aspects of a population for the purpose of achieving the valued goals.

Psychologists who are interested in population research are also dealing with population theories and policies. The population policies which are designed to bring about changes in a population are dependent upon population theories to some extent, because the theories attempt to explain how changes in a population are occurring. Though the modern textbooks on population problems or population studies generally start with the work of Thomas Robert Malthus's (1766-1834), the origin of population theories goes back to the writings of the Chinese philosopher and teacher of ethics, Confucius (551-479 B.C.), whose doctrines were compiled after his death under the title of *'The Analects of Confucious'*, and the Greek philosopher, Plato (427-347 B.C.), whose teacher was Socrates (470-399 B.C.) and his pupil Aristotle (384-322 B.C.), was regarded as the founder of Western philosophy. Malthus was an English economist. He propounded his population theory in 1798 under the title of *"An Essay on the Principle of Population As It Affects the Future Improvement of Society"*.

Malthusian theory in essence is that the increase of population tends to exceed the increase of the means of existence and that therefore sexual restraint should be exercised. Malthus during his life time has observed important changes in the social and economic organizations of Western Europe that were favourable to slow down the rise of population. There was slow improvement in the agricultural productivity and industry which had facilitated the improvement in the living conditions of sections of population. It was thought that a nation's strength depends upon its economic sufficiency and upon the number of people. The population growth was considered as the sign of nation's health and vigour irrespective of the conditions prevailed. Malthus has observed that the increase of population mainly depends upon the increase in the means of subsistence. Because according to his observation that many people live close to the level of subsistence. Malthus was of the view that any permanent improvement for the lot of mankind was not possible unless increased food production was made to go with increased population.

The population theory of Malthus has become the classical work of population problems. Subsequently several population theories have emerged in 18th and 19th centuries. All of them have shown their interests upon broad economic considerations. They brought relationships between population, and natural and man-made resources including the means of production and consumption. The formation of law was based upon observation and generalization and no adequate data were available. Therefore these theories were mainly based upon empirical evidences. Malthusian theory was reflected by the sociologists and communists. Karl Max (1819-1883) has expressed his view on this matter which was exactly opposite to that of Malthus. Therefore during 19th century, basic ideological dispute has arisen. Many criticised Malthusian thesis. The prominent critics were Lorimer (1963) and Robinson (1964).

The population trends before the time of Malthus were determined mainly by the interaction of two important forces. Malthus saw that the trend toward increase of population resulted from (1) the attraction between the two sexes and the (2) positive checks of death and fertility. Deaths and sterility were caused by famine and hunger, disease and vices. Therefore attempts were made to check them. According to Malthus, production of food and other necessities of life in any country was a slow process of development and mainly determined by natural resources. An increase of population soon absorbs the production and causes scarcity of food and misery. Therefore, Malthus was of the view that the only way for a nation to escape from famine and poverty, because of the population pressure on the resources, was to put a restriction on the population growth by the exercise of sound judgment cautiously to restrict the population. Malthus did not give importance to the potentialities of science and technology and also minimized the importance of changes in social, cultural and economic institutions.

During the first-half of nineteenth century the socialist and marxist theorists have not adopted the population problem. They have not only denied the existence of population problem but also stated that the problem can be solved through recognization of society. These socialists and marxists have attributed the human misery not to the excessive population growth. According to them, the human miseries were due to the maldistribution of wealth of the nations and to her defects in the existing social order. They have held the view that the new form of society which they were advocating would have preventive check on the population growth and the working people would increase the production more rapidly than the number of people increaseed in the population.

Malthus firmly believed that two of man's characteristics were unchangeable in the maintenance of life. They were also antagonistic to each other. One was the *need for food* and the other was the *passion between sexes*. Of which the latter was more powerful and made most people to marry at an early age and therefore it resulted in large number of births and the population rapidly increased, as it was not checked by miseries. *Misery*, for Malthus, was the sufferings which caused by the lack of necessities of life, which led often to premature death. The *Positive checks*, according to him, referred to all factors that were operating as determiners of death rate. They were the destroyers of life. Some of the positive checks were vicious customs with respect to women, unwholesome or morally harmful manufacturers, luxury, pestilence and war. All these were resolved into misery. The preventive checks were referred to the factors operating to reduce the birth rate. The postponement of marriage would be the chief preventive check of birth rate.

Malthus was of the view that these two checks, the positive checks and the preventive checks would be the true causes of slow increase of population. He states that the preventive checks would reduce the reproduction rate of human beings, whereas the positive checks would not reduce as they could not be often operating continuously in causing deaths by miseries. The human institutions however good they would serve only to slow down the positive checks for a short time, then the population grows again up to the productive capacity and man would again put into miseries of famine, hunger, disease, war and all those ills that man had in the past. But even the preventive checks which may operate in different degrees in various ranks of society would not be strong to eliminate the population pressure of the subsistence. Therefore Malthus, all his life had the strong view that men's "sex passion" and his "material needs" were always in conflict. The subsistence could not be reduced to a level below the minimum without causing great hardships. Even at this stage there would not be any indication that man's "sex passion" underwent any change. In this way man is destined to the tragic fate of suffering by inevitable causes and still trying to maintain the population which was much greater than the production needed. Malthus has stated that man was not dare enough to face the truth because it was unpleasing and what was expected was the most harmful mischief from the unmanly conduct.

There were severe criticism on the Malthus and on his work by many writers. Some of them might have been genuine and many of them were greatly misrepresented. Thompson and Lewis (1965) state that the chief sinners in this respect were those who did not read his works carefully. Those who hold the belief that Malthus was responsible for all the practices, were now called 'neo-Malthusians.' Thompson and Lewis (1965) state that the classical contribution, that Malthus had made to the study of population, made him the 'real father of modern population study'. Malthus was more responsible than any one else for bringing the population study into the field of social sciences. His work is still very much valued in population studies, because of the facts of supporting his theory about the dynamics of population growth, and the changes in their relation to the human welfare.

Natural Theories of Population

The second half of eighteenth century and the whole of nineteenth century were noted for the industrial and agricultural revolutions, resulting with the increasing efficiency in production and increasing efficiency of agricultural labour in England, in Western European countries and in the United States. The increased efficiency in transportation moved the agricultural products rapidly all over the Europe. Malthus was a contemporary of these developments and his population theory was slowly losing hold among those who are interested in population studies. Malthus's population theory was considered as the 'natural law' in general terms, as he stated that population increased faster than the production and other subsistences for life, because of the passion between sexes. Since passion was natural vice, his theory was called natural law.

A few years later, a contemporary of Malthus, an English social reformer and economist Michael Thomas Sadler (1780-1835) propounded a natural law which was exactly contrary to the natural law founded by Malthus. He was of the view that the tendency of man to increase the population would disappear naturally when the density of the people in the community increased, and on the other hand, the number would stop to grow at the time when the people would enjoy the greatest happiness of life. Sadler was having the view that this tendency among human beings was natural. But he did not produce any evidence to support his theory as during his time there was no significant decline in fertility rate in the cities of England, what could be stated as decline in reproduction naturally. Sadler's theory did not arouse so much enthusiasm among the students of population studies as the Malthus's theory as there were certain inexplicable jargons in Sadler's theory.

At the time when Sadler was explaining this natural law, another economist and social philosopher, a contemporary to Malthus and Sadler, Thomas Doubleday (1790-1870) by name founded different natural law of population concerning the growth of population. Doubleday believed that the increase of population was directly opposite to food production. The higher the food production or the better the food supply the slower the increase in number of people.

The famous English philosopher, Herbert Spencer (1820-1903) was also interested in explaining the population problem through his theory, which was also called natural law. According to him population growth was a social and biological development by natural forces. He had the view that there was a natural law that would release man from the blame, sin or punishment or responsibility for controlling of the increase of population, and the nature was achieving this end by weakening man's interest in reproduction as the nature put him to devote more time, energy and effort to personal, scientific and economic developments. Spencer was of the view that in nature there is an antagonism between individuation and genesis. If individual takes more strenuous effort in his personal achievement in any field, then less will be his interest in reproduction. In this way there was a natural decrease in the reproduction capacity in man, especially in women as personal development was given more importance.

Social Theories of Population Growth

Some of the natural theorists felt that their natural laws of population growth, controls human population or number automatically to the desired level. These theorists criticised Malthus's theory of natural law and founded new theories. Some of these were social theories of population. Quite a number of social theories of population have emerged since Malthus. An American economist and social reformer, Henry George (1839-1897) has brought out a social theory called single tax. According to him what people were paying for the right of using the land, were taken as the tax by the public which the economists called as the rent of the land. The improvements were not included in this tax or rent. The public need not pay any other tax. George (1905) believed that if the landlords were not having any right to collect rent for the land, then the use of the land would go into the control of those who could produce more out of the land. Now the land would be made to yield more than what it was yielding previously under private ownership. Then there would be no need to worry about the increase of population and about the production of subsistence and its shortage.

The author of this theory felt that his theory would solve all the social problems. George did not accept the principle of antagonism between man's natural tendency to increase the numbers and his potentiality to produce more food. He strongly asserts that the increase of population or numbers involved also the increase of man's food products. But this condition would be possible if only man had equal right to approach the resources of the earth without any monopoly. George had stated that if the real law of population was made known to all, then the tendency to increase the production would be stronger and the increase or growth of population would be given greater relief from the distress of shortage of food. Though George's theory appears like that of Spencer's natural law, this has been placed one among the social theories. George also thought of contraception as an important method of reducing fertility rate. Many of the western countries were already practising voluntary control of the size of the family even before George's work, *'The Progress and Poverty'* (1879) was published.

At the end of nineteenth century a French Professor in the University of Strasbourg named Arsane Dumont (1849-1902) formulated a population theory, which he called as 'the theory of social capillarity'. Dumont (1901) has stated that the individual is very much inclined to claim higher in his social environment by the process similar to physical capillarity. In this process of claiming upward in the social environment, man is not so much interested in the reproduction process. As a result of it he slowly loses interest in the family and also in the welfare of the society. His chief interest is moving upward to gain the personal achievement. He does not bother whether it would benefit his society or not. Dumont was of the view that the upward movement of the individual in the social environment is a direct cause of decline in the birth rate which may vary from class to class. The increase of population of a nation is in the inverse ratio to the development of the individual in the social environment. But Dumont did not think whether it is possible for everybody in a nation to climb always upward in the social environment, forgetting his family and society, caring only the individual's personal achievement. Dumont's theory is somewhat similar to the theory of Spencer, but with little improvement over it.

Another social theory of population has been formulated by Alexander Morris Carr-Saunders in the first quarter of twentieth century. Carr-Saunders was an English economist, interested in the study of population. According to his theory man is constantly striving to achieve an optimum number. This optimum number is referred to the nature of the environment, the degree of proficiency put forth, the habits and customs of the people concerned, and all the related facts provide the highest average return per head. Man has always been controlling his numbers to maintain the optimum number and this number may vary from time to time. The optimum number is not fixed for ever. This may constantly going on varying when the said conditions vary. As the proficiency tends to increase so also the number economically desired tends to increase. According to Carr-Saunders the population growth was determined by the economically desired numbers under the conditions of life. This means that man has to develop practices such as abortion, infanticide, segregation of woman, postponing the marriage and so on as the birth control measures. Therefore Carr-Saunders puts more stress on man's actual control on his growth in number, whereas Malthus left this to the positive checks. Carr-Saunders thought that the population growth or man's growth was fully within his control and also depends upon conditions and the attitude of mind that man has developed in his society and also the physical conditions of his life. Carr-Saunder's social theory was quite in contrast to the natural theories.

Communist Theory of Population

The communist theory of population also was considered as the social theory of population. Karl Hinrich Marx (1818-1883) a German social philosopher, who in collaboration with Friedrich Engels (1820-1895) another German socialist leader and political philosopher founded the modern communist theory. The population theory was an incidental and supplement to their general theory of communism. According to the theory founded by Marx, communism was the only cure for all the economic hardships of human beings. According to Marx when the communist doctrines were in operation there would be no poverty and hardship irrespective of the increase of population. Marx's population theory is quite opposite of the population theory of Malthus. Marx was an extremist and was strongly viewed that communism was a panacea for all the ills of the world and that poverty and hardships were solely due to man's innate tendency to grow in numbers faster than what he would produce for his subsistence. He was also of the view that man's tendency to put more stress on the production was due to the evils of capitalism and this would vanish if the systems of communism were put into operation.

According to Marx, poverty was wholly as a result of unemployment or under employment conditions. This was because of the inability of the capitalistic system to provide jobs for all, irrespective of the speed of the population growth. The present communistic doctrines are maintained in the same general principle as Marx presented with regard to population growth and the economic system. Therefore under communism there is no need to worry about the increase of population. The Soviet deligates at the United Nations Population Commission

(1961) often stressed that there cannot be surplus population under a socialist regime inspite of rapid demographic growth.

The two kinds of theories, the natural theories and social theories have explained the causes and the consequences of a population and the dynamics of change. Thompson and Lewis (1965) have clearly brought a distinction between natural theories and the social theories of population. The natural theories are based upon a mechanistic and deterministic view of man and nature. The social theories of population have the assumption that population growth is not exposed to any unchangeable natural law. But population growth is determined by man's innate tendency that man has developed in his society in which he lives. The historical tendency of population was from natural theories (Malthus *et al.*) toward social theories.

Modern Social Theory

The modern social theory is also stated as the *theory of demographic transition.* This was founded by Coale and Hoorer (1958). This is not having the same characteristics as the other theories of population. Therefore, this cannot be called as fully propounded theory. But it has certain merits to be called as theory as it is formulated from empirical evidences. According to the demographic transition theory, the agrarian low income economy is described with high birth rates and low death rates. The birth rate of them is considerably stable. The death rate is found to be fluctuating due to varying conditions. But the economy of the society may change its form. Then it becomes an interdependent and specialized market-dominated economy and the average death rate declines. The decline continues under the influence of better organization and improves the medical knowledge and care. After sometimes the birth rate begins to decline. Both the birth rates and the death rates reach almost a parallel level moving downward, and the declining of birth rates fall behind. At last a further reduction in the death rate was not achieved and the birth rate again approaches the death rate and both of them become equal and a gradual growth rate is again established. There would be low level of mortality and the family pattern becomes smaller. Now the mortality rate is stable and the birth rate would fluctuate year to year according to the prevailing conditions. Though there were some criticisms made on this theory, it is a useful theory as it represents the demographic events.

In conclusion, we may state that all the natural and social theories including the modern social theory seem to endorse the 'population problem' expounded by Malthus. All the theories, except the communist theory, accept that the increase of population is a problem and it has to be solved by some means. Malthus has stated that population would rapidly increase if it was not checked by miseries and miseries are the positive checks that determine the death rates. Further, he wanted that man must adopt preventive checks and must be restrained from the sex passion and accept postponement of marriage to check the birth rates. Some theories state that population problem would be naturally solved by increasing the production, and also by the interest, people have for self-improvement. When people wanted to climb up in the social environment, they would not be interested in procreation and the fertility rate would be reduced. But the communist theory states that in communist society there would not be any population problem.

8. PSYCHOLOGICAL PERSPECTIVE OF POPULATION POLICIES : CHANGES IN POPULATION AND ACHIEVING THE VALUED GOALS

Aims of Population Policies

In the history of nation the population growth has been identified with prosperity and strength of the nation more than the economic prosperity. But today many of the nations are on the way to reduce the rapid population growth by means of reducing their birth rates. They are driven to such decision by some urgent problems. Now the population problem has turned from conceptual stage to policy making and action stage and also governments are interested in implementing it quickly and successfully. There are about forty nations which have formulated their policies and action plans to reduce population growth with their resources and with the help of private and international organizations. The degree of acceptance of the policy has been very impressive and unanimous. The opinion held by all is family planning. The American President, Johnson declared, that the United States will assist family planning programmes in nations which request such help, as early as 1965. Pandit Nehru (1967) the Prime Minister of India said, "We must press forward into family planning and this is a programme of the highest importance." The Singapore republican Government created

Family Planning and Population Board to initiate population control programmes.

The family planning programme, to limit the population growth, is to concentrate on providing new and efficient contraceptive methods on a national basis through mass programme under public health departments or which should function under the action of a separate Government department. Population control may be achieved through dissemination of new contraceptive methods excluding the women who want more children. In the population policy it is very difficult to state the long range goals. However the growth of population must be reduced by implementing vigorously the family planning programme. It should be taken for evidence that family planning can solve the problem of population growth.

The aimed goal of the population policy is to limit population growth to solve the population problems. Generally population policies are concerned with only the growth and size of population. These may result from birth rates, death rates, and migrations. The control of population would require deliberate attempt upon the factors causing rise in all these three factors. Generally a nation's current population policy with regard to population control does not deal with mortality rate and migrations. The policy is concerned only with control of births. A similar term fertility control is also used to describe current policies.

The family planning programmes are aiming simply to achieve a reduction in the birth rate. Therefore the success of the programme is to bring out a reduction as it is assumed that the reduction of birth will reduce the population growth. In the demographic language the achieved goal is said to be a short run decline in a given period of time. Pakistan (1966) adopted a plan in 1961, the aim was to reduce the birth rate from 50 to 40 per thousand by 1970. India (1966) adopted the family planning programmes and the aim was to reduce the birth rate from 40 to 25 per thousand as early as possible. The South Korean (1967) Government's aim was to reduce the population growth from 2.5 to 1.2 per cent by 1980. The problem with these nations is that these nations allow rapid population growth. Under the existing condition the mortality rate is very low and permitting a crude birth rate of 25 to 30 per one thousand would multiply the population. They state that their aim is population control but what exactly taking place is rapid growth of population. This is opposite to what has been expected. For example, Indian population in 1981 was 695 millions. This is little less than twice the size of the population of 1951. In 1995

Indian population is 920 millions. That is, in about 30 years period the population increased about two times, and in about 14 years period from 1980 to 1995 there is an increase of 225 millions. Davis (1970) states that this is the population control irony in developing nations.

Therefore the statistics of the present goals and measures are only an intermediate programme. A real start of controlling the population is yet to begin in India. What is happening in population problem in India? Is that the actual runs contrary to what has been planned and expected? Therefore the population policies should have zero population growth as the goal in the family planning programmes, and not to have as many children as people wish, and also not whenever they want to have as the Turkish (1965) population planning declared.

Zero Population Growth

Therefore, any discussion on population problems may lead to zero population growth and this must be the ultimate goal. But current population policies do not consider such goals. Because it is not acceptable to many nations. Some of the world religions and many of the cultural groups do not accept this. Zero population growth means the number of births in a region in a specific period should be the same as the number of deaths in that area during the period. The birth rate and the death rate should be the same.

Population Policies and Theories

While population theories study about the causes and consequences, population policies deal with changes in population and also achieving the valued goods. Population policies are depending upon population theories. Population policies attempt to explain how changes occur. The most clearly relevant policies for psychologists are those dealing with fertility. The other policies relevant for psychologists are the policies on migration and population distribution. These policies are also having potential relevance. With regard to fertility the current issue of population policy is in relation to matters of degree of urgency for fertility reduction and the most impressive moral method of bringing it and implementing population policies. These are the exclusive privilege of man's efforts. Man with his intelligence and abilities, is able to organize his life problems, not only for his survival but also to lead a better and happy life. Most of man's efforts for better life appear to be the consequences of his planned efforts, but several of his efforts for survival and to live a better life were the results of accidental occurrences. But however man alone can formulate and adopt customs and traditions and can transmit them to his posterity. These process are based on certain plans and hence called policies.

Generally, policy may be defined as a plan or action adapted or possessed by an individual or Government, or political party, or business or industrial organization. This definition may be applied to the population of a nation or to the world. For example, if we want to control the size of a group or its characteristics, we must see whether the group has had any population policy. Our view on this must confine to the current policy prevailing. Population policy cannot be discussed without reference to social goals and values, since changes in the rate of growth structure will reverberate in many ways in the social system. For example, Coale (1968) states that a stationary population results from a zero population growth under conditions of low mortality. This group may have an older age structure. This indicates a conservation of political and social adjustment. A population policy is a part of a coordinated programme of planned social change. It is explicitly a long term social goal. A population policy in a more realistic sense would take into consideration the way in which the current social values are functioning in the population and relate them in between evolved social goals.

Some Early Population Policies

The population policies in the primitive societies were unwritten documents and their customs and traditions alone may provide some information about their way of life. The primitive people considered the survival as more important than birth of the additional children. They also exposed the handicapped, crippled and weak babies or children and the old people who could not take care of themselves to death from the point of view of survival of the existing people. In such groups there was polygamy, one man marrying more than one wives and in some group there was polyandry, one woman marrying two or more husbands. This shows in some cultural groups men were short and in some cultural groups women were short. Whether these groups had population policies or social policies or even it would have been the cultural policies, the cultural groups have practised the same customs and traditions with regard to survival value. But generally such practices may be stated as social policies. It appears that they were also concerned with genetic characteristics of their group people. But their practice of exposing the deformed and crippled children to death, was motivated whether from engenic point of view or from the point of view of healthy group survival? This type of practice of the groups appears to be more of birth population policy and social policy.

Some ancient groups have given importance to strong and healthy population growth. The Romans, the Greeks, the Spartans and the Egyptians seem to have developed their society with strong, sturdy and tough people in their groups since they often involved in fighting with the rival groups. They considered that the crippled and deformed babies and old people who could not take care of themselves are liabilities of healthy people of the population. This policy greatly affected the population growth of the groups. Similarly, their policy was tough in training and educating the able bodied citizens. Though some of the ancient societies did not have much of scientific and technological development of the modern type with regard to their manpower they have very healthy and tough principle to bring up men as great warriors to protect their group people from other rival groups' attack. This may be considered as rigorous population policy. The numbers of the groups were very important, but the vitality of the group was considered as more important. Offsprings were made through strong and tough male members to have children free from deforming and crippling. But when the leaders of the groups became the rulers of big states their power and greatness of their kingdoms were identified with numbers of growth of the population and high birth rates were encouraged gradually. The Spartan type of population policy changed and numbers were considered as the sign of strength and power of the groups and therefore fertility rates were very much encouraged. It is believed that the authoritarian rulers have encouraged high fertility. In Soviet Union special rewards were given to women who gave birth to more number of children.

Policies of High Birth Rates

Some of the advocates of the population policy had the view that high birth rate assures longer survival and also it was the indication of population growth. This is viewed as social policy. It was believed whether this policy would have any effect on birth rates, when there were restrictions on the marital relations and lengthy purification periods after the child birth. The policy of high fertility rates would have effect if only these restrictions were removed. The purification period after the child birth should be shortened, widows should be allowed to remarry, the duration of breast feeding should be reduced to two years, the practice of abortion should be restricted, early marriage should be encouraged. These conditions may increase the fertility rates. If there were no restrictions imposed upon people since the natural marital relations and the reproductive drives are very powerful, then there may be increase of birth rates rapidly.

The social policy of a group encouraging high birth rate may lead to rapid growth of population. This policy, no doubt may increase the birth rate. But the continuance of this policy of some groups, clans, tribes and small groups may sometimes be put into strong population pressures which may result in higher death rates than the birth rates. With all the high birth rate policy for more than one thousand years the population growth in most of the societies was considerably low. Some small groups practically went to the extent to extinction. It was not due to the low birth rates, but due to other conditions. The food production was very low, not able to meet the requirements. People met with famine, poverty and starvation. They were not able to protect themselves from infectious and epidemic diseases. Manpower was wasted enormously in various ways. More energy was invested for less products, conflicts and wars were caused death of many. A man who works hard the whole day could support only himself and his family members were often put into starvation.

There were no organised efforts to reduce man's death rates and also there was realization that the increase of birth rate alone can assure the rapid growth of population. Meanwhile man has made certain important improvements which had some effects on the numbers of his group. The improvements also include increasing agricultural products, making improvements to protect him from other elements. It has taken many decades to cultivate land and produce more foodgrains. The gradual development in agriculture farming increased production considerably. But they often had difficulties. There was failure of crops due to rains or some other calamities. But however improved methods were discovered in agricultural farming, and the subsistence increased, which resulted in reducing the death rates and the numbers increased. On the other side there was also improvements in their way of life particularly in clothing, housing and the use of natural resources and minerals. These improvements have taken place as they were to support the increasing population time to time. The increased numbers were to occupy larger areas for housing and living.

It is quite but natural for a man to have the desire to live comfortably and peacefully without having much friction with others in all respects. This is more psychological than demographical . But man's comfortable living depends upon two things, one is the numbers—the population strength, and the other is production of subsistences. These two should not come to clash. The numbers should be in line with the production of food and other things which are essential for maintaining a decent level of life. This has been realized by man long ago and has been living accordingly for thousands of years. But he has not brought this idea under some explicit policy. The adjustment was going on under customs and tradition or they treated this problem as a social policy. A definite population policy has not been evolved and effected successfully. Even in the more developed countries it was not thought of until Malthus's work was published at the end of eighteenth century. However severe criticism were levelled against Malthus's work, it was his work that has made many people to think of the population problems and population theories and population policies. But every population theory propounded after Malthus has its own merits and demerits.

Though there were both agricultural and industrial developments in the European countries and in the United States, until Malthus's proclamation, that it would be wiser to control the reproduction rates in proportion to the production of food and other subsistences if human beings are interested in a decent level of living, no one thought about it and only after that many people realized about this problem. Further, they have also believed that man's productivity was increasing rapidly and that a new era in man's life was possible and the Government's policy of non-interference (laissez-faire) regarding the reproduction would be also applied to commerce and industry which would increase food and other subsistences needed for the fast increasing population and that there would not be any pressure of the population on the subsistences. People have this faith even today that man's economic demands would be met by the commerce and industry if there were no meddling with his natural reproduction. This view was held by many for the whole of nineteenth century that the increased productivity was more than what was needed for the rapidly increasing population. During this period there was also decline in the death rate and the death was slow in European countries. Similar conditions prevailed also in Eastern countries except deaths by wars.

Another factor that was favourable to meet the situation was the personal control of the size of the family. Certain sections of the people in Western countries kept their family sizes at an optimum level in view of the increasing numbers in industrial and urban areas. People in western European countries adopted the method of *Preventive checks* as suggested by Malthus, specifically increasing the marriageable age. Even contraceptive methods also were adopted in the later part of the nineteenth century. In Japan during first quarter of 20th century there was steady growth of population. The birth rate was slow and there was increased agricultural production. The health services have been found to be more effective and the mortality rate also declined. In China cultivable lands were vastly expanded and the agriculture was very much improved. Though China had suffered with many miseries like frequent famines, poverty, starvation, plagues, floods, the population rate was steadily increasing. When Thompson (1965) went to China in 1923, he observed that Malthusian was known to them and they also practised in checking the population growth. Famine and starvation, disease and war (Civil war) were the important checks on population growth in China. The medical services were such that within a short time the death rate was reduced. Thus in every country without a well defined population policy, some social policy was maintained to keep the birth rates and death rates at some desired level. The situation would have been much better if a population policy was adopted effectively.

9. NEED FOR A UNIVERSAL POPULATION POLICY

Therefore there has been a desire universally in almost all the countries to have well defined population policy which should be implemented effectively by which they would improve their health services and reduce their death rates as much as possible and have a check on the birth rates. It appears that the adoption of population policy would be health oriented. It is estimated that two-thirds of the world population rested in the developing countries. Health services should be established in all the developing countries for reducing the birth rates and the death rates. There were evidences available from the developing nations that the longevity of the people increased considerably. This means that death rates were reduced. But whether birth rates were reduced or not was doubtful in the developing countries. Instead it was increasing rapidly. Health services were active in dealing with the infectious and epidemic diseases. Thomspon and Lewis (1965) state that if attempts were made or even were under consideration for evolving a world population policy an efficient public health service would be required before hand in the developing countries. The purpose of the public health services would be to bring down the birth rate to the level of the production and other subsistence rate and to meet the services man needed for a decent level of living. Therefore a better health service would be needed first of all if we go for a universal population policy.

A universal or a world population policy cannot be evolved so easily. There are certain obstacles for establishing a universal population policy. There are few nations in the world not ready to adopt population policy as a national policy. It appears that some developing countries clearly stated that they cannot implement any population policy so quickly. These Governments have stated that until the people of the country willingly come forward to control the size of their families they cannot give any assurance to other nations for the formulation of a world population policy. There are also other obstacles for the world population policy. The developing nations mostly have faith in traditionalism. The people of these countries do not go against their traditional practices in reproduction. There are also other factors like nationalism, racism, religious affiliation and ideologies. People of the developing countries strongly stick to their customs and traditions and Governments cannot go against the wishes of the people. Further a population policy cannot be forcibly enforced on a population when they are not ready.

Another view prevalent in some countries is that control of population is not a very urgent problem as some countries feel. It is because that some countries' population is also not growing fastly. Another view is that their natural resources are so wealthy that there would not be any shortage of food and other subsistences. The need for slower growth of population was already felt by many developing countries. But to what desirable size the family members can be limited cannot be enforced by any of these Governments. Or within how many years they can enforce a policy and implement it with people of a size of the family, is also not possible. Whether people of a country are ready to set up a most desirable size of the family or not, it is the responsibility and duty of the government to make the people know the consequences of the population growth when the national resources are limited and the production of food is just meeting the needs of the people and make them to realize that a desirable family size is a must, and towards achieving it they must cooperate with the Government in reducing the growth of the population. It is possible for the Governments to educate the people through suitable mass media and also to make wide publicity about the importance and necessity of controlling the size of the family and thereby reducing the population growth to the requirements of its national sources and production. There can be also certain incentives and rewards to motivate people to adopt small family size. But some of the developing countries, which are politically democratic, are depending upon the adult franchise, become nervous in enforcing any policy and implementing it against the wishes of the voters.

There are only few countries in the world which are having low birth rate and low death rate and their natural resources are also at fairly low level in agreement with their ability to provide the requirements for all the people of the country for a decent level of living. The government and the leaders of many countries of the world cannot give any assurance of their people's standard as equal to world's standard. They cannot predict how long the people of their country would adopt the birth control and at what rate the death rate would decline in the next few years. People cannot for long time adopt a restraint policy. They may change their attitudes any time either way. Therefore, some criterion must be used. According to Thompson and Lewis (1965), any world population policy first of all should be based upon certain primary objectives for the next few years like the reducing the rates of population growth in countries where there are high birth rates and falling of death rates. But unless there is an agreement among the people who have high birth rates without any difference of opinion it will not be possible to formulate a world population policy. As a result of it, Thompson and Lewis (1965) feel that a world population policy can never be effectively formulated and reduce the population growth and achieve the goals in the coming years.

National Population Policies

There are some nations who adopted population policies that are applicable to them. The necessity of a population policy for a nation depends upon the nation's population position and other conditions. The conditions are efficient health services, good educational system, and an efficient economy, a low birth rate and a low death rate. If these conditions prevailed in a country naturally, the question is whether such countries should have population policy. For example, Sweden was already in possession of efficient health services, and all other desirable facilities. But that did not mean that it should not have a population policy. The population was growing slowly and if the same situation continued it will result in any harmful consequences on the welfare of the people. The population growth did not have any effect on the economic growth of the country. The national economy was steadily increasing and it was providing a decent level of living to the people of the nation. The poor people in Sweden were having the family size above the average of the nation and therefore they could not provide for their families all the necessities under the existing conditions. They were not able to provide for themselves a decent level of living. Therefore the country should come for rescuing them to a certain limited level. If they maintain a desirable family size then their children may be much benefited and get better opportunities and may contribute their might to the development of the nation. Many families had more children than what was desired. Therefore every husband and wife had easy access to the information centre for reducing the size of the family. The people themselves should decide their size of the family and Government has not pressure on them. In Sweden two methods were adopted with the view of controlling the population growth. All couples were getting contraceptive information easily, and reproduction of mentally subnormal was strongly discouraged. The population policy of Sweden was with the view of improving the quality of population by not giving birth to subnormal children. Though a population policy at world level was not adopted, Sweden had its own population policy which was adopted by the people of the country.

National Population Policy of France

France was one of the Western European countries which was much affected by its population by wars. France is a republican country in Western Europe between the English Channel, the Mediterranean and the Atlantic. It is the largest country in the whole of Europe. France first became a republic in 1793 after the French Revolution and it became an empire in 1804 under Nepoleon, reverted to monarchy during 1815-1848, followed by the second republic during 1848-1852, again the second Empire during 1852-1870, then the third republic in 1890-1940 and fourth and fifth Republic in 1946 and 1958. All these changes, particularly the French Revolutions and the wars faught by Nepoleon reduced the population of France considerably. Also the Franco-Prussian war, fought during 1870-1871 between France and Prussia (the old Germany) resulted in the fall of France, the second empire, and the founding of the German empire. In this war France met with heavy loss of men. After this, France was very much worried over its slow growth of the population compared to other neighbouring countries. There was no natural growth after 1900 in France for few years. The World War I, brought great setback in its population as France had lost 2 million men in the War. Therefore population growth has become an important factor. A family policy was developing which resulted in the rise of three or four children in most of the families which induced a steady growth of population. This policy was adopted till the World War II. At this time France has increased its population at the rate of 6 per every one thousand per year.

Since France had some economic difficulties, slow increase of population was preferred for few years. After World War II France had stabilized her economic difficulties. Secondly the loss of men between 18 and 35 years in World War I also was stabilized by the end of World War II. But the growth of population after World War I was 18 per every one thousand per year as her military loss in World War I was much greater than World War II. The people's opinion also was in favour of increasing the average family size. Therefore the policy of France was increasing the numbers and the policy did not put any emphasis on improving the quality of the population through public health service, educational and recreational facilities. The population policy of France was accepted by the people and greater proportion of people voluntarily came forward to control the size of their families.

National Population Policy of Japan

Japan is an archipelago and an Empire in East Asia extending over 2000 miles between the sea of Japan and the Pacific ocean and consisting of the main islands and over 3000 smaller islands. Its feudalism was abolished in 1871 followed by industrialization and expansion of territories especially during World Wars I and II when most of South East Asia came under Japanese control. The dogma of the Emperor's divinity was abolished in 1946 under the new democratic constitution. Rapid economic growth has made Japan the most industrialised nation in the Far East. Japan, like the other western authoritarian countries wanted a rapid growth of population. The leaders of Japan believed that such growth would provide them strength to enlarge the Japanese empire and widen their territory where they can put more settlers under their control.

When Japan was engaged in the expansion of her territory with an ambition in building an empire, the birth control programme was stopped. Japan, had easily at a low cost was able to expand its territory and had sufficient lands and other natural resources and was able to support the rapidly increasing population. But her ambitions for expanding her territory and in building an empire in the east were not successful and were completely destroyed by her defeat in the World War II. The loss of war brought great economic difficulties for Japan. A large number of army men who were young joined their families and got married. There were also large number of repatriated young adults and also there was speedy demobilizations. As a result of these there was rapid increase of birth rate in Japan during the period 1946-1950 and the death rate was declined remarkably.

The rapid and sudden population growth and the decline of death rate raised the total population strength very much. Already Japan had economic difficulties and also the loss of colonies very much affected her trade and commerce and there was breakdown in her economic position. The problem of supporting millions of families was the pressing issue and the reduction of the family size was then adopted with all seriousness and all practical methods were followed. Japanese people were more cultured and they can easily understand the national problems and adopt any practical solutions. The cultivable lands remained the same. The death rate was increased. There were more deaths of infants and young children. Abortion as a method of birth control was practised nation wide and it was approved by the society. Within a short period, the balance between the increased population and food production and other subsistence was maintained. The other advantages Japan had in dealing with the population problem was that all Japanese speak one language and therefore they had no difficulty in communicating any solution to be urgently dealt with, unlike China and India where there are many languages, where national solidarity is difficult. Any idea to be propagated takes no time and brings no conflict and no differences of opinion among the people. Further the public health services in Japan were very much efficient and large number of experts in the field of medicine were available easily to the people of Japan. The Japanese, whether they have formulated a well defined population policy to be taken into consideration for world population policy or not, they had their own national policy which was now and then adopted to suit to the conditions and situations and in which they were successful.

10. NATIONAL POPULATION POLICY OF INDIA

It is estimated that approximately two-thirds of the people of the world population are living in developing countries and one-third of the people of the world population are willing to control their birth rates. These people can keep their numbers within limits of their ability to maintain balance between the population and production. But the problems in the developing countries are not realized in the real sense. Unlike Japan and other European countries, India is a nation of multiple of races, religions, cultures, languages, and communities and there are many diversity of views politically, socially, economically and communally. More than eighty per cent of the people are illiterates and poor, live under the poverty line. Any national problem to be communicated to the people of the nation and make them to understand is a very difficult task. The illiterate poor people in India mostly work in the fields or on daily wages. They do not eat nutritious food nor have any recreation. Therefore they find the procreation as a means of spending the time happily. They do not bother about pregnancy or number of children they are producing. The only reply to the miseries of a poor Indian citizen gives is that "God has given it. The one who has planted the tree will certainly give water to it." People have such faith in India and it is very difficult to dispel this type of faith associated with Almighty.

At present (1995) population of India is 92 crores. The first census of India was taken in 1872 during the time of the British rule. It was done with a view to get the correct picture of Indian population growth and the composition of the population. Then the birth rates and death rates were registered regularly by a Government department, from which it is possible to find out the population every year. India's population from 1872 to 1921 did not show considerable increase. India during this period had many miseries. There were shortages of food, violent attack of epidemic diseases, failure of monsoons, inadequate rains, unusual infectious diseases, and also famines, poverty and starvations—all contributed to the slow rise of population. There were positive checks on the population, in Malthus's sense, in India. The famines and the deaths were eliminated by supplying food materials through transportations which were improved for this purpose. Such improvements in agricultural cultivation were also made to meet the large demand of supply. The population increased considerably from 28 crores in 1931 to 44 crores in 1961. The rate of increase was 2 per cent. Then there was rapid increase in India's population. In 1971 it was 53 crores; in 1981, 70 crores; and in 1995 it was 92 crores. Such was the rapid increase of population in India. During Second World War the public health service was very much improved.

Pandit Jawaharlal Nehru, when he became the Prime Minister of India after India's independence in 1947 seriously felt that India was suffering from overpopulation and that birth control was seriously needed, if the death rate of the people was reduced and kept at low and a decent level of living was provided to the people of India. Therefore the Government of India had decided to promote family planning and birth control programmes as a part of her integrated plan of modernizing the Indian economy. Funds were allotted to implement the family planning programme in the first and second Five Year Plans.

The family planning and birth control movement in India became more progressively organized and the Family Planning Association of India was started in 1949. The Association convened the first All India Conference of Family Planning in 1951 under the presidentship of Prcfessor S. Chandrasekhar, and an International conference in Bombay was organized on Family Planning and Dr. S. Radhakrishnan, the Vice President of India inaugurated. Even before founding the Family Planning Association of India there were controversies over the birth control in India. Mahatma Gandhi accepted the family planning programme, but he did not accept the mode implementation of the programme by birth control or by abortions. He wrote with all seriousness in his journal *Young India* and *Harijan* about his views. He wrote in his *Young India* (1947) that it is our duty at the present moment to suspend bringing forth heirs to our slavery. According to him there cannot be two opinions about the necessity of birth control, but the method should be self control or Brahmacharya which was handed over from ages past. He has stated that it is inflexible sovereign remedy doing good to those who practice it. He was not convinced of the modern methods of contraception. He did not discuss it with anybody. He was so uncompromising in this issue that he did not agree with anybody. He suggested the method of avoidance of sexual union during unsafe periods and confining it to the safe period of about ten days during a month. Gandhi's birth control method was not given sufficient publicity either in India or in foreign countries. If sufficient publicity was given to his method, many European and Eastern countries also would have adopted it instead of contraceptive method.

The Indian National Congress, held in 1938, was presided by Subhas Chandra Bose. This session had given importance to the population problems. Subhas Chandra Bose (1947) in his presidential address had stated that where poverty, starvation and diseases are stalking the land we cannot afford to have our population mounting up by thirty millions during a single decade. Therefore it will be desirable to restrict our population until we are able to feed, clothe and educate those who exist already. In the same session, the National Planning Committee of the National Congress under the Chairmanship of Pandit Jawaharlal Nehru was constituted. The sub-committee presented its report on population in 1940 and several resolutions were adopted. One of the resolutions of the sub-committee (1947) was that the size of the Indian population is a basic issue in national economic planning, in so far as its unrestricted increase, out of proportion to means of subsistence, affects adversely the standard of living and tends to defeat many social and ameliorative measures and in the interest of social economy, family happiness and national planning, family planning and a limitation of children are essential. The State should adopt a policy to encourage these. It is desirable to stress on self-control as well as to spread knowledge of cheap and safe methods of birth control. Birth control clinics should be established and other necessary measures should be taken on this behalf and the harmful methods should be prevented.

The recommendations of the National Planning Committee of the National Congress were taken up for consideration in 1951 by the Indian Republic Government. The Government of India introduced the central planning for social and economic development. Population policy was the part of planning and it has passed through with the evaluation of the planning. The annual increase rate for 1951-1961 was 2.15 per cent whereas it was 1.25 per cent from 1941-1951. The First Five Year Plan was started in 1951 and a short amount of four crores were earmarked for encouraging family planning. In the Second Five Year Plan (1956) period (1957-1961) the allotment was raised to 24 crores. It was observed that a high rate of population growth is likely to affect adversely the rate of economic development and the living standards per capita. Taking into account the overall shortage of land and capital equipment relatively to population, the conclusion was that effective curb on population growth is an important one for rapid improvement in incomes and for the decent level of living. During the Third Five Year Plan period (1961) (1961-1966) it was observed that due to the improvement in conditions of health and sanitation, the death rate was lowered, particularly the infant mortality. The birth rate thereby increased. The Fourth Five Year Plan (1969) put more emphasis on limitation of family size, was an essential ingredient of development.

The overall execution of these programmes for controlling the rate of population growth was left with the responsibility of the Ministry of Health. The men in the Ministry of Health and Family Planning were with strong conviction, enthusiasm and devotion to the cause of family planning. In 1966 the Government of India had created a full fledged department, exclusively dealing with family planning headed by S. Chandrasekhar, an eminent demographer, as the Minister of State. Dr. S. Chandrasekhar had been studying the population problem from 1940 and was associated with the population problems for a long time. After seven years of study in U.S.A. in economics and demography returned to India in 1947 and joined Annamallai University as Professor of Economics. Then he went to UNESCO, Paris, for a short period as incharge of Demographic Research. Back to Annamallai in 1950 as Professor of Economics and started the Indian Institute of Population Studies and became the Director of the Institute. With his erudite scholarship background he became the Minister of State for Health and Family Planning.

During the First Five Year Plan the programme was mainly directed to create an active public opinion in favour of family planning. It was presenting the accurate picture of rapid increase of population, and making people to gain better understanding of fertility and the method of regulating it. By the end of the First Plan period there were about 126 clinics set up in urban areas and 20 in rural areas. During the Second Plan period the National Family Planning Programme has created a Family Planning Directorate under the Minister of Health, formed State Family Planning offices in various States. The programme consisted of four types of important activities. They were, (1) propagating knowledge about the need of practicing family planning and stressing on the use of contraceptive method, (2) opening family planning clinics and door-to-door field visits by health visitors, (3) distributing contraceptives in the fields, and (4) promoting sterilization with free facilities for operations and also cash rewards to meet the incidental expenses and loss of income.

The family planning clinics were increased considerably to 1435 and there were 1864 rural and 330 urban health centres specially for family planning. The statistics were going on increasing every year with regard to the number of cases of sterilization, number of vasectomy and tubectomy operations. The intensification of implementing the programme resulted in increasing the number of family planning centres. About ten thousand new centres were opened during the Third Plan period and the total centres were 11,474 at the end of the Plan period. During the end of this Plan period the Intra Uterine Device (IUD) was introduced as a method of birth control. The sterilization programme also received importance at this time. About fifteen lakhs of operations were made.

By the end of the Third Five Year Plan period the reorganization of administration set-up was completed. The family planning programme in the Fourth Plan period was intensified. This started functioning with much greater vigour. The Intra Uterine Device (IUD) which was emphasised in the early years has gain momentum in the Fourth Five Year Plan period. The procedure for proper pre-insertion education was checked up. The post-insertion and follow-up check-ups were strengthened. The propaganda had given better effect on this issue. The Fourth Five Year Plan's work toward the progress of the policy of controlling of the population growth was mainly to make the family planning programme a centrally sponsored one for a minimum period of ten years and the entire expenditure must be met by the Central Government. Further, the Ministry of Health and Family Planning also wanted to integrate the maternity and child welfare with family planning. A nutritional programme for mother and children for controlling of blindness caused by vitamin A deficiency was also implemented through Family Welfare Planning Centres. The draft plan (1969) for 1969-75 was also further materializing the programme to achieve the goals.

The Fifth Five Year Plan was drafted keeping in mind the aim of reducing the population growth at 32 for every one thousand by 1973-74. The targets for sterilization and for IUD insertion were also proposed. The other methods suggested and proposed to introduce during this period were oral contraception and injection. These methods were tried through medical and community welfare centres. The conventional contraceptive methods were also accelerated. This programme was implemented among 2.4 million persons in 1969-1970 and ten million persons in 1973-1974. Thus by 1973-74 about 28 million couples were prevented from giving birth to children. But during the plan period (1969) it was expected to avert only 18 million births. The implementation of the programme was very much successful with 28 millions.

But the claims of reduction in birth rates in certain areas cannot be accounted at national level. The Directorate of Central Family Planning Institute (1967) has reported a downward trend in certain areas. In Tamil Nadu, at the Athur block there was a decline of birth rate from 43.6 in 1959 to 36.3 in 1964. In East Bengal in 1959 the birth rate was 42, it was declined to 34 in 1965. A remarkable reduction has been reported from Tea plantations in Assam where the birth rate was declined from 44.3 in 1959 to 25.6 in 1967. In certain other areas also the birth rate was having a downward trend. In the implementation of the population policy in India, it is to be noted that the public opinion was very much favourable in limiting the population growth. The programme also wanted to involve the people nation wide with the help of the voluntary agencies. So, an appeal was made by a National Conference of Population Policy and Programmes (1969) and leaders of various sections had participated in the programme. All of them were asked to work for the social and economic betterment of the people at large.

Therefore in conclusion, we may state that since population problem is a world problem, no nation can be disinterested in studying it nor can show utter indifference to it stating that there is no such problem in their nations. Though Marx's population theory rejected it, later on after enduring the miseries of positive checks like, the famine and starvation, Soviet Russia has accepted it. Therefore a universal policy that can be agreeable to the nations of the world was felt. Towards evolving a universal population policy every nation had its own limitations on the basis of race, religion, nationality, community, customs and traditions. Therefore every nation had evolved its own population policy and methods agreeable to their people. France and Japan had evolved progressive policies. Similarly other nations and India also had her own population policy and programmes for reducing the growth of population. Dr. Chandrasekhar, an eminent demographer, has played an important role in this.

11. PSYCHOLOGICAL ANALYSIS OF INDIA'S FAMILY PLANNING PROGRAMMES

Evolving Family Planning Programmes

If the population problems were recognized, then the immediate practical response or programme would be the formation of family planning programme and implementing it. In the past few years there has been significant increase of interest and activities in the family planning programmes sponsored by Governments of various countries. In some countries, formerly family planning has been of private concern and of voluntary groups. Then the programme has gone rapidly into the public domain with increasing awareness of the socio-economic involvement of population growth with birth control programme. It was very sensitive matter for the people and for the nation. At present, Nortman (1969) states that there are about forty developing countries where family planning programmes are being implemented as Government sponsored programmes. Even in highly industrialized countries like the United States there is greater amount of Government participation in the family planning programme.

As a part of public health service some psychologists have involved themselves in the family planning programmes. Berelson (1969a) has given the course of events in the development of a public family planning programme in the United States. The pressure for family planning policy originates in the planning boards, generally in the development programmes when the demographers and economists come and pay serious attention on current rate of population growth. In some countries the family planning programme originates in medical fields since the medical men show interest in high incidence of induced abortions. The ground for the family planning programme should be prepared by some local experts and it should be recognized by other experts and the experts in the related fields. Then some experts should review the population situation and make recommendation which then call for the adoption of a family planning policy. Though the policy is declared, it may remain without any action, as at some high level politically based review and acceptance should be sought.

When all these efforts are taken at various levels it will be placed under the medical care. The programme is left under the responsibility of the Ministry of Health and considered as one of the programmes of maternai and child care services and health centres. Then a medical man with some experience in public health becomes the director of the programme. The medical man treats the family planning programme as another health service to be looked upon along with the existing services. This is how in any country the family planning programme being brought into a service programme. In India also the same type of procedure was followed, but the policy was originated at political level.

The National Planning Committee of the National Congress under the presidentship of Pandit Jawaharlal Nehru was entrusted with the task of studying the population problem and present its recommendations to the National Congress. It was first mooted out by Subhas Chandra Bose at the National Congress Session (1947) held in 1938 under his presidentship. When India attained its independence in 1947 the matter was taken into consideration. Pandit Jawaharlal Nehru on becoming the Prime Minister of India expressed his anxiety of the population problem. These were the grounds for the origin of India's population policy and the formation of family planning programmes.

We need not go into the demographic data and information to deal with the family planning programme. But we cannot also deny that the demographic data have provided the source of information for evolving a population policy for India and to formulate the family planning programme. But the Government of India was giving continued support for the Demographic Research ever since the First Five Year Plan from 1951. In 1966 a separate Department of Family Planning was started in the Ministry of Health. The significant development in the field of demographic research and in population policy was the incorporation of Dr. S. Chandrasekhar in 1967 as the Minister of Health and Family Planning of the Government of India. Dr. Chandrasekhar has been constantly and very enthusiastically advocating for a national population policy and for starting a family planning programme for more than twenty years since 1947. Dr. Chandrasekhar (1942, 1943a, 1943) was vigorously expressing his deep concern over India's population growth rate, his concern was as a scholar, as demographer and as the citizen of India. Once Dr. Chandrasekhar (1946) has said that the air is today thick with shouts of planning. Blue prints and plans galore are offered for present post-war agricultural planning, industrial planning, educational planning and so on. While planning all these fields relevant and necessary, there has been no talk of specific population planning. He gave the outline of population policy for India.

The first All India Conference on Family Planning was held in 1951 under the leadership of Lady Rama Rao and Dr. Chandrasekhar inaugurated the Conference. His address later on was published under the title of *'Demographic Documentation of India'*. Dr. Chandrasekhar (1952) made another important contribution in 1952 under the title of *'Hungry People and Empty Lands'*. This was dealing with population problem and international tensions. He stressed in this more on family planning. According to him family planning is easier. The more backward a nation in economy and more pressing the need for birth control, the greater the cultural and material obstacles in the path of this reform. He states that one should be reminded of the miserable and gloomy fact that the issue of birth control was the only one in which the Vatican (the Pope) and the Kremlin (the Russian leaders) were in an agreement.

Subsequently Dr. Chandrasekhar (1967) brought out another work on population problem, *'Asia's Population Problem'*. He made certain interesting observations and soon after this he became the Minister of Health and Family Planning. He has stated that a Population Ministry could train a large group of dedicated men and women to go into the rural areas, change their under privileged fellow citizens to the philosophy of small families if with sufficient funds were at its disposal. There may be resistance to change which is universal, but there are methods by which it can be found to overcome. With all the resources and vehement attacks on the population problem to make a reduction in the birth rate no commendable change has taken place in the population in the early period of Family Planning Programme in India. The United Nations Advisory Mission has pointed out in its report. The report (1969) was with regard to the lack of communication and motivational processes in the early years of the Programme. Then Dr. Chandrasekhar took charge of the portfolio of the Minister of Health and Family Planning. Soon, new programmes were enunciated.

Dr. Chandrasekhar is a prolific writer. He has written quite a number of books on population problems. Many of his articles, published in periodicals and journals in India and abroad, attracted great many young Indians and foreigners to study his books and articles and some of them even started studying demography. His article, 'Why are Indians Poor?—Populations and Poverty', published in 1942 in *'Asia'*, written when he was in New York.

Dr. Chandrasekhar has been one of the greatest orator of his time. He has the capacity to keep the audience absorbed in his lectures. Any one who had the chance of hearing him deliver a full length speech on a platform can never forget the experience. His oratory had a charm and appeal that makes the listeners spell-bound, moved and persuaded. He never hesitated to make use of his oratorial talent to explain the miseries of population explosion. Once Mrs. Lakshmi Menon (1951) then Deputy Minister for External Affairs of Government of India was a delegate to the First All India Conference on Population and Family Planning under the Presidentship of Dr. S. Chandrasekhar held in Bombay in 1951, has paid an encomium on his oration. She has stated that the presidential address of Dr. Chandrasekhar was delivered extempore, at a speed which was terrific and with a remarkable facility of language and extraordinary force which reminded one of the torrential eloquence of M. Anderi Vyshinsky (Russian representative in U.N.). She said that she had no hesitation in extolling the superb facility with which the young Professor spoke and swayed the audience.

Another encomium paid by Taurus (1951) a Journalist of Free Press under the caption, 'In a China Shop'. It was the conference lecture delivered by Dr. Chandrasekhar on population and Family Planning. Dr. Chandrasekhar's presidential address consisted of forty printed pages. He abandoned his prepared speech but poured out such a torrent of words at breath-taking speed and extempore that the reporter's finger involuntarily touched his nose in genuine surprise. Dr. Chandrasekhar is a powerful orator and his words came rushing out in colossal rapidly dumb founding perfection in phraseology. He reduced the forty page speech in a forty minutes oration and left the news men gaping open mouthed at his amazing performance.

Dr. Chandrasekhar was often invited to address conferences, seminars, universities and many academic bodies from more than ninety countries in the world. Dr. Chandrasekhar was one of the few Indians invited by Communist China and Soviet Union. The Russians and Chinese have attended his lectures with great interest though they disagreed his basic idea of his theory.

Dr. Chandrasekhar, as a Minister of Health and Family Planning has brought out many changes to give a new life to the Family Planning Programmes of Indian Government. The population explosion is the most serious problem India facing today. But there were no so much political and national commitments on this problem. Yet many thoughtful citizens of the nation become aware of the much disturbing characteristics of India's population growth, taking into consideration the overall India's economic development. He has been pointing out

India's population problem and the urgent necessity of family planning and birth control with all courage and conviction with an anxiety of rescuing India from the disastrous consequences to be caused by the population explosion for more than twenty-five years. He stated that India is a developing country which covers 2.4 per cent of the area of the world's land, but India has to feed fourteen per cent of the world's population with a world's total income of only 1.5 per cent. Therefore the only way that India can reduce the widening gap between the population growth and the agricultural and industrial production and other subsistences is to adopt the family planning and birth control programmes and reduce the population and to take revolutionary steps to increase the agricultural products. The Family Planning Programme should be implemented intensively on an *en masse* scale level. The population problem is a serious and formidable one and it needs urgent attention.

The democratic positive population policy for the first time was formulated by Dr. S. Chandrasekhar at the highest Government level and also the ways and means to implement the policy. Under his quick guidance the programmes gained rapid momentum and soon encompassed the entire country. Dr. Chandrasekhar has launched a massive campaign with the missionary zeal and as dedicated crusader to make every ordinary citizen of India to be aware of the value and desirability of a small family. He was of the view that once the desire was created and the value was understood, it would be easy to make them to accept the contraceptive methods Further, he also took care to see that the contraceptive services were provided them through the community health centres and at the clinical centres near their homes.

Of the number of steps Dr. Chandrasekhar has taken at various levels, a few of them received special attention and importance. The first of which may be stated as the *mass communication programme*. The second has been the *'cafeteria' or self service approach* about the contraceptive methods and the third has been *roping or fastening* into the Family Planning Programme the groups and organizations which were apathetic and hostile to family planning. These efforts were implemented with all seriousness and enthusiasm.

In spreading out the message of the Family Planning to the most remote places of the country the services of every means of art and science of mass media and advertisement techniques were used. For example, posters, bill boards, big banners, cinema slides, sound tracks, radio broadcastings, short films, public announcements, popular entertainments, dramas, advertisements in newspapers were used to publicise the Family Planning. The elephants also were used in the publicity. The symbol of the programme was designed, the design of *inverted red triangle*. This is made known every where as the symbol of Family Planning (1970). This was how the climate was created to make people of the country to know the programme.

The acceptance of the family planning was considered as the socio-economic instrument for maintaining the welfare and happiness of the people. The next step was organizing clinical services at the door steps of the people. Since India is consisting of people of hetrogeneous cultures and traditions couples have different opinions, different levels of motivation and religious cannotations, it was felt that it was necessary to provide all contraceptive methods scientifically suitable and approved, socially and culturally accepted, including the oral pill and injection. Dr. Chandrasekhar has stated that his approach is *cafeteria approach*, which he considered as the best course as the aim of the programme has been not applying any particular method, but how fast the birth rate could be reduced. Therefore these services included sterilization, vasectomy, tubectomy, the loop, the oral pill, injection and condom. The post conception abortion also was recommended.

Formerly, before Dr. Chandrasekhar taking over the task, at Government there were only name sake services and works were entrusted with the medical people. Dr. Chandrasekhar wanted to make it a people's programme and he sought the cooperation of all party people to make the family planning successful. He appealed through Parliament and through letters to enlist the support and services of the large influential groups and private practitioners who were working mainly in rural areas. Dr. Chandrasekhar has attempted a very big triumph of associating various types of professionals and people like the indigenous medical practitioners, Ayurvedic, Siddha, Unani and also homeopathy, various women organizations, trained social workers, the Christian missionaries—the Catholic and Protestants missionary hospitals and doctors, business men, industrial executives who care for industrial labourers, the Sarvodaya workers under the leadership of Jayaprakash Narayan, the Orthodox Muslims and their leaders, the Imams, the army and civil servants of all ranks in all Government Departments, the various religious sects of the Hindus, Panchayat Raj and other rural elected agencies, municipalities, local Government bodies, the Young Men and Young Women Christian Association,

Rotarians, the Lions and other service organizations and other groups. Dr. Chandrasekhar (1968) spoke about the population problems and the family planning among the countless groups of people, addressed meetings relentlessly all over the country for several years for obtaining strong national support from all sections of the people. He is a man of very rare species. Dr. Chandrasekhar (1970) has raised his louder voice of service for the nation continuously and consistently with all zeal and zest, and with dauntless devotion for twenty-five years on the population problems of his nation. But it was very unfortunate that his relentless services were not adequately recognized and rewarded. Whereas his services were recognized in the foreign countries and he was rewarded.

Methods of Family Planning

While discussing about India's Family Planning Programmes we have also discussed certain methods of family planning. Generally, family planning may be defined as the process of controlling of the number of children in a family and of the increased intervals between two children by the use of contraceptive method. Mainly, family planning refers to limiting of the number of children by a couple. The limiting children in the family also means reducing the size of the family or maintaining a small family size. Small family size can be maintained in various ways. Several methods are adopted for this. There are certain artificial methods used to prevent pregnancy or conception. This is generally called contraceptive method. This method is useful for controlling births.

Contraceptive Method

Psychological studies of certain specific methods have been mainly concerned with contraception, serilization and abortion as the part of large research programme on population psychology. Contraception is a method used to prevent conception or pregnancy by artificial means. It is referring to tending to prevent impregnation' or pregnancy. It is medically approved and found to be no harmful. Contraceptive methods are offered free of charge on voluntary basis. It is recognized that the method of contraception used by most of the people are having low birth rates. Therefore, it is more practicable to use in developing countries. To make it acceptable the practice of contraception, the new improved methods must be made known. The new contraceptive methods are very cheap, highly effective, very easy to use, not having any side effects, they are also usable under any living conditions. The two new developments in contraceptive methods are, one is the pill or oral contraception and the other is 'intra uterine coil spring' device (IUD).

The oral contraception has received increasing attention for psychological research in recent years. It is because of the mood and behavioural changes that are associated with hormonal medications. Glick (1967) has reviewed such studies. The pill is given for women. The pill prevents pregnancy by keeping the ovum from getting maturity. Therefore there cannot be any impregnation. If the pill is taken for twenty days continuously there is tremendous effect. The pill should be started taking for a few days, say, 4 or 5 days after menstruation and should be continued for few days, 4 or 5 days, before the menstruation. In between there are twenty days. The pill is entirely free from any side effect. It costs very low and everybody in developing country like India can take it regularly. It is also possible that the number of pills required for a month can be reduced.

There is also pill for men. Now, the pill is developed. This pill is taken by men once in a month. The pill is very effective in men. It makes the sperm cell incapable of fertilizing the female cells, the ovum. Pohlman (1969) has reviewed studies on psychological aspects of all methods of birth control. Many studies according to him were focussed on resistance to contraception. This was very much useful, because attention was directed on individual perception, attitudes and motivations.

Many of the psychological studies on contraception were made by psychoanalysts. They were mainly interested in the sexual symbolic results of the use of the contraceptives and the unconscious motivation for child bearing and its avoidance. A reference to the use of contraception was also found in Freud's writings. Freud (1893, 1894, 1898), in some of his early writings on neuroses, had stated that coitus interruption was a significant factor in the development of neurasthenia and anxiety neurosis and also stated that the use of condom was not a method of fulfilling the needs. He states that by harmful means of controlling conception, society is doomed and fall victim to incurable neuroses. The method reduces the enjoyment of life to a minimum and it destroys the marriage relation, and brings ruins to the coming generation.

The psychoanalytic studies on contraception provide some valuable insight, into the emotional factors related to the use of contraception. The reports are based upon a small number of cases who were under psychiatric care. But psychoanalytic reports of research had no doubt that contraception had emotional significance for some people. Devereaux (1965) had given prominence in his study to the unconscious meaning of contraception. Lehfeldt (1965) has discussed a study of wilful exposure to unwanted pregnancy in relation to the practice of contraception. There are some medical-psychiatric studies based upon case studies. Zell and Crisp (1964) have conducted a study on the effects of oral contraceptives. The study was made by interviews with private patients. They state that fears were experienced by the patients in using the new method. They concluded with an important result that the use of oral contraception was an improvement in sexual adjustment. The effects of oral contraception were studied by Bakker and Dightman (1964) by rigorous psychometric methods on women who were using the pills and also their husbands. A follow-up study was made for two years. They were rated on two variables. One was the occurrence of forgetting the pills and the other was the presence and the type of somatic complaints. The researchers have stated that the pill forgetters were immature women who avoided responsibilities.

The other development, is the intrauterine (IUD) coil spring, used as a contraceptive device. This is manufactured from plastic material in desired shape. It also costs very little. It is more acceptable for women than taking the pills. But it needs certain skill to place it in the correct place. The device can be left for few months in body. This device was introduced in India in 1965. This is the remarkable year in the history of family planning work in India. The intrauterine coil spring device was set in operation as a mass force throughout India. In this year the monthly insertion by the device was increased to the maximum and the Inter-State competition became very keen to win the award. Even within the state, every district workers in the field of family planning put strenuous efforts to make their district to be on the top in using the device. This revolutionary device (IUD) is also a new discovery in the medical field. This has come as the most wanted and satisfactory device to all the workers in the field of family planning and also those who were in the technical and administrative side. The personnel of the family planning department were preaching with all confidence that, here was the device most effective and successful in preventing pregnancy about ninety-nine per cent to those who use it.

It is a suitable method for the very big mass of the Indian people who live with limited facilities.

This device of intrauterine coil spring (IUD) was first introduced in 1964 at the Family Planning Training and Research Centres as the clinical trials. This was performed under the care of the Indian Council of Medical Research. This was supplied to couples along with other methods used for limiting and spacing pregnancy. During the four years period (1964-1968) there were cases who changed over to intrauterine (IUD) from other methods. During the period, Demerath (1967) states that about two thousand women resorted to IUD method. Many white collar couples who have taken advice from family planning training centres had the insertion of lippes loops. Of which more than ninety per cent were between the age group of 20 and 34 years. Of which about eight per cent had four pregnancies and about forty-five per cent of them had one or two pregnancies. Those who had the insertion of lippes loops were mostly younger age group of women. The higher age groups were encouraged for sterilization. Few of the women who were given loops had no living boys and four had no living girls.

Since there were complaints that the intrauterine was causing some bleeding, pain, backache and discomfort for the husband, the IUD for medical reasons was removed. There were also complaints that certain women experienced abdominal pain and some had irregular extra bleeding. There were also few cases that inspite of the IUD insertion, incidences of pregnancies happened. Many of the couples might have had abortion. Therefore, they were advised to use some other method of fertility control than the intrauterine device.

Sterilization

According to Tietize's (1965) study, psychological studies have paid more attention on sterilization and abortion. He states that out of 97 studies classified as psychological and psychiatric, 64 focussed on sterilization or on abortion. Sterilization and abortion have drawn the attention of psychologists more than other aspects because of the potential psychiatric effect in the individual when these procedures were carried out. This is one of the methods used for family planning. By this method one is made infertile to produce children. It is mainly applicable to men. It is a medical device and only a medical man can do this small operation. Sterilization is also made for women. Sterilization as a device of birth control was carried out since 1956 in some of the states in India. But the Government of India had given its approval only in 1959 officially. An intensive device of vasectomy operations were carried out from 1956. The Public Health Department People at all levels were made to cooperate and participate in this effort. This programme was accompanied by payment of money to each person who had underwent this operation. The incentive has increased the number of cases all over the country. All the District Medical Officers and their staffs were also involved in this apart from private practitioners. The National Family Planning Programme of India has fixed family planning programmes which were guided and administered by the suggestion of the Central Government, based upon the grant-in-aid funds available for this propose. But the programmes were constantly changing time to time and growing fast.

The effects of sterilization was studied by Bakker and Dightman (1964) by psychometric methods. Studies have been conducted on men after having vasectomy ranging from 1 to 5 years by Ferber, Tieze and Lewit (1967). Interviews were conducted with a carefully prepared questionnaire. Analyses of the responses showed a highly favourable sexual and psychosocial adjustment to the operation.

Men who went for sterilization were having a high fertility rate. The normal age for fertility has been taken into account for men when they went for sterilization. The pregnancy interval was expected to be three years or 36 months.

Abortion

Abortion is a social revolution that is practised all over the world. It is a means of birth control. It is practised by the people of a nation to make the population proportional to the production and other subsistences. Abortion is a procedure practised by the women of a country to terminate pregnancy before the child gets full development into a child. Abortion is also a way of giving up the unwanted child after pregnancy. The inherent capacity of lawful abortion as a population control has been demonstrated in some of the Eastern European countries and in Japan. These countries have also brought out legislations to legalize abortions. Abortion is a post-conception measure and therefore it does not require a woman or her spouse to exercise planning and foresee to control births. There is some psychological significance in this. Having conceived a child and accepting to disown and stop its birth by both husband and wife is a psycho-social revolution. Abortion as practised at present time is simple technically, and safe method to practice. But it is to be done with the consultation of an experienced physician and it is partially a surgical operation or procedure.

Abortion can be also practised by taking up post-conception-pill or injection. These two procedures are now available. New birth control methods have been devised with much greater effectiveness and they are also acceptable. By these means the birth rates can be changed more quickly in response to changes in attitudes and values in relation to the size of the family. Lehfeldt (1965) was of the view that abortion is a wilfull exposure to an unwanted pregnancy. In any population, abortion is still a significant factor in determining the birth rate. In medical language abortion includes spontaneous miscarriage as well as induced abortion or removal. Sometimes, it is also observed in some women that abortion is taking place spontaneously without any wilfull action or effort. Formerly, before the emergence of population problem and evolving methods of reducing population, the spontaneous abortion was called, the 'abortion' in real sense. The induced abortion is only eliminating the unwanted child or pregnancy. Wiehl (1938) has reviewed the abortion cases in the United States in 1938. He observed that in the total number of pregnancies, about fifteen per cent of pregnancies were terminated in abortions. Out of these fifteen per cent two-thirds were spontaneous abortions and only one-third were induced abortions.

Taussing (1944) states that in induced abortions there were much wide variations in different countries. Even in the United States, according to Taussing out of one-third of the induced abortions, half of them were illegal, while some were therapeutic cases. The therapeutic abortions were normally performed when the life of the mother was at danger. These things have little effect on the size of the population. In such cases, one life is saved, while the other life is lost. There is no gain or loss or change. In the illegal and spontaneous abortions there is direct wastage of pregnancy. This reduces the birth rates, but in some cases it affects the health of the women badly. Since the contraceptive methods are acceptable by the couples and they adopt some method, abortions are becoming less and less and rare. If the contraceptive methods are sincerely adopted and successful there is no chance for any abortion.

Due to improper use of contraceptive methods, or adopting them carelessly there are chances for pregnancy. Further, the sexual union is a feeling aspect and when one is highly aroused with a strong motive for sexual union he or she does not bother about contraceptive method of pregnancy. Further, now-a-days there are more premarital pregnancies in India due to promiscuous relation among young men and women. They could not resist their temptations for sexual union. Once they became victims, to the temptations they cannot stop it after wards. Without any conscious attempt to have child, the young girl becomes pregnant and she seeks some secret and illegal ways and means to get rid of her pregnancy. They were mostly tempted by the motion pictures and television dramas which display mainly the premarital promiscuous relations and the rock music and dance which corrupt the minds of young men and women mostly and they easily go astray. If a statistics is taken about the secret and illegal abortions that are taking place among the present generation of adolescent girls or young adult females from the private practitioners, the numbers certainly would be alarming. Parents are helpless against the dirty tricks they play to get access into such illicit sexual union. There were quite a large number of cases referred to the counselling centre of the author in 1980s. More than 70 per cent of the girls were adolescents and only 30 per cent were above 20 years of age, studying in various courses like nursing, dental, medicine, agriculture and engineering. There were no cases from students studying in Arts and Science courses. While analysing the causes of such incidents, it was found that in these courses the boys and girls were freely mixing among themselves and have free access to each other living places, they were often having private meetings, going for picnics and pleasure trips and so on. All these activities make them emotionally restless and often tempted to be in the company of the other sex. These were the reasons for their premarital pregnancies and seeking for secret and illegal abortions. It was also noted that there were more than one abortion in the case of some girls. These abortions have nothing to do with national policy of reducing the population growth by the method of abortion.

By the way of summarising the whole, the Government of India on recognizing the population problems had evolved a population policy quite suitable for the people of India on the basis of population theories and formulated programmes for controlling the high fertility rates. The programmes included family planning and birth control. India before implementing these programmes made a nation-wide publicity and brought an awareness in the minds of the people that these programmes were inevitable for the nation and also collected support through all mass media of communication. The aim was to maintain a small family size. Several methods were suggested to prevent pregnancy. Contraception is a method by which pregnancy can be controlled artificially. The methods include sterilization, oral contraception, intrauterine device (IUD) and the use of condom. In case of high fertility, sterilization for men was suggested. The pill was found to be successful for both males and females. Abortion as a means of birth control was also practised. It was a way of giving up an unwanted child on becoming pregnant. The Government of India had encouraged people in all possible ways to maintain a small family size.

12. CONCLUSIONS AND SUGGESTIONS

However effectively the family planning programme is explained, and propagated, since most of the people in India are illiterates and poor, they do not stick to the principles for long time. The family planning or birth control is rooted in sexual union. However one controls his/her desires for the sexual union with the opposite sex, instances may be occurring in their life, which cannot be avoided by them even though the family planning is remembered. The chances for avoiding sexual union in the past were more. For example, forty or fifty years ago the Indian families were joint families, each and every member would have been engaged in some kind of work to earn their living. Therefore, they will be away for most of the hours during day time and may not be having more chances for sexual union with the spouse. Further there were no stimulations outside to arouse sexual desires. Therefore the fertility rate was low. But now inspite of knowing the miseries of the population growth and the necessities of family planning, fertility rate is increasing considerably. The reasons are rooted in the scientific development of the mass media of communication. The mass media of communication are like the double edged swords either side can be used.

Generally, the newspapers, weeklies, monthlies and other periodicals carry more pages relating to sex oriented pictures, stories, advertisements. The sex oriented pictures are printed in very attractive multi-colours with more obscene or naked poses. The film world magazines are full of such pictures which corrupt the modesty of young men and women and they become manic in seeing such pictures. The motion picture world has already lost its balance and has become fully a sex perverted field with poor artistic imagination and producing meaningless noise on the name of rock music. The more close body attachment roles, the tribal type of dances in half naked dresses, the meaningless chord music—all have demoralizing effect on young men and women and they are made to think all the times that only sex is real life and they all go in for premarital and promiscuous sexual activities. All these, result in very early marriage and ends in producing three or four children before they reach thirty years. Further production of children is not ruled out.

The present television programmes are also full of vulgar sex jokes which have only demoralizing effect on young men and women. Many wanted to become cine or television stars by resorting themselves to promiscuous way of life. This promiscuous way of life soon converts one as sex starving and makes him/her sex perverted. The normal way of life becomes thoroughly bitter and anything that is sex oriented and show off attracts him/her and he/she fails to maintain the normal way of life, not able to adjust with others and ultimately begins to lead the hippi-like life. In this way the modern mass media of communication at present are misused on the name of entertainment. Generally the youth of the nation are misled, corrupted and demoralized at present by the mass media of communication. Persons who are honestly interested in the future course of the nation should come forward to curb all these unethical and uncultured way of life. This type of life has mostly developed only during the course of ten to fifteen years time.

Since there are very early marriages in rural and urban areas at present and as they are likely to procreate two or three children by the time they become twenty-five years, it is time for all marriages should be registered, indicating the age. If a statistics is taken regarding the early marriages, beginning with 1980 and ending with 1995 for a period of fifteen years and how many children these married couple have produced, it will be known that how the national policy is thoroughly disregarded, and how we are increasing the unhealthy citizens in our nation. India's Family Planning and birth control programmes are not only intended to reduce the number or the population growth, but it is also meant for mentally and physically healthy citizens. The Governments both at the Centre and the State levels are very much worried over the number of deformed, handicapped, mentally retarded children increasing year by year. The institutions for mentally and physically handicapped were increasing in our nation day by day. Why this kind of pathological conditions which did not exist thirty to forty years ago. How so many physically and mentally handicapped children were born during the course of fifteen or twenty years? Though the correct answer can be given only after an investigation into this phenomenon, the apperant causes are quite clear. People thoroughly neglected the national policy of the country regarding the Family Planning and birth control and the marriageable age. Mahatma Gandhi (1947), the father of the nation stressed these two points as early as 1925, the early marriages should be abolished and avoiding sexual union during unsafe periods, confining to the safe period of about ten days during a month.

It is to be noted here that the ancient Greeks, Spartans, Romans, the Egyptians, and the Babylonians strongly stressed the birth of healthy children, to make them great warriors with strong and tough body built. They did not protect the sick or deformed children as they were the liability of the nation. Why do you produce such children and create miseries for yourself and to the nation? Japan had indirectly done away this without any publicity. The deformed, physically and mentally handicapped and diseased persons whose disease like leprosy which cannot be cured were all utilized in World War II and they were all disposed of with the view of building up a nation of healthy, strong and tough citizens. Now they have mentally physically strong and tough people. Still it is not too late for India to strictly enforce the Family Planning and Birth Control programmes and to increase the marriageable ages for both men and women and get all the marriages registered in a Government Office. If this is followed strictly for about twenty years then India will see only healthy, tough and strong citizens without any deformed or handicapped persons. Just like what Mahatma Gandhi (1947) said, let us not bring forth heirs for our slavery and poverty, let us state, let us not bring forth heirs for our poverty and illiteracy, and let us not bring forth increased heirs for the deformed and mentally and physically handicapped citizens of our nation, and let us not bring forth increased heirs for our sex perverts and lazy cine fans through motion pictures in our nation. What had been conceived and implemented by the ancient Greeks, Spartans, Romans, Egyptians and the Babylonians two thousand five hundred years ago is not yet conceived by us even in two thousand A.D. Unless the Indian leaders develop progressive thinking in the case of population problems, all her scientific technological and industrial developments would be a gross waste as they are not going to meet the pressure that the population growth is going to exert on the nation within few years.

Malthus, the father of population studies as early as 1798 had suggested to postpone the marriage for few years both in the case of men and women if the nation really interested in solving the population problems. According to him, it is very simple and easy process, any one can carry out without the help of others. When Dr. S. Chandrasekhar formulated India's population policy and family planning programme, he did not include it in his thesis. The reason might have been that he sought the help and cooperation of all sections of the country's population. The powerful section of the nation's population is the political leaders who always depend upon the adult franchise for their existence. There might have put forth strong protest for this. The Government just only state that the marriageable age for a girl is twenty-one. But how many in the country follow this. Whether this is followed or not, who is checking? Unless all marriages are registered it will not be possible to know at what age a girl or boy gets married. The Government fixed the age for girls twenty-one years for marriage. But in practice at twenty-one the girl might have given birth to two or three children. Many girls get married from the age of 14 years to 18 years of age.

On 7th August 1995 the Maharashtra Government had passed a resolution that persons who are having more than two children are not qualified to contest in local board elections. This is a bold attempt, tried by the Maharashtra Government to make every one to realize that to have more than two children is not desirable. Since this is the beginning venture of the Government with regard to the population problems, they may bring forth still progressive resolutions in the State Assembly. It is a guideline for other State Governments to think of the population growth in their States. There should be also rewarding and punitive methods with regard to the adoption of the Family Planning Programme. Those who are having one child and those who are having no children should be given some rewards and recognized their national feeling or their patriotism. Those who are having more than two children on the basis of increasing numbers should be penalized or taxed on each extra child born and should be considered as unpatriotic citizen. Couples who give birth to deformed or handicapped children should be made to stop further reproduction as their heirs are becoming liability on the parents and on the nation. Such births should be discouraged in the interest of the nation. A leading critic of populations studies, Davis (1967) has advocated measures such as tax and welfare incentives and penalties, providing alternative roles for women and legislation or other actions for fixing the age of marriage at a higher level.

The recommendations of Davis to solve the population problems appear to be little rigid for a democratic country like India. Since this is a very sensitive issue, whichever political party capture power and form Government in India, they would not be inclined to adopt measures like, tax and penalties, unless they are very progressive and radical in their views. But measures of welfare incentives, diverting the females' attention to different roles do not involve any problems in implementing them. The higher age level of marriage is not a new idea, Malthus himself had suggested it two hundred years ago, but a constitution for this depends upon the willingness of the people to accept it and the positive decision taken by the Government. People must be made to involve in problem situations to understand the consequences of it.

While the Government of India was vigorously advocating the family planning programme with the aim of controlling the rapid growth population, having Dr. Chandrasekhar, an eminent demographer, as the Minister for Health and Family Planning, the activities relating to family planning and birth control were going on with all zeal and zest. It was highly exciting to see that there were frequent meetings, seminars, conferences, and publishing pamphlets, books and journals on the problems of population and also providing the ways and means to solve the problems. But in 1990s there is no any sign of talk about population problems and controlling the rapid growth of population. The Government of India seem to have totally disregarded the issue and also they have changed the name of the Department, as Health and Family Welfare. The easiest way of controlling the rapid growth of population is to introduce a legislation regarding the age of marriage and registration of all marriages in the registration office, which would solve the problem without much effort.

The methods of family planning and birth control, discussed in the preceding pages, need a permanent department in the Government for carrying out a regular work in the respective area. All categories of medical people, the community health centres and other organizations should be involved in the task, and collecting statistics and so on. A separate establishment is also necessary. Further, the progress of the work also must be evaluated now and then, periodically. The effects of contraceptive methods need to be checked. The sterilization has to be performed by an experienced physician. This makes a male infertile. At what age this has to be done? It has to be done at a high fertility age or it must be after giving birth to one or two children. But there were instances reported in the newspapers that unmarried youngmen were also sterilized by some physicians. The other contraceptive methods are vasectomy, tubectomy, oral contraception—taking pill, conventional birth control method of using the condom. All these methods are intended for stopping the pregnancy.

Of all these methods, sterilization alone can stop fertility in males permanently. The other methods are only temporary devices. Persons who have taken vasectomy were found to be fertilizing the ovum. Similarly females who underwent tubectomy, also become pregnant. Therefore these methods are not permanent solution to stop pregnancy. The oral contraception, taking the pill is said to be reliable and also very effective. By taking the pill the male sperm cell becomes incapable of fertilizing the female cell, the ovum. But there is every likelihood of forgetting to take the pill at the time of sexual union, as it is to be taken once in a month. In the case of females the pill has to be taken five days before and five days after every menstruation. Regarding the use of intrauterine coil spring device and the lippes loops, there are certain complaints of bleeding, pain, backache, discomfort for the husbands and therefore they were removed for medical reasons.

The non-contraceptive method is abortion, which is a post-conception device. Generally people hesitate to eliminate the pregnancy for religious or cultural reasons. Sometimes it may cause danger to the mother. Since sex is highly exciting feeling aspect of humans, the use of condom is not many times successful. If people sincerely carry out any one of these methods with all seriousness, then it is good. Otherwise there is no use of trusting these methods.

The one simple and easiest method, suggested is the age of marriage, that can be carried out and, it is also within the control of every human being. The Government has already made an announcement that the marriageable age of a female is twenty-one years. If this is carried out sincerely by all people living in rural and urban areas and getting the marriage registered in an office, producing the certificate of age of male and female, it would solve the population problem of India. Indian females particularly the rural females before attaining the age of twenty-one give birth to two or three children. These two or three children in each family can be controlled by sticking to the increased marriageable age.

Unless men, in power in India, think every national problem progressively with courage and conviction, no national problem can find a permanent solution. The problems would only multiplying one after the other and finally we may not find where the root cause is. India for generations had been depending upon temporary solutions which were done in a haphazard way. Unless every Indian citizen feels that every national problem is his personal problem, no national programme can be successfully implemented. When we promote such feelings then there would not be any difficulty in finding out a permanent solution to any national problem.

Psychologists of the present times are showing more interest in the national and world problems, because all problems are emerging only from human behaviour. It can be easily understood that over population is the cause of the very fundamental form of human sexual behaviour. Though extensive works on sexual behaviour have been made by psychologists they did not relate them to the problem of population explosion and birth control. Buckout (1972) states that there has been more talks on population problems, but no action. One of the natural effects of overpopulation is overcrowding everywhere. We are realizing this overcrowding and also the effects of it. People are now, not finding out enough shelter to live in, do not find place in transports, in buses and trains to go to their work places and to come back. There is overload everywhere and the behaviour of people is much affected. The basis of overcrowding is too many births everywhere in short time. If the crowds are to be reduced the birth rates should be reduced. People of conservative and reactionary attitudes feel that it is a controversial issue and in no time in India, we had such issue. But progressive thinkers, demographers, economists and those who are interested in the population problems advocate vigorously birth control. The most sensitive factor in this is, that it is a highly emotion loaded and feeling aspect issue and it has a backlashing potential effect. Another alternative, possible suggestion is to change the attitudes of the people. Therefore unless people understand the consequences of over population and rapid growth and change, their existing attitudes toward parenthood, motherhood, age of marriage, sexual union, child birth, contraceptive methods, and abortion, no substantial progress in any area can be achieved in India. What are all the progress and developments that we find in statistics, are only temporary and to meet the emergency needs.

Psychologists can do some valuable service to the nation by measuring the attitudes of the people in the above mentioned aspects of life. A better understanding of these attitudes may probably modify them for developing some effective birth control programmes. A concentrated effect to educate the people on the crises of overpopulation must be carried out. This may, not only modify the attitudes, beliefs and the concept of sexual behaviour of the people, but also may establish a system of encouragement for remaining with one or two children or single or childless. Though this appears to be difficult, may in due course become a national method. This will also stop bringing forth the heirs to our deformed citizens, illiteracy and poverty.

Psychologists approach to deal with population problems is mainly based upon the change of the existing attitudes of people about aspects of life, of which the most important are the concept of parenthood, marriageable age for both males and females and sex behaviour. If change of attitudes in these areas have taken place, then people would themselves take care of the problems, like the Japanese people. What urgently needed is properly educating the people about the crises caused by the population explosion. It must be made so intelligibly that they must adopt any one of the methods with all willingness and interest and they must also advice others about the necessity of adopting a method.

The educating strategy should be evolved so pleasantly that people should be drawn with interest towards it. There should not be any discouraging and distasteful words on any account. Till most of the people understand the crux of the problem the educating processes must be with pleasant feeling and viable. When the people approach for some clarification of some points or issues they should be explained with very simple words, the words they often use in their everyday life, so that they will not forget the contents of the issues. Technical jargons as far as possible should be avoided.

EXPERIMENT 9

Measurement of Attitude toward Family Planning and Birth Control

1. INTRODUCTION

Population refers to all the persons inhabiting a country, city, town or other specified place or area. It is also referring to the number of such inhabitants. Sometimes it is stated as the functioning of all the people of a particular race or class in a specified area. Ecologically population meant a group of individuals of the same species inhabiting a given area. Generally population is meant all the living people in a country or in a region. The concept of population is used to indicate a human aggregate. Most of the times population is applied to the total number of persons residing in a given area at a given time.

We use here the concept, population to the aggregate of people who can be brought under the influence of demographic processes of fertility, mortality and migration. Thus population is a living and changing organism. Therefore, wherever people are assembled or crowded is not called population. For example, the people who are assembled in a public meeting, the people assembled in a picture house, people assembling in a fair are not populations in the real sense. They are not populations because of their size and character. They are influenced by the economic cultural and political factors and they are not influenced by the demographic factors. Generally populations are identified with areas such as villages, towns, cities, regions, states, countries and continents. According to this description, India is a country having a specified area in the continent of Asia and the residents or the people of India are called population because they are subjected to demographic influences such as fertility, mortality and migration. Sometimes a part of all the people of the country is called population. This may be called sub-population.

India's Population Problem and Family Planning

India is one of the countries considered as having the highest population in the world. Population as it is not a problem, but when it goes beyond the limit of its resources then it becomes a problem. In 1995, India's population is 92 crores. Till 1931 the population of India was not a problem. After that and particularly after 1941 India's population has increased rapidly and started causing several problems. Demographers like Dr. Chandrasekhar [1942, 1943(a), 1943(b), 1946, 1956] has been raising voice on this issue and was giving warnings constantly that India is going to face severe problems if we do not take proper steps to control the growth of population. Pandit Jawaharlal Nehru, after independence in 1947, on becoming the Prime Minister of India, was very much worried over the rapid increase of Indian population and has stated that India was suffering from overpopulation that birth control was badly needed if her death rates was to be reduced and kept at low rate and if a better level of living was to be assured to the people of India. Therefore the Indian Union Government had decided to promote family planning and birth control as part of her plan for modernizing and improving her economy. Nehru's view on this issue has been accepted nation-wide and a considerable amount of money was allotted for encouraging the family planning and birth control programmes. In every Five Year Plan funds were allotted and also raised plan to plan.

When Dr. S. Chandrasekhar (1967, 1968) became the Minister for Health and Family Planning the programmes were accelerated and wider publicity was made and all categories of people were made to involve in the family planning and birth control programmes.

Psychologists now-a-days began to pay more attention on the population problem in every country. The main reason has been that population problems cause more miseries and unhappiness in the life of the people. The American Psychological Association in 1969 has set up a task force on psychology and family planning and population policy were entrusted with them. This responsibility was entrusted with them for encouraging greater research and professional service participation by psychologists in this newly emerging area. Psychologists in various countries pay similar attention and study the problem caused by the population growth. The Indian psychologists have not yet aroused from the dogmatic slumber to pay attention on this issue. This is the time for them to plunge into the issue and study various aspects of the population problems.

What has taken place in India is population explosion. The population at present is several crores more than what it should be. There is immense pressure of population upon the food production and other subsistences. India with all her natural resources is not able to produce to feed the whole population. Food is not available in certain remote areas. It may be due to insufficient food products or lack of proper transportation or maldistribution of food. As a result of it people starve or reduce their demands and live with whatever is available for them.

The second serious problem is unemployment. Because of the increased population, people are not getting jobs. This also leads to underemployed. Many educated and uneducated unemployed young men roam about in search of jobs. Now there are also many educated young women unemployed. Government's programme of lending money through Banks or some organizations do not reach them properly. As a result of unemployment and under-employment these young men in due course get frustrated and become delinquents and engaged themselves in anti-social and criminal activities. Everyday innumerable number of criminal activities are reported by the press and the police. Government cannot keep one police man behind every unemployed person and watch him. We do not know when an unemployed youth becomes an anti-social element. These people ultimately become impoverished and they cannot live honest way of life.

The third important problem is the living place. Since the cost of materials have become very exorbitant it is not easy for many people to build houses for them. Within the small income many could not afford to spend for the construction of a house or to pay the exorbitant rents demanded by the house owners. These are the problem caused by increased population. Therefore, it becomes an urgent need to reduce the growth of population. This becomes a national problem and therefore everyone must contribute his/her might to solve this problem. The only way is to adopt family planning and reduce the birth rates in every family. Other nations have implemented this programme successfully and solved the problem. But we are not active in this venture. Having formulated a population policy and evolved the family planning and birth control programmes it becomes the duty of every citizen of this great nation to carry out the programmes and help the government to solve the national problem of the population explosion.

Therefore it is a matter of interest for the psychologists to go into many aspects of the population crises. Their interest is mainly, how this problem affects the behaviour of the individuals and the group. There are reports all over the world sometimes about the population disaster, like food shortage, famine, starvation, hunger and death. There were instance in the past that millions of people were affected by these consequences of population. Food shortage and famine were cause of many civil war, and revolution. These disasters were followed by infectious and epidemic diseases causing death of millions of people. The main reason has been the food production and other subsistences were inadequate to meet the pressure of the growing population. The growth of population should be limited to the level of natural resources and production. If the growth of population exceeds the limits of natural resources and production level the problem arises. The over population is due to unlimited birth rates and this is not controlled spontaneously. The fundamental reason according to Malthus (1798) is the sexual behaviour. The sexual behaviour is natural and instinctual. Psychologists and researchers who have studied sexual behaviour of humans earlier did not relate it to birth rates.

India's population problem at present has become a very big issue. One of the reasons is that even after the introduction of family planning and birth control programmes by the Government of India the birth rate was not reduced. They produce some statistics with regard to the number of vasectomy operations conducted by the physicians and the number of people to whom they distributed the pills and condoms for birth control. But were those people really applying these birth control methods and stopped the births? Even persons who were well informed of the consequences of the growth of population and those who are in government services occupying big posts did not carry out the family planning and birth control programmes. Some are of the view that population is the property of the nation.

The small population alone is not considered as the property of a nation. Sometimes at certain crucial conditions rapid increase of population by migration or by natural growth has been considered as property. What is more vital for a nation, is a steady growth of economic and cultural conditions to feed the increasing population. The economic development of a nation should not face any pressure from the population size. These two trends should begin in diverse ways to each other when the economic growth continues steadily in an upward trend, the population growth should take a downward trend. The production of food and other subsistences should maintain a balance with the growth of population. Or the population growth should be limited to the level of economic growth. Therefore it is necessarily to launch a technological and attitudinal change as one of the programmes of modernizing economy. This may result in economic-cum-industrial change on one side and social-cum-attitudinal change on the other. In other words economic change and population control may lead to achieving the goal. Therefore the Planning Commission of the Indian Government should assert that family planning is an essential programme for economic development. Any economic planning in India without taking into account the consequences of family planning programmes may face only a deficit economy.

Unless surveys are conducted it will not be possible for us to know what amount of knowledge people have acquired regarding the family planning, birth control and contraceptive methods. Therefore the KAP surveys regarding family planning are made. It is the measure of knowledge, attitudes and practices, (KAP) concerning fertility control. But in developing countries a servey usually is conducted with family planning action programmes which is more concerned with mainly the

KAP variables. The 'K' stands for knowledge about the physiology of reproduction and method of contraception. The 'A' stands for attitudes, what the individual considers about the size of family, pregnancy, family limitation, the use of sterilization, abortion and methods of contraception. The 'P' stands for practices of the individual as to how far he carries out the practices of birth control.

The nature of KAP surveys and the purpose of which they have been used have been discussed in a recent report made by Mauldin, Watson and Noe (1970). The reliability and validity of the KAP data were also reviewed and certain results were selected and compared with large number of KAP surveys. The American Population Council [1967(a), 1976(b)] was very keen in making the KAP surveys by using carefully developed standard instruments and procedures.

Indian Servey

India has been showing much interest in the population studies and research since 1951. The demographic researchers have collected large amount of information through the censuses of 1951 and 1961. There were a number of surveys. The most important surveys were the National Sample Surveys (NSS) a large number of ad hoc surveys, which included fertility and mortality surveys and the KAP surveys of family planning. The National Sample Survey was continuously engaged in collecting data on different aspects like the economic and social aspect of the people. Most of the data had demographic contents. The data were concerned mainly referring to birth and death rates morbidity, internal migration, fertility and family planning.

Family Planning Methods

The population problem was recognized by the crises that were revealed in various forms of miseries. Then the immediate response is the promotion of family planning. Prior to the implementation of family planning, various surveys were conducted, the important of which was the KAP survey. About forty developing nations are supporting the family planning activities. India is one of the nations showing very much interest in family planning action programmes. Though the crises of population explosion was realized by the leaders of India as early as 1951 and started the family planning programme, a systematic action programme to curb the population growth was accelerated when Dr.

S. Chandrasekhar became the Minister of Health and Family Planning in the Government of India.

Several Family Planning methods were applied in the past few years. Family Planning, in the Indian context, may be defined as the control of number of children in a family and of the intervals between two children by the use of contraceptive devices. The definition of family planning varies from country to country. The Turkish (1965) law concerning population planning declared that population planning meant that individuals can have as many children as they wish and whenever they want to. Planning means what each couple exercise to control the size of their family.

The couples by the application of the method, it is possible for them to obtain the number of births saved each year from the time of the initial use of the method. If every family, in the country, adopt some methods and save or prevent the births, each one family is contributing to the solution of the nation's population problems.

Abortion

Induced abortion is one of the surest means of controlling reproduction. This method has also been proved to be capable of reducing birth rates rapidly. It was the method used by the Japanese very successfully which has reduced the birth to half. In the East European countries abortion was an important factor in reducing the fertility rate in the early 1950's. In the Latin America, According to Armijo *et al.* (1964) abortion is the foremost birth control method. But the United Nations have excluded abortion from family planning methods. But few nations prefer abortion to contraception. The extent of the use of abortion in any society depends upon the cultural values of the society. Some societies may permit and some do not. Abortion has become safe and technically simple, but it is a surgical or quasi-surgical procedure.

Abortion may mean an operation or other procedure to terminate pregnancy before the foetus is visible or it may mean premature termination of pregnancy by spontaneous or by induced expulsion of a nonviable foetus from uterus. In medical language abortion included spontaneous miscarriage as well as induced abortion.

Further, abortions are practiced also in many parts of the world, where it is illegal or considered as immoral. In India, it has been observed that there are increasing illegal abortions during the course of fifteen to twenty years. These illegal abortions were practiced mostly by adolescent girls and early adult females below 25 years of age. The pregnancies were occurring due to premarital sexual unions. In India, of late the adolescent boys and girls are engaged in freely mixing among themselves and also having often social meetings which result in premarital casual and indiscriminate sexual relationships. There is a general attitudinal change in different age groups toward premarital, permissive and promiscuous sexual relations. There are also experimental evidences that the amount of education at the school and college levels is positively associated with permissive attitudes toward premarital sex relations. Glenn and Weaver (1979) have observed in their nation-wide study in United States and elsewhere that at each age level permissiveness increased as the educational level increased. The premarital sexual behaviour among the males and females was almost the same and the level is much more higher than the previous era. This results in pregnancy among the girls and the only way of eliminating it is abortion and they go in search of some method of getting it eliminated. Once they do this, it is not a difficult task for them to repeat the same. This type of illegal and immoral abortions are becoming common occurrences. The abortion helps a girl to get rid of her guilty act secretly.

Contraceptive Method

Birth control is made by practising various contraceptive methods. Contraception means preventing conception or pregnancy by artificial method. It is referred to tending to prevent impregnation or pregnancy. Contraceptive method is practised by using Pill and Intra-Uterine Contraceptive Device (IUCD), sterilization, vasectomy, salpingectomy, and conventional contraceptive methods and the use of condom.

Oral Contraceptives

The pill is available everywhere. There is now a new and improved pill available. This is given to females. This pill prevents pregnancy by holding the ovum from becoming mature. Therefore the ovum cannot be impregnated. When the pill is taken for twenty days continuously pregnancy will not occur. This pill must be taken five days after menstruation and five days before next menstruation. It is very effective and is not having side effects. It is also called oral contraception. Oral contraception has been approved by the Indian Council of Medical Research. Earlier it was supplied in the project centres. It is found that the women wanting the oral pills are generally lower age groups, lower parity, higher education and from higher income groups. Whereas others were wanting of the intra uterine contraceptive device (IUCD) and sterilization. Therefore large number of women were taking the pills regularly for longer period of time. In some places injections and mini-dose pills are also practised.

Sterilization

This is one of the method of family planning, practised in India for more than twenty years. Sterilization means making one not to produce children (offspring). It is making one medically infertile to produce children. It is done for both males and females. The male sterilization is called vasectomy and the female sterilization is called salpingectomy.

Conventional Contraceptives: The use of Condom

The use of condom is stated as conventional contraceptive method. Those who have higher age specific fertility rate may use this. And also those who wanted to delay child birth can use it. It is used by males when the couple wanted to postpone the pregnancy. But it is not a reliable contraceptive method. The problem is whether the use of this method of really preventing conception. The condom is used only at the time of a coitus. What is taking place if the condom is missed at the time of a coitus? If the couple fail to use five times out of ten times during coitus the chance is only fifty per cent of preventing the conception. If they failed to use two times out of ten times during coitus the chance of avoiding conception is only twenty per cent. Further condom can be used only during the risk or unsafe period. During safe period, for ten days the couples need not use condom. But newly married and young couple have more number of coituses and if they fail or forget to use condom during the unsafe period there are chances for conception. The Indian study made by Mony Nag (1965) states that the average number of coitus in a month is six times. But it varies on the basis of age. The newly married couple can save number of births in the first year and also in the second year by using condom during the unsafe periods.

Fertility

Fertility means the ability to produce children. Generally, fertility refers to the number of births occurring in a specified population in a given period of time. Population growth occurs due to high fertility and low mortality. But what is the cause of high fertility? According to demographers and sociologists it is the social stratification variables that are responsible for high fertility. For example, education, religion, culture, urban and rural residences, work status of females are the main reasons. From psychological point of view, it is due to the result of many individuals' acts and decisions from the biological and environmental compulsions. There are measures of study of fertility such as crude birth rate, age specific birth rate, the general fertility rate and gross reproduction rate. The fertility potentiality, in India even after twenty years of the implementation of family planning and birth control programmes, is not reduced. Instead it is increased. Therefore the other way of reducing population growth is increasing the marriageable age apart from using contraceptive methods and abortion.

Age of Marriage

The marriageable age varies from place to place. According to Kale's (1965) study, in Karnataka state the median marriageable age of women was 11 years. About 84 per cent of women were married before the age of 13 years. About seven per cent were married at the age of 15 years and above. Out of 101 cases, only three were married at the age 18 years. In another Baroda Fertility Study made by Bhanot and Gandotra (1970), it was observed that the median marriage age was 15 years in urban areas and 12 years in rural areas. In Baroda city, the Gujarati speaking backward community people's marriage age was 13 years. The age varies in the case of other cultural groups. The marriageable age of males varies on the basis of their socio-economic, educational status. Therefore, Indian women who were married at the age of 13 to 15 years would give birth to two or three children before they reach the age of 20 years and sometimes more as it is the age of high fertility period.

Problem

Assess a person's attitude toward family planning and birth control by using suitable instrument and compare it with a small group of persons.

2. METHOD

Participant

Choose a person who shows some interest in the national problem of population growth and collect other personal information such as age, sex, home town (urban or rural), number brothers, and sisters, if married number of children, qualification. Father's occupation, mother's occupation if employed, approximate annual income of the family, whether the person is with sound health or handicapped and so on.

Material

The material used in this study to assess the attitude of the person is, The Family Planning and Birth Control Attitude Scale, Manual, Test booklet, Scoring key and Scoring sheet.

Description of the Material

The Family Planning and Birth Control Attitude Scale was designed and developed by Prof. M. Rajamanickam (1996) to measure the attitudes of the students, the employed persons and the general public toward the Family Planning and Birth Control. Since the population problem is a very crucial one that is having very bad effect upon the decent level of living of the people in India and since the growth of population is rapid, leaders of the nation are wanting to reduce the growth of population to the level of food production and other subsistences is our country. Therefore, it is an urgent need to reduce the population growth and studies were made in the past by the demographers and other social scientists to know the level of decrease in the birth rates. But no satisfactory report has been received. Therefore psychologists wanted to know what type of attitude that the people of the country are having on this issue. In the United States Psychologists made several KAP studies. In India studies on population problem were not made from psychological point of view. The population problems and their consequences are becoming more of psychological problems since people's various aspects of behaviour are determined by the changes. Therefore psychological studies on population problems and their consequences become a must at the present situation in India. Therefore a scale involving important factors of population problems is designed and developed. It is a five-point scale, developed according to Likert scaling technique.

This scale includes eight important variables of population problems. They are (a) Population problem, (b) Family planning, (c) Birth control, (d) Fertility control, (e) Birth control method : Abortion, (f) Contraceptive method, (g) Sterilization, and (h) Age of marriage.

It is also important to know whether the (subject) has understood the *population problem.* The difficulties in getting the food supplies and other materials, the exorbitant price-rise, the difficulties in getting employment or the unemployment problems, criminal and anti-social activities, the problem of getting living places, or getting a house at a considerable rent, the problem of overcrowding everywhere—are all due to the population explosion problems. Human behaviour is thoroughly changing from fair dealings to unfair dealings in everything. Crime rates are increasing due to unemployment. People get irritated, frustrated and become aggressive on trivial things and attack each other. Killing rates are increasing rapidly every day. These are all the consequences of population growth. Whether people of the nation have realized all these or not, psychologists are very anxious to know about all these.

To get rid of such problems the Government of India have launched a nation-wide *Family Planning Programme.* This involves reducing the family size by giving birth to limited number of children and also to increase the intervals between births. This leads to birth control and also reducing the *fertility* rates. Various birth control methods are practised all over the nation. Whether the methods are genuinely practised? *Abortion* is a post-conception method of birth control. Scholars state that abortion is more reliable than other contraceptive methods. Abortion is a quasisurgical method. Abortion is not a contraceptive method.

Contraceptive methods are intended to prevent pregnancies. By these methods conception is being prevented either by taking *Contraceptive pills*, or injection. The contraceptive methods also include the insertion of loops or the *Intra Uterine Device (IUD).* All these methods are for females. Pills for males also are invented. The effective contraceptive method for males and also for females is the *sterilization.* By this process one is made infertile to produce children. Another method suggested is *the increase of marriageable age* for both male and female.

All these eight components are included in the Family Planning and Birth Control Attitude Scale. The scale consisted of 64 statements, eight statements for each component. Among the eight statements on each variable or component there are four positive statements and four negative statements. Thus, on the whole there are 32 positive statements and 32 negative statements. Each statement expresses one idea, generally, about family planning and birth control and specifically about the particular problem of the variable. The ideas expressed in the statements are far and against the problem. The subject may agree with certain ideas given in the statements or disagree with certain ideas given in the statements. The subject has to read each statement carefully and express his/her agreement or disagreement by underlining any one of the five responses, such is strongly agree, agree, unable to decide, disagree and strongly disagree, given under each statement.

The responses are assigned with scores. The strongly agree of the positive statement is given a score 5, agree 4, unable to decide 3, disagree 2, and strongly disagree 1. For the negative statements the reverse order is used. The strongly agree of the negative statement is given a score 1, agree 2, unable to decide 3, disagree 4, and strongly disagree 5. The individual score is the total score of all the 64 statements. The scores of the eight variables may be also scored separately and treated separately for the purpose of analysis of answers. The highest score in the scale is 320 and the lowest score is 64. If the individual score falls in between 64 and 128 he/she is having unfavourable attitude toward family planning and birth control. He/she is against family planning and birth control. If the score falls between 129 and 192 it is neutral attitude. The individual is unable to decide and therefore remains neutral. If the individual's score falls in between 193 and 320 it is favourable attitude toward family planning and birth control. The individual wants that family planning and birth control programmes should be implemented and population should be reduced.

The scores of eight variables may be also treated separately to know whether the subjects accept the problem and the implementation of the programmes. Since in each variable there are eight statements the scores may be obtained for each variable separately. Thus the lowest score in each variable is $(8 \times 1) = 8$ and the highest score is $(8 \times 5) = 40$. For example, in the case of first variable the lowest score for population problem is 8 and the highest score is 40. If the individual's score falls in between 8 and 16 he/she is having unfavourable attitude toward population problem. A score falling in between 17 and 24 it is neutral attitude. The individual is unable to decide it. A score falling in between 25 and 40 is favourable attitude toward of the population problem. He/she is of the view that there is population problem is our country. The individual's score in this variable is the total score of all the eight statements of population problem. The scores may be treated in the same manner for all other variables.

The statements were framed from the ideas collected from contemporary literature, journals, and speeches made by eminent scholars in the field of population studies. One hundred statements were written and after carefully editing in consultation with eminent demographers 72 statements were retained. These statements were cyclostyled and distributed among fifty final year post-graduate students of three universities. On the basis of the responses 8 statements were omitted as they appeared to be ambiguous. Finally 64 statements were retained. These statements were printed and bound into booklet forms and distributed among 350 university students, teachers and persons engaged in various occupations. The split-half method of correlation worked out and the correletion co-efficient was treated with Spearman-Brown Formula for determining the reliability of the scale. The reliability was found to be 0.78 which was significant at one per cent level. The intrinsic validily was worked out for the scale. It was 0.88 which was significant at one per cent level. This scale can be used for individual testing and also for group testing.

Procedure

The experimenter should check whether the test materials are correct with the manual, test booklet, scoring key and the scoring sheet. Than he/she should keep the participant seated in front of his/her in a well illuminated room, where there is no auditory disturbances. The experimenter, then, should give the following instructions to the participant.

• This is a test to assess your opinion about family planning and birth control in our country. It is not an intelligence test or personality test. Therefore you can freely express your view on family planning and birth control. There are 64 statements in this test booklet, each one expressing one idea about family planning and birth control. Please read each statement carefully. You may agree with the idea in some statements and disagree with the idea in some statements. Whatever opinion you have about it, express it by underlining any one of the five responses given under each statement. If you strongly agree with the idea then underline the response, 'strongly agree', if you simply agree, underline the response 'agree'. If you are unable to decide underline 'unable to decide', if you disagree with the idea, then underline response 'disagree', and if you strongly disagree, then underline the response 'strongly disagree'. You must carry the same procedure for all the 64 statements. You should not omit any of them. You can return it to me as soon you complete all the statements. Now you can start, "Ready go". Saying this experimenter hands over the test booklet to the participant.

As the participant started answering the items, the experimenter should also watch how much time the participant takes to complete it. When he/she completed, the experimenter should collect the test booklet and ask the participant to give the introspective report. On getting it the participant may be allowed to go away.

Method of Scoring

The experimenter should scrutinize the test booklet whether the participant has answered all the items correctly. Then with the help of the scoring key he/she should score the responses of the participant for all the 64 statements. There are both positive and negative statements toward family planning and birth control. The positive statements are supporting family planning and birth control while the negative statements are against family planning and birth control. This is scored according to the scoring key. The strongly agree response of the positive statement is given a score of 5, the agree response is given 4, the unable decide response 3, the disagree response is given 2, and strongly disagree is given one. The scores for the negative statements are on the reverse. The strongly agree of the negative statements is given 1, the agree response 2, the unable to decide response 3, the disagree response is given 4, the strongly disagree response is given 5. The individual score is the total score of all 64 statements. The high score indicates favourable attitude toward family planning and birth control. The low score indicates unfavourable attitude toward family planning and birth control.

The score falling in between 64 and 128 indicates unfavourable attitude toward family planning and birth control, the score falling in between 129 and 192 indicates neutral attitude toward family planning and birth control and the score falling in between 193 and 320 indicates favourable attitude toward family planning and birth control.

The norm of the scores for discussion is that a score falling in between 64 and 96 is extremely unfavourable attitude or anti-attitude toward family planning and birth control. The score in between 97 and 160 is moderately unfavourable. The score falling in between 161 and 224 indicates neutral attitude. The score in between 225 and 288 is moderately favourable toward family planning and birth control. The score falling in between 289 and 320 is extremely favourable attitude toward family planning and birth control.

3. RESULTS

The experimenter should score all the items according to the procedure and obtain the individual score. The scores should be treated statistically and presented in Table 4.1. There are eight variables in the scale. All of them should be treated separately and the scores of them should be presented in Table 4.1.

In Table 4.1 the score of each variable is presented in the order A to H. The highest score of a variable is 40 and the lowest score is 8. The individual's score falls in between these two scores which is depending upon his/her preference toward the particular issue. The individual's total score of all the 8 variables is his/her score on the scale.

Table 4.1 : Showing the scores of the individual on the Family Planning and Birth Control attitude Scale

S.No.	*Variables*	*Scores*
1	A. Population Problem	
2	B. Family Planning	
3	C. Birth Control	
4	D. Fertility Control	
5	E. Birth Control Method : Abortion	
6	F. Contraceptive Method	
7	G. Sterilization	
8	H. Age of Marriage	
	Total score	

Work out the scores of favourable attitude, unfavourable attitude and the neutral attitude and list the respective items for all the eight variables and present them in Table 4.2. Collect the group data from other experimenters and present them in Table 4.3.

Table 4.2 : Showing the favourable, unfavourable and neutral attitude scores and the respective items for all the eight variables separately on the Family Planning and Birth Control Attitude Scale

S.No.	*Variables*	*Favourable Scores and Item Nos.*	*Unfavourable scores and Item Nos.*	*Neutral scores and item Nos.*
1	A. Population Problem			
2	B. Family Planning			
3	C. Birth Control			
4	D. Fertility Control			
5	E. Birth Control Method: Abortion			
6	F. Contraceptive Method			
7	G. Sterilization			
8	H. Age of Marriage			
	Total Scores			

State the individual's total score on the family planning and birth control attitude scale. The score of the individual is supposed to fall in between 64 and 320. If the score falls in between 64 and 128 the individual is against the family planning and birth control. If the score falls in between 129 and 192 the individual is neutral toward family planning and birth Control. If the score falls in between 193 and 320 the individual is favourable toward family planning and birth control. State where the individual's score falls. Is it favourable toward family planning and birth control or unfavourable. State the score of each variable and state whether it is favourable or unfavourable toward the respective variable.

State the three categories of scores for each variable. State the variables in which the individual scored high and in which he/she scored low. State the variables in which the favourable scores are higher than the unfavourable and neutral scores. State whether there is any variable in which the individual has scored higher unfavourable score. State the items answered favourably, unfavourably and neutrally by the individual. State the total score of each category (favourable, unfavourable and neutral) for all the eight variables.

Table 4.3 : Showing the group data with the scores of the variables and the total score on the Family Planning and Birth Control Attitude Scale

			A	B	C	D	E	F	G	H
S. No.	*Name*	*Total Score on the Scale*	*Population Problem*	*Family Planning*	*Birth Control*	*Fertili. Control*	*Abortion*	*Contraceptive Method*	*Sterilization*	*Age of Marriage*
1	P.M.									
2	K.R.									
3	R.V.									
4	P.V.									
5	M.S.									
6	R.M.									
7	S.V.									
8	P.K.									
9	M.R.									
10	V.L.									
	Total									
	Mean									

Work out the total score and the mean score for all the eight variables. State the mean score of the group for the whole scale. Mention the mean scores for all the eight variables. State how many subjects have scored more than the group mean score in the family planning and birth control attitude scale and how many scored below the group mean. Similarly in all eight variables how many scored more than the group means and how many scored below the group means.

4. DISCUSSION

Discuss the score of the individual in the family planning and birth control attitude scale. State whether he/she is favourable toward family planning and birth control or unfavourable. Cite the scores and discuss the nature of the individual's attitude. State the score in each variable and discuss whether he/she is favourable or unfavourable toward the specific variable. Is he/she accepting birth control, abortion, contraceptive methods, sterilization and age of marriage? Discuss the stand of the participant. What are the variables in which the individual has scored above the group mean and the variable in which scored below the group means. Does the score in each variable indicate favourable attitude or unfavourable attitude. Which is the variable in which the individual scored the highest and in which scored the lowest. State the reason if any from his/her personal information. On the whole state whether he/she has scored favourably toward family planning and birth control or unfavourably. State whether the individual has accepted the population problem or not? Support the answers citing the scores.

State whether the individual accepts family planning or not, cite the score and discuss it. Is he/she accepting abortion? State whether the individual approves contraceptive methods or not? State the score and discuss the nature of his/her attitude. What is the score of the individual in sterilization? Is it favourable score or unfavourable score, discuss it. What is the nature of attitude of the individual regarding the marriage? Is he/she favourable toward it or not. State the score and discuss. State and discuss whether any of the personal factors of the individual is having any influence in the attitudes in any of the areas. If so, state the factors, how they are having influence in his/her attitudes.

Where the individual stands in the group mean? State whether his/her score is above the group mean or below the group mean. How many of the subjects in the group scored above the group mean and how many below group mean. State whether the group means is favourable attitude toward family planning and birth control or neutral or unfavourable? How many of them in the group scored above 193 indicating favourable toward family planning and birth control and how many below 192 indicating neutral attitude and how many scored below 128 indicating unfavourable attitude toward family planning and birth control. Compare the mean scores of the eight variables and state how many scored above the group mean in the variables and how many scored below the group means? Who scored the highest in the whole scale and who scored the lowest? How many of them approve population problem, family planning, birth control, fertility control, abortion, contraceptive method, sterilization and age of marriage? How many of them did not approve all or any of them? State whether any of the personal factors had any influence in their attitude toward family planning and birth control. State whether there is any difference between the urban and rural subjects in their attitude. Discuss whether there is any difference in their attitude due to sex, age, and education, number of children in the family and income.

5. CONCLUSIONS

1. What is the nature of attitude of your participant? Whether it is favourable or neutral or unfavourable toward family planning and birth control?
2. What are the variables in which your participant scored high and scored low.
3. How many in the group are favourable toward family planning and birth control and how many are against it.
4. How many in the group accepted abortion and the contraceptive methods? How many did not accept?
5. Give the order of acceptance of the variables by the individual from the score of each variable.
6. Give the order of the variables as accepted by the group from the total scores of each variable.
7. Do the attitudes vary on the basis of sex, age, education, number of members in the family, occupative and income?

BIBLIOGRAPHY

Ackerman, N.W. and M. Jahoda, *Anti-Semitism and Emotional Disorder : A Psychoanalytic Interpretation.* New York : Harper, 1950.

Acknar, B. *Discussion on Physiological measurements of emotional tensions.* Proc. Roy. Soc. Med. 1958, **51**, 76-78.

Aiello, J.R., Epistein, Y.M., and Karlin, R.A., *Field Experimental Research in Human Crowding.* Paper presented at the meeting of the Eastern Psychological Association, 1975.

Albee, G.W., Conceptual models of manpower requirements in Psychology, *American Psychologist*, 1968, **23**, 317-320.

Albert, S. and Dabbs, J.M., Physical distance and persuasion. *Journal of Personality and Social Psychology*, 1970, **15**, 265-270.

Allen, M., *The Single or Representative Case Study : A Justification.* Unpublished paper, 1970.

Allen, M., The human organism as an open system. *Interpersonal Developments.* 1970, **1**, 2, 65-67.

Allgeier, A.R., and Byrne, D., Attraction toward the opposite sex as a determinant of physical proximity. *Journal of Social Psychology*, 1973, **90**, 213-219.

Allport, G.W., *The Nature of Prejudice*, Cambridge, Mass: Addison-Wesley, 1954.

Allport, G.W., The open system in personality theory. *Journal of Abnormal and Social Psychology*, 1960, **61**, 301-310.

Altman, I., Nelson, P.A., and Lett, E.E., The ecology of home Environments. *JSAS Ecology of Selected Documents in Psychology*, 1972, **2**, 65, (Ms. No. 421).

Altman, I., *The Environment and Social Behaviour.* Monterey. C.A. : Brooks/Cube, 1975.

American Psychiatric Association. *Diagnostic and Statistical Manual of Mental Disorders* (1st ed.) Washington D.C., American Psychiatric Association, 1952.

American Psychiatric Association. *Diagnostic and Statistical Manual of Mental Disorders* (2nd Ed.) Washington D.C. : American Psychaiatric Association,

American Psychiatric Association. *Diagnostic and Statistical Manual of Mental Disorders* (third Ed.). Washington D.C. : American Psychiatric Association, 1980.

American Psychiatric Association. *Diagnostic and Statistical Manual of Mental Disorders* (Revised). Washington D.C. : American Psychiatric Association, 1987.

Anderson, T.W., Erwin, N., Flynn, D., Lewis, L., and Erwin, J., Effects of short-term crowding on aggression in captive groups of pigtail monkeys. *Aggressive Behaviour*, 1979, **3**, 33-46.

Appleyard, D. and Lintell, M., The environmental quality of city streets : The residents' view point. *Journal of the American Institute of Planners*, 1972, **38**, 84-101.

Armijo, R. and Moureal, T., Components of Population Change in Latin America (Milbark Fund, New York, 1965), p. 272 : E. Rice-War *Amer. J. Public Health*, 1964, **54**, 313.

Asha Nehamiah. Fighting AIDS with awareness. *Sunday Magazine, Indian Express*, Sept. 8th, 1991.

Ashton, N.L.; Shaw, M.E.; and Worsharm, A.P. Affective reaction to interpersonal distance by friends and strangers. *Bulletin of the Psychonomatic Society*, 1980, **15**, 306- 308.

Ax, A.F. The physiological differentiation between fear and anger in humans. *Psychometric Medicine*, 1953, **15**, 433-442.

Bakker, C.B., and Dightman, C.R. Psychological factors in fertility control. *Fertility and Sterility*, 1964, **15**, 559-567.

Bandura, A. and Walters, R.H. *Social Learning and Personality Development*, New York : Holt Rinehart and Winston, 1963.

Bandura, A. Behavioural psychotherapy. *Scientific American*, 1967, **216**, 78-86.

Bandura, A. *Principles of Behaviour Modification.* New York : Holt, Rinehart and Winston, 1969.

Bandura, A. Influence of Models Reinforcement contingencies on the Acquisition imitative Responses. In A. Bandura (Ed.). *Psychological Modelling : Conflict Theories*. Chicago : Aldine-Atherton, 1971.

Barker, R.C. Ecology and motivation. In M.R. Jones (Ed.). *Nabraska Symposium on Motivation* (Vol. 8). Lincoln : University of Nebraska Press, 1960.

Barker, R.G. and Gamp, P.V., *Big School, Small School.* Stanford Calif : Standford University Press, 1964.

Barker, R.G. *Ecological Psychology : Concepts and Method for Stydying the Environment of Human Behaviour.* Standford University Press, 1968.

Barker, R.G. and Schoggan, R. *Qualitative Community Life.* San Francisco : Jossey Bass, 1973.

Baron, R.A. and Bell, P.A. Aggression and heat : Mediating effects of prior provaction and exposure to an aggressive model. *Journal of Personality and Social Psychology.* 1975, **31**, 825-832.

Baron, R.A., and Bell, P.A. Aggression and heat; The influence of ambient temperature, negative affect and cooling drink on physical aggression. *Journal of Personality and Social Psychology*, 1976, **33**, 205-215.

Baron, R.M., Mandel, D.R., Adams, C.A., and Criffin, L.M. Effects of social density in university residential environment. *Journal of Personality and Social Psychology*, 1976, **34**, 434-446.

Bartz, W.R. While psychologists doze one. *American Psychologist*, 1970, **25**, 6, 500-503.

Baruch, D.W. *Class house of prejudice.* New York : Morrow, 1946.

Baum, A., and Greenberg, C.I. Waiting for a crowd. The behavioural and perceptual effects of anticipated crowding. *Journal of Personality and Social Psychology*, 1975, **32**, 667-671.

Baum, A., and Valins, S. *Architecture and social behaviour : Psychological studies of social density.* Hillsdale, N.J. : Erlbaum, 1977.

Baumeister, R.F., and Steinhilber, A. Paradoxical effects of supportive audiences on performance under pressure : The home field disadvantage in sports championships. *Journal of Personality and Social Psychology*, 1984, **47**, 85-93.

Beard, R.R. and Wertheimer, G.A. Behavioural impairment associated with small doses of carbon monoxide. *American Journal of Public Health.* 1967, **57**, 2012-2022.

Beck, A.T. *Depression : Clinical, experimental and theoretical aspects.* New York : Herper & Row, 1967.

Beck, A.T. and Emery, G. *Anxiety disorder and phobias* : A Cognitive perspective. New York : Basic Book, 1985.

Bell, P.A., Fisher, J.D., and Loomis, R.J. *Environmental Psychology.* Philadelphia : W.B. Saunders Company, 1978.

Bell, G.R. Provins, K.A., and Hiorns, R.F. Visual and auditory vigilance during exposure to hot and humid conditions. *Ergonomics*, 1964, **7**, 279-288.

Bell. P.A. and Baron, R.A. Aggression and ambient temperature : The facilitating and inhibiting effects of hot and cold environments. *Bulletin of the psychonomic Society*, 1977, **9**, 443-445.

Benastein, B. Language and social class, *British Journal of Sociology*, 1960, **11**, 271-276.

Benjamin, B. Tuberculosis and Social conditions in the Metropolitan. *British Journal of Tuberculosis*, 1953, **47**,

Bennett, R., Rafgerty, J.M., Carnivez, G.L. and Smith, J.M. The effects of cold temperature on alturism and aggression. Paper presented at the *Midwestern Psychological Association Meeting*, Chicago, 1983.

Bennett, A.E. Mad doctors. *J. Nerv. Ment. Dis.* 1947, **106**, 11-18.

Bennett, C.C., Anderson, L.S., Cooper, S., Hassol, L., Klien, D.C. and Resenblum (Eds.). *Community Psychology : A report of the Boston Conference on the education of Psychologists for community mental health.* Boston : Boston University Press, 1966.

Berck, P. Building community strengths : A model for conceptualizing and implementing social change. *Unpublished Manuscript*. University of Illinois at Urbana-Champaign, 1976.

Berelson, B. National Family Planning Programmes : Where we stand. In S.J. Behrman, *et al.* (Eds.). *Fertility and family planning* : A world view. Ann Arbor : University of Michigan Press, 1969.

Berg, R.L., and Beebe-Center, J.G. Cardiac stable in man, *Jl. Exp. Psychol.* 1941, **28**, 262-279.

Bergin, A.E. Some implications of psychotherapy research for therapeutic practice. *Journal of Abnormal Psychology*, 1966. **71**, 235-246.

Bergin, A.E. The evaluation of therapeutic outcomes. In A.E. Bergin and S.L. Garfield (Eds.) *Handbook of psychotherapy and behaviour change : An empirical analysis.* New York : Wiley, 1971.

Berkowitz, L. *Aggression : A social psychological analysis.* New York : McGraw-Hill, 1962.

Berlyne, D.E. *Conflict, Arousal and Curiosity.* New York : McGraw-Hill, 1964.

Berlyne, D.E. *Aesthetics and Psychology*. New York : Appleton-Century-Crofts, 1912.

Bertlanffy, L. Von. General system theory and psychiatry. In S. Arieti (Ed.). *American handbook of psychiatry, Vol. III.* New York : Basic Book, 1966.

Bevan, W. Behaviour in unusual environment. In H. Helson and W. Bevan (Ed.) *Contemporary approaches to psychology*. Princeton, N.J. Van Nostrand, 1967.

Bhanot, I.V. and Gandotra, M.M. Baroda Fertility study : A Brief Report. In Asish Bose Desai, P.B., and Jain, S.P. (compiled). *Studies in Demography*, 1970.

Bickman, L., Teger, A., Gabriele, T., Mchughlin, G., Berger, M., and Sundaday, E. Dormitory density and helping behaviour. *Environment and Behaviour*, 1973, **5**, 465-490.

Blackburn, R. Emotionality, Extraversion and aggression in paranoid and non-paranoid schizophrenic offenders. *British Journal of Psychiatry*, 1968, **115**, 1301-02.

Bleda, P.R. and Sandman, P.H. In smoke's way : Socio-emotional reactions to another's smoking. *Journal of Applied Psychology*, 1977, **62**, 452-458.

Bloom, B. *Community mental health : A historical and critical analysis*, Morris Town, N.J. : General Learning Press, 1973.

Blot, W.J., Brinto, L.A., Fraumeni, J.R., Jr and Stone, B.J., Cancer mortality in U.S. Countries with Petroleum industries, *Science*, 1975, **198**, 58-53.

Boas, E.P., and Geldschmidt, E.F. *The heart-rate*, Spring field, III. : Thomas, 1932.

Booth, A. *Urban Crowding and its consequences.* New York : Praeger, 1976.

Boring, E.G. *A. history of experimental psychology.* New York : Appleton-Century-Crofts, 1950.

Borton, T. *Reach, touch and teach : student concerns and process education.* New York : McGraw-Hill, 1970.

Breisecher, P. Neuropsychological effects of air pollution *American Behavioural Scientists.* 1971, **14**, 837-864.

Breuer, J. and Freud, S. Studies on Hysteria, Vol. II of the standard Edition of the *Complete Psychological Works of Sigmund Freud* (1893-1895). London : Hogarth Press, 1955.

Bridges, K.M.B. Emotional development in early infancy. *Child development*, 1932, **3**, 324-334.

Broadbent, D. *Decision and stress.* New York : Academic Press, 1971.

Bromberg, W. *The mind of man.* New York : Harper, 1937.

Bronzaft, A.L. and MaCarthy, D.P. The effects of elevated train noise on reading ability : *Environment and behaviour*, 1975, **7** 517-527.

Brown, C.H. and Van Gelder, D. Emotional reactions before examinations. I : Physiological changes, *Jl. Psychol.* 1938, **5**, 1-9.

Brown, G.W., Goldberg, E.M. and Morrison, S.L. Schizophrenia and social class, *British Journal of Psychiatry*, 1963, **109**, 785-802.

Bryce J. *The American Commonwealth.* Vol. 2. New York : Macmillan Company, 1910.

Buckhout, R. Toward a two-child norm : Changing family planning attitudes. *American Psychologist*, 1972, **27**, 1, 11-26.

Bugental, J.F.T. The humanistic ethics : the individual in Psychotherapy as a societal change agent. *Journal of Humanistic Psychology*, 1971, **11**, 1, 11-25.

Bhuler, C. and Allen, M. *Introduction to Humanistic Psychology.* Monterey, California : Brooks/Cole Publishing Company, 1972.

Burgess J. Development of social spacing in normal and mentally retarded children. *Journal of Nonverbal behaviour*, 1981, **6**, 89-96.

Butler, C. *The Course of Human Life as a Psychological Problem.* Lepziz : S. Hirzel, 1933.

Byrne, D., Ervin, C.R., and Lamberth. Continuity between the experimental study of attraction and real life computer dating. *Journal of Personality and Social Psychology*, 1920, **16**, 157-165.

Byrne, D. The attraction paradigm. New York : Academic Press, 1971.

Calhoun, J.B. Population density and social pathology. *Science,* 1962, **206**, 139-148.

Calhoun, J.B. Ecological factors in the development of behaviour anomalies. In. J. Zubin. and H.E. Hunt (Eds.). *Comparative Psychopathology.* New York : Grune and Stratton, 1967.

Candland, D.K. *Psychology : The Experimental Approach.* New York McGraw-Hill Book Company, 1968.

Caplan, G. *Principles of Preventive Psychiatry.* New York : Basic Books, 1969.

Caplan, R.B. *Psychiatry and community in Nineteenth century in America*, New York : Basic Books, 1969.

Carr-Saunders, Am. M. The Population Problem : *A Study in Human Evaluation.* Oxford : Clarendon Press, 1922.

Cervone, J.C. An environmental-social approach to an arousal behaviour relationship. *Unpublished Master's thesis.* Colorado State University, 1977.

Champman, B., Masterpasque, F., and Lore, R. The effects of crowding during pregnancy on offspring emotional and sexual behaviour in rats. *Bulletin of the Psychonomic Society*, 1976, 7, 475-477.

Chandrasekhar, S. *Why are Indians Poor?—Population and Poverty.* Asia, New York, 1942.

Chandrasekhar, S. Population Pressure in India. *Pacific Affairs*, U.S.A., Vol. XVI, No. 2, June 1943(a) pp. 161-184.

Chandrasekhar, S. Growth and Characteristics of India's Population. *The Scientific Monthly* (Washington DC). September 1943 (b).

Chandrasekhar, S. *India's Population--Facts and Policy.* New York : The John Day Company, 1946.

Chandrasekhar, S. *Hungry People and Empty Lands.* Baroda : M.S. University of Baroda, 1952, Later on it was published by George Allen and Unwin, London, in 1956.

Chandrasekhar, S. (ed.). *Asia's Population Problems.* London : George Allen and Unwin, 1967.

Chandrasekhar, S. How India is Tackling Her Population Problem. *Foreign Affairs* (New York), October 1968.

Chassin, L., Presson, C.C., Sherman, S.J. Corty, E., and Olshavasky. R.W. Self-images and cigarette-smoking in adolescents. *Personality and Social Psychology Bulletin*, 1984, **7**, 670-676.

Chesney M.A., Eagleston, J.R., and Rosenman, R.H. The Type : A Structured Interview : A behavioural assessment in the rough. *Journal of Behaviour Assessment,* 1980, **2**, 255-272.

Child I.L. *Humanistic Psychology and the Research Tradition : Their Several Virtues.* New York : John Wiley & Sons, Inc., 1973.

Cialdini, R. Ittering Effects of Social Influence. *Unpublished manuscript*, Arozona State University, 1977.

Clement, U., Schmidt, G., Kruse, M. Changes in sex differences in sexual behaviour : A replication of a study on West German students (1966-1981), *Archives of Sexual Behaviour*, 1984, **13,** 99-120.

Coale, A.J. and Hoover, E.M. *Population Growth and Economic Development in Low Income Countries.* Princeton, J : Princeton University Press, 1958.

Cohen, A. Industrial noise and medical absence and accident record data on exposed workers. In W.D. Ward (Ed.). *Proceedings of the International Congress on Noise as a Public Health Problem.* Washington, D.C. U.S. Government Printing Office, 1973.

Cohen, S. Glass, D.C. and Singer, J.E. Apartment noise, auditory discrimination and reading ability in children. *Journal of Experimental Social Psychology*, 1973, **9**, 407- 422.

Cohen, S. Environmental load and the allocation of attention. In A. Barum, and S. Valins, (Eds.). *Advances in environmental research,* Hillsdale, N.J. : Lawrence Erlbaum, 1977.

Coleman, J.C. *Abnormal Psychology and Modern Life* (5th ed.). Bombay : Taraporevala & Sons Co., Private Ltd., 1976.

Comas, J. Scientific Racism Again. *Current Anthropology*. 1961, **2**, No. 4, 304.

Corcoran, D.W.J. Noise and loss of sleep. *Quarterly Journal of Experimental Psychology*, 1962, **14**, 178-182.

Cotton, J.L. Ambient temperature and violent crime. *Journal of Applied Social Psychology*, 1986.

Cowen, E.L. Social and community intervention. *Annual Review of Psychology*, 1973, **24**, 423-472.

Cowen, E.L., Dorr, D., Clarfield, S., Kreling, B., McWilliams, S.A., Pokracki, D., Prett, M., Terrell, D., and Wilson, A. The AMC : A quick screening device for early identification of school maladaptation. *American Journal of Community Psychology*, 1973, **1**, 12-35.

Cowen, E.L. Social and Community intervention. *Annual Review of Psychology*. 1973, **24**, 423-472.

Cowen, E.L., Weissberg, R.P., and Eotyczewski, B.S. Physical contact in helping interactions with young children. *Journal of Community and Clinical Psychology*, 1982, **50**, 219-225.

Cox, V.C., Paulus, P.B., and McCain, G. Prison crowding research : The revelance for prison housing standards and a general approach regarding crowding phenomena. *American Psychologist*. 1984, **39**, 1148-1160.

Craik, K.H. Environmental Psychology, *Annual Review of Psychology*, 1973, **24**, 403-422.

Crockford, G.W. Heat problems and protective clothing in iron and steel work. In C.N. Davis, R.R. Davis and F.H. Tyrer (Eds.). *The Effects of Abnormal Physical Conditions at Work*. London : E & S. Livingston, 1967.

Crook, M.A. and Langdon, F.J. The effects of aircraft noise in schools around London Airport. *Journal of Sound and Vibration*. 1974, **34**, 221-232.

Crowe, M.J. Toward a definitional model of public perceptions of air polution. *Journal of the Air Pollution Control Association*. 1968, **18**, 154-157.

Darrow, C.W. Continuous records of systolic and diastolic blood pressure, *Arch. Neruel Psychiat* (Chicago).

Davis, W.A. *Social Class Influences Upon Learning*. Cambridge Mass : Harward Unit Press, 1948.

Davis, K. The sociology of demographic behaviour, In R.K. Merton, *et al.* (Eds.). *Sociology today : Problems and Prospects*. New York : Basic Book, 1959.

De Fronzo, J. Climate and Crime : Tests of an FBI Assumption. *Environment and Behaviour*, 1984, **16**, 185-210.

Dellinger, R.W. Jet roar : Health Problems take off near airports. *Human Behaviour*, 1979, **8**, 50-51.

Demerath, M.J. Organization and Management Needs of National Family Planning Programme : The case of India. *The Journal of Social Issues*, October, 1967, XXIII (4).

Dennison, G. The lives of children. New York : Vintage, 1969.

Devereaux, G.A.A. Psychoanalytic study of Contraception. *Journal of Sex Research*, 1965, **1**, 105-134.

Dilthey, W. *Pattern and Meaning in History*. New York : Torchbooks, 1961.

Dollard, J., Doob, L.W., Miller, N.E., Mower, O.H. and Sears R.R. *Frustration and aggression*. New Haven, Connecticut : Yale University Press, 1939.

Dooley, B.B. Crowding Stress : *The effects of social density on men with close or far personal space*. Unpublished doctoral dissertation. University of California at Los Angeles, 1974.

Dorothy Wedderbun. *Poverty inequality and class structure*. Cambridge : Cambridge University Press, 1947.

Dosey, M., and Meisels, M. Personal space and self-protection. *Journal of personality and Social Psychology*, 1969, **11**, 93-97.

Dubos, R. *Man adaption*. New Haven : Yale University Press, 1965.

Dukes, W.F. N=1. *Psychological Bulletin*, 1965, **64**, 74- 79.

Dumont, A. *La Morale basee sur la dimographic*. Paris : Schelicher Freres, 1901.

Eston, D.M. *Mechanism of Body Function*, New Delhi : Prentice-Hall of India Private Limited, 1978.

Edney. J.J. Property, Possession and permanance : A field study in human territoriality. *Journal of Applied Social Psychology*, 1972, **2**, 275-282.

Edwards, D.J.A. Approaching the Unfamiliar : A study of human interaction distances. *Journal of Behavioural Sciences*, 1972, 1, 240-250.

Eels, K., Davis, A., Havighurst, R., Herrick, V. and Tyler, R. *Intelligence and cultural difference*. Chicago : Chicago Univ. Press, 1951.

Eiser, J.R. Smoking addiction and decision-making. *Journal of Applied Social Psychology*, 1983, 32, 11-28.

Epstein. W. and Shontz, F. *Psychology in Progress*, New York : Holt Rinehart and Winston, Inc., 1971.

Epistein, Y.M., and Karlin, R.A. Effects of acute experimental crowding *Journal of Applied Social Psychology*, 1979, **5**, 34-53.

Evans, G.W. Behavioural and physiological consequences of crowding in humans. *Journal of Applied Social Psychology*, 1979, **9**, 27-46, 1975.

Eysenck. H.J. The effects of psychotherapy : An evaluation. *Journal of consulting psychology*. 1952, **16**, 319-324.

Fairweather, G.W. *Social change : The Challenge survival*. Morristown, N.J. : General Learning Press, 1972.

Fawcett, J.M. *Psychology and Population : Behavioural Research Issues in Fertility and Family Planning*. New York : The Population Council, 1970.

Ferber, A.S., Tieze, C., and Lewit, S. Men with vasectomies : A study of medical, sexual and psychosocial changes. *Psychosomatic Medicine*, 1967, **29**, 354-366.

Fisher, J.D. Situation—specific variables as determinants of perceived environmental aesthetic quality and perceived crowdedness. *Journal of Research in Personality*. 1974, **8**, 177-188.

Fisher, J.D., and Byrne, D. Too close for comfort : Sex differences in response to invasions of personal space. *Journal of personality and Social Psychology*, 1975, **32**, 15-21.

Folk, C.E. *Textbook of Environmental Psychology*. Philadelphia : Lea & Febiger, 1974.

Fourth Five Year Plan, India. Planning Commission, *A Draft Out-line*, New Delhi, 1969.

Fox, W.F. Human performance in the cold. *Human Factors*, 1967, **9**, 203-270.

Freedman, J.L., Levy, A.S., Buchanan, R.W. and Price, J. Crowding and human aggressiveness. *Journal of Experimental Social Psychology*, 1972, **8**, 528-548.

Freud, S. The aetiology of the neuroses (1893). In J. Strachey (Ed.). *The standard edition of the Complete Psychological Works of Sigmund Freud.* Vol. 1. London : Hogarth Press, 1966.

Freud, S. On the grounds of detaching a particular syndrome from neurasthenia under the description of Anxiety neurosis (1984). In J. Strachy (ed.) *The standard edition of the Complete Psychological Works of Sigmund Freud.* Vol. III. London : Hogarth Press, 1961.

Freud, S. Sexuality in the aetiology of the neuroses (1898). In. J. Strachey (Ed.). *The standard edition of the Complete Psychological Works of Sigmund Freud.* Vol. III. London : Hogarth Press, 1962.

Freud, S. *The Interpretation of Dreams* (1900) Volumes IV and V of the Standard Edition. London : Hogarth Press, 1953.

Freud, S. *A General Introduction to Psychoanalysis*. New York : Garden City Books, 1947, (First German ed., 1917).

Freud, S. *Beyond the Pleasure Principle*. In Vol XIII of The Standard Edition. London : Hogarth Press, (1920), 1957.

Freud, S. *Mourning and Melancholia* (1917) In collected papers (Vol-4). London : Hogarth Press, 1934.

Frick, W.B. *Humanistic Psychology : Interview with Maslow, Murphy and Rogers*. Columbus, Ohio : Charles E. Merrill Publishing Company, 1971.

Friedman, M. *Pathogenesis of Coronary artery disease*. New York : McGraw Hill, 1969.

Fromm, E. *Man for Himself*. Greenwich, Conn: Faweett Books, 1947.

Fromm, E. *The Revolution of Hope : Towards a Humanized Technology*. New York : Holt Rinehart and Wiston, 1968.

Galle, O.R., Gove, W.R. and McPherson, J.M. Population density and pathology : What are the relationships for man? *Science*, 1972, **176**, 23-30.

Gandlin, M.K. *Self-Restraint vs Self-Indulgence*. Ahmedabad : Navjivan Publishing House, 1947.

Gardner, E. *Fundamentals of Neurology*. Philadelphia, W.B. Saunders, 1975.

Garland, H. and Pearce, J. Neurological Complication of Carbon Monoxide Poisoning. *Quarterly Journal of Medicine*, 1967, **36**, 445-455.

Garrett, H.E. *General Psychotopy*. New York : American Book Company, 1961.

Garver N. What Violence is. *The Nation*, June 24, 1969.

Geen, R.G., and O'Neel, E.C. Activation of cue-elicited aggression by general arousal. *Journal of Personality and Social Psychology*, 1969, **11** 289-292.

Geen, R.G., O'Neel, E.C. (Eds.). *Perspectives on Aggression*. New York : Academic Press, 1976.

George, H. *Progress and Poverty : An Inquiry into the causes of Industrial Depressions and Increase of want with increase of wealth : A. Remedy*. New York : Dobleday, Doran & Company, 1905.

Gezwirtv, J.L. Learning analysis of the effect of effective privation in childhood. *Acta Psychologia*, 1961, **19**, 404-405.

Getzels, J.W. A. Social Psychology of Education. In Lindzey, G. ed. Aronson, E. (Eds.). *The Handbook of Social Psychology*, Vol. 5, New York : Addison Wesley, 1969.

Gilula, M.F. and Daniels, D.N. Violence and man's struggle to adopt, *Science,* 1969, **164**, 396-405.

Glass, D.C., and Singer, J.E. *Urban Stress*. New York : Academic Press, 1972.

Glenn, N.D., and Wever, C.N. Attitudes toward premarital, extramarital and homosexual relations in the U.S. in the 1970s. *Journal of Sex Research,* 1979, **15**, 108-118.

Glick, I.D. Mood and behavioural changes associated with the use of oral contraceptive agents : A review of the literature. *Psychopharmacologia* 1967, **10**, 363-374.

Glidewell, J.C. Priorities for psychologists in community mental health. In G. Rosenblum (Ed.). *Issues in community psychology and preventive mental health*. New York : Behavioural Publication, 1971.

Goffman, E. *Ayslums*. Garden City, New York : Doubleday, 1961.

Goldstein, K. *The Organism*, New York : American Book, 1939.

Goranson, C.E. & King, D. Rioting and daily temperature : Analysis of the U.S. riots in 1967. Unpublished manuscript, *York University*, 1970.

Gorden, T. *Teacher Effectiveness Training* (TET). New York : Peter H. Wyden, 1974.

Gormley, F.F. and Aiello, J.R. Social density, interpersonal relationships, and residential crowding stress, *Journal of Applied Social Psychology*, 1982, **12**, 22-236.

Garhman Saxon and Reeder Leo. G. *Social Factors in the Chronic Diseases*, New Jersey : Prentice-Hall, Inc., 1972.

Grether, W.F. Vibration and human performance. *Human Factors*, 1971, **13**, 203-216.

Griffiths, I.d. and Boyce, P.R. Performance and Thermal Comfort. *Ergnonomics*, 1971, **14**, 457-468.

Griffitt, W. Environmental effects on interpersonal effective behaviour : Ambient effective temperature and attraction. *Journal of Personality and Social Psychology*, 1970, **15**, 240-244.

Grobb, G.N. *Mental institutions in America : Social Policy to 1875*, New York : Free Press, 1973.

Grossman, S.P. *A Textbook of Physiological Psychology*, New York, John Willey Sons, INC, 1967.

Gunderson, E.K.E. Mental health problem in Antartica. *Archives of Environmental Health*, 1968, **17** 558-564.

Gump, P.V., Schoggen, P., and Redl, F. The camp milieu and its immediate effects. *J. Soc. Issues*, 1957, **13**, 40-46.

Gump, P.V. Schoggen, P., and Redl, F. The behaviour of the same child in different milieus. In R.C. Barker (Ed.). *The stream of behavior.* New York : Appleton-Century-Crofs, 1963.

Gurin, G. and Gurin, P. Expectancy theory in the study of Poverty. *Journal of Social Issues*, 1970, **26,** 83-104.

Hall, E.T. *The hidden dimension.* New York : Doubleday, 1966.

Hallowitz, E. The challenge to group psychotherapist created by a society in flux, *Inter. Jl. Group Psychother*, 1970, **20**, 315-336.

Handbook of Social Psychology, 1954.

Hart, R.H. The concept of APS : Air Pollution Syndrome (S). *Journal of the South Carolina Medican Association*, 1970, **66**, 71-73.

Hartnett, J.J., Bailey, F. and Gibson, W. Personal space as influenced by sex and type of movement. *Journal of Psychology.* 1970, **76**, 139-144.

Harvey, W. *Anatomical Studies on the motion of the Heart and Blood.* Springfield, Illinoss : Charles E. Thomas Publishers, 1931.

Hathway, S.L. and McKinley, J.C., *Minnesota Multiphasic Personality Inventory Manual*, Revised. New York, 1967.

Hauser, P.M. and Dancean, U.D. *The study of population : An inventory and appraisal.* Chicago : University of Chicago Press, 1959.

Hebb, D.O. *Textbook of Psychology* (3rd ed.). Philadelphia : W.B. Saunders, 1972.

Hegal, G.W.F. *The Phenomonology of Mind*, 1807.

Heidegger, M. *Was it Metaphysik.* Frankfurt : V. Klostermann, 1949.

Heidegger, M. *Being and Time*, 1927.

Heidegger, M. *Platons Lehre von der Wahrhest*, mit eirem bridf Uber den Humanisumus, Bern : A frencke AG., 1947.

Heimstra, N.W. and A.L. McDonald. *Psychology and Contemporary Problems.* Monterey, California : Brooks/Cole Publishing Company, 1973.

Heimstra, N.W. and McFarling, L.H. *Environmental Psychology.* Monterey. California : Brooks Kole, 1974.

Helson, H. *Adaptation : Level Theory*, New York : Harper & Row, 1964.

Henry, F. A direct reading cardio-Chronoscope. *Journal of Exp. Psychol.* 1938, **22,** 598-601

Herburg, E., Herfurt, J.C., Hauenstein, L.S., Chapa, C., Schull, W.J. and Schork, M.A. Sociological Stress, suppressed hostility, skin colour and black-white male blood pressure : Detroit, *Psychosomatic Medicine*, 1973, **35**, 276-296.

Herridge, C.F. and Lowbeeze, Observations of the effects of aircraft noise near Heathrow Airport and mental health. In W.D. Ward (Ed.).

Proceedings of the International Congress on Noise as a Public Health Problem. Washington, D.C. : U.S. Government Printing Office, 1973.

Herridege, C.F. Aircraft noise and mental health. *Journal of Psychomatic Research*, 1974, **18**, 239-243.

Hersch, C. From mental health social action. Clinical Psychology in historical perspective. *American Psychologist*, 1969, **24**, 809-819.

Herskovits, M.J. *The Anthropometry of the American Negro.* New York : Columbia University Press, 1930.

Hilgard, R.H., Atkinson, R.C. and Atkinson, R.L. *Introduction to Psychology* (6th ed.) : New Delhi. Oxford IBH Publishing Co., 1975.

Hill, J.W. Applied problems of hot work in the glass industry. In C.N. Davis, P.R. Davis, & F.H. Tyres (Eds.) *The effect of abnormal physical conditions at work.* London : E and S Livingston, 1967.

Hirt, E., and Kimble, C.E. *The home-field advantage in sports : Differences and Correlates.* Paper presented at the Midwestern Psychological Association, Detroit, 1981.

Ho, D., Rota, R., Schooley, R., Kaplan, J., Allen, Groopman, J., Resnick, L., Felsenstein, L., Andrews, C., and Hirsch, M. Isolation of H TLV-III form cerebrospinal fluid and neural tissues of patients with neurologic symptoms related to the acquired immune deficiency syndrome (AIDS). *New England Journal of Medicine*, 1985, **313**, 1493-1497.

Hobbs, N. Mental Health's third revolution. *American Journal of Orthopsychiatry*, 1964, **34**, 822-833.

Holahn, C.J. Environmental Psychology. In M.R. Rosenzweig and L.W. Proter (eds.). *Annual review of psychology*, 1986 Vol., **37**, 381-407, Polo Alto. CA : Annual Reviews, Inc.,

Hollingshead, B.B. and Redlich, F.C. *Social class and mental illness : A Community study.* New York : Wiley, 1958.

Hull, C.L. *Principles of behaviour.* New York : Appleton-Century-Crofts, 1943.

Horner, A. and Buhler, C., Existential and humanistic psychology. A hope for the future in philosophy, Psychotherapy and research. *International Psychiatric Clinics*, 1969, **6**, 3, 55-73.

Hummel, A.L., Levitt. L., and Loomis, R.J. Rearch strategies for measuring attitudes toward pollution. *Unpublished Manuscript,* Colorado State University, 1973.

Hummel, C.F., Loomis, R.J., and Jebert, J.A. Effects of city labels and cue utilization on air pollution judgments (working papers in Environmental Social Psychology, No. 1) *Unpublished manuscript,* Colorado State University, 1975.

Hummel, C.F. Effects of induced cognitive sets in viewing air pollution scenes. *Unpublished doctoral dissertation,* Colorado State University, 1977.

Hurt, H. The hottest place in the whole U.S.A. *Texes Monthly,* 1975, **3,** 50.

Hutt, C., and Vaizey, M.J., *Differential effects of group density on social behaviour*, 1966, **209**, 1371, 1372.

Huxley. J. *The human crises*. Seattle : University of Washington Press, 1963.

Ilfeld, F.W. Over view of the causes and prevention of violence. *Archives of General Psychiatry*, 1969, **20**, 675-689.

Innes, G., Miller, W.M., and Valentine, M. Emotion and blood pressure. *Journal of Mental sciences*. 1959, **105**, 840- 851.

Jansen, G. Non-auditory effects of noise : Physiological and psychological reactions in man. In W.D. Ward (Ed.), *Proceedings of the International Congress on Noise as a Public Health Problem.* Washington, D.C., U.S. Government Printing Office, 1973.

Jankins, C.D. Psychologic and social precurors of coronary disease. *New England Journal of Medicine*, 1971, 284, 244-255.

Jenkins, C.D. Recent evidence supporting psychologic and social risk factors for coronary disease. *New England Journal of Medicine*, 1976, **294,** 987-994.

Jespers, K. *Existenz philosophie*. Berlin Gryter and Co., 1938.

Joffee, J.M. and Albee, G.W. Powerlessness and psychopathology. In J.M. Joffee and C.W. Albee (Eds.). *Prevention through political action and social change : Primary prevention of psychopathology*. Vol. 5. Hevner, N.W. : University Press of New England, 1981.

Joint Commission on mental health and illness. *Action for Mental Health*. New York : Willey, 1961.

Journard, S.M. and Paul Lasaknw. Some factors in Self-disclosure, *Journal of Abnormal and Social Psychology*, 1958, **56**, 91-98.

Jourard, S.M. Self-disclosure and Cathexis. *Journal of Abnormal and Social Psychology*, 1959, **59**, 428-431.

Jourard, S.M. The effects of Experimenter's self disclosure on subject's Behaviour. In C.. Spielberger (Ed.) *Current Topics in Clinical and Community Psychology*. New York, 1962.

Jourard, S.M. Personal adjustment : *An approach through the study of healthy personality.* New York : MacMillan, 1963.

Jourard, S.M. *The transparent self.* Princeton : Van Nostrand, 1964.

Jourard, S.M. *Disclosing man to himself.* New York : D. Van Nostrand Company, 1968.

Kahneman, D. *Attention and effort.* Englewood Cliffs, N.J. : Prentice-Halls, 1973.

Kale, B.D. Family Planning Enquiry is Dharwar Taluka, *Demographic Research Centre.* Institute of Economic Research, Dharwar, 1965.

Kantowitz, B.H. *Environmental Psychology : Behaviour in the Physical World* : In R.A. Baron. D. Byrane, and B.H. Kantowitz. Psychology : Understanding behaviour, Philadelphia. W.B. Saunders, 1977.

Kaplan, S., Kaplan, R., and Wendt, J.S., Rated preference and complexity for natural and urban visual material. *Perception and Psychophysics,* 1972, **12**, 354-356.

Kaplan, S. The Challenge of environmental psychology : A Proposal for a new functionalism. *American Psychologists*, 1972, **27**, (2), 140-143.

Kaplan, R. Some methods and strategies in the prediction of preference. In E.H. Zube, J.G. Fabos, and R.O. Brush (Eds.). *Landscape assessment : Values, Perceptions and Researchers.* Strandsburg, Pa. : Dowden, Hutichison & Ross, 1978.

Karlin, R.A. Rosen, L., and Epistein, Y. Three into two does not go : A follow up of the effects of overcrowded dormitory rooms. *Personality and Social Psychology Bulletin*, 1979, **5**, 391-395.

Kasl, S.V., and Cobb, S. Blood pressure changes in men undergoing job loss : A preliminary report. *Psychosomatic Medicine*, 1970, **32**, 19-38.

Katz, P. Animals and men. London : Longmans, Green, 1937.

Kaufmann, W. (Ed.). *Existentialism form Dostoerksy to Sartra.* New York : Meridian, 1956.

Kelly, J.E. Ecological constraints on mental health service. *American Psychologist*, 1966, **21**, 535-539.

Kelly, J.G. Naturalistic observation in contrasting social environment. In E.P. Williams and H.L. Raush (Eds.). *Naturalistic view points in psychological research.* New York : Rinehart and Winston, 1969.

Khattri, P.K. A Comparison of Frustration-Aggression in Recent Amputees and Git Trainers. *Journal of Community Guidance and Research*, 1993, **10**, 3, 185-197.

Kierkegaard, S.A. *Either/Or*, 1943.

Keirkegaard, S.A. *The Concept Dread*, 1944.

Kierkegaard, S.A. *The Sickness upto Death*, 1949.

Kleitman, N. Sleep and Wakefulness. Chicago : University of Chicago Press, 1939.

Knowles, E.S., and Johnson, L. Interpersonal consistency and interpersonal distance. *JSAS Catalogue of Selected Documents in Psychology*, 1974, **4**, 124.

Kogan, T.P. Socio-economic community variables as prediction of Cognitive test performance of school children. *Dissertation Abstract*, 1970, **31**, 29-59.

Kohl, H.R. *The open classroom*, New York : Vintage, 1969.

Konecni, V.J., Libuser, L., Morton, H., and Ebbesen, E.B. Effects of a violation of personal space and escape and helping responses. *Journal of Experimental Social Psychology,* 1975, **11**, 288-299.

Kryter, K.D. *The effects of noise on man*. New York : Academic Press, 1970.

Lacey. J.I. Somatic response pattering and stress : Some revisions of activation theory. In W.H. Appley., and R. Trumbell, (Eds.). *Psychological Stress*. New York : Appleton-Century-Crofts, 1967.

Lahfeldt, H. Psychological aspects of planned parenthood. *Journal of Sex Research*, 1965, **1**, 97-103.

Lakshmi N. Menon. The First All India Family Planning Conference. *National Herald (Lucknow)* December 20, 1951.

Landis, C. Changes in blood pressure during sleep as determined by Erlanges method. *Amer. Jl. Physiol*. 1925a, **73**, 551-555.

Landis, C., and Gullettle, R. Studies in emotional reaction, III : Systolic blood pressure and inspiration-expiration ratio. *Jl. Comp. Psychol.* 1926, **5**, 221-250.

Landis, C. Studies of emotional reaction, V : Severe emotional upset. *Jl. Comp. Psychol*. 1926, **6,** 221-242.

Landsberg. H.E. *Weather and Health*, New York. Doubleday, 1969.

Lange, C.E. Om Sindsberagelser. *It psyko fisiolog. studie*. Copenhagen : Kronar, 1885.

Lazarus, R.S. *Patterns of Adjustment* (3rd ed.). New York : McGraw-Hill, 1976.

Lazarus, R. *Psychological stress and the coping process*. New York : McGraw-Hill, 1966.

Lebo, C.P. and Oliphant, K.P. Music as a source of acoustic trauma. *Laryngoscope,* 1968, **78**, 1211-1218.

Leonard, C.B. *Education and ecstasy*, New York : Dell, 1968.

Leverne, A.A. Nonspecific Air Pollution Syndrome (NAPS) Preliminary report. *Behavioural Neuropsychiatry*, 1970, 2, 19-21.

Lindemann, E. Sympotomatology and management of acute grief. *American Journal of Psychiatry*, 1944, **101,** 141-148.

Linton, R. *The Study of Man : An Introduction.* New York : D. Applaton-Century-Company Inc., 1936.

Little, K.B. Cultural variations in social schemata, *Journal of Personality and Social Psychology*, 1968, **10**, 1-7.

Laewi, O. On the Humoral Transmission of Heart Nerves. In *Great Experiments in Biology* Ed. by M.L. Gabriel and S. Fogel Englewood Cliffs, NJ. Prentice-Harr, INC. 1953.

Loo, C. The effects of spatial density on the social behaviour of children. *Journal of Applied Social Psychology*, 1972, **4**, 372-381.

Lorion, R.P. Socio-economic status and traditional treatment approaches reconsidered. *Psychological Bulletin*, 1973, **79**, 263-270.

Lorimer, F. Issues of Population Policy. In P.M. Hauser (Ed.). *The Population Dilemma*. Englewood Cliffs, N.J. Prentice-Hall 1963.

Lowrie, W. *Kierkegaard*, New York : Oxford University Press, 1938.

Lussell, W.L. A Psychopathic department of an American general hospital in 1808. *Amer. J. Psychiat.*, 1941, **98**, 229-237.

Macey, R.I. *Human Physiology,* New Delhi : Prentice-Hall of India Private Limited, 1973.

Mack, R.W. *Race, Class and Power.* New York : American Book Company 1963.

Mackanzie, S.T. Noise and office work. Employee and Employer concerns. Ithaca : *New York State Schools of Industrial and Labour Relations*. Cornell University, 1975.

Mallory, W.H. *China : Land of Famine*, American Geographical Society, New York : 1926.

Maloney, M.P., Ward, M.O. and Braucht, C.N. A revised scale for a new functionalism. *American Psychologists*, 1972, **27**, (2)-140-143.

Malthus, T.R. *An Essay on the Principle of Population As It Affects the Future Improvement of Society.* London : J. Johnson is St. Pals's Churchyard 1798.

Marsden, H.M. Crowding and animal behaviour. In. J.F. Wohlwill and D.H. Carson (Eds.). *Environment and the social sciences: Perspectives and applications*. Washington, D.C.: American Psychological Association, 1972.

Martindale, D.A. Territorial dominance behaviour in ydyadic verbal interactions. Proceedings of the *Annual Convention of the American Psychological Association*, 1971, **6**, 305, 306.

Maslow A.H. Motivation and personality, New York : Harper and Row Publication, INC, 1954.

Maslow, A.H. *The Psychology of Science : A reconnaissance*, New York : Harper and Row 1966.

Maslow, A.H. Lessons from the peak-experiences, *Journal of Humanistic Psychology., 1962,* **2**, 9-18.

Maslow, A.H. *Motivation and Personality* (2nd ed.). New York : Harper and Row Publishers, 1970.

Maslow, A.H. The dominance drive as a determiner of the social and sexual behaviour of infra-human primates, I-IV, *Journal of Genetic Psychology*, 1976, **48**, 338, 278, 49, 161-190.

Maslow, A.H. *The Farther Reaches of Human Nature*. New York : Viking Press, 1971.

Maslow, A.H. Further notes on the Psychology of Being. *Journal of Humanistic Psychology*, 1963, **3**, 120-135.

Maslow, A.H. Notes on Being Psychology. *Journal of Humanistic Psychology*, 1962, 2, 47-71.

Maslow, A.H. Synergy in the Society and in the Individual. *Journal of Individual Psychology*, 1964, 20, 153-164.

Maslow, A.H. A Theory of Metamotivation : The Biological Rooting of the Value-Life. *Journal of Humanistic Psychology*. 1967, **7**, 2, 93-127.

Massey, A., and Vandenburgh, J.G. Puberty delay by a urinary cue from female house mice in feral populations. *Science*, 1980, 209, 821-822.

Mauldin, W.P. Watson, W.P., and Neo. L.F. *KAP surveys and evaluation of family planning programmes*. New York : The Population Council, April 1970.

May, R. The origin and significance of the existential movement in Psychology. In R. May, E. Angel, and H. Ellenberger (Eds.). *Existence*. New York : Basic Books, 1958.

McDougall, W. *Outline of Psychology*. New York : Scribner, 1923.

McDougall, W. *An introduction to social psychology :* Botnon Luce and Co., 1926.

McDougall, W. *The energies of man*. New York : Scribner, 1933.

Meecham, W.C., and Smith. H.G. *British Journal of audiology*. Quoted in N. Napp Noise drives you crazy-jets and mental hospitals. *Psychology Today*, 1977.

Meer, J. The strife of bath. *Psychology Today*, 1986, 20(5), p. 6.

Megargee, E.I. and Mendulshon, G.A. Across validation of twelve MMPI indices of hostility and control. *Journal of Abnormal and Social Psychology*, 1962, **20**, 675-689.

Mehrabian, A., and Russell, J.A. *An Approach to Environmental Psychology*. Cambridge, Mass : M.I.T. Press, 1974.

Milgram, S. The experience of living in cities. *Science*, 1970, **167**, 1461-1468.

Miller, N. and Dollard, J. *Social Learning and Imitation*. New Haven : Yale University Press, 1941.

Mischel, W. *Personality and assessment*. New York : Wiley, 1968.

Misra, G. and Tripathi, L.B. *Manual for Psychological deprivation scale* (PDS). Agra : National Psychological corporation; 1978.

Misra, G. and Tripathi, L.B. *Psychological consequences of Prolonged Deprivation*. Agra : National Psychological Corporation, 1980.

Mitachall, H.W. Implementing Family Planning Programmes in the State Level in India. In Bose, A, Desai, P.B., and S.P. Jain (Eds.). *Studies in Demography*. George Allen and Unwin Ltd., 1970.

Moni Nag, Family, Type and Fertility : *World Population Conference*. Vol. II, p. 167, 1965.

Monte, C.F. *Beneath the Mask : An Introduction to Theories of Personality*. New York : Praeger Publishers, 1977.

Morison, T. *The Industrial Organization of an Indian Province* London : John Murray (Publishers) Ltd., 1918.

Morris, C.G. *Psychology : An Introduction*. Englewood Cliffs, New Jersey : Prentice-Hall, Inc., 1973.

Murphy, G. *Personality : A Biosocial Approach to Origin and Structure*. New York : Harper and Brothers, 1947.

Murphy, G. *An Introduction Psychology*, New Delhi : Oxford and IBH Publishing Co., 1964.

Murrell, S.A. *Community Psychology and Social Systems*. New York : Behavioural Publications 1973.

Myrdal, G. *An American Dilemma*. New York : Casnegie Corporation, 1944.

National Conference on Population Policy. National Planning Committee, Population : Report of the Sub-Committee Bombay : Vora and Co., Publishers Ltd., 1947.

Neill, A.S. *Summerhill : A radical approach to child rearing*. New York : Hart, 1960.

Ng. L.K.Y., Marsden, H.M., Coluburn, R.W., and Thoa, N.B. Population density and social pathology in mice. Differences in catecholamine matabolism associated with differences in behaviour, *Brian Research*, 1937, **59**, 323-330.

Nietzal, M.T., Winett, R.A., MacDonald, M.L., Davidson, W.S. *Behavioural Approaches to Community Psychology*. New York : Pergamon Press, 1977.

Nortman, D. Population and family planning programmes : *A Fact Book Report on Population Family Planning*. December 1969, 1-48.

Pareek Udai, Devi, R.S. and Saul Rosenzweig. Manual of the Indian Adaptation of the *Rosenzweig Picture Frustration Study-Adult Form*, Varanasi : Rupa Psychological Centre, 1968.

Parr, A.E. Psychological aspects of Urbanology. *Journal of Social Issues*, 1966, **22,** 39-45.

Pasamanick, B., Rogers, M.E. and Lilienfeld, A.M. Pregnancy experience and the development of behaviour disorder in children. *American Journal of Psychiatry*, 1956, **112**, 613-618.

Patterson, M.L. Compensation in non-verbal immediacy behaviour : *A review. Sociometry*, 1973, **36**, 237-252.

Patterson, M.L. *Factors affecting interpersonal proximity*. Paper presented at the meeting of the American Psychological Association. New Orleans, September 1974.

Paulus, P.B., Annis, A.B., Seta, J.J., Schkade, J.K., and Mathews, R.W. Crowding does affect task performance. *Journal of Personality and Social Psychology*, 1976, **34**, 248-253.

Paulus, P.B., Crowding, In P.B. Paulus (ed.). *Psychology of group influence*. Hillsadale, NJ : Evlbaum, 1980.

Penwarden, A.D. Acceptable wind speeds in towns, *Building Science*, 1973, **8** 250-267.

Pepler, R.D. Performance and wellbeing in heat, In C.M. Herfeld (Ed.). *Temperature : Its measurement and control in science and industry* (Vol. II., Pt. 3) New York : Reinhold, 1963.

Pepler, R. The thermal, comfort and students in climate controlled and non-climate controlled schools. *ASHRAE Transaction.* 1972, **78**, 97-109.

Petrarch, F. *Secretum : a spiritual self-analysis*, 1342.

Phillis, D.E. and Gromko, M.H. Sex differences in sexual activity : Reality or illusion? *Journal of Sex Research*, 1985, **21** 437-448.

Pohlman, E. Birth control : Independent and dependent variable for psychological research. *American Psychologist*. 1966, 21, 967-970.

Pohlman, E.A. Psychologists introduction to the birth planning literature. *Journal of Social Issues*, 1967, **23**, 13-28 (a).

Pohlman, E. Some effects of being able to control sex of offspring. *Erugencs Quarterly*, 1967, **14**, 274-281 (b).

Pohlman, E. *The psychology of birth planning*, Cambridge, Mass : Sahenkman Publishing Company, 1969.

Polanyi, M. *Personal knowledge*, Chicago : University of Chicago Press, 1958.

Postman, N. and Weingartner, C. *The soft revolution*. New York : Delacorte Press, 1971.

Postman, L, and Egan, J.P. *Experimental Psychology : An Introduction.* New York : Harpet & Row, 1949.

Poulton, E.C. and Kerslake, M. Mak. Initial stimulating effect of warmth upon perceptual efficiency, *Aerospace Medicine*, 1965, **36**, 29-32.

Poulton, E.C. *Environment and human efficiency*. Springfield III : Charles C. Thomas, 1970.

Poulton, E.C., Hunt, J.C.R., Mumford, J.C. and Poulton, J. Mechanical disturbance produced by steady and gusty winds of moderate strength: Skilled performance and semantic assessments. *Ergonomics*, 1975, **18**, 651-673.

Price, G.H., and Dabbs, J.M. Sex setting and personal space : changes as children grow older. *Personality and Social Psychology Bulletin*, 1974, **1**, 362-363.

Proshansky. H.M., Ittalson, W.H., and Rivlin, L.G. (Eds.). *Environmental Psychology : Man and his physical setting*. New York : Rinehart and Winston, 1970.

Proshansky. H.M. Environmental Psychology and the real world. *American Psychologists*, 1976, **31**, 303-310.

Provins, K.A. and Clarke, R.S.J. The effect of cold on neural Performance. *Journal of Occupational Medicine*, 1960, 2, 169-176.

Provins, K.A. Environmental heat, body temperature and behaviour. *Australian Journal of Psychology*, 1966, **18**, 118-129.

Provins, K.A. and Bell, C.R. Effects of heat stress on the Performance of two tasks running concurrently. *Journal of Experimental Psychology*, 1970, **85**, 40-44.

Purkey, W.W. *Inviting school success : a self-concept approach to teaching learning*, Belmont, Calif : Wadsworth, 1978.

Rabinson, W.C. The development of modern population theory. *The American Journal of Economics and Sociology*, 1964, **23**, 375-392.

Rahe, R.H., and Lind, E. Psychosocial factors and sudden cardiac death : A Pilot study. *Journal of Psychomatic Research*, 1971, **15**, 19-24.

Rajamanickam, M. and Venkatammal, P. A study of prolonged deprivation among tenth standard students. *Indian Journal of Community Guidance Service*, 1984, 1, 2, 35-50.

Rajamanickam, M. and Arumugam, R. Aggression and Violence among the University Students. *Indian Journal of Community Guidance Service*, 1991, **8**, 1, 15-38.

Rajamanickam, M. *Family Planning and Birth Control Attitude Scale*. Madras : Institute of Community Guidance and Research, 1995.

Rajamanickam, M. *Environmental Pollution Attitude Scale*. Madras : Institute of Community Guidance and Research, 1995.

Rajamanickam, M. *Noise Pollution Attitude Scale*. Madras : Institute of Community Guidance and Research, 1995.

Rajamanickam, M. *Temperature Attitude Scale*. Madras : Institute of Community Guidance and Research, 1995.

Rajamanickam, M. *Air Pollution Attitude Scale*. Madras : Institute of Community Guidance and Research, 1995.

Rajecki, D.W,. Nernz, D.R., Freedenberg, T.G. and McGarthy, P.J. Components of aggression in chickens and conceptualization of aggression in general. *Journal of Personality and Social Psychology*, 1981, **37**, 1902-1914.

Ramachandran, K.V. and Deshpande, V.A. Sex Ratio at Birth in India by Regions, *Malbark Memorial Fund Quarterly*, 1964, 42, 2, Part 1, 84-95.

Rankin, N.O. The effects of selective social deprivation in a neutral setting. *Dissortation Abstract*, 1970, 30, 4820- 4821.

Rappaport, J. *Community Psychology*. New York : Holt Rinehart and Winston, 1977.

Rappaport, J. In praise of paradox : A social policy of empowerment of prevention. *American Journal of Community Psychology*, 1981, **9**, 1-25.

Rappaport, J. and Chinsky, J.M. Model for delivery of service from a historical and conceptual perspective. *Professional Psychology*, 1974, **5**, 42-50.

Rath, R. and Dash, A.S. Cognitive growth and class room learning of neutrally deprived children in the primary schools. *Paper presented at the East-work Centre for Cross-Culture Studies*. Honolulu, 1972.

Reitan, R.M. The neurological model. In L.L. Abate (Ed.). *Models of Clinical Psychology*. Atlanta, GR : School of Arts & Science, Georgia State College, 1969.

Riegal, K.R. Influence of economic and political ideologies on the developmental psychology. *Psychological Bulletin*, 1972. **78**, 129-141.

Rogers, C. *Counselling and Psychotherapy*. Boston : Houghton Mifflin, 1942.

Rogers, C.A. Theory of Therapy, Personality, and Interpersonal Relationship as Developed in the Client-Centred framework, Psychology : *A study of a science,* Vol. 3. Foundations of the person in the social context. S. Loch, (Ed.). New York : McGraw-Hill, 1959.

Rogers, C. The actualizing Tendency in Relation to Motives and to Consciousness. *Nebraska Symposium on Motivation.* Vol. 4. Marshall R. Jones, ed. Lincoln : University of Nebraska Press, 1963.

Rogers, C. *Client-centred therapy : Its current practice implications and theory.* Boston : Houghton Mifflin, 1951.

Rohles, F.H. Jr. The model comfort envelope and its use in current standards. *Human Factors,* 1974, 16, 314-322.

Rose, A. *The Negro in America.* Boston, Mass : Beacon Press, 1956.

Rose, E.F., and Rose, M. Carbon monoxide : A challenge to Physician. *Clinical Medicine,* 1971, **78**, 17-18.

Rosenfeld, H.H. Effect of an approval—seeking induction on interpersonal proximity. *Psychological Reports,* 1965, **17**, 120-122.

Rosenman, R.H., Friedman, M., Strans, R., Wurm, M., Lositicheck R., Hahn, W., and Werthessen, N.T. A predictive study of coronary heart disease. *Journal of the American Medical Association,* 1964, **189**, 103-110.

Rosenman, R.H., Brand, R.J., Jenkins, C.D., Friedman, M., Strans, R., and Wurm, M., Coronary heart disease in the Western collaborative group study : Final follow-up experience of 8-1/2 years, *Journal of American Medical Association,* 1975, 283, 872-877.

Rosenzweig, S. Frustration as an experimental problem: I. The significance of frustration as a problem of research. *Char. & Pers.* 1938, **7**, 126-128.

Rosenzweig, S. Frustration as an experimental problem: VI. General outline of frustration. *Char. & Pers.*, 1938, **7**, 151-160.

Rosenzweig, S. An experimental study of repression with special reference to need persistence and ego-defensive reactions to frustration. *Journal of Experimental Psychology,* 1943, **32**, 64-74.

Rosenzweig, S. A outline of frustration theory. In J. Mcv. Hunt (Ed.) *Personality and the behaviour disorders.* Vol. 1. New York : Ronald Press, 1944.

Rosenzweig, S. *The Rosenzweig. P.F. Study form for Adults,* 1944, (Distributed by the author).

Rosenzweig, S., Clarke, H.J., Garfield, M.S. and Lenndorff, S., Scoring Samples for the Rosenzweig Picture Frustration study. *Journal of Psychology,* 1946, **21**, 45-72.

Rozenzweig, S., Fleming. E.E. and Clarke, H.J. Revised scoring manual for the Rosenzweig Picture Frustration Study. *Journal Psychology,* 1947, **24**, 165-208.

Rosenzweig, S. *The Rosenzweig P.F. Study, Revised Form for Adults*, 1948, (Distributed by the author).

Rosenzweig, S., Fleming, E.E. and Rosenzweig, L. The children's Form of Rosenzweig Picture Frustration Study. *Journal of Psychology*, 1948, **26**, 141-191.

Rosenzweig, S. Revised norms for the Adult form of Rosenzweig Picture-Frustration Study. *Journal of Personality*, 1950, **18**, 344-346.

Ross, M., Layton, B., Erickson, B., and Schopler, J. Affect Facial regard, and reactions to crowding. *Journal of Personality and Social Psychology*, 1973, **28**, 69-76.

Rotter, J.B. *Clinical Psychology*, Englewood Cliffs, N.J. : Prentice-Hall Inc., 1964.

Ruskin, A., Board, O.W., and Schaffer, R.L. Blast Hypertension: Elevated arterial pressure in victims of the Texas City disaster. *American Journal of Medicine*, 1948, **4**, 228-236.

Rustemli, A. Male and female personal space needs and escape reactions under intrusion : A Turkish sample. *International Journal of Psychology*, 1986.

Saegert, S. *Effects of Spatial and Social density on arousal mood, and social orientation.* Unpublished Doctoral dissertation. University of Michigan, 1974.

Sanders, R., Smith, R.S. and Weinman, B. *Chronic psychosis and recovery : An experiment in socio-environmental therapy*. San Francisco : Jossey-Bass, 1967.

Sartre, J.P. *Existentialisme est un humanisme*. Paris : Editions Nagal, 1946.

Satir, V. *Peoplemaking*. Pilo Alto, Calif : Science and Behaviour Books, 1972.

Scheff, T.J. (Ed.) *Mental illness and social processes*. New York : Harper & Row, 1967.

Scherer, S.E. Proxemic behaviour of primary school children as a function of their socio-economic class and sub-culture. *Journal of Personality and Social Psychology*, 1974, **29**, 800-805.

Schiller, F.C.S. *Truth in Humanism.*

Schofield, W. *Psychotherapy : The purchase of friendship*. Englewood Cliffs, N.J. : Prentice-Hall, 1964.

Schulte, J.H. Effects of mild carbon monoxide intoxication. *Archives of Environmental Health*, 1963, **7**, 524-530.

Schultz, D.B. *Sensory restriction.* New York : Academic Press, 1965.

Scott, J.A. Comfort and seating distance in living rooms : The relationship of interactions and topic of conversation. *Environment and Behaviour*, 1984, 16, 30-34.

Second Five Year Plan, India, Planning Commission, New Delhi, 1956.

Seligman, M.E.P. *Helplessness*, San Francisco : W.H. Freeman, 1975.

Selling, L.S. *Men against madness.* New York : Garden City Books, 1943.

Sells, S.B. Ecology and the science of psychology. *Multivariate Behavioural Research*, 1966, **1**, 131-144.

Selye, H. *The physiology and pathology of exposure to stress*, Montreal : Acta, 1950.

Selye, H. *The Stress of Life,* New York : McGraw-Hill, 1956.

Shea, J.D.C. Changes in interpersonal distance and categories of play behaviour in the early weeks of preschool. *Development Psychology*, 1981, **17**, 417-425.

Shephard, J.F. Organic changes and feeling. *Amer. Jl. Psychol.* 1906, **17,** 522-584.

Shephard J.F. *The circulation and sleep with atlas.* New York : Macmillan, 1914.

Shontz, F.C. Research methods in personality. New York:

Silver Jubilee Souvenir : Residents' Welfare Association, Annanagar, Chennai, 1995.

Simon, S.S. Howe, L.W. and Krischenbaum, H. *Values Classification a hand book of practical strategies for teachers and students.* New York : Hart Publishing Co., 1972.

Sinha, D. and *et al. Deprivation.* New Delhi : Concept Publishing Company, 1982.

Smith, B.M. *Social psychology and Human Values.* Chicago : Aldite Publishing Co., 1969.

Smith, M.B. and Hobbs, N. The community and the community mental Health Centre. *American Psychologist*, 1966, **15**, 113-118.

Smith, M.B. Ethical implications of population policies: a Psychological view. *American Psychologists*, 1972, **27**, 1, 11-15.

Smith, R.J., and Knowles, E.S. Attributional consequences of personal space invasions. *Personality and Social Psychology. Bulletin*, 1979, **4**, 429-433.

Smuts, Jan C. *Holism and Evolutions.* New York : MacMillan, 1926.

Sommer, R. Man's proximate environment. *Journal of Social Issues*, 1966, 22, 59-70.

Sommer, R. *Personal space*, Engleword Cliffs, N.J. Prentice-Hall, 1969.

Sommer, R. Environmental Psychology. A blueprint for the future. *APA Monitor*, 1980, **11**, 47.

Sonnenfled, J. Variable values in space and landscape : An inquiry into the nature of environmental necessity. *Journal of Social Issues*, 1966, **22**, 71-82.

Spiegal, J.P. Psychological factors in riots—old and new. *American Journal of Psychiatry*, 1968, **125**, 281-285.

Spielberger, C.D. and London, P., Rage Boomarangs : A key to preventing coronaries is emerging : Learn to handle anger and avoid seven deadly responses. *Indian Journal of Community Guidance Service*, 1984, **1**, 15-19.

Spielberger, C.D. *State-trait anger expression inventory* : Professional Manual, Odessa, Fla : Psychological Assessment Resources, 1988.

Steovkis, B. A method for the uninterrupted registering of blood pressure as a psycho-physiological research technique for the study of psychic stimuli on the blood pressure. *Jl. Exp. Psychol.* 1938, **22,** 365-376.

Stokols, D., Rall, M., Pinner, B., and Schopler, J. Physical, social and personal determinants of the perception of crowding. *Environment and Behaviour*, 1973, **5**, 87-177.

Stone, L.J. and Hekanson, J.E. Arousal reaction via self-punitive behaviour. *Journal of Personality and social psychology*, 1967, **12**, 72-72.

Strange, J.R. *Abnormal Psychology*, New York : MacGraw- Hill, 1965.

Storms, M., and Thomas, G.C. Reactions to physical closeness. *Journal of Personality and Social Psychology*, 1977, **35**, 412-418.

Subhas Chandra Bose. *National Planning Committee. Population : Report of the sub-committee*. Bombay : Vora and Co., Publishers Ltd., 1947.

Sundstrom, E., and Sundstrom, M.G. Personal space invasion : What happens when the invaders asks permission? *Environmental Psychology and Non-verbal Behaviour*, 1981, 41, 76-82.

Symmodns, M. Disadvantage children growing in a climate of hopelessness and despair. *American Journal of Psycho-analysis*, 1968, **28**, 15-24.

Tarlok Singh. Policy and Administration for poverty concentration Area, *IASSI Quarter*, 1983, Vol. 2. No.

Taunus, *In a China Shop*, Free Press, (Bombay) December 3, 1951.

Taussing, F.J. *The Abortion Problem.* Proceedings of the Conference Held Under the Ausipices of the National Committee of Maternal Health, Inc, Baltimore : The Williams and Wilkin, Company, 1944.

Taylar, R.B. and Lanni, J.C. Teritorial dominance : The influence of the resident advantage in triadic decision making. *Journal of Personality and Social Psychology*, 1981, **41**, 909-915.

The First Five Year Plan. Planning Commission Government of India, New Delhi, 1952.

The American Population Council. *A manual for surveys of fertility and family planning : Knowledge, attitudes, and practices.* New York : The Population Council, 1967 (a).

The American Population Council. S.S.S.R. Views on population and family planning, *Studies in family Planning*, 1967 (b), 49, 661.

The Collins English Dictionary, London : Collins, 1979.

Third Five Year Plan, India, Planning Commission, New Delhi.

Thompson. W.S., and Lewis, D.T. *Population Problems (5th ed.).* New York : McGraw-Hill, 1965.

Tieze, C. *Bibliography of fertility control*, 1950-1965. New York : National Committee on Maternal Health, Publication No. 23., 1965.

Tolman, E.C. *Purposive behaviour in animal and man.* New York : Appleton-century-crofts, 1932.

Tornatzky, L.G. Howa, Ph.D. Programme aimed at survival issues survived. *American Psychologist*, 1976, 31, 189-192.

Tulkin, S.R. An analysis of the concept of cultural deprivation. *Developmental Psychology*, 1972, **6**, 326-339.

Turkish Population Planning. *Official Gazettee*, 15 April 1965, p. 1 & 7.

Tutoo, D.N. Psychodynamics of violence in university students in A.K.P. Sinha and S.L. Dass (Ed.). *Violent Behaviour : A synopsium.* New Delhi : S. Chand and Co. Pvt. Ltd., 1975.

Ullmann, L.P. and Krasnea, L. *A psychological approach to abnormal behaviour.* New York : Holt, Rinehart and Winston, 1969.

United Nations, Report on the Family Planning Programme of the Government of India, New York, 1969, 4-5.

U.S.A. Surgeon General's Scientific Advisory Committee on Television and Social Behaviour. *Television and Growing up : The impact of television violence.* U.S. Government Printing Office, Washington, D.C. 1072.

Veblen, T. *The Theory of the Leisure Class.* New York : Mac- Millan, 1899.

Warner, H.D. The effects of intermittent noise on human target detection. *Human Factors*, 1969, **11**, 245-250.

Warner, H.D. and Heimstra, N.W. Effects of intermittent noise on visual search tasks of various complexity, *Perceptual and Motor Skills*, 1971, **32**, 219-226.

Warner, H.D. and Heimstra, N.W. Effects of Noise intensity on visual target-detection performance. *Human Factors*, 1972, **14**, 2, 177-181.

Washington Post, July 28, 1985.

Watson, J.B. Psychology as the Behaviourist Views It. *Psychological Review*, 1913, **20**, 158-177.

Watson, J.B. *Behaviour : An introduction to comparative psychology* : New York : Holt, Rinehart and Winston, 1914.

Watson, J.B *Psychology from the standpoint of behaviourist.* Philadelphia : J.B. Lippincott, 1919.

Watson, J.B. *The Universalized in human behaviour. Psychological Review*, 31, 273-280.

Watson, J.B. *Behaviourism*, New York : Norton, 1925.

Watson, O.M. and Graves, T.T. Quantitative research in proximate behaviour. *American Anthropologist*, 1966, **68**, 917-985.

Weinger, F.H. Altruism, Abiance, and Action : The effects of rural and urban rearing on helping behaviour. *Journal of Personality and Social Psychology*, 1976, **34**, 112-124.

Werner, N., Latane, B., and Pendey, J. *Social Loafing in the United States and India*. Paper presented at the Joint Asian Meeting of the International Association for cross-cultural psychology and the international council of Psychologists, Taipei, Taiwan, 1981.

Whitehorn, J.C., Kaufman, M.R. & Thomas, J.M. *Heart rate in relation to emotional disturbances*. Arch. Neurl. Psychiat. (Chicago), 1935, ***33***, 712-731.

Whitehorn, J.C. and Richter, H. *Unsteadiness of the heart rate in psychotic neurotic states*. Arch. Neurl. Psychiat (Chicago) 1937, **38,** 62-70.

Whiteman, M. and Dentsch, M. Social disadvantage as related to intellective and language development. In Deutsch, M. et al. (Eds.). *Social Class, Race, and Psychological Development*, New York : Holt, 1968.

Whitwell, J.R. *Historical notes on psychiatry*. London : H.K. Lewis, 1936.

Wiehl, D.G. A Summary of Data on Reported Incidence of Abortion. *Milbank Memorial Fund Quarterly*, Vol. 16, p. 88, 1938.

Wilkinson, R.T. Individual differences in response to the environment, *Ergonomics*, 1974, **17,** 745-756.

Willcox, W.F. *U.S. Bureau of the Census*. Proportion of Children in the United States, 1905.

Williams, E.P. An ecological orientation in psychology. *Marrill-Palmer Quart.*, 1965, **11**, 317-343.

Williams, E.P. and Raush, H.L. (Eds.) *Naturalistic view point in psychological research,* New York : Holt Rinehart and Winston, 1969.

Willis, F.N. Initial speaking distance as a function of the speaker's relationship. *Psychonomic Science*, 1966, **5**, 221-222.

Wirth, L. and Goldhamer, H. *The Hybird and the Problem of Miscegenation in : Otto Klinberg (editor). Characteristics of the American Negro.* New York : Harper Row Brothers, 1944.

Wohlwill, J.F. The physical environment : A Problem for a Psychology of Stimulation, *Journal of Social Issues*, 1966, 22, 29-38.

Wohlwill, J.F. and Carson, D.M. (Eds.). *Environment and Social Sciences : Perspectives and applications.* Washington, D.C. : American Psychological Association, 1972.

Wohlwill, J.F. Human adaptation to level of environmental stimulation. *Human Ecology*, 1974, **2**, 127-147.

Wohlwill, J.F. The emerging discipline of environmental psychology. *American Psychologist*, 1970. **25**, 303-512.

Wolfgang, M.E. Violence and human behaviour. In F.F. Korten, S.W. Cook and J.I. Lacey (Eds.). *Psychology and the problem of society.* Washington, D.C. : American Psychological Association. 1970. 309-326.

Woodworth, R.S. and Marquis, D.G. *Psychology*, London : Metheun & Co., 1952.

Woodworth, R.S. *Contemporary Schools of Psychology.* London : Metheun & Co., 1955.

Worchel, S., and Teddlie, C. The experience of crowding : A two factor theory. *Journal of Personality and Social Psychology*, 1976, 34, 30-40.

Worchel, S., and Brown, E.H. The role of plausibility in influencing environmental attributions. *Journal of Experimental Social Psychology*, 1984, **20**, 86-96.

Wright, B.W., Gloniques, M.F. and Krene, P.J. Cultural deprivation : Operational definition in terms of language development, *American Journal of Orthopsychiatry*, 1970, **40**, 77-86.

Zax, M. and Cowen, E.L. Research on early detection and prevention of emotional dysfunction in young school children. In C.D. Spielberger (Ed.) *Current topics in clinical and Community Psychology* (Vol. 1) New York : Academic Press, 1969.

Zax, M. and Cown, E.L. Abnormal Psychology : *Changing conceptions* : New York : Holt, Rinehart and Winston, 1972.

Zax, M. and Specter, G.A. *An Introduction to Community Psychology*, New York : Wiley, 1974.

Zell, J.R. and Crisp. W.E. A psychiatric evaluation of the use of oral contraceptive : A study of 250 private patients. *Obstetric and Gynaecology*, 1964, **23**, 657-661.

Zilboorg, G., and Henry, G.W. *A History of Medical Psychology* : New York : Norton, 1941.

Zubek, J.P. (Ed.) *Sensory Deprivation : Fifteen Years of Research*. New York : Appleton-Century-Crofts, 1969.

INDEX